Praise for *Prompt Engineering for Generative AI*

The absolute best book-length resource I've read on prompt engineering. Mike and James are masters of their craft.

—*Dan Shipper, cofounder and CEO, Every*

This book is a solid introduction to the fundamentals of prompt engineering and generative AI. The authors cover a wide range of useful techniques for all skill levels from beginner to advanced in a simple, practical, and easy-to-understand way. If you're looking to improve the accuracy and reliability of your AI systems, this book should be on your shelf.

—*Mayo Oshin, founder and CEO, Siennai Analytics,
early LangChain contributor*

Phoenix and Taylor's guide is a lighthouse amidst the vast ocean of generative AI. Their book became a cornerstone for my team at Phiture AI Labs, as we learned to harness LLMs and diffusion models for creating marketing assets that resonate with the essence of our clients' apps and games. Through prompt engineering, we've been able to generate bespoke, on-brand content at scale. This isn't just theory; it's a practical masterclass in transforming AI's raw potential into tailored solutions, making it an essential read for developers looking to elevate their AI integration to new heights of creativity and efficiency.

—*Moritz Daan, Founder/Partner,
Phiture Mobile Growth Consultancy*

Prompt Engineering for Generative AI

Future-Proof Inputs for Reliable
AI Outputs at Scale

James Phoenix and Mike Taylor

Beijing · Boston · Farnham · Sebastopol · Tokyo

Prompt Engineering for Generative AI

by James Phoenix and Mike Taylor

Published by O'Reilly Media, Inc., 1005 Gravenstein Highway North, Sebastopol, CA 95472.

O'Reilly books may be purchased for educational, business, or sales promotional use. Online editions are also available for most titles (*http://oreilly.com*). For more information, contact our corporate/institutional sales department: 800-998-9938 or *corporate@oreilly.com*.

Acquisitions Editor: Nicole Butterfield	**Indexer:** nSight, Inc.
Development Editor: Corbin Collins	**Interior Designer:** David Futato
Copyeditor: Piper Editorial Consulting, LLC	**Cover Designer:** Karen Montgomery
Proofreader: Kim Wimpsett	**Illustrator:** Kate Dullea

May 2024:   First Edition

Revision History for the First Edition

2024-05-15:   First Release

See *http://oreilly.com/catalog/errata.csp?isbn=9781098153434* for release details.

The O'Reilly logo is a registered trademark of O'Reilly Media, Inc. *Prompt Engineering for Generative AI*, the cover image, and related trade dress are trademarks of O'Reilly Media, Inc.

978-1-098-15343-4

[LSI]

Table of Contents

Preface

The rapid pace of innovation in generative AI promises to change how we live and work, but it's getting increasingly difficult to keep up. The number of AI papers published on arXiv is growing exponentially (*https://oreil.ly/EN5ay*), Stable Diffusion (*https://oreil.ly/QX-yy*) has been among the fastest growing open source projects in history, and AI art tool Midjourney's Discord server (*https://oreil.ly/ZVZ5o*) has tens of millions of members, surpassing even the largest gaming communities. What most captured the public's imagination was OpenAI's release of ChatGPT, which reached 100 million users in two months (*https://oreil.ly/FbYWk*), making it the fastest-growing consumer app in history. Learning to work with AI has quickly become one of the most in-demand skills.

Everyone using AI professionally quickly learns that the quality of the output depends heavily on what you provide as input. The discipline of *prompt engineering* has arisen as a set of best practices for improving the reliability, efficiency, and accuracy of AI models. "In ten years, half of the world's jobs will be in prompt engineering," claims Robin Li (*https://oreil.ly/IdIfO*), the cofounder and CEO of Chinese tech giant Baidu. However, we expect prompting to be a skill required of many jobs, akin to proficiency in Microsoft Excel, rather than a popular job title in itself. This new wave of disruption is changing everything we thought we knew about computers. We're used to writing algorithms that return the same result every time—not so for AI, where the responses are non-deterministic. Cost and latency are real factors again, after decades of Moore's law making us complacent in expecting real-time computation at negligible cost. The biggest hurdle is the tendency of these models to confidently make things up, dubbed *hallucination*, causing us to rethink the way we evaluate the accuracy of our work.

We've been working with generative AI since the GPT-3 beta in 2020, and as we saw the models progress, many early prompting tricks and hacks became no longer necessary. Over time a consistent set of principles emerged that were still useful with the newer models, and worked across both text and image generation. We have written this book based on these timeless principles, helping you learn transferable skills that will continue to be useful no matter what happens with AI over the next five years. The key to working with AI isn't "figuring out how to hack the prompt by adding one magic word to the end that changes everything else," as OpenAI cofounder Sam Altman asserts (*https://oreil.ly/oo262*), but what will always matter is the "quality of ideas and the understanding of what you want." While we don't know if we'll call it "prompt engineering" in five years, working effectively with generative AI will only become more important.

Software Requirements for This Book

All of the code in this book is in Python and was designed to be run in a Jupyter Notebook (*https://jupyter.org*) or Google Colab notebook (*https://colab.research.goo gle.com*). The concepts taught in the book are transferable to JavaScript or any other coding language if preferred, though the primary focus of this book is on prompting techniques rather than traditional coding skills. The code can all be found on GitHub (*https://oreil.ly/BrightPool*), and we will link to the relevant notebooks throughout. It's highly recommended that you utilize the GitHub repository (*https://oreil.ly/Bright Pool*) and run the provided examples while reading the book.

For non-notebook examples, you can run the script with the format `python con tent/chapter_x/script.py` in your terminal, where x is the chapter number and `script.py` is the name of the script. In some instances, API keys need to be set as environment variables, and we will make that clear. The packages used update frequently, so install our *requirements.txt* (*https://oreil.ly/BPreq*) in a virtual environment before running code examples.

The *requirements.txt* file is generated for Python 3.9. If you want to use a different version of Python, you can generate a new *requirements.txt* from this *requirements.in* (*https://oreil.ly/YRwP7*) file found within the GitHub repository, by running these commands:

```
`pip install pip-tools`
`pip-compile requirements.in`
```

For Mac users:

1. Open Terminal: You can find the Terminal application in your Applications folder, under Utilities, or use Spotlight to search for it.

2. Navigate to your project folder: Use the `cd` command to change the directory to your project folder. For example: `cd path/to/your/project`.

3. Create the virtual environment: Use the following command to create a virtual environment named venv (you can name it anything): `python3 -m venv venv`.

4. Activate the virtual environment: Before you install packages, you need to activate the virtual environment. Do this with the command `source venv/bin/activate`.

5. Install packages: Now that your virtual environment is active, you can install packages using `pip`. To install packages from the *requirements.txt* file, use `pip install -r requirements.txt`.

6. Deactivate virtual environment: When you're done, you can deactivate the virtual environment by typing **deactivate**.

For Windows users:

1. Open Command Prompt: You can search for `cmd` in the Start menu.

2. Navigate to your project folder: Use the `cd` command to change the directory to your project folder. For example: `cd path\to\your\project`.

3. Create the virtual environment: Use the following command to create a virtual environment named `venv`: `python -m venv venv`.

4. Activate the virtual environment: To activate the virtual environment on Windows, use `.\venv\Scripts\activate`.

5. Install packages: With the virtual environment active, install the required packages: `pip install -r requirements.txt`.

6. Deactivate the virtual environment: To exit the virtual environment, simply type: `deactivate`.

Here are some additional tips on setup:

- Always ensure your Python is up-to-date to avoid compatibility issues.

- Remember to activate your virtual environment whenever you work on the project.

- The *requirements.txt* file should be in the same directory where you create your virtual environment, or you should specify the path to it when using `pip install -r`.

Access to an OpenAI developer account is assumed, as your `OPENAI_API_KEY` must be set as an environment variable in any examples importing the OpenAI library, for which we use version 1.0. Quick-start instructions for setting up your development environment can be found in OpenAI's documentation (*https://oreil.ly/YqbrY*) on their website.

You must also ensure that *billing is enabled* on your OpenAI account and that a valid payment method is attached to run some of the code within the book. The examples in the book use GPT-4 where not stated, though we do briefly cover Anthropic's competing Claude 3 model (*https://oreil.ly/jY8Ai*), as well as Meta's open source Llama 3 (*https://oreil.ly/BbXZ3*) and Google Gemini (*https://oreil.ly/KYgij*).

For image generation we use Midjourney (*https://www.midjourney.com*), for which you need a Discord account to sign up, though these principles apply equally to DALL-E 3 (available with a ChatGPT Plus subscription or via the API) or Stable Diffusion (available as an API (*https://oreil.ly/cmTtW*) or it can run locally (*https://oreil.ly/Ha0T5*) on your computer if it has a GPU). The image generation examples in this book use Midjourney v6, Stable Diffusion v1.5 (as many extensions are still only compatible with this version), or Stable Diffusion XL (*https://oreil.ly/S0P4s*), and we specify the differences when this is important.

We provide examples using open source libraries wherever possible, though we do include commercial vendors where appropriate—for example, Chapter 5 on vector databases demonstrates both FAISS (an open source library) and Pinecone (a paid vendor). The examples demonstrated in the book should be easily modifiable for alternative models and vendors, and the skills taught are transferable. Chapter 4 on advanced text generation is focused on the LLM framework LangChain, and Chapter 9 on advanced image generation is built on AUTOMATIC1111's open source Stable Diffusion Web UI.

Conventions Used in This Book

The following typographical conventions are used in this book:

Italic
Indicates new terms, URLs, email addresses, filenames, and file extensions.

`Constant width`
Used for program listings, as well as within paragraphs to refer to program elements such as variable or function names, databases, data types, environment variables, statements, and keywords.

`Constant width bold`
Shows commands or other text that should be typed literally by the user.

`Constant width italic`
Shows text that should be replaced with user-supplied values or by values determined by context.

This element signifies a tip or suggestion.

This element signifies a general note.

 This element indicates a warning or caution.

Throughout the book we reinforce what we call the Five Principles of Prompting, identifying which principle is most applicable to the example at hand. You may want to refer to Chapter 1, which describes the principles in detail.

 Principle Name

This will explain how the principle is applied to the current example or section of text.

Using Code Examples

Supplemental material (code examples, exercises, etc.) is available for download at *https://oreil.ly/prompt-engineering-for-generative-ai*.

If you have a technical question or a problem using the code examples, please send email to *bookquestions@oreilly.com*.

This book is here to help you get your job done. In general, if example code is offered with this book, you may use it in your programs and documentation. You do not need to contact us for permission unless you're reproducing a significant portion of the code. For example, writing a program that uses several chunks of code from this book does not require permission. Selling or distributing examples from O'Reilly books does require permission. Answering a question by citing this book and quoting example code does not require permission. Incorporating a significant amount of example code from this book into your product's documentation does require permission.

We appreciate, but generally do not require, attribution. An attribution usually includes the title, author, publisher, and ISBN. For example: "*Prompt Engineering for Generative AI* by James Phoenix and Mike Taylor (O'Reilly). Copyright 2024 Saxifrage, LLC and Just Understanding Data LTD, 978-1-098-15343-4."

If you feel your use of code examples falls outside fair use or the permission given above, feel free to contact us at *permissions@oreilly.com*.

O'Reilly Online Learning

O'REILLY® For more than 40 years, *O'Reilly Media* has provided technology and business training, knowledge, and insight to help
companies succeed.

Our unique network of experts and innovators share their knowledge and expertise
through books, articles, and our online learning platform. O'Reilly's online learning
platform gives you on-demand access to live training courses, in-depth learning
paths, interactive coding environments, and a vast collection of text and video from
O'Reilly and 200+ other publishers. For more information, visit *https://oreilly.com*.

How to Contact Us

Please address comments and questions concerning this book to the publisher:

O'Reilly Media, Inc.
1005 Gravenstein Highway North
Sebastopol, CA 95472
800-889-8969 (in the United States or Canada)
707-827-7019 (international or local)
707-829-0104 (fax)
support@oreilly.com
https://www.oreilly.com/about/contact.html

We have a web page for this book, where we list errata, examples, and any additional information. You can access this page at *https://oreil.ly/prompt-engineering-
generativeAI*.

For news and information about our books and courses, visit *https://oreilly.com*.

Find us on LinkedIn: *https://linkedin.com/company/oreilly-media*.

Watch us on YouTube: *https://youtube.com/oreillymedia*.

Acknowledgments

We'd like to thank the following people for their contribution in conducting a technical review of the book and their patience in correcting a fast-moving target:

- Mayo Oshin, early LangChain contributor and founder at SeinnAI Analytics
  (*https://www.siennaianalytics.com*)

- Ellis Crosby, founder at Scarlett Panda (*https://www.scarlettpanda.com*) and AI agency Incremen.to (*https://incremen.to*)
- Dave Pawson, O'Reilly author of *XSL-FO* (*https://oreil.ly/XSL-FO*)
- Mark Phoenix, a senior software engineer
- Aditya Goel, GenAI consultant

We are also grateful to our families for their patience and understanding and would like to reassure them that we still prefer talking to them over ChatGPT.

## CHAPTER 1

The Five Principles of Prompting

Prompt engineering is the process of discovering prompts that reliably yield useful or desired results.

A *prompt* is the input you provide, typically text, when interfacing with an AI model like ChatGPT or Midjourney. The prompt serves as a set of instructions the model uses to predict the desired response: text from *large language models* (LLMs) like ChatGPT (*https://chat.openai.com*), or images from *diffusion models* like Midjourney (*https://www.midjourney.com*).

Here is a simple example of a prompt input for a product name generator (inspired by one of OpenAI's examples (*https://oreil.ly/Fc8cq*)), and the resulting output from ChatGPT.

Input:

```
Can I have a list of product names for a pair of shoes that
can fit any foot size?
```

Output:

```
Certainly! Here's a list of product names for a pair of shoes
that can fit any foot size:

UniFit SoleStrides
FlexiSize All-Fit Shoes
OmniFit FootFlex
...
AnyStep AdaptiWalkers
FlexiRange UniversalSteps
PerfectGlide MultiFit Shoes
```

This is already a remarkable response for a naive prompt, which feels like magic because we got here with very little effort. As the state-of-the-art models improve, the likelihood you will get *good enough* results on your first try goes up. For any throwaway interactions with an AI, where you don't plan to do the same task again, the naive approach is all you need.

However, if you planned to put this prompt into production, you'd benefit from investing more work into getting it right. Mistakes cost you money in terms of the fees OpenAI charges based on the length of the prompt and response, as well as the time spent fixing mistakes. If you were building a product name generator with thousands of users, there are some obvious issues you'd want attempt to fix:

Vague direction
> You're not briefing the AI on what style of name you want, or what attributes it should have. Do you want a single word or a concatenation? Can the words be made up, or is it important that they're in real English? Do you want the AI to emulate somebody you admire who is famous for great product names?

Unformatted output
> You're getting back a list of separated names line by line, of unspecified length. When you run this prompt multiple times, you'll see sometimes it comes back with a numbered list, and often it has text at the beginning, which makes it hard to parse programmatically.

Missing examples
> You haven't given the AI any examples of what *good* names look like. It's auto-completing using an average of its training data, i.e., the entire internet (with all its inherent bias), but is that what you want? Ideally you'd feed it examples of successful names, common names in an industry, or even just other names you like.

Limited evaluation
> You have no consistent or scalable way to define which names are good or bad, so you have to manually review each response. If you can institute a rating system or other form of measurement, you can optimize the prompt to get better results and identify how many times it fails.

No task division
> You're asking a lot of a single prompt here: there are lots of factors that go into product naming, and this important task is being naively outsourced to the AI all in one go, with no task specialization or visibility into how it's handling this task for you.

Addressing these problems is the basis for the core principles we use throughout this book. There are many different ways to ask an AI model to do the same task, and even slight changes can make a big difference. LLMs work by continuously predicting the next token (approximately three-fourths of a word), starting from what was in your prompt. Each new token is selected based on its probability of appearing next, with an element of randomness (controlled by the *temperature* parameter). As demonstrated in Figure 1-1, the word *shoes* had a lower probability of coming after the start of the name *AnyFit* (0.88%), where a more predictable response would be *Athletic* (72.35%).

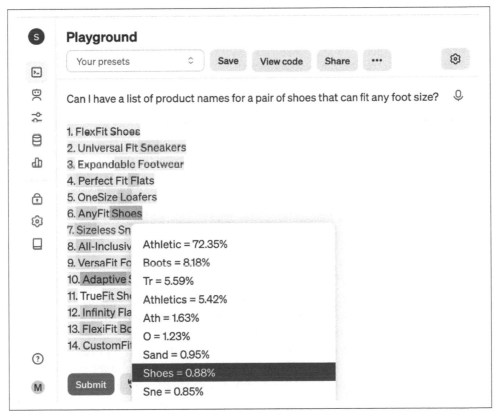

Figure 1-1. How the response breaks down into tokens

LLMs are trained on essentially the entire text of the internet, and are then further fine-tuned to give helpful responses. Average prompts will return average responses, leading some to be underwhelmed when their results don't live up to the hype. What you put in your prompt changes the probability of every word generated, so it matters a great deal to the results you'll get. These models have seen the best and worst of what humans have produced and are capable of emulating almost anything if you know the right way to ask. OpenAI charges based on the number of tokens used (*https://openai.com/pricing*) in the prompt and the response, so prompt engineers need to make these tokens count by optimizing prompts for cost, quality, and reliability.

Here's the same example with the application of several prompt engineering techniques. We ask for names in the style of Steve Jobs, state that we want a comma-separated list, and supply examples of the task done well.

Input:

```
Brainstorm a list of product names for a shoe that fits any
foot size, in the style of Steve Jobs.

Return the results as a comma-separated list, in this format:
Product description: A shoe that fits any foot size
Product names: [list of 3 product names]

## Examples
Product description: A refrigerator that dispenses beer
Product names: iBarFridge, iFridgeBeer, iDrinkBeerFridge

Product description: A watch that can tell accurate time in
space
Product names: iNaut, iSpace, iTime

Product description: A home milkshake maker
Product names: iShake, iSmoothie, iShake Mini
```

Output:

```
Product description: A shoe that fits any foot size
Product names: iFitFoot, iPerfectFit, iShoeSize
```

While no prompt is ever perfect, this prompt is optimized to reliably deliver solid product names in the right format. The user of your product name generator can choose somebody other than Steve Jobs to get the types of names they like, they can change the response format if needed, and the output of this prompt can become the input of another. Finally, you could periodically update the examples you use in the prompt based on user feedback, making your system smarter over time.

Overview of the Five Principles of Prompting

The process for optimizing this prompt follows the *Five Principles of Prompting*, which we will dissect using this example in the remainder of this chapter, and recall throughout the book. They map exactly to the five issues we raised when discussing the naive text prompt. You'll find references back to these principles throughout the rest of the book to help you connect the dots to how they're used in practice. The Five Principles of Prompting are as follows:

Give Direction
> Describe the desired style in detail, or reference a relevant persona

Specify Format
> Define what rules to follow, and the required structure of the response

Provide Examples
> Insert a diverse set of test cases where the task was done correctly

Evaluate Quality
> Identify errors and rate responses, testing what drives performance.

Divide Labor
> Split tasks into multiple steps, chained together for complex goals

These principles are not short-lived *tips* or *hacks* but are generally accepted conventions that are useful for working with any level of intelligence, biological or artificial. These principles are model-agnostic and should work to improve your prompt no matter which generative text or image model you're using. We first published these principles in July 2022 in the blog post "Prompt Engineering: From Words to Art and Copy" (*https://oreil.ly/RYYiV*), and they have stood the test of time, including mapping quite closely to OpenAI's own Prompt Engineering Guide (*https://oreil.ly/dF8q-*), which came a year later. Anyone who works closely with generative AI models is likely to converge on a similar set of strategies for solving common issues, and throughout this book you'll see hundreds of demonstrative examples of how they can be useful for improving your prompts.

We have provided downloadable one-pagers for text and image generation you can use as a checklist when applying these principles. These were created for our popular Udemy course The Complete Prompt Engineering for AI Bootcamp (*https://oreil.ly/V40zg*) (70,000+ students), which was based on the same principles but with different material to this book.

- Text Generation One-Pager (*https://oreil.ly/VCcgy*)
- Image Generation One-Pager (*https://oreil.ly/q7wQF*)

To show these principles apply equally well to prompting image models, let's use the following example, and explain how to apply each of the Five Principles of Prompting to this specific scenario. Copy and paste the entire input prompt into the Midjourney Bot in Discord, including the link to the image at the beginning, after typing **/imagine** to trigger the prompt box to appear (requires a free Discord (*https://discord.com*) account, and a paid Midjourney (*https://www.midjourney.com*) account).

Input:

```
https://s.mj.run/TKAsyhNiKmc stock photo of business meeting
of 4 people watching on white MacBook on top of glass-top
table, Panasonic, DC-GH5
```

Figure 1-2 shows the output.

Figure 1-2. Stock photo of business meeting

This prompt takes advantage of Midjourney's ability to take a base image as an example by uploading the image to Discord and then copy and pasting the URL into the prompt (*https://s.mj.run/TKAsyhNiKmc*), for which the royalty-free image from Unsplash is used (Figure 1-3). If you run into an error with the prompt, try uploading the image yourself and reviewing Midjourney's documentation (*https://oreil.ly/UTxpX*) for any formatting changes.

Figure 1-3. Photo by Mimi Thian on Unsplash (https://oreil.ly/J4Hkr)

Let's compare this well-engineered prompt to what you get back from Midjourney if you naively ask for a stock photo in the simplest way possible. Figure 1-4 shows an example of what you get without prompt engineering, an image with a darker, more stylistic take on a stock photo than you'd typically expect.

Input:

```
people in a business meeting
```

Figure 1-4 shows the output.

Although less prominent an issue in v5 of Midjourney onwards, community feedback mechanisms (when users select an image to resize to a higher resolution, that choice may be used to train the model) have reportedly biased the model toward a *fantasy* aesthetic, which is less suitable for the stock photo use case. The early adopters of Midjourney came from the digital art world and naturally gravitated toward fantasy and sci-fi styles, which can be reflected in the results from the model even when this aesthetic is not suitable.

Figure 1-4. People in a business meeting

Throughout this book the examples used will be compatiable with ChatGPT Plus (GPT-4) as the text model and Midjourney v6 or Stable Diffusion XL as the image model, though we will specify if it's important. These foundational models are the current state of the art and are good at a diverse range of tasks. The principles are intended to be future-proof as much as is possible, so if you're reading this book when GPT-5, Midjourney v7, or Stable Diffusion XXL is out, or if you're using another vendor like Google, everything you learn here should still prove useful.

1. Give Direction

One of the issues with the naive text prompt discussed earlier was that it wasn't briefing the AI on what *types* of product names you wanted. To some extent, naming a product is a subjective endeavor, and without giving the AI an idea of what names you like, it has a low probability of guessing right.

By the way, a human would also struggle to complete this task without a good *brief*, which is why creative and branding agencies require a detailed briefing on any task from their clients.

 Although it's not a perfect mapping, it can be helpful to imagine what context a human might need for this task and try including it in the prompt.

In the example prompt we gave direction through the use of *role-playing*, in that case emulating the style of Steve Jobs, who was famous for iconically naming products. If you change this aspect of the prompt to someone else who is famous in the training data (as well as matching the examples to the right style), you'll get dramatically different results.

Input:

```
Brainstorm a list of product names for a shoe that fits any
foot size, in the style of Elon Musk.

Return the results as a comma-separated list, in this format:
Product description: A shoe that fits any foot size
Product names: [list of 3 product names]

## Examples
Product description: A refrigerator that dispenses beer
Product names: Teslacool, FridgeX, Neuradrink

Product description: A watch that can tell accurate time in
space
Product names: WatchX, iSpace, The Watch Company

Product description: A home milkshake maker
Product names: ShakeX, The Milkshake Company, HyperShake
```

Output:

```
ShoeX, MarsFit, The Shoe Company
```

There are also some rules or best practices you would do well to follow, which could be included in the prompt as context to guide the AI toward a name that works. This technique is sometimes referred to as *prewarming* or *internal retrieval*, and it is simple but effective (Liu et al., 2021 (*https://oreil.ly/1lqzK*)). Starting the conversation asking for best practice advice, then asking it to follow its own advice, can help a lot. In effect, you are using it to generate its own direction.

Input:

> Please give me 5 tips for naming products based on expert
> industry advice.

Output:

> Certainly! Naming a product is crucial as it often gives the
> first impression to potential customers. Here are five expert
> tips to guide you in naming products:
>
> 1. **Simplicity & Memorability**: Opt for names that are
> short, easy to spell, and memorable. Long, complicated names
> can be difficult for customers to recall. Remember, the
> easier the name is to remember, the more likely it is that
> consumers will think of your product when making a purchase
> decision.
>
> ...
>
> 5. **Positive Connotations**: Names that evoke positive
> emotions or imagery can create a favorable perception of
> your product. Avoid names that have negative or
> controversial associations in any of the primary languages
> or cultures where you intend to do business. It's often
> worthwhile to conduct linguistic checks and market testing
> to ensure there aren't unintended meanings.
>
> Lastly, once you've shortlisted a few names, it's a good
> idea to run them by diverse focus groups or conduct surveys
> to gauge reactions. Also, ensure that the name you choose is
> available for trademarking and doesn't infringe on existing
> trademarks.

Then within the same chat window, where the model has the context of the past advice it gave, you ask your initial prompt for the task you wanted to complete.

Input:

> Using this advice, can I have a list of product names for a
> pair of shoes that can fit any foot size?

Output:

> Certainly! Based on the criteria given:
>
> 1. **Simplicity & Memorability**
> 2. **Relevance & Descriptiveness**
> 3. **Differentiation & Uniqueness**
> 4. **Adaptable & Scalable**
> 5. **Positive Connotations**
>
> Here's a list of potential product names for shoes that can
> fit any foot size:

```
1. **FitAll Walkers**: A simple and memorable name that
instantly suggests a universal fit.

...

10. **TrueFit Universals**: Emphasizing genuine comfort and
fit for all.

Before finalizing any name, remember to check for trademarks
to ensure there's no conflict with existing products or
brands.
```

Another fruitful strategy in our experience is to take the best advice out there for the task you want to accomplish and insert that context into the prompt. For example, you could take Brandwatch's 5 Golden Rules for naming a product (*https://oreil.ly/ 3bWjz*) or another trusted external resource you find, and insert that as context into the prompt. This will increase the length of the prompt significantly, which costs more money (when using the API as a developer), but may be worth the trade-off if the quality of the response improves.

Input:

```
Can I have a list of product names for a pair of shoes that
can fit any foot size? Please follow the five rules below:

1. It should be readable and writable.
If your product name is hard to pronounce, people won't talk about it,
and if they can't write it down (and spell it correctly!)
when they hear it, how do you expect them to Google it?

Keep it simple and don't go with any wacky spellings just for the sake of it.

...

5. It should evoke an emotion, feeling, or idea.
Your product name should tie back into what your product is, what the
feeling you want people to have when experiencing your product is, and/or
what idea are you trying to get across.

It should be emotive and inspiring.
```

Output:

```
1. FlexFit Footwear
2. OmniSize Sneakers
3. AdaptStride Shoes
...
18. OmniComfort Kicks
19. FlexSize Footwear
20. Boundless Soles
```

There are other myriad ways of providing direction. In the image generation example, direction was given by specifying that the business meeting is taking place around a glass-top table. If you change only that detail, you can get a completely different image, as detailed in Figure 1-5.

Input:

```
https://s.mj.run/TKAsyhNiKmc stock photo of business meeting
of four people gathered around a campfire outdoors in the
woods, Panasonic, DC-GH5
```

Figure 1-5 shows the output.

Figure 1-5. Stock photo of business meeting in the woods

Role-playing is also important for image generation, and one of the quite powerful ways you can give Midjourney direction is to supply the name of an artist or art style to emulate. One artist that features heavily in the AI art world is Van Gogh, known for his bold, dramatic brush strokes and vivid use of colors. Watch what happens when you include his name in the prompt, as shown in Figure 1-6.

Input:

```
people in a business meeting, by Van Gogh
```

Figure 1-6 shows the output.

Figure 1-6. People in a business meeting, by Van Gogh

To get that last prompt to work, you need to strip back a lot of the other direction. For example, losing the base image and the words *stock photo* as well as the camera *Panasonic, DC-GH5* helps bring in Van Gogh's style. The problem you may run into is that often with too much direction, the model can quickly get to a conflicting combination that it can't resolve. If your prompt is overly specific, there might not be enough samples in the training data to generate an image that's consistent with all of your criteria. In cases like these, you should choose which element is more important (in this case, Van Gogh) and defer to that.

Direction is one of the most commonly used and broadest principles. It can take the form of simply using the right descriptive words to clarify your intent, or channeling the personas of relevant business celebrities. While too much direction can narrow the creativity of the model, too little direction is the more common problem.

2. Specify Format

AI models are universal translators. Not only does that mean translating from French to English, or Urdu to Klingon, but also between data structures like JSON to YAML, or natural language to Python code. These models are capable of returning a response in almost any format, so an important part of prompt engineering is finding ways to specify what format you want the response to be in.

Every now and again you'll find that the same prompt will return a different format, for example, a numbered list instead of comma separated. This isn't a big deal most of the time, because most prompts are one-offs and typed into ChatGPT or Midjourney. However, when you're incorporating AI tools into production software, occasional flips in format can cause all kinds of errors.

Just like when working with a human, you can avoid wasted effort by specifying up front the format you expect the response to be in. For text generation models, it can often be helpful to output JSON instead of a simple ordered list because that's the universal format for API responses, which can make it simpler to parse and spot errors, as well as to use to render the front-end HTML of an application. YAML is also another popular choice because it enforces a parseable structure while still being simple and human-readable.

In the original prompt you gave direction through both the examples provided, and the colon at the end of the prompt indicated it should complete the list inline. To swap the format to JSON, you need to update both and leave the JSON uncompleted, so GPT-4 knows to complete it.

Input:

```
Return a comma-separated list of product names in JSON for
"A pair of shoes that can fit any foot size.".
Return only JSON.

Examples:
[{
            "Product description": "A home milkshake maker.",
            "Product names": ["HomeShaker", "Fit Shaker",
            "QuickShake", "Shake Maker"]
    },
    {
            "Product description": "A watch that can tell
            accurate time in space.",
            "Product names": ["AstroTime", "SpaceGuard",
            "Orbit-Accurate", "EliptoTime"]}
]
```

Output:

```
[
    {
            "Product description": "A pair of shoes that can \
            fit any foot size.",
            "Product names": ["FlexFit Footwear", "OneSize Step",
            "Adapt-a-Shoe", "Universal Walker"]
    }
]
```

The output we get back is the completed JSON containing the product names. This can then be parsed and used programmatically, in an application or local script. It's also easy from this point to check if there's an error in the formatting using a JSON parser like Python's standard *json* library, because broken JSON will result in a parsing error, which can act as a trigger to retry the prompt or investigate before continuing. If you're still not getting the right format back, it can help to specify at the beginning or end of the prompt, or in the system message if using a chat model: You are a helpful assistant that only responds in JSON, or specify JSON output (*https://oreil.ly/E7wua*) in the model parameters where available (this is called *grammars* with Llama models (*https://oreil.ly/yU27T*).

 To get up to speed on JSON if you're unfamiliar, W3Schools has a good introduction (*https://oreil.ly/Xakgc*).

For image generation models, format is very important, because the opportunities for modifying an image are near endless. They range from obvious formats like stock photo, illustration, and oil painting, to more unusual formats like dashcam footage, ice sculpture, or in Minecraft (see Figure 1-7).

Input:

```
business meeting of four people watching on MacBook on top of
table, in Minecraft
```

Figure 1-7 shows the output.

Figure 1-7. Business meeting in Minecraft

When setting a format, it is often necessary to remove other aspects of the prompt that might clash with the specified format. For example, if you supply a base image of a stock photo, the result is some combination of stock photo and the format you wanted. To some degree, image generation models can generalize to new scenarios and combinations they haven't seen before in their training set, but in our experience, the more layers of unrelated elements, the more likely you are to get an unsuitable image.

There is often some overlap between the first and second principles, Give Direction and Specify Format. The latter is about defining what type of output you want, for example JSON format, or the format of a stock photo. The former is about the style of response you want, independent from the format, for example product names in the style of Steve Jobs, or an image of a business meeting in the style of Van Gogh. When there are clashes between style and format, it's often best to resolve them by dropping whichever element is less important to your final result.

3. Provide Examples

The original prompt didn't give the AI any examples of what you think *good* names look like. Therefore, the response is approximate to an average of the internet, and you can do better than that. Researchers would call a prompt with no examples *zero-shot*, and it's always a pleasant surprise when AI can even do a task zero shot: it's a sign of a powerful model. If you're providing zero examples, you're asking for a lot without giving much in return. Even providing one example (*one-shot*) helps considerably, and it's the norm among researchers to test how models perform with multiple examples (*few-shot*). One such piece of research is the famous GPT-3 paper "Language Models are Few-Shot Learners" (*https://oreil.ly/KW5PS*), the results of which are illustrated in Figure 1-8, showing adding one example along with a prompt can improve accuracy in some tasks from 10% to near 50%!

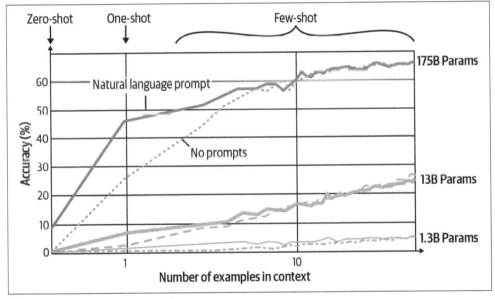

Figure 1-8. Number of examples in context

When briefing a colleague or training a junior employee on a new task, it's only natural that you'd include examples of times that task had previously been done well. Working with AI is the same, and the strength of a prompt often comes down to the examples used. Providing examples can sometimes be easier than trying to explain exactly what it is about those examples you like, so this technique is most effective when you are not a domain expert in the subject area of the task you are attempting to complete. The amount of text you can fit in a prompt is limited (at the time of writing around 6,000 characters on Midjourney and approximately 32,000 characters for the free version of ChatGPT), so a lot of the work of prompt engineering involves selecting and inserting diverse and instructive examples.

There's a trade-off between reliability and creativity: go past three to five examples and your results will become more reliable, while sacrificing creativity. The more examples you provide, and the lesser the diversity between them, the more constrained the response will be to match your examples. If you change all of the examples to animal names in the previous prompt, you'll have a strong effect on the response, which will reliably return only names including animals.

Input:

```
Brainstorm a list of product names for a shoe that fits any
foot size.

Return the results as a comma-separated list, in this format:
Product description: A shoe that fits any foot size
Product names: [list of 3 product names]

## Examples:
Product description: A home milkshake maker.
Product names: Fast Panda, Healthy Bear, Compact Koala

Product description: A watch that can tell accurate time in
space.
Product names: AstroLamb, Space Bear, Eagle Orbit

Product description: A refrigerator that dispenses beer
Product names: BearFridge, Cool Cat, PenguinBox
```

Output:

```
Product description: A shoe that fits any foot size
Product names: FlexiFox, ChameleonStep, PandaPaws
```

Of course this runs the risk of missing out on returning a much better name that doesn't fit the limited space left for the AI to play in. Lack of diversity and variation in examples is also a problem in handling edge cases, or uncommon scenarios. Including one to three examples is easy and almost always has a positive effect, but above that number it becomes essential to experiment with the number of examples you include, as well as the similarity between them. There is some evidence (Hsieh et al., 2023 (*https://oreil.ly/6Ixcw*)) that direction works better than providing examples, and it typically isn't straightforward to collect good examples, so it's usually prudent to attempt the principle of Give Direction first.

In the image generation space, providing examples usually comes in the form of providing a base image in the prompt, called *img2img* in the open source Stable Diffusion (*https://oreil.ly/huVRu*) community. Depending on the image generation model being used, these images can be used as a starting point for the model to generate from, which greatly affects the results. You can keep everything about the prompt the same but swap out the provided base image for a radically different effect, as in Figure 1-9.

Input:

```
stock photo of business meeting of 4 people watching on
white MacBook on top of glass-top table, Panasonic, DC-GH5
```

Figure 1-9 shows the output.

Figure 1-9. Stock photo of business meeting of four people

In this case, by substituting for the image shown in Figure 1-10, also from Unsplash, you can see how the model was pulled in a different direction and incorporates whiteboards and sticky notes now.

 These examples demonstrate the capabilities of image generation models, but we would exercise caution when uploading base images for use in prompts. Check the licensing of the image you plan to upload and use in your prompt as the base image, and avoid using clearly copyrighted images. Doing so can land you in legal trouble and is against the terms of service for all the major image generation model providers.

Figure 1-10. Photo by Jason Goodman on Unsplash (https://oreil.ly/ZbzZy)

4. Evaluate Quality

As of yet, there has been no feedback loop to judge the quality of your responses, other than the basic trial and error of running the prompt and seeing the results, referred to as *blind prompting* (*https://oreil.ly/42rSz*). This is fine when your prompts are used temporarily for a single task and rarely revisited. However, when you're reusing the same prompt multiple times or building a production application that relies on a prompt, you need to be more rigorous with measuring results.

There are a number of ways performance can be evaluated, and it depends largely on what tasks you're hoping to accomplish. When a new AI model is released, the focus tends to be on how well the model did on *evals* (evaluations), a standardized set of questions with predefined answers or grading criteria that are used to test performance across models. Different models perform differently across different types of tasks, and there is no guarantee a prompt that worked previously will translate well to a new model. OpenAI has made its evals framework (*https://oreil.ly/ wolEL*) for benchmarking performance of LLMs open source and encourages others to contribute additional eval templates.

In addition to the standard academic evals, there are also more headline-worthy tests like GPT-4 passing the bar exam (*https://oreil.ly/txhSZ*). Evaluation is difficult for more subjective tasks, and can be time-consuming or prohibitively costly for smaller teams. In some instances researchers have turned to using more advanced models like GPT-4 to evaluate responses from less sophisticated models, as was done with the release of Vicuna-13B (*https://oreil.ly/NW3WX*), a fine-tuned model based on Meta's Llama open source model (see Figure 1-11).

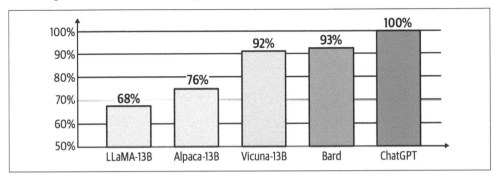

Figure 1-11. Vicuna GPT-4 Evals

More rigorous evaluation techniques are necessary when writing scientific papers or grading a new foundation model release, but often you will only need to go just one step above basic trial and error. You may find that a simple thumbs-up/thumbs-down rating system implemented in a Jupyter Notebook can be enough to add some rigor to prompt optimization, without adding too much overhead. One common test is to see whether providing examples is worth the additional cost in terms of prompt length, or whether you can get away with providing no examples in the prompt. The first step is getting responses for multiple runs of each prompt and storing them in a spreadsheet, which we will do after setting up our environment.

You can install the OpenAI Python package with `pip install openai`. If you're running into compatability issues with this package, create a virtual environment and install our *requirements.txt* (*https://oreil.ly/2KDV6*) (instructions in the preface).

To utilize the API, you'll need to create an OpenAI account (*https://oreil.ly/oGv4j*) and then navigate here for your API key (*https://oreil.ly/oHID1*).

 Hardcoding API keys in scripts is not recommended due to security reasons. Instead, utilize environment variables or configuration files to manage your keys.

Once you have an API key, it's crucial to assign it as an environment variable by executing the following command, replacing `api_key` with your actual API key value:

```
export OPENAI_API_KEY="api_key"
```

Or on Windows:

```
set OPENAI_API_KEY=api_key
```

Alternatively, if you'd prefer not to preset an API key, then you can manually set the key while initializing the model, or load it from an *.env* file using *python-dotenv* (*https://oreil.ly/IaQjS*). First, install the library with `pip install python-dotenv`, and then load the environment variables with the following code at the top of your script or notebook:

```python
from dotenv import load_dotenv

load_dotenv()  # take environment variables from .env.
```

The first step is getting responses for multiple runs of each prompt and storing them in a spreadsheet.

Input:

```python
# Define two variants of the prompt to test zero-shot
# vs few-shot
prompt_A = """Product description: A pair of shoes that can
fit any foot size.
Seed words: adaptable, fit, omni-fit.
Product names:"""

prompt_B = """Product description: A home milkshake maker.
Seed words: fast, healthy, compact.
Product names: HomeShaker, Fit Shaker, QuickShake, Shake
Maker

Product description: A watch that can tell accurate time in
space.
Seed words: astronaut, space-hardened, eliptical orbit
Product names: AstroTime, SpaceGuard, Orbit-Accurate,
EliptoTime.

Product description: A pair of shoes that can fit any foot
size.
Seed words: adaptable, fit, omni-fit.
Product names:"""

test_prompts = [prompt_A, prompt_B]

import pandas as pd
from openai import OpenAI
import os

# Set your OpenAI key as an environment variable
# https://platform.openai.com/api-keys
client = OpenAI(
  api_key=os.environ['OPENAI_API_KEY'],  # Default
)

def get_response(prompt):
    response = client.chat.completions.create(
```

```
        model="gpt-3.5-turbo",
        messages=[
            {
                "role": "system",
                "content": "You are a helpful assistant."
            },
            {
                "role": "user",
                "content": prompt
            }
        ]
    )
    return response.choices[0].message.content

# Iterate through the prompts and get responses
responses = []
num_tests = 5

for idx, prompt in enumerate(test_prompts):
    # prompt number as a letter
    var_name = chr(ord('A') + idx)

    for i in range(num_tests):
        # Get a response from the model
        response = get_response(prompt)

        data = {
            "variant": var_name,
            "prompt": prompt,
            "response": response
        }
        responses.append(data)

# Convert responses into a dataframe
df = pd.DataFrame(responses)

# Save the dataframe as a CSV file
df.to_csv("responses.csv", index=False)

print(df)
```

Output:

```
   variant                                              prompt
  \
0        A  Product description: A pair of shoes that can ...
1        A  Product description: A pair of shoes that can ...
2        A  Product description: A pair of shoes that can ...
3        A  Product description: A pair of shoes that can ...
4        A  Product description: A pair of shoes that can ...
5        B  Product description: A home milkshake maker.\n...
6        B  Product description: A home milkshake maker.\n...
7        B  Product description: A home milkshake maker.\n...
```

```
8          B  Product description: A home milkshake maker.\n...
9          B  Product description: A home milkshake maker.\n...

                                                       response
0   1. Adapt-a-Fit Shoes \n2. Omni-Fit Footwear \n...
1   1. OmniFit Shoes\n2. Adapt-a-Sneaks \n3. OneFi...
2   1. Adapt-a-fit\n2. Flexi-fit shoes\n3. Omni-fe...
3   1. Adapt-A-Sole\n2. FitFlex\n3. Omni-FitX\n4. ...
4   1. Omni-Fit Shoes\n2. Adapt-a-Fit Shoes\n3. An...
5   Adapt-a-Fit, Perfect Fit Shoes, OmniShoe, OneS...
6         FitAll, OmniFit Shoes, SizeLess, AdaptaShoes
7         AdaptaFit, OmniShoe, PerfectFit, AllSizeFit.
8   FitMaster, AdaptoShoe, OmniFit, AnySize Footwe...
9        Adapt-a-Shoe, PerfectFit, OmniSize, FitForm
```

Here we're using the OpenAI API to generate model responses to a set of prompts and storing the results in a dataframe, which is saved to a CSV file. Here's how it works:

1. Two prompt variants are defined, and each variant consists of a product description, seed words, and potential product names, but `prompt_B` provides two examples.

2. Import statements are called for the Pandas library, OpenAI library, and os library.

3. The `get_response` function takes a prompt as input and returns a response from the `gpt-3.5-turbo` model. The prompt is passed as a user message to the model, along with a system message to set the model's behavior.

4. Two prompt variants are stored in the `test_prompts` list.

5. An empty list `responses` is created to store the generated responses, and the variable `num_tests` is set to 5.

6. A nested loop is used to generate responses. The outer loop iterates over each prompt, and the inner loop generates `num_tests` (five in this case) number of responses per prompt.

    a. The `enumerate` function is used to get the index and value of each prompt in `test_prompts`. This index is then converted to a corresponding uppercase letter (e.g., 0 becomes *A*, 1 becomes *B*) to be used as a variant name.

    b. For each iteration, the `get_response` function is called with the current prompt to generate a response from the model.

    c. A dictionary is created with the variant name, the prompt, and the model's response, and this dictionary is appended to the `responses` list.

7. Once all responses have been generated, the `responses` list (which is now a list of dictionaries) is converted into a Pandas DataFrame.

8. This dataframe is then saved to a CSV file with the Pandas built-in `to_csv` function, making the file *responses.csv* with `index=False` so as to not write row indices.

9. Finally, the dataframe is printed to the console.

Having these responses in a spreadsheet is already useful, because you can see right away even in the printed response that `prompt_A` (zero-shot) in the first five rows is giving us a numbered list, whereas `prompt_B` (few-shot) in the last five rows tends to output the desired format of a comma-separated inline list. The next step is to give a rating on each of the responses, which is best done blind and randomized to avoid favoring one prompt over another.

Input:

```python
import ipywidgets as widgets
from IPython.display import display
import pandas as pd

# load the responses.csv file
df = pd.read_csv("responses.csv")

# Shuffle the dataframe
df = df.sample(frac=1).reset_index(drop=True)

# df is your dataframe and 'response' is the column with the
# text you want to test
response_index = 0
# add a new column to store feedback
df['feedback'] = pd.Series(dtype='str')

def on_button_clicked(b):
    global response_index
    # convert thumbs up / down to 1 / 0
    user_feedback = 1 if b.description == "\U0001F44D" else 0

    # update the feedback column
    df.at[response_index, 'feedback'] = user_feedback

    response_index += 1
    if response_index < len(df):
        update_response()
    else:
        # save the feedback to a CSV file
        df.to_csv("results.csv", index=False)

        print("A/B testing completed. Here's the results:")
        # Calculate score and num rows for each variant
        summary_df = df.groupby('variant').agg(
            count=('feedback', 'count'),
            score=('feedback', 'mean')).reset_index()
```

```
        print(summary_df)

def update_response():
    new_response = df.iloc[response_index]['response']
    if pd.notna(new_response):
        new_response = "<p>" + new_response + "</p>"
    else:
        new_response = "<p>No response</p>"
    response.value = new_response
    count_label.value = f"Response: {response_index + 1}"
    count_label.value += f"/{len(df)}"

response = widgets.HTML()
count_label = widgets.Label()

update_response()

thumbs_up_button = widgets.Button(description='\U0001F44D')
thumbs_up_button.on_click(on_button_clicked)

thumbs_down_button = widgets.Button(
    description='\U0001F44E')
thumbs_down_button.on_click(on_button_clicked)

button_box = widgets.HBox([thumbs_down_button,
thumbs_up_button])

display(response, button_box, count_label)
```

The output is shown in Figure 1-12:

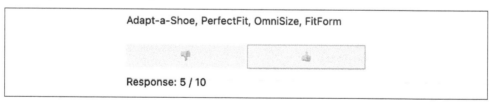

Figure 1-12. Thumbs-up/thumbs-down rating system

If you run this in a Jupyter Notebook, a widget displays each AI response, with a thumbs-up or thumbs-down button (see Figure 1-12) This provides a simple interface for quickly labeling responses, with minimal overhead. If you wish to do this outside of a Jupyter Notebook, you could change the thumbs-up and thumbs-down emojis for *Y* and *N*, and implement a loop using the built-in input() function, as a text-only replacement for iPyWidgets.

Once you've finished labeling the responses, you get the output, which shows you how each prompt performs.

Output:

```
A/B testing completed. Here's the results:
  variant  count  score
0       A      5    0.2
1       B      5    0.6
```

The dataframe was shuffled at random, and each response was labeled blind (without seeing the prompt), so you get an accurate picture of how often each prompt performed. Here is the step-by-step explanation:

1. Three modules are imported: `ipywidgets`, `IPython.display`, and `pandas`. `ipywidgets` contains interactive HTML widgets for Jupyter Notebooks and the IPython kernel. `IPython.display` provides classes for displaying various types of output like images, sound, displaying HTML, etc. Pandas is a powerful data manipulation library.

2. The pandas library is used to read in the CSV file *responses.csv*, which contains the responses you want to test. This creates a Pandas DataFrame called `df`.

3. `df` is shuffled using the `sample()` function with `frac=1`, which means it uses all the rows. The `reset_index(drop=True)` is used to reset the indices to the standard 0, 1, 2, …, n index.

4. The script defines `response_index` as 0. This is used to track which response from the dataframe the user is currently viewing.

5. A new column `feedback` is added to the dataframe `df` with the data type as `str` or string.

6. Next, the script defines a function `on_button_clicked(b)`, which will execute whenever one of the two buttons in the interface is clicked.

   a. The function first checks the `description` of the button clicked was the thumbs-up button (`\U0001F44D; 👍`), and sets `user_feedback` as 1, or if it was the thumbs-down button (`\U0001F44E 👎`), it sets `user_feedback` as 0.

   b. Then it updates the `feedback` column of the dataframe at the current `response_index` with `user_feedback`.

   c. After that, it increments `response_index` to move to the next response.

   d. If `response_index` is still less than the total number of responses (i.e., the length of the dataframe), it calls the function `update_response()`.

   e. If there are no more responses, it saves the dataframe to a new CSV file *results.csv*, then prints a message, and also prints a summary of the results by variant, showing the count of feedback received and the average score (mean) for each variant.

7. The function `update_response()` fetches the next response from the dataframe, wraps it in paragraph HTML tags (if it's not null), updates the `response` widget to display the new response, and updates the `count_label` widget to reflect the current response number and total number of responses.

8. Two widgets, `response` (an HTML widget) and `count_label` (a Label widget), are instantiated. The `update_response()` function is then called to initialize these widgets with the first response and the appropriate label.

9. Two more widgets, `thumbs_up_button` and `thumbs_down_button` (both Button widgets), are created with thumbs-up and thumbs-down emoji as their descriptions, respectively. Both buttons are configured to call the `on_button_clicked()` function when clicked.

10. The two buttons are grouped into a horizontal box (`button_box`) using the `HBox` function.

11. Finally, the `response`, `button_box`, and `count_label` widgets are displayed to the user using the `display()` function from the `IPython.display` module.

A simple rating system such as this one can be useful in judging prompt quality and encountering edge cases. Usually in less than 10 test runs of a prompt you uncover a deviation, which you otherwise wouldn't have caught until you started using it in production. The downside is that it can get tedious rating lots of responses manually, and your ratings might not represent the preferences of your intended audience. However, even small numbers of tests can reveal large differences between two prompting strategies and reveal nonobvious issues before reaching production.

Iterating on and testing prompts can lead to radical decreases in the length of the prompt and therefore the cost and latency of your system. If you can find another prompt that performs equally as well (or better) but uses a shorter prompt, you can afford to scale up your operation considerably. Often you'll find in this process that many elements of a complex prompt are completely superfluous, or even counterproductive.

The *thumbs-up* or other manually labeled indicators of quality don't have to be the only judging criteria. Human evaluation is generally considered to be the most accurate form of feedback. However, it can be tedious and costly to rate many samples manually. In many cases, as in math or classification use cases, it may be possible to establish *ground truth* (reference answers to test cases) to programmatically rate the results, allowing you to scale up considerably your testing and monitoring efforts. The following is not an exhaustive list because there are many motivations for evaluating your prompt programmatically:

Cost

Prompts that use a lot of tokens, or work only with more expensive models, might be impractical for production use.

Latency

Equally the more tokens there are, or the larger the model required, the longer it takes to complete a task, which can harm user experience.

Calls

Many AI systems require multiple calls in a loop to complete a task, which can seriously slow down the process.

Performance

Implement some form of external feedback system, for example a physics engine or other model for predicting real-world results.

Classification

Determine how often a prompt correctly labels given text, using another AI model or rules-based labeling.

Reasoning

Work out which instances the AI fails to apply logical reasoning or gets the math wrong versus reference cases.

Hallucinations

See how frequently you encouner hallucinations, as measured by invention of new terms not included in the prompt's context.

Safety

Flag any scenarios where the system might return unsafe or undesirable results using a safety filter or detection system.

Refusals

Find out how often the system incorrectly refuses to fulfill a reasonable user request by flagging known refusal language.

Adversarial

Make the prompt robust against known prompt injection (*https://oreil.ly/KGAqe*) attacks that can get the model to run undesirable prompts instead of what you programmed.

Similarity

Use shared words and phrases (BLEU or ROGUE (*https://oreil.ly/iEGZ9*)) or vector distance (explained in Chapter 5) to measure similarity between generated and reference text.

Once you start rating which examples were good, you can more easily update the examples used in your prompt as a way to continuously make your system smarter over time. The data from this feedback can also feed into examples for fine-tuning, which starts to beat prompt engineering once you can supply a few thousand examples (*https://oreil.ly/DZ-br*), as shown in Figure 1-13.

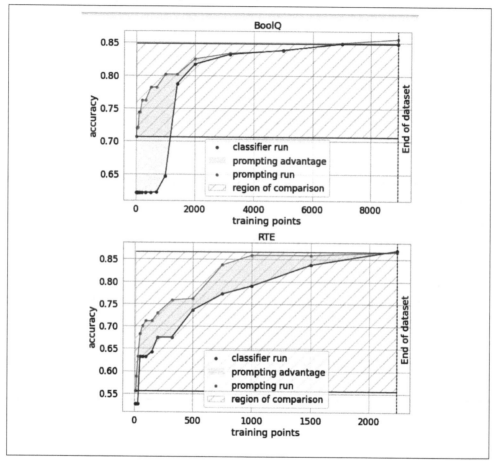

Figure 1-13. How many data points is a prompt worth?

Graduating from thumbs-up or thumbs-down, you can implement a 3-, 5-, or 10-point rating system to get more fine-grained feedback on the quality of your prompts. It's also possible to determine aggregate relative performance through comparing responses side by side, rather than looking at responses one at a time. From this you can construct a fair across-model comparison using an *Elo rating (https://oreil.ly/TlldE)*, as is popular in chess and used in the Chatbot Arena (*https://oreil.ly/P2IcU*) by *lmsys.org*.

For image generation, evaluation usually takes the form of *permutation* prompting, where you input multiple directions or formats and generate an image for each combination. Images can than be scanned or later arranged in a grid to show the effect that different elements of the prompt can have on the final image.

Input:

```
{stock photo, oil painting, illustration} of business
meeting of {four, eight} people watching on white MacBook on
top of glass-top table
```

In Midjourney this would be compiled into six different prompts, one for every combination of the three formats (stock photo, oil painting, illustration) and two numbers of people (four, eight).

Input:

```
1. stock photo of business meeting of four people watching
on white MacBook on top of glass-top table

2. stock photo of business meeting of eight people watching
on white MacDook on top of glass-top table

3. oil painting of business meeting of four people watching
on white MacBook on top of glass-top table

4. oil painting of business meeting of eight people watching
on white MacBook on top of glass-top table

5. illustration of business meeting of four people watching
on white MacBook on top of glass-top table

6. illustration of business meeting of eight people watching
on white MacBook on top of glass-top table
```

Each prompt generates its own four images as usual, which makes the output a little harder to see. We have selected one from each prompt to upscale and then put them together in a grid, shown as Figure 1-14. You'll notice that the model doesn't always get the correct number of people (generative AI models are surprisingly bad at math), but it has correctly inferred the general intention by adding more people to the photos on the right than the left.

Figure 1-14 shows the output.

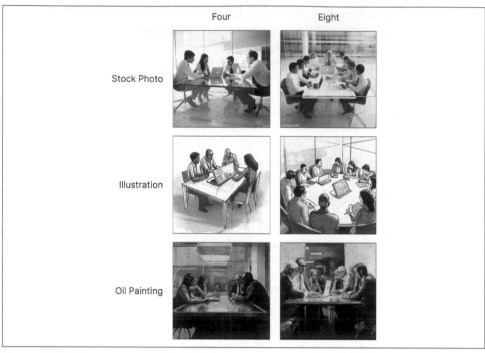

Figure 1-14. Prompt permutations grid

With models that have APIs like Stable Diffusion, you can more easily manipulate the photos and display them in a grid format for easy scanning. You can also manipulate the random seed of the image to fix a style in place for maximum reproducibility. With image classifiers it may also be possible to programmatically rate images based on their safe content, or if they contain certain elements associated with success or failure.

5. Divide Labor

As you build out your prompt, you start to get to the point where you're asking a lot in a single call to the AI. When prompts get longer and more convoluted, you may find the responses get less deterministic, and hallucinations or anomalies increase. Even if you manage to arrive at a reliable prompt for your task, that task is likely just one of a number of interrelated tasks you need to do your job. It's natural to start exploring how many other of these tasks could be done by AI and how you might string them together.

One of the core principles of engineering is to use task decomposition to break problems down into their component parts, so you can more easily solve each individual problem and then reaggregate the results. Breaking your AI work into multiple calls that are chained together can help you accomplish more complex tasks, as well as provide more visibility into what part of the chain is failing.

There are lots of factors that go into product naming, and an important task is naively outsourced to the AI with no visibility into how it's weighing the importance of these factors (if at all). The way our current system works, we're getting a list of names, but all names are displayed with equal importance with no further context for helping us decide. Fortunately AI tools are capable of self-evaluation; if we add a second step to our task, we can automatically check for nondesirable outputs.

Input:

```
Rate this list of product names for a pair of shoes that can
fit any foot size. The rating should be out of 10, inline
next to the product name:

UniFit SoleStrides
FlexiSize All-Fit Shoes
OmniFit FootFlex

...

AnyStep AdaptiWalkers
FlexiRange UniversalSteps
PerfectGlide MultiFit Shoes
```

Output:

```
UniFit SoleStrides: 7/10
FlexiSize All-Fit Shoes: 8/10
OmniFit FootFlex: 7/10

...

AnyStep AdaptiWalkers: 7/10
FlexiRange UniversalSteps: 7.5/10
PerfectGlide MultiFit Shoes: 9/10

This ranking is based on clarity, memorability, and how well
the name communicates the unique selling point of the
product (that they can fit any foot size). Remember, these
ratings are subjective and the ultimate success of a product
name also depends on the target market, branding, and
marketing efforts.
```

In running this multiple times, it consistently rates the name "OneSize Glovewalkers" as the worst, providing context (if you ask) that the concept might be confusing in a shoe context. You may be wondering why, if the model *knows* this is a bad name, does it suggest it in the first place? LLMs work by predicting the next token in a sequence and therefore struggle to know what the overall response will be when finished. However, when it has all the tokens from a previous response to review, it can more easily predict whether this would be labeled as a good or bad response.

We can continue to chain multiple calls together to improve the results of our task. For example, we could split this into three separate ratings: clarity, memorability, and how well the name communicates the unique selling point of the product. These ratings could then be given to a human as additional context on the final decision, or even calculated together to select the final name programmatically.

The real unlock in learning to work professionally with AI versus just playing around with prompting is realizing that every part of the system can be broken down into a series of iterative steps. Even with a single prompt this principles applies, as simply appending Let's think step by step to the prompt can lead to demonstrable gains in reasoning and proficiency, as well as provide an audit trail for quality assurance and debugging. When taking the time and tokens to reason, the ratings change and are more consistent with the scoring criteria.

Input:

```
Let's think step by step. Rate this list of product names
for a pair of shoes that can fit any foot size. The rating
should be out of 10, inline next to the product name:

UniFit SoleStrides
FlexiSize All-Fit Shoes
OmniFit FootFlex
...
AnyStep AdaptiWalkers
FlexiRange UniversalSteps
PerfectGlide MultiFit Shoes
```

Output:

```
Here's a rating out of 10 for each product name, considering
factors like descriptiveness, catchiness, and overall
appeal:

1. **UniFit SoleStrides**: 7/10 - Sounds unifying but may
not immediately convey the "fit any size" idea.
2. **FlexiSize All-Fit Shoes**: 8.5/10 - Combines
flexibility and the notion that it fits all sizes.
3. **OmniFit FootFlex**: 8/10 - Omnipresence (fitting all)
and flexibility nicely conveyed.
...
18. **AnyStep AdaptiWalkers**: 7.5/10 - "AnyStep" suggests
versatility, but the overall name might be less direct.
19. **FlexiRange UniversalSteps**: 8/10 - Combines
flexibility and universal fit.
20. **PerfectGlide MultiFit Shoes**: 8.5/10 - "MultiFit" is
clear, and "PerfectGlide" suggests a comfortable experience.
```

```
Remember, the best name can also be influenced by your
target audience, branding strategy, and the overall message
you want to convey.
```

OpenAI calls this (*https://oreil.ly/0MZ3-*) "giving the model time to think," and it is a key tenet of prompt engineering. In effect, *chain of thought* techniques like this, where the model is encouraged to list out its steps, are like dividing a task within the same prompt. Once we've automated product naming given a product idea, we can call ChatGPT again to describe each product, which in turn can be fed into Midjourney to generate an image of each product. Using an AI model to generate a prompt for an AI model is *meta prompting*, and it works because LLMs are human-level prompt engineers (Zhou, 2022 (*https://oreil.ly/Dwszu*)).

Input:

```
Describe the new product "OneFit UltraStride Shoes," a shoe
that can fit any foot size, in great detail:
```

Output:

```
Introducing the revolutionary "OneFit UltraStride Shoes,"
the footwear innovation designed to fit any foot size with
unparalleled comfort and style. These shoes are a result of
cutting-edge technology and meticulous craftsmanship,
ensuring a truly personalized and enjoyable walking or
running experience for everyone.

Design and Materials:
The OneFit UltraStride Shoes boast an elegant and modern
design that appeals to both fashion-forward individuals and
sports enthusiasts. They feature a sleek and streamlined
silhouette, crafted using premium materials for durability
and aesthetic appeal. The shoe's upper is constructed from a
combination of breathable mesh and flexible synthetic
materials, allowing for excellent airflow and a lightweight
feel.

...

Color and Customization:
OneFit UltraStride Shoes are available in a variety of
vibrant colors and stylish patterns, catering to diverse
personal preferences. You can choose from classic
monochromatic options for a timeless look or opt for bold
and vibrant hues to make a fashion statement. The ability to
customize the shoe's appearance allows individuals to
express their unique style while enjoying the benefits of
the OneFit technology.

Conclusion:
The OneFit UltraStride Shoes represent a breakthrough in
footwear technology, eliminating the hassle of finding the
```

perfect fit for your feet. With their adaptive design,
superior comfort, and stylish aesthetics, these shoes offer
a truly personalized experience for individuals of all foot
sizes. Stay comfortable, confident, and on-trend with the
OneFit UltraStride Shoes, the ultimate choice for those
seeking unmatched versatility and a perfect fit.

DALL-E is well-known by GPT-4, and therefore you can invoke its name within
ChatGPT and it does a reasonable job at crafting a prompt for an image generation
tool. If you were planning on using this prompt in production, you may consider
applying the prompting principle of providing examples, but it does a good enough
job for our purposes without examples.

Input:

```
Convert this description into a short prompt for an AI image
generation model such as DALL-E:
```

Output:

```
Create an eye-catching image that visually represents the
"OneFit UltraStride Shoes," a revolutionary footwear product
that adapts to any foot size. Showcase a sleek and modern
shoe design incorporating a stretchable upper, an adjustable
lacing system, and a cushioned insole for optimal comfort.
Emphasize the shoe's versatility by displaying it in action
on various surfaces, highlighting its excellent traction.
Incorporate vibrant colors and patterns to convey the
customizable nature of the product. The image should capture
the essence of innovation, style, and personalized fit that
the OneFit UltraStride Shoes offer.
```

The output of this prompt can now be plugged into image generation tools like
DALL-E or Midjourney as a prompt, which can give you a good starting point for
visualizing what the product might look like. Although this might not be the final
design you go with, seeing an image is more evocative and helps people form an
opinion faster. It's easier cognitively to criticize or compliment an existing image than
it is to imagine a new image from a blank page or section of text.

Figure 1-15 shows the output.

Figure 1-15. OneFit UltraStride shoes

It's common practice when working with AI professionally to chain multiple calls to AI together, and even multiple models, to accomplish more complex goals. Even single-prompt applications are often built dynamically, based on outside context queried from various databases or other calls to an AI model. The library LangChain (*https://www.langchain.com*) has developed tooling for chaining multiple prompt templates and queries together, making this process more observable and well structured. A foundational example is progressive summarization, where text that is too large to fit into a context window can be split into multiple chunks of text, with each being summarized, before finally summarizing the summaries. If you talk to builders of early AI products, you'll find they're all under the hood chaining multiple prompts together, called *AI chaining*, to accomplish better results in the final output.

The Reason and Act (ReAct) (*https://oreil.ly/tPPW9*) framework was one of the first popular attempts at AI agents, including the open source projects BabyAGI (*https://oreil.ly/TEiQx*), AgentGPT (*https://oreil.ly/48lq6*) and Microsoft AutoGen (*https://oreil.ly/KG5Xl*). In effect, these agents are the result of chaining multiple AI calls together in order to plan, observe, act, and then evaluate the results of the action.

Autonomous agents will be covered in Chapter 6 but are still not widely used in production at the time of writing. This practice of self-reasoning agents is still early and prone to errors, but there are promising signs this approach can be useful in achieving complex tasks, and is likely to be part of the next stage in evolution for AI systems.

There is an AI battle occurring between large tech firms like Microsoft and Google, as well as a wide array of open source projects on Hugging Face, and venture-funded start-ups like OpenAI and Anthropic. As new models continue to proliferate, they're diversifying in order to compete for different segments of the growing market. For example, Anthropic's Claude 2 had an 100,000-token context window (*https://oreil.ly/NQcFW*), compared to GPT-4's standard 8,192 tokens (*https://oreil.ly/iZhMl*). OpenAI soon responded with a 128,000-token window version of GPT-4 (*https://oreil.ly/3TTZ9*), and Google touts a 1 million token context length with Gemini 1.5 (*https://oreil.ly/cyhR4*). For comparison, one of the Harry Potter books would be around 185,000 tokens, so it may become common for an entire book to fit inside a single prompt, though processing millions of tokens with each API call may be cost prohibitive for most use cases.

This book focuses on GPT-4 for text generation techniques, as well as Midjourney v6 and Stable Diffusion XL for image generation techniques, but within months these models may no longer be state of the art. This means it will become increasingly important to be able to select the right model for the job and chain multiple AI systems together. Prompt templates are rarely comparable when transferring to a new model, but the effect of the Five Prompting Principles will consistently improve any prompt you use, for any model, getting you more reliable results.

Summary

In this chapter, you learned about the importance of prompt engineering in the context of generative AI. We defined prompt engineering as the process of developing effective prompts that yield desired results when interacting with AI models. You discovered that providing clear direction, formatting the output, incorporating examples, establishing an evaluation system, and dividing complex tasks into smaller prompts are key principles of prompt engineering. By applying these principles and using common prompting techniques, you can improve the quality and reliability of AI-generated outputs.

You also explored the role of prompt engineering in generating product names and images. You saw how specifying the desired format and providing instructive examples can greatly influence the AI's output. Additionally, you learned about the concept of role-playing, where you can ask the AI to generate outputs as if it were a famous person like Steve Jobs. The chapter emphasized the need for clear direction and context to achieve desired outcomes when using generative AI models. Furthermore, you discovered the importance of evaluating the performance of AI models and the various methods used for measuring results, as well as the trade-offs between quality and token usage, cost, and latency.

In the next chapter, you will be introduced to text generation models. You will learn about the different types of foundation models and their capabilities, as well as their limitations. The chapter will also review the standard OpenAI offerings, as well as competitors and open source alternatives. By the end of the chapter, you will have a solid understanding of the history of text generation models and their relative strengths and weaknesses. This book will return to image generation prompting in Chapters 7, 8, and 9, so you should feel free to skip ahead if that is your immediate need. Get ready to dive deeper into the discipline of prompt engineering and expand your comfort working with AI.

## CHAPTER 2

Introduction to Large Language Models for Text Generation

In artificial intelligence, a recent focus has been the evolution of large language models. Unlike their less-flexible predecessors, LLMs are capable of handling and learning from a much larger volume of data, resulting in the emergent capability of producing text that closely resembles human language output. These models have generalized across diverse applications, from writing content to automating software development and enabling real-time interactive chatbot experiences.

What Are Text Generation Models?

Text generation models utilize advanced algorithms to understand the meaning in text and produce outputs that are often indistinguishable from human work. If you've ever interacted with ChatGPT (*https://chat.openai.com*) or marveled at its ability to craft coherent and contextually relevant sentences, you've witnessed the power of an LLM in action.

In natural language processing (NLP) and LLMs, the fundamental linguistic unit is a *token*. Tokens (*https://oreil.ly/3fOsM*) can represent sentences, words, or even subwords such as a set of characters. A useful way to understand the size of text data is by looking at the number of tokens it comprises; for instance, a text of 100 tokens roughly equates to about 75 words. This comparison can be essential for managing the processing limits of LLMs as different models may have varying token capacities.

Tokenization, the process of breaking down text into tokens, is a crucial step in preparing data for NLP tasks. Several methods can be used for tokenization, including Byte-Pair Encoding (BPE) (*https://oreil.ly/iSOp7*), WordPiece, and SentencePiece. Each of these methods has its unique advantages and is suited to particular use cases. BPE is commonly used due to its efficiency in handling a wide range of vocabulary while keeping the number of tokens manageable.

BPE begins by viewing a text as a series of individual characters. Over time, it combines characters that frequently appear together into single units, or tokens. To understand this better, consider the word *apple*. Initially, BPE might see it as *a, p, p, l*, and *e*. But after noticing that *p* often comes after *a* and before *l* in the dataset, it might combine them and treat *appl* as a single token in future instances.

This approach helps LLMs recognize and generate words or phrases, even if they weren't common in the training data, making the models more adaptable and versatile.

Understanding the workings of LLMs requires a grasp of the underlying mathematical principles that power these systems. Although the computations can be complex, we can simplify the core elements to provide an intuitive understanding of how these models operate. Particularly within a business context, the accuracy and reliability of LLMs are paramount.

A significant part of achieving this reliability lies in the pretraining and fine-tuning phases of LLM development. Initially, models are trained on vast datasets during the pretraining phase, acquiring a broad understanding of language. Subsequently, in the fine-tuning phase, models are adapted for specific tasks, honing their capabilities to provide accurate and reliable outputs for specialized applications.

Vector Representations: The Numerical Essence of Language

In the realm of NLP, words aren't just alphabetic symbols. They can be tokenized and then represented in a numerical form, known as *vectors*. These vectors are multidimensional arrays of numbers that capture the semantic and syntactic relations:

$$w \rightarrow \mathbf{v} = [v_1, v_2, ..., v_n]$$

Creating word vectors, also known as *word embeddings*, relies on intricate patterns within language. During an intensive training phase, models are designed to identify and learn these patterns, ensuring that words with similar meanings are mapped close to one another in a high-dimensional space (Figure 2-1).

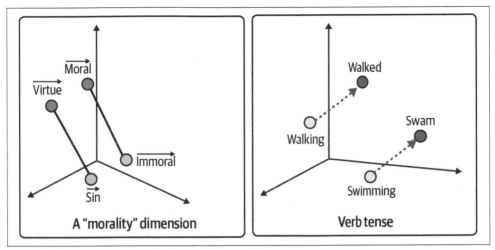

Figure 2-1. Semantic proximity of word vectors within a word embedding space

The beauty of this approach is its ability to capture nuanced relationships between words and calculate their distance. When we examine word embeddings, it becomes evident that words with similar or related meanings like *virtue* and *moral* or *walked* and *walking* are situated near each other. This spatial closeness in the embedding space becomes a powerful tool in various NLP tasks, enabling models to understand context, semantics, and the intricate web of relationships that form language.

Transformer Architecture: Orchestrating Contextual Relationships

Before we go deep into the mechanics of transformer architectures, let's build a foundational understanding. In simple terms, when we have a sentence, say, *The cat sat on the mat*, each word in this sentence gets converted into its numerical vector representation. So, *cat* might become a series of numbers, as does *sat*, *on*, and *mat*.

As you'll explore in detail later in this chapter, the transformer architecture takes these word vectors and understands their relationships—both in structure (syntax) and meaning (semantics). There are many types of transformers; Figure 2-2 showcases both BERT and GPT's architecture. Additionally, a transformer doesn't just see words in isolation; it looks at *cat* and knows it's related to *sat* and *mat* in a specific way in this sentence.

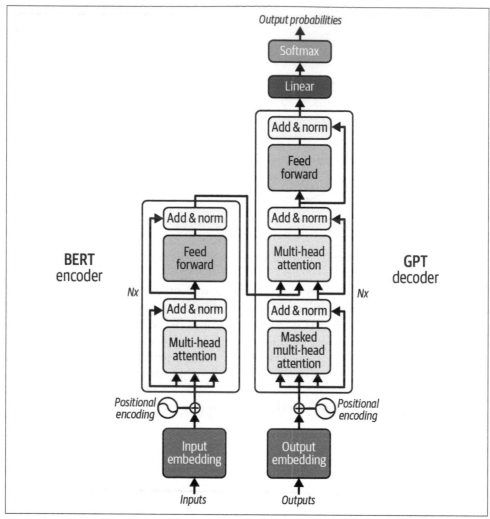

Figure 2-2. BERT uses an encoder for input data, while GPT has a decoder for output

When the transformer processes these vectors, it uses mathematical operations to understand the relationships between the words, thereby producing new vectors with rich, contextual information:

$$\mathbf{v}'_i = \text{Transformer}(\mathbf{v}_1, \mathbf{v}_2, ..., \mathbf{v}_m)$$

One of the remarkable features of transformers is their ability to comprehend the nuanced contextual meanings of words. The self-attention (*https://oreil.ly/xuovP*) mechanism in transformers lets each word in a sentence look at all other words to understand its context better. Think of it like each word casting votes on the importance of other words for its meaning. By considering the entire sentence, transformers can more accurately determine the role and meaning of each word, making their *interpretations more contextually rich.*

Probabilistic Text Generation: The Decision Mechanism

After the transformer understands the context of the given text, it moves on to generating new text, guided by the concept of likelihood or probability. In mathematical terms, the model calculates how likely each possible next word is to follow the current sequence of words and picks the one that is most likely:

$$w_{next} = \text{argmax}\, P(w \mid w_1, w_2, ..., w_m)$$

By repeating this process, as shown in Figure 2-3, the model generates a coherent and contextually relevant string of text as its output.

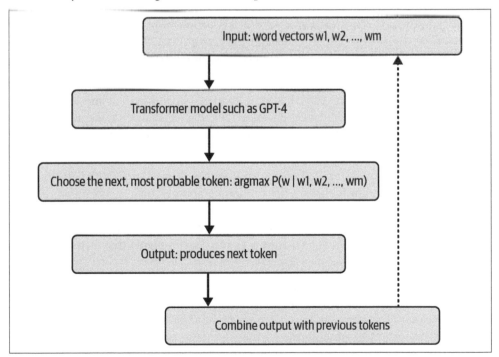

Figure 2-3. How text is generated using transformer models such as GPT-4

The mechanisms driving LLMs are rooted in vector mathematics, linear transformations, and probabilistic models. While the under-the-hood operations are computationally intensive, the core concepts are built on these mathematical principles, offering a foundational understanding that bridges the gap between technical complexity and business applicability.

Historical Underpinnings: The Rise of Transformer Architectures

Language models like ChatGPT (the *GPT* stands for *generative pretrained transformer*) didn't magically emerge. They're the culmination of years of progress in the field of NLP, with particular acceleration since the late 2010s. At the heart of this advancement is the introduction of transformer architectures, which were detailed in the groundbreaking paper "Attention Is All You Need" (*https://oreil.ly/6NNbg*) by the Google Brain team.

The real breakthrough of transformer architectures was the concept of *attention*. Traditional models processed text sequentially, which limited their understanding of language structure especially over long distances of text. Attention transformed this by allowing models to directly relate distant words to one another irrespective of their positions in the text. This was a groundbreaking proposition. It meant that words and their context didn't have to move through the entire model to affect each other. This not only significantly improved the models' text comprehension but also made them much more efficient.

This attention mechanism played a vital role in expanding the models' capacity to detect long-range dependencies in text. This was crucial for generating outputs that were not just contextually accurate and fluent, but also coherent over longer stretches.

According to AI pioneer and educator Andrew Ng (*https://oreil.ly/JQd53*), much of the early NLP research, including the fundamental work on transformers, received significant funding from United States military intelligence agencies. Their keen interest in tools like machine translation and speech recognition, primarily for intelligence purposes, inadvertently paved the way for developments that transcended just translation.

Training LLMs requires extensive computational resources. These models are fed with vast amounts of data, ranging from terabytes to petabytes, including internet content, academic papers, books, and more niche datasets tailored for specific purposes. It's important to note, however, that the data used to train LLMs can carry *inherent biases from their sources*. Thus, users should exercise caution and ideally employ human oversight when leveraging these models, ensuring responsible and ethical AI applications.

OpenAI's GPT-4, for example, boasts an estimated 1.7 trillion parameters (*https://oreil.ly/pZvMo*), which is equivalent to an Excel spreadsheet that stretches across thirty thousand soccer fields. *Parameters* in the context of neural networks are the weights and biases adjusted throughout the training process, allowing the model to represent and generate complex patterns based on the data it's trained on. The training cost for GPT-4 was estimated to be in the order of $63 million (*https://oreil.ly/_NAq5*), and the training data would fill about 650 kilometers of bookshelves full of books (*https://oreil.ly/D7jT5*).

To meet these requirements, major technological companies such as Microsoft, Meta, and Google have invested heavily, making LLM development a high-stakes endeavor.

The rise of LLMs has provided an increased demand for the hardware industry, particularly companies specializing in graphics processing units (GPUs). NVIDIA, for instance, has become almost synonymous with high-performance GPUs that are essential for training LLMs.

The demand for powerful, efficient GPUs has skyrocketed as companies strive to build ever-larger and more complex models. It's not just the raw computational power that's sought after. GPUs also need to be fine-tuned for tasks endemic to machine learning, like tensor operations. *Tensors*, in a machine learning context, are multidimensional arrays of data, and operations on them are foundational to neural network computations. This emphasis on specialized capabilities has given rise to tailored hardware such as NVIDIA's H100 Tensor Core GPUs, explicitly crafted to expedite machine learning workloads.

Furthermore, the overwhelming demand often outstrips the supply of these top-tier GPUs, sending prices on an upward trajectory. This supply-demand interplay has transformed the GPU market into a fiercely competitive and profitable arena. Here, an eclectic clientele, ranging from tech behemoths to academic researchers, scramble to procure the most advanced hardware.

This surge in demand has sparked a wave of innovation beyond just GPUs. Companies are now focusing on creating dedicated AI hardware, such as Google's Tensor Processing Units (TPUs), to cater to the growing computational needs of AI models.

This evolving landscape underscores not just the symbiotic ties between software and hardware in the AI sphere but also spotlights the ripple effect of the LLM *gold rush*. It's steering innovations and funneling investments into various sectors, especially those offering the fundamental components for crafting these models.

OpenAI's Generative Pretrained Transformers

Founded with a mission to ensure that artificial general intelligence benefits all of humanity, OpenAI (*https://openai.com*) has recently been at the forefront of the AI revolution. One of their most groundbreaking contributions has been the GPT series of models, which have substantially redefined the boundaries of what LLMs can achieve.

The original GPT model by OpenAI was more than a mere research output; it was a compelling demonstration of the potential of transformer-based architectures. This model showcased the initial steps toward making machines understand and generate human-like language, laying the foundation for future advancements.

The unveiling of GPT-2 was met with both anticipation and caution. Recognizing the model's powerful capabilities, OpenAI initially hesitated in releasing it due to concerns about its potential misuse. Such was the might of GPT-2 that ethical concerns took center stage, which might look quaint compared to the power of today's models. However, when OpenAI decided to release the project as open-source (*https://oreil.ly/evOQE*), it didn't just mean making the code public. It allowed businesses and researchers to use these pretrained models as building blocks, incorporating AI into their applications without starting from scratch. This move democratized access to high-level natural language processing capabilities, spurring innovation across various domains.

After GPT-2, OpenAI decided to focus on releasing paid, closed-source models. GPT-3's arrival marked a monumental stride in the progression of LLMs. It garnered significant media attention, not just for its technical prowess but also for the societal implications of its capabilities. This model could produce text so convincing that it often became indistinguishable from human-written content. From crafting intricate pieces of literature to churning out operational code snippets, GPT-3 exemplified the seemingly boundless potential of AI.

GPT-3.5-turbo and ChatGPT

Bolstered by Microsoft's significant investment in their company, OpenAI introduced GPT-3.5-turbo, an optimized version of its already exceptional predecessor. Following a $1 billion injection (*https://oreil.ly/1C8qm*) from Microsoft in 2019, which later increased to a hefty $13 billion for a 49% stake in OpenAI's for-profit arm, OpenAI used these resources to develop GPT-3.5-turbo, which offered improved efficiency and affordability, effectively making LLMs more accessible for a broader range of use cases.

OpenAI wanted to gather more world feedback for fine-tuning, and so ChatGPT (*https://chat.openai.com*) was born. Unlike its general-purpose siblings, ChatGPT was fine-tuned (*https://oreil.ly/6ib-Q*) to excel in conversational contexts, enabling a dialogue between humans and machines that felt natural and meaningful.

Figure 2-4 shows the training process for ChatGPT, which involves three main steps:

Collection of demonstration data
> In this step, human labelers provide examples of the desired model behavior on a distribution of prompts. The labelers are trained on the project and follow specific instructions to annotate the prompts accurately.

Training a supervised policy
> The demonstration data collected in the previous step is used to fine-tune a pretrained GPT-3 model using supervised learning. In supervised learning, models are trained on a labeled dataset where the correct answers are provided. This step helps the model to learn to follow the given instructions and produce outputs that align with the desired behavior.

Collection of comparison data and reinforcement learning
> In this step, a dataset of model outputs is collected, and human labelers rank the outputs based on their preference. A reward model is then trained to predict which outputs the labelers would prefer. Finally, reinforcement learning techniques, specifically the Proximal Policy Optimization (PPO) algorithm, are used to optimize the supervised policy to maximize the reward from the reward model.

This training process allows the ChatGPT model to align its behavior with human intent. The use of reinforcement learning with human feedback helped create a model that is more helpful, honest, and safe compared to the pretrained GPT-3 model.

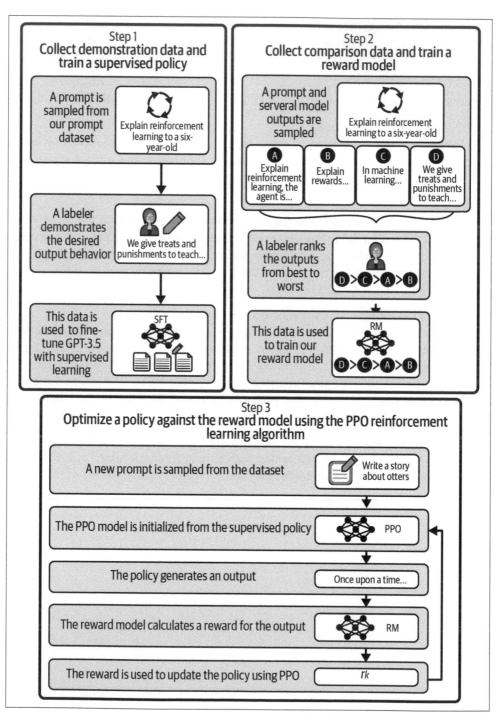

Figure 2-4. The fine-tuning process for ChatGPT

According to a UBS study (*https://oreil.ly/2Ivq2*), by January 2023 ChatGPT set a new benchmark, amassing 100 million active users and becoming the fastest-growing consumer application in internet history. ChatGPT is now a go-to for customer service, virtual assistance, and numerous other applications that require the finesse of human-like conversation.

GPT-4

In 2024, OpenAI released GPT-4, which excels in understanding complex queries and generating contextually relevant and coherent text. For example, GPT-4 scored in the 90th percentile of the bar exam with a score of 298 out of 400. Currently, GPT-3.5-turbo is free to use in ChatGPT, but GPT-4 requires a monthly payment (*https://oreil.ly/UOEBM*).

GPT-4 uses a mixture-of-experts approach (*https://oreil.ly/v45LZ*); it goes beyond relying on a single model's inference to produce even more accurate and insightful results.

On May 13, 2024, OpenAI introduced GPT-4o (*https://oreil.ly/4ttmq*), an advanced model capable of processing and reasoning across text, audio, and vision inputs in real time. This model offers enhanced performance, particularly in vision and audio understanding; it is also faster and more cost-effective than its predecessors due to its ability to process all three modalities in one neural network.

Google's Gemini

After Google lost search market share due to ChatGPT usage, it initially released Bard on March 21, 2023. Bard was a bit rough around the edges (*https://oreil.ly/Sj24h*) and definitely didn't initially have the same high-quality LLM responses that ChatGPT offered (Figure 2-5).

Google has kept adding extra features over time including code generation, visual AI, real-time search, and voice into Bard, bringing it closer to ChatGPT in terms of quality.

On March 14, 2023, Google released PaLM API (*https://oreil.ly/EbI8-*), allowing developers to access it on Google Cloud Platform. In April 2023, Amazon Web Services (AWS) released similar services such as Amazon Bedrock (*https://oreil.ly/4fNQX*) and Amazon's Titan FMs (*https://oreil.ly/FJ-7D*). Google rebranded Bard to Gemini (*https://oreil.ly/EO42O*) for their v1.5 release in February 2024 and started to get results similar to GPT-4.

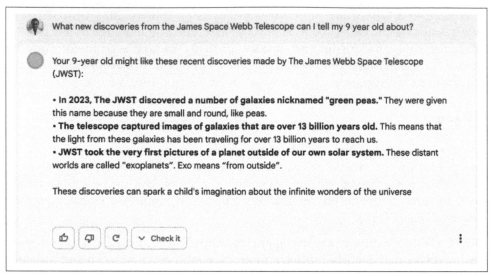

Figure 2-5. Bard hallucinating results about the James Webb Space Telescope

Also, Google released two smaller open source models (*https://oreil.ly/LWIwv*) based on the same architecture as Gemini. OpenAI is finally no longer the only obvious option for software engineers to integrate state-of-the-art LLMs into their applications.

Meta's Llama and Open Source

Meta's approach to language models differs significantly from other competitors in the industry. By sequentially releasing open source models Llama (*https://oreil.ly/LroPn*), Llama 2 (*https://oreil.ly/NeZLw*) and Llama 3 (*https://oreil.ly/Vwlo-*), Meta aims to foster a more inclusive and collaborative AI development ecosystem.

The open source nature of Llama 2 and Llama 3 has significant implications for the broader tech industry, especially for large enterprises. The transparency and collaborative ethos encourage rapid innovation, as problems and vulnerabilities can be quickly identified and addressed by the global developer community. As these models become more robust and secure, large corporations can adopt them with increased confidence.

Meta's open source strategy not only democratizes access to state-of-the-art AI technologies but also has the potential to make a meaningful impact across the industry. By setting the stage for a collaborative, transparent, and decentralized development process, Llama 2 and Llama 3 are pioneering models that could very well define the future of generative AI. The models are available in 7, 8 and 70 billion parameter versions on AWS, Google Cloud, Hugging Face, and other platforms.

The open source nature of these models presents a double-edged sword. On one hand, it levels the playing field. This means that even smaller developers have the opportunity to contribute to innovation, improving and applying open source models to practical business applications. This kind of decentralized innovation could lead to breakthroughs that might not occur within the walled gardens of a single organization, enhancing the models' capabilities and applications.

However, the same openness that makes this possible also poses potential risks, as it could allow malicious actors to exploit this technology for detrimental ends. This indeed is a concern that organizations like OpenAI share, suggesting that some degree of control and restriction can actually serve to mitigate the dangerous applications of these powerful tools.

Leveraging Quantization and LoRA

One of the game-changing aspects of these open source models is the potential for quantization (*https://oreil.ly/bkWXk*) and the use of LoRA (*https://oreil.ly/zORsB*) (low-rank approximations). These techniques allow developers to fit the models into smaller hardware footprints. Quantization helps to reduce the numerical precision of the model's parameters, thereby shrinking the overall size of the model without a significant loss in performance. Meanwhile, LoRA assists in optimizing the network's architecture, making it more efficient to run on consumer-grade hardware.

Such optimizations make fine-tuning these LLMs increasingly feasible on consumer hardware. This is a critical development because it allows for greater experimentation and adaptability. No longer confined to high-powered data centers, individual developers, small businesses, and start-ups can now work on these models in more resource-constrained environments.

Mistral

Mistral 7B, a brainchild of French start-up Mistral AI (*https://mistral.ai*), emerges as a powerhouse in the generative AI domain, with its 7.3 billion parameters making a significant impact. This model is not just about size; it's about efficiency and capability, promising a bright future for open source large language models and their applicability across a myriad of use cases. The key to its efficiency is the implementation of sliding window attention, a technique released under a permissive Apache open source license. Many AI engineers have fine-tuned on top of this model as a base, including the impressive Zephr 7b beta (*https://oreil.ly/Lg6_r*) model. There is also Mixtral 8x7b (*https://oreil.ly/itsJG*), a mixture of experts model (similar to the architecture of GPT-4), which achieves results similar to GPT-3.5-turbo.

For a more detailed and up-to-date comparison of open source models and their performance metrics, visit the Chatbot Arena Leaderboard (*https://oreil.ly/ttiji*) hosted by Hugging Face.

Anthropic: Claude

Released on July 11, 2023, Claude 2 (*https://claude.ai/login*) is setting itself apart from other prominent LLMs such as ChatGPT and LLaMA, with its pioneering Constitutional AI (*https://oreil.ly/Tim9W*) approach to AI safety and alignment—training the model using a list of rules or values. A notable enhancement in Claude 2 was its expanded context window of 100,000 tokens, as well as the ability to upload files. In the realm of generative AI, a *context window* refers to the amount of text or data the model can actively consider or keep in mind when generating a response. With a larger context window, the model can understand and generate based on a broader context.

This advancement garnered significant enthusiasm from AI engineers, as it opened up avenues for new and more intricate use cases. For instance, Claude 2's augmented ability to process more information at once makes it adept at summarizing extensive documents or sustaining in-depth conversations. The advantage was short-lived, as OpenAI released their 128K version of GPT-4 only six months later (*https://oreil.ly/ BWxrn*). However, the fierce competition between rivals is pushing the field forward.

The next generation of Claude included Opus (*https://oreil.ly/NH0jh*), the first model to rival GPT-4 in terms of intelligence, as well as Haiku, a smaller model that is lightning-fast with the competitive price of $0.25 per million tokens (half the cost of GPT-3.5-turbo at the time).

GPT-4V(ision)

In a significant leap forward, on September 23, 2023, OpenAI expanded the capabilities of GPT-4 with the introduction of Vision, enabling users to instruct GPT-4 to analyze images alongside text. This innovation was also reflected in the update to ChatGPT's interface, which now supports the inclusion of both images and text as user inputs. This development signifies a major trend toward *multimodal models*, which can seamlessly process and understand multiple types of data, such as images and text, within a single context.

Model Comparison

The market for LLMs is dominated by OpenAI at the time of writing, with its state-of-the-art GPT-4 model widely considered to have a significant lead. The closest competitor is Anthropic, and there is widespread excitement at the potential of smaller open source models such as Llama and Mistral, particularly with respects to fine-tuning. Although commentators expect OpenAI to continue to deliver world-beating models in the future, as open source models get *good enough* at more tasks, AI workloads may shift toward local fine-tuned models. With advances in model performance and quantization (methods for trading off accuracy versus size and compute cost), it may be possible to one day run LLMs on your mobile phone or other devices.

For now, the best way to get a sense for what the models are good at is to run the same prompt across multiple models and compare the responses. One thing that regularly stands out in our work is that GPT-4 is much better at following instructions, as is demonstrated in the following example where it was the only model to respond in the right format, with names that matched the examples (starting with the letter *i*), as desired.

Input:

```
Brainstorm a list of product names for a shoe that fits any foot size,
in the style of Steve Jobs.

Return the results as a comma-separated list, in this format:
Product description: A shoe that fits any foot size
Product names: [list of three product names]

## Examples
Product description: A refrigerator that dispenses beer
Product names: iBarFridge, iFridgeBeer, iDrinkBeerFridge

Product description: A watch that can tell accurate time in space
Product names: iNaut, iSpace, iTime

Product description: A home milkshake maker
Product names: iShake, iSmoothie, iShake Mini
```

Output (GPT-4):

```
Product description: A shoe that fits any foot size
Product names: iFit, iShoe, iFlexible
```

Output (Claude 3):

```
Product description: A shoe that fits any foot size
Product names: iFit, iComfort, iSole
```

Output (Llama 3 70b):

```
Here is the list of product names for a shoe that fits any foot size,
in the style of Steve Jobs:

Product description: A shoe that fits any foot size Product names:
iFit, OneSize, iWalkFree
```

Summary

The journey of LLMs from their inception to their current advanced states is a tale of relentless innovation, collaboration, and intense competition. As these models continue to evolve, they are likely to become even more integral parts of our daily lives, changing the way we interact with technology and even with each other.

By understanding the historical context and capabilities of these models, you can better appreciate the tools at our disposal for various applications, from prompt engineering to the development of intelligent virtual agents. It's important to note, however, that while these models offer expansive possibilities, data privacy remains a crucial concern. If these models use your data for retraining or fine-tuning, exercise caution and refrain from inputting sensitive information.

In the next chapter, you will learn all the basic prompt engineering techniques for working with text LLMs. You'll learn the essential skills needed to get the most out of powerful language models like GPT-4. Exciting insights and practical methods await you as you unlock the true potential of generative AI.

## CHAPTER 3

Standard Practices for Text Generation with ChatGPT

Simple prompting techniques will help you to maximize the output and formats from LLMs. You'll start by tailoring the prompts to explore all of the common practices used for text generation.

Generating Lists

Automatically generating lists is incredibly powerful and enables you to focus on higher-level tasks while GPT can automatically generate, refine, rerank, and de-duplicate lists on your behalf.

Input:

```
Generate a list of Disney characters.
```

Output:

```
Sure, here is a list of some popular Disney characters:

1. Mickey Mouse
2. Minnie Mouse
...
30. Bagheera (The Jungle Book)
```

GPT-4 is perfectly capable of providing a list of characters. However, there are some pitfalls with this approach:

- GPT has decided to provide 30 examples as a numbered list, separated by \n characters. However, if your downstream Python code was expecting to split on bullet points, then you'll likely end up with undesirable results or a runtime error.

- GPT has provided preceding commentary; removing any preceding/succeeding commentary would make parsing the output easier.

- The list size wasn't controlled and was left to the language model.

- Some of the characters have the name of their corresponding film within brackets—for example, *Bagheera (The Jungle Book)*—and others don't. This makes names harder to extract because you would need to remove the movie titles.

- No filtering or selection has been applied to the LLM generation based on our desired result.

Following you'll find an optimized prompt.

Input:

```
Generate a bullet-point list of 5 male Disney characters.
Only include the name of the character for each line.
Never include the film for each Disney character.
Only return the Disney characters, never include any commentary.

Below is an example list:

* Aladdin
* Simba
* Beast
* Hercules
* Tarzan
```

Output:

```
* Woody
* Buzz Lightyear
* Stitch
* Jack Sparrow
* Prince Charming
```

Provide Examples

Simply rephrasing your prompt to include examples *(few-shot prompting)* can greatly impact the desired output.

By optimizing the prompt, you've achieved the following:

- Restricted the list to a fixed size of five
- Generated only male characters
- Correctly formatted the list with bullet points
- Removed any preceding commentary

Simple lists are fine for most tasks; however, they are less structured, and for some tasks it's beneficial to obtain nested data structures from a GPT-4 output.

Three typical data structures include:

- Nested text data (hierarchical lists)
- JSON
- YAML

Hierarchical List Generation

Hierarchical lists are useful for when your desired output is nested. A good example of this would be a detailed article structure.

Input:

```
Generate a hierarchical and incredibly detailed article outline on:

What are the benefits of data engineering.

See an example of the hierarchical structure below:

Article Title: What are the benefits of digital marketing?

* Introduction
    a. Explanation of digital marketing
    b. Importance of digital marketing in today's business world
* Increased Brand Awareness
    a. Definition of brand awareness
    b. How digital marketing helps in increasing brand awareness
```

Output:

```
Article Title: What are the benefits of data engineering?

* Introduction
    a. Explanation of data engineering
    b. Importance of data engineering in today's data-driven world

...(10 sections later)...
```

```
      * Conclusion
          a. Importance of data engineering in the modern business world
          b. Future of data engineering and its impact on the data ecosystem
```

To generate an effective article outline in the preceding output, you've included two key phrases:

Hierarchical

To suggest that the article outline needs to produce a nested structure.

Incredibly detailed

To guide the language model towards producing a larger output. Other words that you could include that have the same effect would be *very long* or by specifying a large number of subheadings, *include at least 10 top-level headings.*

 Asking a language model for a fixed number of items doesn't guarantee the language model will produce the same length. For example, if you ask for 10 headings, you might receive only 8. Therefore, your code should either validate that 10 headings exist or be flexible to handle varying lengths from the LLM.

So you've successfully produced a hierarchical article outline, but how could you parse the string into structured data?

Let's explore Example 3-1 using Python, where you've previously made a successful API call against OpenAI's GPT-4. Two regular expressions are used to extract the headings and subheadings from `openai_result`. The `re` module in Python is used for working with regular expressions.

Example 3-1. Parsing a hierarchical list (https://oreil.ly/A0otS)

```python
import re

# openai_result = generate_article_outline(prompt)
# Commented out to focus on a fake LLM response, see below:

openai_result = '''
* Introduction
    a. Explanation of data engineering
    b. Importance of data engineering in today's data-driven world
* Efficient Data Management
    a. Definition of data management
    b. How data engineering helps in efficient data management
* Conclusion
    a. Importance of data engineering in the modern business world
    b. Future of data engineering and its impact on the data ecosystem
'''
```

```python
# Regular expression patterns
heading_pattern = r'\* (.+)'
subheading_pattern = r'\s+[a-z]\. (.+)'

# Extract headings and subheadings
headings = re.findall(heading_pattern, openai_result)
subheadings = re.findall(subheading_pattern, openai_result)

# Print results
print("Headings:\n")
for heading in headings:
    print(f"* {heading}")

print("\nSubheadings:\n")
for subheading in subheadings:
    print(f"* {subheading}")
```

This code will output:

```
Headings:
- Introduction
- Efficient Data Management
- Conclusion

Subheadings:
- Explanation of data engineering
- Importance of data engineering in today's data-driven world
- Definition of data management
- How data engineering helps in efficient data management
- Importance of data engineering in the modern business world
- Future of data engineering and its impact on the data ecosystem
```

The use of regular expressions allows for efficient pattern matching, making it possible to handle variations in the input text, such as the presence or absence of leading spaces or tabs. Let's explore how these patterns work:

```python
heading_pattern = r'\* (.+)'
```

This pattern is designed to extract the main headings and consists of:

- * matches the asterisk (*) symbol at the beginning of a heading. The backslash is used to escape the asterisk, as the asterisk has a special meaning in regular expressions (zero or more occurrences of the preceding character).

- A space character will match after the asterisk.

- (.+): matches one or more characters, and the parentheses create a capturing group. The . is a wildcard that matches any character except a newline, and the +

is a quantifier that means *one or more* occurrences of the preceding element (the dot, in this case).

By applying this pattern you can easily extract all of the main headings into a list without the asterisk.

```
subheading_pattern = r'\s+[a-z]\. (.+)
```

The `subheading pattern` will match all of the subheadings within the `openai_result` string:

- `\s+` matches one or more whitespace characters (spaces, tabs, and so on). The `+` means *one or more* occurrences of the preceding element (the `\s`, in this case).

- `[a-z]` matches a single lowercase letter from *a* to *z*.

- `\.` matches a period character. The backslash is used to escape the period, as it has a special meaning in regular expressions (matches any character except a newline).

- *A space character will match after the period.*

- `(.+)` matches one or more characters, and the parentheses create a capturing group. The `.` is a wildcard that matches any character except a newline, and the `+` is a quantifier that means *one or more* occurrences of the preceding element (the dot, in this case).

Additionally the `re.findall()` function is used to find all non-overlapping matches of the patterns in the input string and return them as a list. The extracted headings and subheadings are then printed.

So now you're able to extract headings and subheadings from hierarchical article outlines; however, you can further refine the regular expressions so that each heading is associated with corresponding `subheadings`.

In Example 3-2, the regex has been slightly modified so that each subheading is attached directly with its appropriate subheading.

Example 3-2. Parsing a hierarchical list into a Python dictionary (https://oreil.ly/LcMtv)

```
import re

openai_result = """
* Introduction
  a. Explanation of data engineering
  b. Importance of data engineering in today's data-driven world
* Efficient Data Management
  a. Definition of data management
```

```
        b. How data engineering helps in efficient data management
        c. Why data engineering is important for data management
* Conclusion
        a. Importance of data engineering in the modern business world
        b. Future of data engineering and its impact on the data ecosystem
"""

section_regex = re.compile(r"\* (.+)")
subsection_regex = re.compile(r"\s*([a-z]\..+)")

result_dict = {}
current_section = None

for line in openai_result.split("\n"):
    section_match = section_regex.match(line)
    subsection_match = subsection_regex.match(line)

    if section_match:
        current_section = section_match.group(1)
        result_dict[current_section] = []
    elif subsection_match and current_section is not None:
        result_dict[current_section].append(subsection_match.group(1))

print(result_dict)
```

This will output:

```
{
    "Introduction": [
        "a. Explanation of data engineering",
        "b. Importance of data engineering in today's data-driven world"
    ],
    "Efficient Data Management": [
        "a. Definition of data management",
        "b. How data engineering helps in efficient data management"
    ],
    "Conclusion": [
        "a. Importance of data engineering in the modern business world",
        "b. Future of data engineering and its impact on the data ecosystem"
    ]
}
```

The section title regex, r'* (.+)', matches an asterisk followed by a space and then one or more characters. The parentheses capture the text following the asterisk and space to be used later in the code.

The subsection regex, r'\s*([a-z]\..+)', starts with \s*, which matches zero or more whitespace characters (spaces or tabs). This allows the regex to match subsections with or without leading spaces or tabs. The following part, ([a-z]\..+), matches a lowercase letter followed by a period and then one or more characters. The parentheses capture the entire matched subsection text for later use in the code.

The for loop iterates over each line in the input string, `openai_result`. Upon encountering a line that matches the section title regex, the loop sets the matched title as the current section and assigns an empty list as its value in the `result_dict` dictionary. When a line matches the subsection regex, the matched subsection text is appended to the list corresponding to the current section.

Consequently, the loop processes the *input string line by line*, categorizes lines as section titles or subsections, and constructs the intended dictionary structure.

When to Avoid Using Regular Expressions

As you work to extract more structured data from LLM responses, relying solely on regular expressions can make the control flow *become increasingly complicated*. However, there are other formats that can facilitate the parsing of structured data from LLM responses with ease. Two common formats are *.json* and *.yml* files.

Generating JSON

Let's start by experimenting with some prompt design that will direct an LLM to return a JSON response.

Input:

```
Compose a very detailed article outline on "The benefits of learning code" with a
JSON payload structure that highlights key points.

Only return valid JSON.

Here is an example of the JSON structure:
{
    "Introduction": [
        "a. Explanation of data engineering",
        "b. Importance of data engineering in today's data-driven world"],
    ...
    "Conclusion": [
        "a. Importance of data engineering in the modern business world",
        "b. Future of data engineering and its impact on the data ecosystem"]
}
```

Output:

```
{
    "Introduction": [
        "a. Overview of coding and programming languages",
        "b. Importance of coding in today's technology-driven world"],
    ...
    "Conclusion": [
        "a. Recap of the benefits of learning code",
```

```
        "b. The ongoing importance of coding skills in the modern world"]
}
```

Give Direction and Provide Examples

Notice that in the preceding prompt, you've provided direction on the type of task, the format, and an example JSON output.

Common errors that you'll encounter when working with JSON involve invalid payloads, or the JSON being wrapped within triple backticks (```), such as:

Output:

```
Sure here's the JSON:
```json
{"Name": "John Smith"} # valid payload
{"Name": "John Smith", "some_key":} # invalid payload
```
```

Ideally you would like the model to respond like so:

Output:

```
{"Name": "John Smith"}
```

This is important because with the first output, you'd have to split after `json` and then parse the exact part of the string that contained valid JSON. There are several points that are worth adding to your prompts to improve JSON parsing:

```
You must follow the following principles:
* Only return valid JSON
* Never include backtick symbols such as: `
* The response will be parsed with json.loads(), therefore it must be valid JSON.
```

Now let's examine how you can parse a JSON output with Python (*https://oreil.ly/MoJHn*):

```python
import json

# openai_json_result = generate_article_outline(prompt)

openai_json_result = """
{
    "Introduction": [
        "a. Overview of coding and programming languages",
        "b. Importance of coding in today's technology-driven world"],
    "Conclusion": [
        "a. Recap of the benefits of learning code",
        "b. The ongoing importance of coding skills in the modern world"]
}
"""
parsed_json_payload = json.loads(openai_json_result)
```

```
print(parsed_json_payload)
```

```
'''{'Introduction': ['a. Overview of coding and programming languages',
"b. Importance of coding in today's technology-driven world"],
'Conclusion': ['a. Recap of the benefits of learning code',
'b. The ongoing importance of coding skills in the modern world']}'''
```

Well done, you've successfully parsed some JSON.

As showcased, structuring data from an LLM response is streamlined when requesting the response in valid JSON format. Compared to the previously demonstrated regular expression parsing, this method is less cumbersome and more straightforward.

So what could go wrong?

- The language model accidentally adds extra text to the response such as `json output:` and your application logic only handles for valid JSON.
- The JSON produced isn't valid and fails upon parsing (either due to the size or simply for not escaping certain characters).

Later on you will examine strategies to gracefully handle for such edge cases.

YAML

.yml files are a structured data format that offer different benefits over *.json*:

No need to escape characters
YAML's indentation pattern eliminates the need for braces, brackets, and commas to denote structure. This can lead to cleaner and less error-prone files, as there's less risk of mismatched or misplaced punctuation.

Readability
YAML is designed to be human-readable, with a simpler syntax and structure compared to JSON. This makes it easier for you to create, read, and edit prompts, especially when dealing with complex or nested structures.

Comments
Unlike JSON, YAML supports comments, allowing you to add annotations or explanations to the prompts directly in the file. This can be extremely helpful when working in a team or when revisiting the prompts after some time, as it allows for better understanding and collaboration.

Input:

```
- Below you'll find the current yaml schema.
- You can update the quantities based on a User Query.
- Filter the User Query based on the schema below, if it doesn't match and
  there are no items left then return `"No Items"`.
```

```
  - If there is a partial match, then return only the items that are
  within the schema below:

  # schema:
  - item: Apple Slices
    quantity: 5
    unit: pieces
  - item: Milk
    quantity: 1
    unit: gallon
  - item: Bread
    quantity: 2
    unit: loaves
  - item: Eggs
    quantity: 1
    unit: dozen

  User Query: "5 apple slices, and 2 dozen eggs."

  Given the schema below, please return only a valid .yml based on the User
  Query.If there's no match, return `"No Items"`. Do not provide any
  commentary or explanations.
```

Output:

```
  - item: Apple Slices
    quantity: 5
    unit: pieces
  - item: Eggs
    quantity: 2
    unit: dozen
```

Notice with the preceding example how an LLM is able to infer the correct *.yml* format from the User Query string.

Additionally, you've given the LLM an opportunity to either:

- Return a valid *.yml* response
- Return a filtered *.yml* response

If after filtering, there are no *.yml* items left, then return *No Items*.

Filtering YAML Payloads

You might decide to use this same prompt for cleaning/filtering a *.yml* payload.

First, let's focus on a payload that contains both valid and invalid schema in reference to our desired schema. Apple slices fit the criteria; however, Bananas doesn't exist, and you should expect for the User Query to be appropriately filtered.

Input:

```
# User Query:
- item: Apple Slices
  quantity: 5
  unit: pieces
- item: Bananas
  quantity: 3
  unit: pieces
```

Output:

```
# Updated yaml list
- item: Apple Slices
  quantity: 5
  unit: pieces
```

In the preceding example, you've successfully filtered the user's payload against a set criteria and have used the language model as a *reasoning engine*.

By providing the LLM with a set of instructions within the prompt, the response is closely related to what a human might do if they were manually cleaning the data.

The input prompt facilitates the delegation of more control flow tasks to a language learning model (LLM), tasks that would typically require coding in a programming language like Python or JavaScript.

Figure 3-1 provides a detailed overview of the logic applied when processing user queries by an LLM.

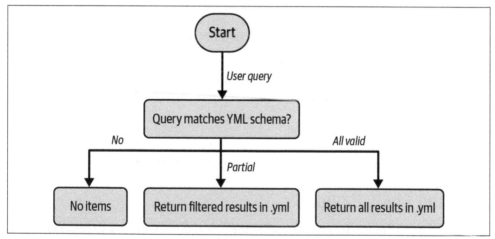

Figure 3-1. Using an LLM to determine the control flow of an application instead of code

Handling Invalid Payloads in YAML

A completely invalid payload might look like this:

Input:

```
# User Query:
- item: Bananas
  quantity: 3
  unit: pieces
```

Output:

```
No Items
```

As expected, the LLM returned `No Items` as none of the `User Query` items matched against the previously defined `schema`.

Let's create a Python script that gracefully accommodates for the various types of LLM results returned. The core parts of the script will focus on:

- Creating custom exceptions for each type of error that might occur due to the three LLM response scenarios
- Parsing the proposed schema
- Running a serious of custom checks against the response so you can be sure that the YML response can be safely passed to downstream software applications/microservices

You could define six specific errors that would handle for all of the edge cases:

```python
class InvalidResponse(Exception):
    pass


class InvalidItemType(Exception):
    pass


class InvalidItemKeys(Exception):
    pass


class InvalidItemName(Exception):
    pass


class InvalidItemQuantity(Exception):
    pass


class InvalidItemUnit(Exception):
    pass
```

Then provide the previously proposed YML schema as a string:

```
# Provided schema
schema = """
- item: Apple Slices
  quantity: 5
  unit: pieces
- item: Milk
  quantity: 1
  unit: gallon
- item: Bread
  quantity: 2
  unit: loaves
- item: Eggs
  quantity: 1
  unit: dozen
"""
```

Import the yaml module and create a custom parser function called validate_response that allows you to easily determine whether an LLM output is valid:

```python
import yaml

def validate_response(response, schema):
    # Parse the schema
    schema_parsed = yaml.safe_load(schema)
    maximum_quantity = 10

    # Check if the response is a list
    if not isinstance(response, list):
        raise InvalidResponse("Response is not a list")

    # Check if each item in the list is a dictionary
    for item in response:
        if not isinstance(item, dict):
            raise InvalidItemType('''Item is not a dictionary''')

        # Check if each dictionary has the keys "item", "quantity", and "unit"
        if not all(key in item for key in ("item", "quantity", "unit")):
            raise InvalidItemKeys("Item does not have the correct keys")

        # Check if the values associated with each key are the correct type
        if not isinstance(item["item"], str):
            raise InvalidItemName("Item name is not a string")
        if not isinstance(item["quantity"], int):
            raise InvalidItemQuantity("Item quantity is not an integer")
        if not isinstance(item["unit"], str):
            raise InvalidItemUnit("Item unit is not a string")

        # Check if the values associated with each key are the correct value
        if item["item"] not in [x["item"] for x in schema_parsed]:
```

```
        raise InvalidItemName("Item name is not in schema")
    if item["quantity"] > maximum_quantity:
        raise InvalidItemQuantity(f'''Item quantity is greater than
        {maximum_quantity}''')
    if item["unit"] not in ["pieces", "dozen"]:
        raise InvalidItemUnit("Item unit is not pieces or dozen")
```

To test these edge cases, following you'll find several mocked LLM responses:

```
# Fake responses
fake_response 1 = """
- item: Apple Slices
  quantity: 5
  unit: pieces
- item: Eggs
  quantity: 2
  unit: dozen
"""

fake_response_2 = """
# Updated yaml list
- item: Apple Slices
  quantity: 5
  unit: pieces
"""

fake_response_3 = """Unmatched"""
```

Finally, now you can:

- Use `yaml.safe_load(response)` to safely parse the *.yml* schema

- Call the `validate_response` function for each LLM response to test it against custom *.yml* validation logic

```
# Parse the fake responses
response_1_parsed = yaml.safe_load(fake_response_1)
response_2_parsed = yaml.safe_load(fake_response_2)
response_3_parsed = yaml.safe_load(fake_response_3)


# Validate the responses against the schema
try:
    validate_response(response_1_parsed, schema)
    print("Response 1 is valid")
except Exception as e:
    print("Response 1 is invalid:", str(e))

try:
    validate_response(response_2_parsed, schema)
    print("Response 2 is valid")
except Exception as e:
    print("Response 2 is invalid:", str(e))
```

```
try:
    validate_response(response_3_parsed, schema)
    print("Response 3 is valid")
except Exception as e:
    print("Response 3 is invalid:", str(e))

Response 1 is valid
Response 2 is valid
Response 3 is invalid: Response is not a list
```

Diverse Format Generation with ChatGPT

ChatGPT is not only capable of generating *.json* or *.yml* files but can also support many other data formats. For example, it can aid you in creating a mermaid diagram or generating a mock *.csv* document. Its versatility stretches to even generating code, conversations, and scripts.

Let's explore in detail how ChatGPT can produce diverse formatted content. Mermaid is a markdown-like scripting language for generating charts, diagrams, and other visualizations.

Input:

```
Create a flowchart diagram in mermaid syntax showing a simple food ordering
process that starts with "Choose food" and ends with "Pay for meal."
Include steps for "Add food to cart" and "Confirm cart."
```

Output:

```
graph TD
    ChooseFood[Choose Food] --> AddToCart[Add to Cart]
    AddToCart --> ConfirmCart[Confirm Cart]
    ConfirmCart --> PayForMeal[Pay for Meal]
```

This output, when input to a mermaid diagram renderer, will create a precise flowchart reflecting the food ordering process (Figure 3-2).

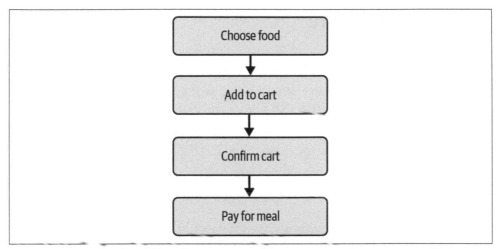

Figure 3-2. A streamlined flow diagram created using mermaid syntax via an LLM

Mock CSV Data

ChatGPT can also generate mock CSV data that can be utilized for testing purposes or other uses.

Input:

```
Generate a sample CSV data for five students with the following fields:
name, age, grade.
```

Output:

```
name,age,grade
John,16,A
Alex,17,B
Emma,16,A
Sophia,16,B
Liam,17,A
```

The example generated is a well-formatted CSV file, which can be loaded directly into many tools that read CSV data.

Remember, GPT models rely heavily on the format you specify. For instance, specifying CSV implies the AI should use commas as separators. Be clear about the desired format for optimal results.

You've explored different ways of extracting structured data from language models including regular expressions, JSON, YML, and other formats. You can also now use LLMs to direct parts of your application's control flow.

Explain It like I'm Five

The *Explain It like I'm Five* prompt focuses on explaining a given section of text *as if you were talking to a five-year-old child.*

This style of prompting is very effective and is a great way to convert technical documents into simple summaries that anyone can understand.

Let's apply this prompt to an abstract of "Tumor Microenvironment: Recent Advances in Various Cancer Treatments" (*https://oreil.ly/MDOsz*).

Input:

```
Explain the following text as if I was 5 years old. Explain it like I'm 5.

Text: This is a review regarding different types of cancer treatments.
We aimed at analyzing the tumor microenvironment and the recent trends
for the therapeutic applications and effectiveness for several kinds
of cancers. Traditionally the cancer treatment was based on the
neoplastic cells.

...(shortened for brevity)...
```

Output:

```
Cancer is a sickness that makes your body's cells grow and divide in a way
that is not normal. Doctors have different ways to treat cancer, like
cutting it out, giving you medicine, or using special rays to kill the
cancer cells...
```

The ChatGPT output from the preceding example is much more digestible than the abstract.

Universal Translation Through LLMs

Additionally, language models can potentially act as *universal translators* due to their proficiency in understanding and generating human-like text across multiple languages.

Let's investigate this with a simple example:

1. Generate some simple text.
2. Change the simple text and make it difficult to read.
3. Then transform the same text back into an easy to read format in Spanish (instead of English).
4. Revert the simplistic text back into English.

Input:

    Create some simple text.

Output:

    The sun gently rises, painting the sky with hues of orange and pink. Birds
    chirp merrily as they welcome the new day. The cool breeze whispers through
    the trees, carrying the scent of fresh grass and blooming flowers. Life
    awakens with a sense of tranquility and promise.

    ...(shortened for brevity)...

Input:

    Now make the text incredibly complex and hard to read.

Output:

    In the ethereal realm of celestial ascendancy, wherein the resplendent
    orb of the sun commences its gradual ascent, an exquisite phenomenon
    unfolds,engendering a symphony of chromatic brilliance upon the
    expansive canopy of the firmament. Avian denizens, endowed with
    mellifluous voices, bespeak their jubilant salutations, punctuating
    the aural tapestry with notes of felicity. The zephyr, tenderly
    wafting amidst arboreal sentinels, carries upon its gentle currents
    the redolence of verdant blades and blossoming flora.
    ...(shortened for brevity)...

Input:

    Now transform the text into a simple, easy to read format that's in Spanish
    , make sure that it is very easy to understand and read. You must ensure
    that it is as simple to comprehend as possible.

    - Use simple language.
    - Make it concise.

Output:

    En un lugar mágico y celestial, cuando el sol empieza a salir, ocurre algo
    hermoso en el cielo. Los pájaros cantan alegremente, llenando el aire con
    sus dulces melodías. Una brisa suave sopla entre los árboles, llevando
    consigo el olor fresco de la naturaleza. Todo cobra vida y promete momentos
    felices. Nos invita a disfrutar de las cosas simples y a encontrar la
    felicidad en los pequeños detalles. En este escenario encantador,
    encontramos paz y aprendemos que hasta los momentos más simples pueden
    ser mágicos.

Input:

    Finally translate it back into English.

Output:

```
In a magical and celestial place, when the sun begins to rise, something
beautiful happens in the sky. The birds sing cheerfully, filling the air
with their sweet melodies. A gentle breeze blows among the trees, carrying
the fresh scent of nature. Everything comes alive and promises happy
moments. It invites us to enjoy the simple things and find happiness in the
little details. In this enchanting setting, we find peace and learn that
even the simplest moments can be magical.
```

As you can see, part of the meaning is lost while doing the translation, and this is to be expected. However, large parts of the original text's intent remains, demonstrating that LLMs can act as *highly effective translators* for languages that have adequate resources on the internet. For languages that do not have a good amount of resources, it will yield bad results.

The same logic applies to coding languages. LLMs are very good at generating code for established programming languages such as Python and JavaScript but perform worse for newer coding languages and packages.

The boundaries between different forms of information are becoming *increasingly fluid*. The essence of information itself is evolving, allowing for effortless transformations of summaries into stories, poems, or other creative expressions, ultimately enriching our understanding and engagement with the content.

Diffusion models are a unique class of generative models utilized in machine learning, specifically designed to produce new images that mimic those found in the training set.

Moreover, when you combine language models with diffusion models, it enables seamless transitions between text, video, and other modalities. This makes it even simpler for you to convey complex ideas across various formats, facilitating a more accessible and comprehensive experience.

Ask for Context

LLMs are not only capable of generating text but can also act as simple agents with a limited amount of *reasoning capability*. This allows you to write a prompt asking the language model to either:

- Return a valid result to a question or statement
- Ask for more context to appropriately answer the question

In this section, you'll learn about the importance of *asking for context* when working with LLMs such as GPT-4. We will start with an example of a prompt that doesn't provide enough context, resulting in a less useful response.

Then, we will provide a better prompt that encourages the model to ask for additional context if needed. Finally, we will use the additional context provided to generate a more informed response.

Input:

```
Should I use MongoDB or PostgreSQL for my project?
```

Output:

```
It's difficult to make a recommendation without knowing more about your
specific software requirements. Both MongoDB and PostgreSQL have their
advantages, but the best choice depends on the specific needs of your
project.
```

In the preceding prompt, the model does not have enough context to make a meaningful recommendation. Instead, you can ask ChatGPT for a list of recommended points that would help it to make an effective decision.

Input:

```
Should I use MongoDB or PostgreSQL for my project?

Provide a list of requirements that would help you to make an informed
and high-quality decision about which database solution I should choose?
```

Output:

```
To make an informed decision between MongoDB and PostgreSQL for your
project, consider the following requirements:

1. Data Structure: Evaluate the structure of your data. If your data
is highly unstructured or schema-less, MongoDB's flexible document model
may be more suitable. On the other hand, if your data has a fixed schema
or requires complex relationships, PostgreSQL's relational model might
be a better fit.

...

10. Cost: Assess the cost implications of each database solution. MongoDB
offers both a community edition (free) and a commercial edition with
additional features and support.PostgreSQL is open-source and free to use,
with optional commercial support available from various vendors.
```

After prompting ChatGPT about how to make an informed decision, now you're aware of what to include within your prompt to help the language model with deciding.

Input:

```
Should I use MongoDB or PostgreSQL for my project?

Context:
- Data Structure: Highly unstructured data with varying document formats
and no fixed schema. Scalability: Project requires the ability to handle
massive amounts of data and distribute it across multiple servers.
- ACID Compliance: Strong data consistency and integrity are crucial for
the project's financial transactions.
- Querying Capabilities: Complex geospatial queries and aggregations on
location-based data.
Community and Ecosystem: Active community with numerous third-party
libraries and tools specifically tailored for the project's industry.
- Data Integrity and Constraints: Enforcing strict foreign key
relationships and complex data validation rules.
- Transactions and Concurrency: Requires handling high levels of
concurrent read and write operations while maintaining data consistency.
- Maturity and Stability: Prioritizing a well-established and extensively
tested database for long-term stability.
- Development and Operational Ease: Agile development approach with a need
for rapid prototyping and iterative schema design.
- Cost: Budget constraints necessitate using an open-source solution with
no additional licensing or support costs.

If you need more context, please specify what would help you to make
a better decision.
```

Output:

```
Based on these considerations, both MongoDB and PostgreSQL have their
strengths, but given the emphasis on strong data consistency, complex
querying, and data integrity constraints, PostgreSQL seems to be a more
suitable choice for your project.
```

In this final example, the model uses the additional context provided to give a well-informed recommendation for using PostgreSQL. By asking for context when necessary, LLMs like ChatGPT and GPT-4 can deliver more valuable and accurate responses.

Figure 3-3 demonstrates how *asking for context* changes the decision-making process of LLMs. Upon receiving user input, the model first assesses whether the context given is sufficient. If not, it prompts the user to provide more detailed information, emphasizing the model's reliance on context-rich inputs. Once adequate context is acquired, the LLM then generates an informed and relevant response.

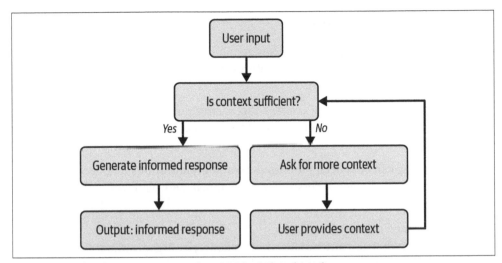

Figure 3-3. The decision process of an LLM while asking for context

Allow the LLM to Ask for More Context by Default

You can allow the LLM to ask for more context as a default by including this key phrase: *If you need more context, please specify what would help you to make a better decision.*

In this section, you've seen how LLMs can act as agents that use environmental context to make decisions. By iteratively refining the prompt based on the model's recommendations, we eventually reach a point where the model has *enough context to make a well-informed decision.*

This process highlights the importance of providing sufficient context in your prompts and being prepared to ask for more information when necessary. By doing so, you can leverage the power of LLMs like GPT-4 to make more accurate and valuable recommendations.

In agent-based systems like GPT-4, the ability to ask for more context and provide a finalized answer is crucial for making well-informed decisions. AutoGPT (*https://oreil.ly/l3Ihy*), a multiagent system, has a self-evaluation step that automatically checks whether the task can be completed given the current context within the prompt. This technique uses an actor–critic relationship, where the existing prompt context is being analyzed to see whether it could be further refined before being executed.

Text Style Unbundling

Text style unbundling is a powerful technique in prompt engineering that allows you to extract and isolate specific textual features from a given document, such as tone, length, vocabulary, and structure.

This allows you to create new content that shares similar characteristics with the original document, ensuring consistency in style and tone across various forms of communication.

This consistency can be crucial for businesses and organizations that need to communicate with a unified voice across different channels and platforms. The benefits of this technique include:

Improved brand consistency
By ensuring that all content follows a similar style, organizations can strengthen their brand identity and maintain a cohesive image.

Streamlined content creation
By providing a clear set of guidelines, writers and content creators can more easily produce materials that align with a desired style.

Adaptability
Text style unbundling allows for the easy adaptation of existing content to new formats or styles while preserving the core message and tone.

The process of text style unbundling involves *identifying the desired textual features* or creating a meta prompt (a prompt to create prompts) to extract these features and then using the extracted features to guide the generation of new content.

Identifying the Desired Textual Features

To successfully unbundle a text style, you must first identify the specific features you want to extract from the input document. Common textual features to consider include:

Tone of voice
The overall mood or attitude conveyed by the text, such as formal, casual, humorous, or authoritative

Length
The desired word count or general length of the content

Vocabulary and phrasing
The choice of words and expressions, including industry-specific jargon, colloquialisms, and complexity

Additionally, you can even create a meta prompt that will dynamically show you these.

Input:

> Analyze the following text and identify core features that will allow
> further documents to imitate the same style, consistency, and formatting
> as the document below.
>
> Provide all of the features as a style writing guide that will be used
> for future documents.
>
> Analyze the following text:
>
> Artificial intelligence is rapidly transforming the world around us,
> opening up new possibilities and revolutionizing industries. From
> health care to entertainment, AI is making our lives better and more
> convenient in countless ways. However, with great power comes great
> responsibility. We must ensure that AI technologies are developed and
> deployed ethically and responsibly to protect our privacy and uphold our
> values.

Output:

> Style Writing Guide:
>
> Tone of Voice
> - Maintain an informative and optimistic tone throughout the document.
> - Emphasize the positive impact of the subject matter while acknowledging
> any potential concerns or responsibilities.
>
> Length:
> ...
>
> Vocabulary:
> ...
>
> Structure:
> ...
>
> Content:
> - Focus on the transformative nature and positive impacts of the subject
> matter.
> - Highlight specific industries or areas where the subject matter has
> made a difference.
> - Acknowledge any associated responsibilities or potential risks,
> emphasizing the need for ethical and responsible practices.
> Stress the importance of privacy protection and upholding values in
> relation to the subject matter.

Generating New Content with the Extracted Features

After you've extracted the desired features from the input document, you can use this information to guide future content generation. Remember to ensure that the AI model incorporates the extracted features into its output by specifying the desired style in your prompt. For example:

```
Write a new blog post on [topic] using the same tone of voice,
length, vocabulary, and structure as the previously analyzed text.
```

By combining this technique with *reference text* (documents that act as grounding truth), you can produce credible, branded content that requires minimal revisions.

Extracting Specific Textual Features with LLMs

You can easily tailor a prompt to guide an LLM in extracting particular textual features from a document. This can be applied beyond just analyzing text for copywriting purposes. For instance, recognizing entities or discerning sentiment from the text can be achieved by crafting a precise instruction for the LLM.

Input:

```
Analyze the following text to identify and list the entities mentioned:

Artificial intelligence is rapidly transforming the world around us,
opening up new possibilities and revolutionizing industries. From
health care to entertainment, AI is making our lives better and more
convenient in countless ways. However, with great power comes great
responsibility. We must ensure that AI technologies are developed
and deployed ethically and responsibly to protect our privacy and
uphold our values.
```

Output:

```
Entities:
- Artificial Intelligence (AI)
- Health care
- Entertainment
- Privacy
- Values
```

Summarization

In the era of information overload, the ability to condense large amounts of text into concise, digestible summaries has become an essential skill. As the volume of data we produce and consume continues to grow, the demand for effective summarization techniques has increased significantly.

AI has made significant advancements in this domain, providing powerful tools for generating summaries that retain the most critical information while discarding less relevant details.

Let's explore how to summarize using a language model.

Input:

```
Summarize the following text:

Whereas the party of the first part, hereinafter referred to as the
"Purchaser," and the party of the second part, hereinafter referred to
as the "Vendor," being fully cognizant of their respective legal
obligations and responsibilities pursuant to the applicable statutory
provisions and common law doctrines, have duly entered into a legally
binding agreement, hereinafter referred to as the "Agreement," for the
purpose of effectuating a transaction involving the transfer of goods,
hereinafter referred to as the "Goods," between the Purchaser and the
Vendor, subject to the terms and conditions set forth herein, the Parties
do hereby solemnly acknowledge and affirm the following:
...
```

Output:

```
This is a legally binding agreement between the Purchaser and the Vendor
for the transfer of goods. The agreement incorporates the recitals as an
integral part, but in case of any conflict, the operative provisions of the
agreement prevail. The interpretation clause states that singular words
include the plural and vice versa, and words referring to a gender include
all genders. References to statutory provisions include any amendments or
replacements.
```

Summarization is an invaluable application of AI, enabling users to quickly extract key insights from lengthy articles, reports, or research papers. This process can help individuals make informed decisions, save time, and prioritize their reading. AI-generated summaries can also facilitate information sharing among teams, allowing for more efficient collaboration and communication.

Summarizing Given Context Window Limitations

For documents larger than an LLM can handle in a single API request, a common approach is to chunk the document, summarize each chunk, and then combine these summaries into a final summary, as shown in Figure 3-4.

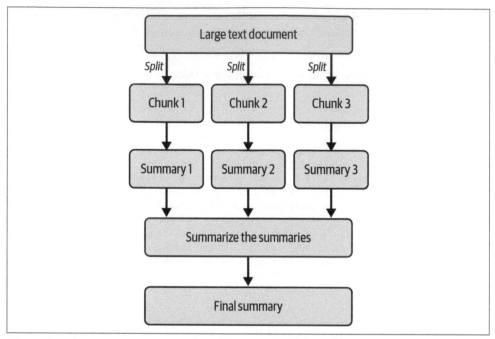

Figure 3-4. A summarization pipeline that uses text splitting and multiple summarization steps

Additionally, people may require different types of summaries for various reasons, and this is where AI summarization comes in handy. As illustrated in the preceding diagram, a large PDF document could easily be processed using AI summarization to generate distinct summaries tailored to individual needs:

Summary A
Provides key insights, which is perfect for users seeking a quick understanding of the document's content, enabling them to focus on the most crucial points

Summary B
On the other hand, offers decision-making information, allowing users to make informed decisions based on the content's implications and recommendations

Summary C
Caters to collaboration and communication, ensuring that users can efficiently share the document's information and work together seamlessly

By customizing the summaries for different users, AI summarization contributes to increased information retrieval for all users, making the entire process more efficient and targeted.

Let's assume you're only interested in finding and summarizing information about the advantages of digital marketing. Simply change your summarization prompt to `Provide a concise, abstractive summary of the above text. Only summarize the advantages: ...`

AI-powered summarization has emerged as an essential tool for quickly distilling vast amounts of information into concise, digestible summaries that cater to various user needs. By leveraging advanced language models like GPT-4, AI summarization techniques can efficiently extract key insights and decision-making information, and also facilitate collaboration and communication.

As the volume of data continues to grow, the demand for effective and targeted summarization will only increase, making AI a crucial asset for individuals and organizations alike in navigating the Information Age.

Chunking Text

LLMs continue to develop and play an increasingly crucial role in various applications, as the ability to process and manage large volumes of text becomes ever more important. An essential technique for handling large-scale text is known as *chunking*.

Chunking refers to the process of breaking down large pieces of text into smaller, more manageable units or chunks. These chunks can be based on various criteria, such as sentence, paragraph, topic, complexity, or length. By dividing text into smaller segments, AI models can more efficiently process, analyze, and generate responses.

Figure 3-5 illustrates the process of chunking a large piece of text and subsequently extracting topics from the individual chunks.

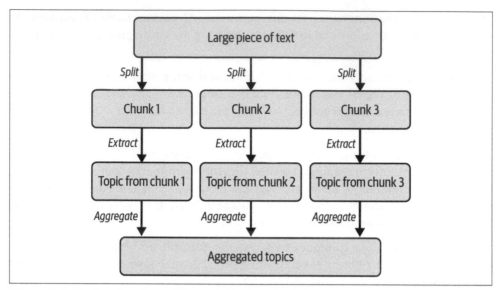

Figure 3-5. Topic extraction with an LLM after chunking text

Benefits of Chunking Text

There are several advantages to chunking text, which include:

Fitting within a given context length
> LLMs only have a certain amount of input and output tokens, which is called a *context length*. By reducing the input tokens you can make sure the output won't be cut off and the initial request won't be rejected.

Reducing cost
> Chunking helps you to only retrieve the most important points from documents, which reduces your token usage and API costs.

Improved performance
> Chunking reduces the processing load on LLMs, allowing for faster response times and more efficient resource utilization.

Increased flexibility
> Chunking allows developers to tailor AI responses based on the specific needs of a given task or application.

Scenarios for Chunking Text

Chunking text can be particularly beneficial in certain scenarios, while in others it may not be required. Understanding when to apply this technique can help in optimizing the performance and cost efficiency of LLMs.

When to chunk

Large documents
> When dealing with extensive documents that exceed the maximum token limit of the LLM

Complex analysis
> In scenarios where a detailed analysis is required and the document needs to be broken down for better comprehension and processing

Multitopic documents
> When a document covers multiple topics and it's beneficial to handle them individually

When not to chunk

Short documents
> When the document is short and well within the token limits of the LLM

Simple analysis
> In cases where the analysis or processing required is straightforward and doesn't benefit from chunking

Single-topic documents
> When a document is focused on a single topic and chunking doesn't add value to the processing

Poor Chunking Example

When text is not chunked correctly, it can lead to reduced LLM performance. Consider the following paragraph from a news article:

> The local council has decided to increase the budget for education by 10% this year, a move that has been welcomed by parents and teachers alike. The additional funds will be used to improve school infrastructure, hire more teachers, and provide better resources for students. However, some critics argue that the increase is not enough to address the growing demands of the education system.

When the text is fragmented into isolated words, the resulting list lacks the original context:

```
["The", "local", "council", "has", "decided", "to", "increase", "the",
"budget", ...]
```

The main issues with this poor chunking example include:

Loss of context
> By splitting the text into individual words, the original meaning and relationships between the words are lost. This makes it difficult for AI models to understand and respond effectively.

Increased processing load
> Processing individual words requires more computational resources, making it less efficient than processing larger chunks of text.

As a result of the poor chunking in this example, an LLM may face several challenges:

- Difficulty understanding the main ideas or themes of the text
- Struggling to generate accurate summaries or translations
- Inability to effectively perform tasks such as sentiment analysis or text `classification`

By understanding the pitfalls of poor chunking, you can apply prompt engineering principles to improve the process and achieve better results with AI language models.

Let's explore an improved chunking example using the same news article paragraph from the previous section; you'll now chunk the text by sentence:

```
["""The local council has decided to increase the budget for education
by 10% this year, a move that has been welcomed by parents and teachers alike.
""",

"""The additional funds will be used to improve school infrastructure,
hire more teachers, and provide better resources for students.""",

"""However, some critics argue that the increase is not enough to
address the growing demands of the education system."""]
```

Divide Labor and Evaluate Quality

Define the granularity at which the text should be chunked, such as by sentence, paragraph, or topic. Adjust parameters like the number of tokens or model temperature to optimize the chunking process.

By chunking the text in this manner, you could insert whole sentences into an LLM prompt with the most relevant sentences.

Chunking Strategies

There are many different chunking strategies, including:

Splitting by sentence
> Preserves the context and structure of the original content, making it easier for LLMs to understand and process the information. Sentence-based chunking is particularly useful for tasks like summarization, translation, and sentiment analysis.

Splitting by paragraph
> This approach is especially effective when dealing with longer content, as it allows the LLM to focus on one cohesive unit at a time. Paragraph-based chunking is ideal for applications like document analysis, topic modeling, and information extraction.

Splitting by topic or section
> This method can help AI models better identify and understand the main themes and ideas within the content. Topic-based chunking is well suited for tasks like text classification, content recommendations, and clustering.

Splitting by complexity
> For certain applications, it might be helpful to split text based on its complexity, such as the reading level or technicality of the content. By grouping similar complexity levels together, LLMs can more effectively process and analyze the text. This approach is useful for tasks like readability analysis, content adaptation, and personalized learning.

Splitting by length
> This technique is particularly helpful when working with very long or complex documents, as it allows LLMs to process the content more efficiently. Length-based chunking is suitable for applications like large-scale text analysis, search engine indexing, and text preprocessing.

Splitting by tokens using a tokenizer
> Utilizing a tokenizer is a crucial step in many natural language processing tasks, as it enables the process of splitting text into individual tokens. Tokenizers divide text into smaller units, such as words, phrases, or symbols, which can then be analyzed and processed by AI models more effectively. You'll shortly be using a package called `tiktoken`, which is a bytes-pair encoding tokenizer (BPE) for chunking.

Table 3-1 provides a high-level overview of the different chunking strategies; it's worth considering what matters to you most when performing chunking.

Are you more interested in preserving semantic context, or would naively splitting by length suffice?

Table 3-1. Six chunking strategies highlighting their advantages and disadvantages

Splitting strategy	Advantages	Disadvantages
Splitting by sentence	Preserves context, suitable for various tasks	May not be efficient for very long content
Splitting by paragraph	Handles longer content, focuses on cohesive units	Less granularity, may miss subtle connections
Splitting by topic	Identifies main themes, better for classification	Requires topic identification, may miss fine details
Splitting by complexity	Groups similar complexity levels, adaptive	Requires complexity measurement, not suitable for all tasks
Splitting by length	Manages very long content, efficient processing	Loss of context, may require more preprocessing steps
Using a tokenizer: Splitting by tokens	Accurate token counts, which helps in avoiding LLM prompt token limits	Requires tokenization, may increase computational complexity

By choosing the appropriate chunking strategy for your specific use case, you can optimize the performance and accuracy of AI language models.

Sentence Detection Using SpaCy

Sentence detection, also known as sentence boundary disambiguation, is the process used in NLP that involves identifying the start and end of sentences within a given text. It can be particularly useful for tasks that require preserving the context and structure of the original content. By splitting the text into sentences, LLMs can better understand and process the information for tasks such as summarization, translation, and sentiment analysis.

Splitting by sentence is possible using NLP libraries such as spaCy (*https://spacy.io*). Ensure that you have spaCy installed in your Python environment. You can install it with `pip install spacy`. Download the en_core_web_sm model using the command `python -m spacy download en_core_web_sm`.

In Example 3-3, the code demonstrates sentence detection using the spaCy library in Python.

Example 3-3. Sentence detection with spaCy (https://oreil.ly/GKDnc)

```
import spacy

nlp = spacy.load("en_core_web_sm")

text = "This is a sentence. This is another sentence."
```

```
doc = nlp(text)

for sent in doc.sents:
    print(sent.text)
```

Output:

```
This is a sentence.
This is another sentence.
```

First, you'll import the spaCy library and load the English model (en_core_web_sm) to initialize an nlp object. Define an input text with two sentences; the text is then processed with doc = nlp(text), creating a doc object as a result. Finally, the code iterates through the detected sentences using the doc.sents attribute and prints each sentence.

Building a Simple Chunking Algorithm in Python

After exploring many chunking strategies, it's important to build your intuition by writing a simple chunking algorithm from scatch.

Example 3-4 shows how to chunk text based on the length of characters from the blog post "Hubspot - What Is Digital Marketing?" This file can be found in the Github repository at *content/chapter_3/hubspot_blog_post.txt (https://oreil.ly/30rlQ)*.

To correctly read the *hubspot_blog post.txt* file, make sure your current working directory is set to the *content/chapter_3 (https://oreil.ly/OHurh)* GitHub directory. This applies for both running the Python code or launching the Jupyter Notebook server.

Example 3-4. Character chunking (https://oreil.ly/n3sNy)

```
with open("hubspot_blog_post.txt", "r") as f:
    text = f.read()

chunks = [text[i : i + 200] for i in range(0, len(text), 200)]

for chunk in chunks:
    print("-" * 20)
    print(chunk)
```

Output:

```
search engine optimization strategy for many local businesses is an optimized
Google My Business profile to appear in local search results when people look for
products or services related to what yo
--------------------
u offer.
```

```
For Keeps Bookstore, a local bookstore in Atlanta, GA, has optimized its
Google My Business profile for local SEO so it appears in queries for
"atlanta bookstore."
-------------------
...(shortened for brevity)...
```

First, you open the text file *hubspot_blog_post.txt* with the open function and read its contents into the variable text. Then using a list comprehension you create a list of chunks, where each chunk is a 200 character substring of text.

Then you use the range function to generate indices for each 200 character substring, and the i:i+200 slice notation to extract the substring from text.

Finally, you loop through each chunk in the chunks list and print it to the console.

As you can see, because the chunking implementation is relatively simple and only based on length, there are gaps within the sentences and even words.

For these reasons we believe that good NLP chunking has the following properties:

- Preserves entire words, ideally sentences and contextual points made by speakers
- Handles for when sentences span across several pages, for example, page 1 into page 2
- Provides an adequate token count for each chunk so that the total number of input tokens will appropriately fit into a given token context window for any LLM

Sliding Window Chunking

Sliding window chunking is a technique used for dividing text data into overlapping chunks, or *windows*, based on a specified number of characters.

But what exactly is a sliding window?

Imagine viewing a long piece of text through a small window. This window is only capable of displaying a fixed number of characters at a time. As you slide this window from the beginning to the end of the text, you see *overlapping chunks of text*. This mechanism forms the essence of the sliding window approach.

Each window size is defined by a *fixed number of characters*, and the *step size* determines how far the window moves with each slide.

In Figure 3-6, with a window size of 5 characters and a step size of 1, the first chunk would contain the first 5 characters of the text. The window then slides 1 character to the right to create the second chunk, which contains characters 2 through 6.

This process repeats until the end of the text is reached, ensuring each chunk overlaps with the previous and next ones to retain some shared context.

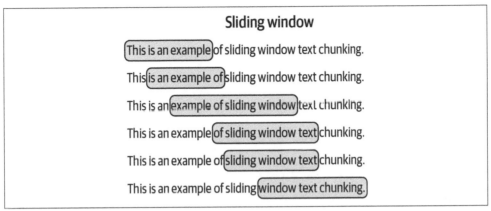

Figure 3-6. A sliding window, with a window size of 5 and a step size of 1

Due to the step size being 1, there is a lot of duplicate information between chunks, and at the same time the risk of losing information between chunks is dramatically reduced.

This is in stark contrast to Figure 3-7, which has a window size of 4 and a step size of 2. You'll notice that because of the 100% increase in step size, the amount of information shared between the chunks is greatly reduced.

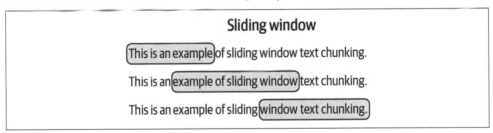

Figure 3-7. A sliding window, with a window size of 4 and a step size of 2

You will likely need a larger overlap if accuracy and preserving semantic context are more important than minimizing token inputs or the number of requests made to an LLM.

Example 3-5 shows how you can implement a sliding window using Python's len() function. The len() function provides us with the total number of characters in a given text string, which subsequently aids in defining the parameters of our sliding windows.

Example 3-5. Sliding window (https://oreil.ly/aCkDo)

```python
def sliding_window(text, window_size, step_size):
    if window_size > len(text) or step_size < 1:
        return []
    return [text[i:i+window_size] for i
    in range(0, len(text) - window_size + 1, step_size)]

text = "This is an example of sliding window text chunking."
window_size = 20
step_size = 5

chunks = sliding_window(text, window_size, step_size)

for idx, chunk in enumerate(chunks):
    print(f"Chunk {idx + 1}: {chunk}")
```

This code outputs:

```
Chunk 1: This is an example o
Chunk 2: is an example of sli
Chunk 3:  example of sliding
Chunk 4: ple of sliding windo
Chunk 5: f sliding window tex
Chunk 6: ding window text chu
Chunk 7: window text chunking
```

In the context of prompt engineering, the sliding window approach offers several benefits over fixed chunking methods. It allows LLMs to retain a higher degree of context, as there is an overlap between the chunks and offers an alternative approach to preserving context compared to sentence detection.

Text Chunking Packages

When working with LLMs such as GPT-4, always remain wary of the maximum context length:

```
maximum_context_length = input_tokens + output_tokens
```

There are various tokenizers available to break your text down into manageable units, the most popular ones being NLTK, spaCy, and tiktoken.

Both NLTK (*https://oreil.ly/wTmI7*) and spaCy (*https://oreil.ly/c4MvQ*) provide comprehensive support for text processing, but you'll be focusing on tiktoken.

Text Chunking with Tiktoken

Tiktoken (*https://oreil.ly/oSpVe*) is a fast *byte pair encoding (BPE)* tokenizer that breaks down text into subword units and is designed for use with OpenAI's models. Tiktoken offers faster performance than comparable open source tokenizers.

As a developer working with GPT-4 applications, using tiktoken offers you several key advantages:

Accurate token breakdown
> It's crucial to divide text into tokens because GPT models interpret text as individual tokens. Identifying the number of tokens in your text helps you figure out whether the text is too lengthy for a model to process.

Effective resource utilization
> Having the correct token count enables you to manage resources efficiently, particularly when using the OpenAI API. Being aware of the exact number of tokens helps you regulate and optimize API usage, maintaining a balance between costs and resource usage.

Encodings

Encodings define the method of converting text into tokens, with different models utilizing different encodings. Tiktoken supports three encodings commonly used by OpenAI models:

Encoding name	OpenAI models
cl100k_base	GPT-4, GPT-3.5-turbo, text-embedding-ada-002
p50k_base	Codex models, text-davinci-002, text-davinci-003
r50k_base (or gpt2)	GPT-3 models like davinci

Understanding the Tokenization of Strings

In English, tokens can vary in length, ranging from a single character like *t*, to an entire word such as *great*. This is due to the adaptable nature of tokenization, which can accommodate even tokens shorter than a character in complex script languages or tokens longer than a word in languages without spaces or where phrases function as single units.

It is not uncommon for spaces to be included within tokens, such as "is" rather than "is " or " "+"is". This practice helps maintain the original text formatting and can capture specific linguistic characteristics.

To easily examine the tokenization of a string, you can use OpenAI Tokenizer (*https://oreil.ly/K6ZQK*).

You can install tiktoken from PyPI (*https://oreil.ly/HA2QD*) with `pip install tiktoken`. In the following example, you'll see how to easily encode text into tokens and decode tokens into text:

```python
# 1. Import the package:
import tiktoken

# 2. Load an encoding with tiktoken.get_encoding()
encoding = tiktoken.get_encoding("cl100k_base")

# 3. Turn some text into tokens with encoding.encode()
# while turning tokens into text with encoding.decode()
print(encoding.encode("Learning how to use Tiktoken is fun!"))
print(encoding.decode([1061, 15009, 374, 264, 2294, 1648,
311, 4048, 922, 15592, 0]))

# [48567, 1268, 311, 1005, 73842, 5963, 374, 2523, 0]
# "Data engineering is a great way to learn about AI!"
```

Additionally let's write a function that will tokenize the text and then count the number of tokens given a `text_string` and `encoding_name`.

```python
def count_tokens(text_string: str, encoding_name: str) -> int:
    """
    Returns the number of tokens in a text string using a given encoding.

    Args:
        text: The text string to be tokenized.
        encoding_name: The name of the encoding to be used for tokenization.

    Returns:
        The number of tokens in the text string.

    Raises:
        ValueError: If the encoding name is not recognized.
    """
    encoding = tiktoken.get_encoding(encoding_name)
    num_tokens = len(encoding.encode(text_string))
    return num_tokens

# 4. Use the function to count the number of tokens in a text string.
text_string = "Hello world! This is a test."
print(count_tokens(text_string, "cl100k_base"))
```

This code outputs 8.

Estimating Token Usage for Chat API Calls

ChatGPT models, such as GPT-3.5-turbo and GPT-4, utilize tokens similarly to previous completion models. However, the message-based structure makes token counting for conversations more challenging:

```python
def num_tokens_from_messages(messages, model="gpt-3.5-turbo-0613"):
    """Return the number of tokens used by a list of messages."""
    try:
        encoding = tiktoken.encoding_for_model(model)
    except KeyError:
        print("Warning: model not found. Using cl100k_base encoding.")
        encoding = tiktoken.get_encoding("cl100k_base")
    if model in {
        "gpt-3.5-turbo-0613",
        "gpt-3.5-turbo-16k-0613",
        "gpt-4-0314",
        "gpt-4-32k-0314",
        "gpt-4-0613",
        "gpt-4-32k-0613",
        }:
        tokens_per_message = 3
        tokens_per_name = 1
    elif model == "gpt-3.5-turbo-0301":
        tokens_per_message = 4  # every message follows
        # <|start|>{role/name}\n{content}<|end|>\n
        tokens_per_name = -1  # if there's a name, the role is omitted
    elif "gpt-3.5-turbo" in model:
        print('''Warning: gpt-3.5-turbo may update over time. Returning
        num tokens assuming gpt-3.5-turbo-0613.''')
        return num_tokens_from_messages(messages, model="gpt-3.5-turbo-0613")
    elif "gpt-4" in model:
        print('''Warning: gpt-4 may update over time.
        Returning num tokens assuming gpt-4-0613.''')
        return num_tokens_from_messages(messages, model="gpt-4-0613")
    else:
        raise NotImplementedError(
            f"""num_tokens_from_messages() is not implemented for model
            {model}."""
        )
    num_tokens = 0
    for message in messages:
        num_tokens += tokens_per_message
        for key, value in message.items():
            num_tokens += len(encoding.encode(value))
            if key == "name":
                num_tokens += tokens_per_name
    num_tokens += 3  # every reply is primed with
    # <|start|>assistant<|message|>
    return num_tokens
```

Example 3-6 highlights the specific structure required to make a request against any of the chat models, which are currently GPT-3x and GPT-4.

Normally, chat history is structured with a `system` message first, and then succeeded by alternating exchanges between the `user` and the `assistant`.

Example 3-6. A payload for the Chat Completions API on OpenAI

```
example_messages = [
    {
        "role": "system",
        "content": '''You are a helpful, pattern-following assistant that
        translates corporate jargon into plain English.''',
    },
    {
        "role": "system",
        "name": "example_user",
        "content": "New synergies will help drive top-line growth.",
    },
    {
        "role": "system",
        "name": "example_assistant",
        "content": "Things working well together will increase revenue.",
    },
    {
        "role": "system",
        "name": "example_user",
        "content": '''Let's circle back when we have more bandwidth to touch
        base on opportunities for increased leverage.''',
    },
    {
        "role": "system",
        "name": "example_assistant",
        "content": '''Let's talk later when we're less busy about how to
        do better.''',
    },
    {
        "role": "user",
        "content": '''This late pivot means we don't have
        time to boil the ocean for the client deliverable.''',
    },
]

for model in ["gpt-3.5-turbo-0301", "gpt-4-0314"]:
    print(model)
    # example token count from the function defined above
    print(f'''{num_tokens_from_messages(example_messages, model)}
    prompt tokens counted by num_tokens_from_messages().''')
```

"role": "system" describes a system message that's useful for *providing prompt instructions*. It offers a means to tweak the assistant's character or provide explicit directives regarding its interactive approach. It's crucial to understand, though, that the system command isn't a prerequisite, and the model's default demeanor without a system command could closely resemble the behavior of "You are a helpful assistant."

The roles that you can have are ["system", "user", "assistant"].

"content": "Some content" is where you place the prompt or responses from a language model, depending upon the message's role. It can be either "assistant", "system", or "user".

Sentiment Analysis

Sentiment analysis is a widely used NLP technique that helps in identifying, extracting, and understanding the emotions, opinions, or sentiments expressed in a piece of text. By leveraging the power of LLMs like GPT-4, sentiment analysis has become an essential tool for businesses, researchers, and developers across various industries.

The primary goal of sentiment analysis is to determine the attitude or emotional tone conveyed in a text, whether it's positive, negative, or neutral. This information can provide valuable insights into consumer opinions about products or services, help monitor brand reputation, and even assist in predicting market trends.

The following are several prompt engineering techniques for creating effective sentiment analysis prompts:

Input:

```
Is this text positive or negative?

I absolutely love the design of this phone, but the battery life is quite
disappointing.
```

Output:

```
The text has a mixed tone, as it contains both positive and negative
aspects. The positive part is "I absolutely love the design of this phone,"
while the negative part is "the battery life is quite disappointing."
```

Although GPT-4 identifies a "mixed tone," the outcome is a result of several shortcomings in the prompt:

Lack of clarity
    The prompt does not clearly define the desired output format.

Insufficient examples

The prompt does not include any examples of positive, negative, or neutral sentiments, which could help guide the LLM in understanding the distinctions between them.

No guidance on handling mixed sentiments

The prompt does not specify how to handle cases where the text contains a mix of positive and negative sentiments.

Input:

```
Using the following examples as a guide:
positive: 'I absolutely love the design of this phone!'
negative: 'The battery life is quite disappointing.'
neutral: 'I liked the product, but it has short battery life.'

Only return either a single word of:
- positive
- negative
- neutral

Please classify the sentiment of the following text as positive, negative,
or neutral: I absolutely love the design of this phone, but the battery
life is quite disappointing.
```

Output:

```
neutral
```

This prompt is much better because it:

Provides clear instructions

The prompt clearly states the task, which is to classify the sentiment of the given text into one of three categories: positive, negative, or neutral.

Offers examples

The prompt provides examples for each of the sentiment categories, which helps in understanding the context and desired output.

Defines the output format

The prompt specifies that the output should be a single word, ensuring that the response is concise and easy to understand.

Techniques for Improving Sentiment Analysis

To enhance sentiment analysis accuracy, preprocessing the input text is a vital step. This involves the following:

Special characters removal
> Exceptional characters such as emojis, hashtags, and punctuation may skew the rule-based sentiment algorithm's judgment. Besides, these characters might not be recognized by machine learning and deep learning models, resulting in misclassification.

Lowercase conversion
> Converting all the characters to lowercase aids in creating uniformity. For instance, words like *Happy* and *happy* are treated as different words by models, which can cause duplication and inaccuracies.

Spelling correction
> Spelling errors can cause misinterpretation and misclassification. Creating a spell-check pipeline can significantly reduce such errors and improve results.

For industry- or domain-specific text, embedding domain-specific content in the prompt helps in navigating the LLM's sense of the text's framework and sentiment. It enhances accuracy in the classification and provides a heightened understanding of particular jargon and expressions.

Limitations and Challenges in Sentiment Analysis

Despite the advancements in LLMs and the application of prompt engineering techniques, sentiment analysis still faces some limitations and challenges:

Handling sarcasm and irony
> Detecting sarcasm and irony in text can be difficult for LLMs, as it often requires understanding the context and subtle cues that humans can easily recognize. Misinterpreting sarcastic or ironic statements may lead to inaccurate sentiment classification.

Identifying context-specific sentiment
> Sentiment analysis can be challenging when dealing with context-specific sentiments, such as those related to domain-specific jargon or cultural expressions. LLMs may struggle to accurately classify sentiments in these cases without proper guidance or domain-specific examples.

Least to Most

The *least to most* technique in prompt engineering is a powerful method for sequentially generating or extracting increasingly detailed knowledge on a given topic. This method is particularly effective when dealing with complex subjects or when a high level of detail is necessary.

Least to most uses a *chain* of prompts where each new prompt is based on the last answer. This step-by-step approach helps gather more detailed information each time, making it easier to dive deeper into any topic.

This technique can also be applied to code generation, as demonstrated in a Flask Hello World app example.

Planning the Architecture

Before diving into the architecture, let's briefly understand what Flask is. Flask (*https://oreil.ly/7N-bs*) is a lightweight web application framework in Python, widely used for creating web applications quickly and with minimal code. (Flask is only used for demonstration purposes here and isn't included within the *requirements.txt* file (*https://oreil.ly/TRK0i*) for the book.

Now, let's ask an LLM to outline the basic architecture for a simple Flask "Hello World" application.

Input:

```
Outline the basic architecture for a simple Flask "Hello World" application.
```

Output:

```
Sure! Here's an outline for a basic Flask "Hello World" application:

Import Flask module: Import the Flask module
to use its ((("Flask module code generation")))functionality.

Create an instance of the Flask application: Create an instance of the
Flask class to represent your web application.
Define a route and view function: ...
Implement the view function: ...
Run the application: Start the Flask development server to run the application.
```

Coding Individual Functions

Before coding, let's clarify what a Flask route is: it's a function linked to a URL pattern that determines what users see on a specific web page. Next, we'll provide the code snippet for a simple "Hello World" route in Flask.

Input:

> Provide a code snippet for a simple "Hello World" route in Flask.

Output:

> Certainly! Here's a simple code snippet for a "Hello World" route using Flask:

```
from flask import Flask

app = Flask(__name__)

@app.route('/')
def hello_world():
    return 'Hello, World!'

if __name__ == '__main__':
    app.run()
```

In this code, we import the Flask module and create a Flask application instance named app. We then define a route using the @app.route decorator, specifying the root URL path '/'. The hello_world function is associated with this route, and it returns the string 'Hello, World!' as the response.

The Flask application will start by calling app.run() when your Python script is executed directly.

Adding Tests

Finally, let's ask it to generate a test case for the "Hello World" route in the Flask application.

Input:

> Provide an example of a test case for the "Hello World" route in a Flask application.

Output:

> Sure! Here's an example of a test case for the "Hello World" route in a Flask application:

```
import unittest
from flask import Flask
from flask.testing import FlaskClient

# Create the Flask application
app = Flask(__name__)

# Create the route
@app.route('/')
def hello_world():
    return 'Hello, World!'
```

```
class FlaskAppTestCase(unittest.TestCase):
    def setUp(self):
        # Create a test client
        self.app = app.test_client()

    def test_hello_world_route(self):
        # Send a GET request to the route
        response = self.app.get('/')

        # Check the response status code
        self.assertEqual(response.status_code, 200)

        # Check the response data
        self.assertEqual(response.data, b'Hello, World!')

if __name__ == '__main__':
    unittest.main()
```

By using the least to most prompt technique, you can gradually build up the knowledge and understanding required for the task at hand.

Benefits of the Least to Most Technique

This method is particularly useful for complex tasks, as it allows an LLM to generate relevant knowledge that will subsequently be used as context for future tasks.

Let's dive deeper into the benefits of using this approach in various other scenarios:

Progressive exploration
Breaking a complex problem into smaller tasks allows an LLM to provide more detailed and accurate information at each step. This approach is especially helpful when working with a new subject matter or a multifaceted problem.

Flexibility
The least to most technique offers flexibility in addressing different aspects of a problem. It enables you to pivot, explore alternative solutions, or dive deeper into specific areas as needed.

Improved comprehension
By breaking down a task into smaller steps, an LLM can deliver information in a more digestible format, making it easier for you to understand and follow.

Collaborative learning
This technique promotes collaboration between you and an LLM, as it encourages an iterative process of refining the output and adjusting your responses to achieve the desired outcome.

Challenges with the Least to Most Technique

Overreliance on previously generated knowledge
Using previous chat history to store the state may lead to larger tasks forgetting their initial tasks/outputs due to limitations in context length.

Dependence on prior prompts
Since each prompt is built upon preceding outputs, it is imperative to ensure that the quality and responses of previous prompts provide ample information for the next step.

Evaluate Quality

In the process of designing prompts, make sure to evaluate the quality of each prior LLM response. The performance of the next task depends upon the quality of information provided by the preceding one.

Role Prompting

Role prompting is a technique in which the AI is given a specific role or character to assume while generating a response. This helps guide the AI's response style and content to better align with the user's needs or desired outcome.

Awesome ChatGPT prompts (*https://oreil.ly/8pf40*) provides an extensive list of role prompts that you can use.

Let's ask ChatGPT to take on the role of a tech reviewer for MongoDB.

Input:

```
I want you to act as a tech reviewer. I will give you the name of a piece
of technology and you will provide me with an in-depth review - including
pros, cons, features, and comparisons to other technologies on the market.
My first suggestion request is: MongoDB.
```

Output:

```
MongoDB is a popular NoSQL, document-oriented database management system
designed to handle high-volume data storage and retrieval.

Features:

1. Document-Oriented Storage: MongoDB stores data in a flexible, JSON-like
format called BSON, making it easy to store complex data structures like
arrays and nested objects.
```

```
...

Pros:
1. High Performance: MongoDB's indexing and caching capabilities deliver
fast read and write operations.
...

Cons:
1. Limited Support for Transactions: While MongoDB supports multidocument
ACID transactions, it may not be the best choice for applications that
require complex transactional operations.
...


Comparisons to other technologies:
1. Couchbase, another popular NoSQL database, offers similar features to
MongoDB, including flexible schema and JSON-based storage. However,
Couchbase is more focused on distributed caching and may be more
suitable for applications requiring low-latency data access.

Conclusion:

MongoDB is a powerful and versatile NoSQL database solution suitable for
various applications, particularly those requiring high performance and
scalability. Its flexible data model, rich query language, and strong
consistency make it a popular choice among developers.
```

The prompt is an excellent example of role prompting, as it clearly defines the role
the AI should assume (a tech reviewer) and sets expectations for the type of response
desired (an in-depth review of MongoDB).

Give Direction

When crafting prompts, consider assigning a specific role to the
AI. This sets the proper context for the response, creating a more
focused and relevant output.

Benefits of Role Prompting

Role prompting helps narrow down the AI's responses, ensuring more focused, contextually appropriate, and tailored results. It can also enhance creativity by pushing
the AI to think and respond from unique perspectives.

Challenges of Role Prompting

Role prompting can pose certain challenges. There might be potential risks for bias
or stereotyping based on the role assigned. Assigning stereotyped roles can lead
to generating biased responses, which could harm usability or offend individuals.

Additionally, maintaining consistency in the role throughout an extended interaction can be difficult. The model might drift off-topic or respond with information irrelevant to the assigned role.

Evaluate Quality

Consistently check the quality of the LLM's responses, especially when role prompting is in play. Monitor if the AI is sticking to the role assigned or if it is veering off-topic.

When to Use Role Prompting

Role prompting is particularly useful when you want to:

Elicit specific expertise
If you need a response that requires domain knowledge or specialized expertise, role prompting can help guide the LLM to generate more informed and accurate responses.

Tailor response style
Assigning a role can help an LLM generate responses that match a specific tone, style, or perspective, such as a formal, casual, or humorous response.

Encourage creative responses
Role prompting can be used to create fictional scenarios or generate imaginative answers by assigning roles like a storyteller, a character from a novel, or a historical figure.

- *Explore diverse perspectives*: If you want to explore different viewpoints on a topic, role prompting can help by asking the AI to assume various roles or personas, allowing for a more comprehensive understanding of the subject.

- *Enhance user engagement*: Role prompting can make interactions more engaging and entertaining by enabling an LLM to take on characters or personas that resonate with the user.

If you're using OpenAI, then the best place to add a role is within the `System Message` for chat models.

GPT Prompting Tactics

So far you've already covered several prompting tactics, including asking for context, text style bundling, least to most, and role prompting.

Let's cover several more tactics, from managing potential hallucinations with appropriate reference text, to providing an LLM with critical *thinking time*, to understanding the concept of *task decomposition*—we have plenty for you to explore.

These methodologies have been designed to significantly boost the precision of your AI's output and are recommended by OpenAI (*https://oreil.ly/QZE8n*). Also, each tactic utilizes one or more of the prompt engineering principles discussed in Chapter 1.

Avoiding Hallucinations with Reference

The first method for avoiding text-based hallucinations is to instruct the model to *only answer using reference text.*

By supplying an AI model with accurate and relevant information about a given query, the model can be directed to use this information to generate its response.

Input:

```
Refer to the articles enclosed within triple quotes to respond to queries.

You must follow the following principles:
- In cases where the answer isn't found within these articles, simply
return "I could not find an answer".

"""
B2B clients tend to have longer decision-making processes, and thus longer
sales funnels. Relationship-building strategies work better for these
clients, whereas B2C customers tend to respond better to short-term offers
and messages.
"""

Example responses:
- I could not find an answer.
- Yes, B2B clients tend to have longer decision-making processes, and thus
longer sales funnels.
```

Output:

```
Yes, B2B clients tend to have longer decision-making processes, which leads
to longer sales cycles.
```

If you were to ask the same reference text this question:

Input:

```
...The rest of the prompt...

Question: Are B2C sales more cost-effective?
```

Output:

```
I could not find an answer.
```

Give Direction and Specify Format

The preceding prompt is excellent as it both instructs the model on how to find answers and also sets a specific response format for any unanswerable questions.

Considering the constrained context windows of GPTs, a method for dynamically retrieving information relevant to the asked query might be necessary to utilize this strategy.

Another approach is to direct the model to *incorporate references* from a given text in its response. When the input is enhanced with relevant information, the model can be guided to include citations in its responses by referring to sections of the supplied documents. This approach has the added benefit that citations in the output can be *authenticated automatically by matching strings* within the given documents.

Input:

```
You will be provided with a document delimited by triple quotes and a
question. Your task is to answer the question using only the provided
document and to cite the passage(s) of the document used to answer the
question. If the document does not contain the information needed to answer
this question then simply write: "Insufficient information." If an answer
to the question is provided, it must be annotated with a citation. Use the
following format to cite relevant passages ({"citation": …}).

"""
A nuclear reactor is a device that initiates, controls, and maintains a
nuclear chain reaction. The nuclear reactor uses the energy released by
nuclear fission to generate heat, which is then often used to produce steam
to drive a turbine and produce electricity.

-Excerpted from https://en.wikipedia.org/wiki/Nuclear_reactor
"""

Question: What is a nuclear reactor?
```

Output:

```
A nuclear reactor is a device that initiates, controls, and maintains a
nuclear chain reaction.It uses the energy released by nuclear fission to
generate heat, which is then often used to produce steam to drive a turbine
and produce electricity. {"citation": "A nuclear reactor is a device that
initiates, controls, and maintains a nuclear chain reaction. The nuclear
reactor uses the energy released by nuclear fission to generate heat, which
is then often used to produce steam to drive a turbine and produce
electricity."}
```

Give GPTs "Thinking Time"

Often, by explicitly guiding an LLM to *derive solutions from first principles* before reaching a verdict, you can garner more accurate responses. Providing an LLM with *thinking time* can often lead to better results.

Input:

```
First, try to solve the problem on your own. Then, see if your answer
matches the proposed solution. Don't judge the given answer until you've
tried solving it yourself.

Problem:
Jane has 5 apples, then John takes 2 from Mary. Mary originally had 15
apples. John then gives his apples to Jane.

How many apples does Jane have?

Proposed solution:
1. Janes originally had 5 apples.
2. John takes 2 apples from Mary, but this doesn't affect Jane's count.
3. John then gives his apples to Jane.

So, Jane's final count of apples is her original 5 apples plus the 2 apples
that John gave her, for a total of 7 apples.
```

Output:

```
Let's break down the problem:

1. Jane originally has 5 apples.
2. John takes 2 apples from Mary. However, this action doesn't directly
impact the number of apples Jane has at this point.
3. John gives his apples to Jane.

Following these steps, we need to add the 2 apples John gave to Jane to
Jane's original number of apples. Therefore:

5 apples (Jane's original number) + 2 apples (given by John) = 7 apples

So, Jane now has 7 apples. My solution matches the proposed solution.
```

In some cases, when using GPT-4 or other generative AI models, you may not want the model's reasoning process to be visible to the user.

You can achieve this by asking an LLM to *generate an inner monologue*. This is particularly useful in tutoring applications, where revealing the model's reasoning might give away the solution prematurely.

The Inner Monologue Tactic

The *inner monologue tactic* instructs the model to structure parts of the output that should be hidden from the user in a specific format. This makes it easy to remove these parts before presenting the final output to the user.

Here's how you can utilize this tactic to answer user queries effectively.

Input:

```
Step 1: Solve the Problem

First, you need to work out your solution to the problem. Be sure not to
rely on the user's solution, as it might be incorrect. You can encapsulate
your workings within triple quotes (`"""`) to indicate that this section
should be hidden.

Step 2: Compare Solutions

Next, compare your solution with the user's solution. Evaluate whether the
user's solution is correct or not. Again, encapsulate this section within
triple quotes (`"""`).

Step 3: Prepare a Hint

If the user made a mistake, determine an appropriate hint that can help
guide them toward the correct answer, without giving it away outright.
This section should also be within triple quotes (`"""`).

Step 4: Deliver the Hint

If a mistake was made, present the hint from the previous step to the user.
Remember not to use triple quotes for this step. Instead of using a title
like "Step 4", use a heading such as `Hint:`


Problem Statement: A deck of cards has 52 cards: 13 hearts, 13 diamonds, 13
clubs, and 13 spades. If two cards are drawn from the deck without
replacement, what is the probability that one of the drawn cards is a heart
and the other one is a club?

User's Solution: (13/52)*(13/51) = 169/2652 = 13/204
```

Output:

```
"""
Step 1 - My Solution:

First, calculate the probability of drawing 1 heart and 1 club from a
deck of 52 cards without replacement.

In the first draw, the probability of drawing a heart is 13/52.
```

```
For the second draw, after removing 1 card (assuming it's a heart), the
total number of cards becomes 51. So, the probability of drawing a club now
is 13/51.

Multiplying these two probabilities gives the probability of both events
happening in sequence,which is P(Heart then Club) = (13/52)*(13/51).

Repeat the calculation assuming the first drawn card is a club and the
second drawn card is a heart. Remember, order matters in this case as
we're dealing with separate events.
"""
"""
Step 2 - Comparison with the User's Solution:

Compare your solution with the user's solution. The user's solution only
considers the sequence of drawing a heart first and then a club. They
have not accounted for the alternate sequence  (Club then Heart), and
thus, the solution is incomplete.
"""
"""
Step 3 - Preparation of Hint:

Given that the user hasn't considered both sequences (Heart then Club
and Club then Heart), a hint at the consideration of both possible
sequences will be helpful. This could nudge the user in the right
direction without revealing the solution outright.
"""
# Step 4 - Delivery of Hint:
# Hint: Remember that the two cards could be drawn in any order. Consider
both possible sequences: Heart then Club and Club then Heart.
```

Self-Eval LLM Responses

Another tactic you can use is to *critque a generated LLM output* and ask whether the LLM missed any information or important facts. You're essentially asking an LLM to *evaluate itself* based on its previous output.

First, create a prompt to generate a `"Hello World"` function.

Input:

```
Generate a "Hello World" Python function.
```

Output:

```
Sure, here's a very simple Python function that prints "Hello, World!" to
the console:

def print_hello_world():
    print("Hello, World!")

print_hello_world()
```

When you run this function, it will print the string "Hello, World!" to the console.

The LLM returns a simple Python function called print_hello_world() that prints the traditional "Hello, World!" greeting.

Then make a second LLM request with the previous chat history, asking for the initial output to be improved.

Input:

```
...Previous Chat History...

Given the previous function, can you improve it again with anything else?
Perhaps defaults or type hints?
```

Output:

```
We can add type hints to make it clear that the function doesn't take any
arguments and doesn't return anything. We can also add a docstring to
describe what the function does.

Here's the improved code:

def print_hello_world() -> None:
    """
    Prints "Hello, World!" to the standard output.
    """
    print("Hello, World!")

If you wanted to make the function more flexible, you could add a default
argument that allows you to print a different message:

def print_message(message: str = "Hello, World!") -> None:
    """
    Prints the given message to the standard output. If no message is given
    , it defaults to "Hello, World!".

    Args:
        message (str, optional): The message to be printed.
        Defaults to "Hello, World!".
    """
    print(message)
```

Consequently GPT-4 returns an upgraded version of the function, now furnished with Python type hints and a default argument. This enriches the function with greater flexibility, allowing it to print not just "Hello, World!" but any user-specified message.

These prompt-response exchanges illustrate how you can easily refine generated LLM outputs until you're satisfied with the final output.

It's possible to critique an LLM's response multiple times, until no further refinement is provided by the LLM.

Classification with LLMs

Classifying, in the context of AI, refers to the process of predicting the class or category of a given data point or sample. It's a common task in machine learning where models are trained to assign predefined labels to unlabeled data based on learned patterns.

LLMs are powerful assets when it comes to classification, even with zero or only a small number of examples provided within a prompt. Why? That's because LLMs, like GPT-4, have been previously trained on an extensive dataset and now possess a degree of reasoning.

There are two overarching strategies in solving classification problems with LLMs: *zero-shot learning* and *few-shot learning*.

Zero-shot learning
> In this process, the LLM classifies data with exceptional accuracy, without the aid of any prior specific examples. It's akin to acing a project without any preparation—impressive, right?

Few-shot learning
> Here, you provide your LLM with a small number of examples. This strategy can significantly influence the structure of your output format and enhance the overall classification accuracy.

Why is this groundbreaking for you?

Leveraging LLMs lets you sidestep lengthy processes that traditional machine learning processes demand. Therefore, you can quickly prototype a classification model, determine a base level accuracy, and create immediate business value.

Although an LLM can perform classification, depending upon your problem and training data you might find that using a traditional machine learning process could yield better results.

Building a Classification Model

Let's explore a few-shot learning example to determine the sentiment of text into either 'Compliment', 'Complaint', or 'Neutral'.

```
Given the statement, classify it as either "Compliment", "Complaint", or
"Neutral":
1. "The sun is shining." - Neutral
2. "Your support team is fantastic!" - Compliment
3. "I had a terrible experience with your software." - Complaint

You must follow the following principles:
- Only return the single classification word. The response should be either
"Compliment", "Complaint", or "Neutral".
- Perform the classification on the text enclosed within """ delimiters.

"""The user interface is intuitive."""

Classification:

Compliment
```

Several good use cases for LLM classification include:

Customer reviews

Classify user reviews into categories like "Positive," "Negative," or "Neutral." Dive deeper by further identifying subthemes such as "Usability," "Customer Support," or "Price."

Email filtering

Detect the intent or purpose of emails and classify them as "Inquiry," "Complaint," "Feedback," or "Spam." This can help businesses prioritize responses and manage communications efficiently.

Social media sentiment analysis

Monitor brand mentions and sentiment across social media platforms. Classify posts or comments as "Praise," "Critic," "Query," or "Neutral." Gain insights into public perception and adapt marketing or PR strategies accordingly.

News article categorization

Given the vast amount of news generated daily, LLMs can classify articles by themes or topics such as "Politics," "Technology," "Environment," or "Entertainment."

Résumé screening

For HR departments inundated with résumés, classify them based on predefined criteria like "Qualified," "Overqualified," "Underqualified," or categorize by expertise areas such as "Software Development," "Marketing," or "Sales."

Be aware that exposing emails, résumés, or sensitive data does run the risk of data being leaked into OpenAI's future models as training data.

Majority Vote for Classification

Utilizing multiple LLM requests can help in reducing the variance of your classification labels. This process, known as *majority vote*, is somewhat like choosing the most common fruit out of a bunch. For instance, if you have 10 pieces of fruit and 6 out of them are apples, then apples are the majority. The same principle goes for choosing the majority vote in classification labels.

By soliciting several classifications and taking the *most frequent classification*, you're able to reduce the impact of potential outliers or unusual interpretations from a single model inference. However, do bear in mind that there can be significant downsides to this approach, including the increased time required and cost for multiple API calls.

Let's classify the same piece of text three times, and then take the majority vote:

```
from openai import OpenAI
import os

client = OpenAI(api_key=os.environ.get("OPENAI_API_KEY"))

base_template = """
Given the statement, classify it as either "Compliment", "Complaint", or
"Neutral":
1. "The sun is shining." - Neutral
2. "Your support team is fantastic!" - Compliment
3. "I had a terrible experience with your software." - Complaint

You must follow the following principles:
- Only return the single classification word. The response should be either
"Compliment", "Complaint", or "Neutral".
- Perform the classification on the text enclosed within ''' delimiters.

'''{content}'''

Classification:
"""

responses = []

for i in range(0, 3):
    response = client.chat.completions.create(
        model="gpt-4",
        messages=[{"role": "system",
            "content": base_template.format(content='''Outside is rainy,
```

```
            but I am having a great day, I just don't understand how people
            live, I'm so sad!'''),}],)
    responses.append(response.choices[0].message.content.strip())

def most_frequent_classification(responses):
    # Use a dictionary to count occurrences of each classification
    count_dict = {}
    for classification in responses:
        count_dict[classification] = count_dict.get(classification, 0) + 1

    # Return the classification with the maximum count
    return max(count_dict, key=count_dict.get)

print(most_frequent_classification(responses))   # Expected Output: Neutral
```

Calling the `most_frequent_classification(responses)` function should pinpoint `'Neutral'` as the dominant sentiment. You've now learned how to use the OpenAI package for majority vote classification.

Criteria Evaluation

In Chapter 1, a human-based evaluation system was used with a simple thumbs-up/thumbs-down rating system to identify how often a response met our expectations. Rating manually can be expensive and tedious, requiring a qualified human to judge quality or identify errors. While this work can be outsourced to low-cost raters on services such as Mechanical Turk (*https://www.mturk.com*), designing such a task in a way that gets valid results can itself be time-consuming and error prone. One increasingly common approach is to use a more sophisticated LLM to evaluate the responses of a smaller model.

The evidence is mixed on whether LLMs can act as effective evaluators, with some studies claiming LLMs are human-level evaluators (*https://oreil.ly/nfc3f*) and others identifying inconsistencies in how LLMs evaluate (*https://oreil.ly/ykkzY*). In our experience, GPT-4 is a useful evaluator with consistent results across a diverse set of tasks. In particular, GPT-4 is effective and reliable in evaluating the responses from smaller, less sophisticated models like GPT-3.5-turbo. In the example that follows, we generate concise and verbose examples of answers to a question using GPT-3.5-turbo, ready for rating with GPT-4.

Input:

```
from openai import OpenAI
import os

client = OpenAI(api_key=os.environ.get("OPENAI_API_KEY"))

responses = []
```

```
for i in range(10):
    # concise if even, verbose if odd
    style = "concise" if i % 2 == 0 else "verbose"

    if style == "concise":
        prompt = f"""Return a {style} answer to the
        following question: What is the meaning of life?"""
    else:
        prompt = f"""Return an answer to the following
        question: What is the meaning of life?"""

    response = client.chat.completions.create(
        # using GPT-3.5 Turbo for this example
        model="gpt-3.5-turbo",
        messages=[{"role": "user",
            "content": prompt}])
    responses.append(
        response.choices[0].message.content.strip())

system_prompt = """You are assessing the conciseness of a
response from a chatbot.
You only respond with a 1 if the response is concise,
and a 0 if it is not.
"""

ratings = []

for idx, response in enumerate(responses):
    rating = client.chat.completions.create(
        model="gpt-4",
        messages=[{"role": "system",
            "content": system_prompt},
            {"role": "system",
            "content": response}])
    ratings.append(
        rating.choices[0].message.content.strip())

for idx, rating in enumerate(ratings):
    style = "concise" if idx % 2 == 0 else "verbose"
    print(f"Style: {style}, ", f"Rating: {rating}")
```

Output:

```
Style: concise,  Rating: 1
Style: verbose,  Rating: 0
Style: concise,  Rating: 1
Style: verbose,  Rating: 0
Style: concise,  Rating: 1
Style: verbose,  Rating: 0
Style: concise,  Rating: 1
Style: verbose,  Rating: 0
Style: concise,  Rating: 1
Style: verbose,  Rating: 0
```

This script is a Python program that interacts with the OpenAI API to generate and evaluate responses based on their conciseness. Here's a step-by-step explanation:

1. `responses = []` creates an empty list named `responses` to store the responses generated by the OpenAI API.

2. The `for` loop runs 10 times, generating a response for each iteration.

3. Inside the loop, `style` is determined based on the current iteration number (`i`). It alternates between "concise" and "verbose" for even and odd iterations, respectively.

4. Depending on the `style`, a `prompt` string is formatted to ask, "What is the meaning of life?" in either a concise or verbose manner.

5. `response = client.chat.completions.create(...)` makes a request to the OpenAI API to generate a response based on the `prompt`. The model used here is specified as "gpt-3.5-turbo."

6. The generated response is then stripped of any leading or trailing whitespace and added to the `responses` list.

7. `system_prompt = """You are assessing..,"""` sets up a prompt used for evaluating the conciseness of the generated responses.

8. `ratings = []` initializes an empty list to store the conciseness ratings.

9. Another `for` loop iterates over each response in `responses`.

10. For each response, the script sends it along with the `system_prompt` to the OpenAI API, requesting a conciseness evaluation. This time, the model used is "gpt-4."

11. The evaluation rating (either 1 for concise or 0 for not concise) is then stripped of whitespace and added to the `ratings` list.

12. The final `for` loop iterates over the `ratings` list. For each rating, it prints the `style` of the response (either "concise" or "verbose") and its corresponding conciseness `rating`.

For simple ratings like conciseness, GPT-4 performs with near 100% accuracy; however, for more complex ratings, it's important to spend some time evaluating the evaluator. For example, by setting test cases that contain an issue, as well as test cases that do not contain an issue, you can identify the accuracy of your evaluation metric. An evaluator can itself be evaluated by counting the number of false positives (when the LLM hallucinates an issue in a test case that is known not to contain an issue), as well as the number of false negatives (when the LLM misses an issue in a test case that is known to contain an issue). In our example we generated the concise and verbose examples, so we can easily check the rating accuracy, but in more complex examples you may need human evaluators to validate the ratings.

 Evaluate Quality

Using GPT-4 to evaluate the responses of less sophisticated models is an emerging standard practice, but care must be taken that the results are reliable and consistent.

Compared to human-based evaluation, LLM-based or synthetic evaluation typically costs an order of magnitude less and completes in a few minutes rather than taking days or weeks. Even in important or sensitive cases where a final manual review by a human is necessary, rapid iteration and A/B testing of the prompt through synthetic reviews can save significant time and improve results considerably. However, the cost of running many tests at scale can add up, and the latency or rate limits of GPT-4 can be a blocker. If at all possible, a prompt engineer should first test using programmatic techniques that don't require a call to an LLM, such as simply measuring the length of the response, which runs near instantly for close to zero cost.

Meta Prompting

Meta prompting is a technique that involves the creation of text prompts that, in turn, generate other text prompts. These text prompts are then used to generate new assets in many mediums such as images, videos, and more text.

To better understand meta prompting, let's take the example of authoring a children's book with the assistance of GPT-4. First, you direct the LLM to generate the text for your children's book. Afterward, you invoke meta prompting by instructing GPT-4 to produce prompts that are suitable for image-generation models. This could mean creating situational descriptions or specific scenes based on the storyline of your book, which then can be given to AI models like Midjourney or Stable Diffusion. These image-generation models can, therefore, deliver images in harmony with your AI-crafted children's story.

Figure 3-8 visually describes the process of meta prompting in the context of crafting a children's book.

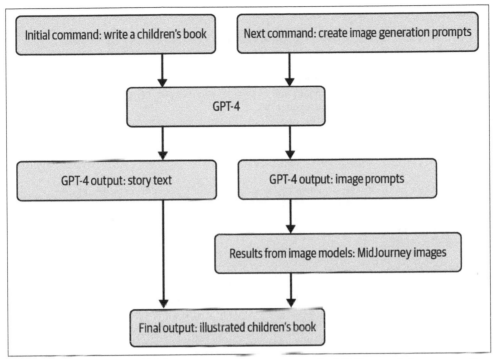

Figure 3-8. Utilizing an LLM to generate image prompts for MidJourney's image creation in the process of crafting a children's book

Meta prompts offer a multitude of benefits for a variety of applications:

Image generation from product descriptions
Meta prompts can be employed to derive an image generation prompt for image models like Midjourney (*https://www.midjourney.com*), effectively creating a visual representation of product descriptions.

Generating style/feature prompts
Let's consider you are a copywriter needing to develop a unique style guide prompt from a couple of blog posts. Given each client has a distinctive tone and style, it's beneficial to utilize a *meta prompt* that encapsulates all the varied features, rather than producing a single prompt output.

Optimizing prompts to achieve specific goals
A common approach is to ask ChatGPT or another language model to refine or improve `Prompt A` in order to attain `Goal 1`, given `Prompt A` and `Goal 1`. This method aids in identifying any missed input features, that by adding could assist the language model in generating a more detailed and desirable response.

Let's experiment with creating a meta prompt for the copywriting example.

Input:

> Act as a GPT Prompt Engineer, you are solely responsible for producing
> highly effective large language model text prompts given a task.
>
> You must follow the following principles:
> - Return only a single prompt, never return the output of a prompt.
> - You must follow the task properly.
> - You must either refine the prompt or create a new prompt depending upon
> the Task.
> - Bullet point out any important features so that another Prompt Engineer
> can easily copy inputs into the prompt.
>
> Task: You must create a copywriting guide ChatGPT several blog posts.
> Include relevant features within the ChatGPT prompt that will allow ChatGPT
> to imitate the writer. You must decide what the most important features are
> to mimic the writer's style etc. You will only be applying this style to
> new blog posts.
>
> Blog post text: You need a variety of soft skills in addition to technical
> skills to succeed in the technology sector. Soft skills are used by
> software professionals to collaborate with their peers...

Output:

> Prompt:
>
> Based on the extensive text provided, your task is to create a series of
> blog posts following the same style and structure of the writer. As a guide
> you should follow these features:
>
> 1. Clear, direct language: Your writing should be in clear and direct
> language, breaking down complex subjects into easily understandable
> concepts.
> 2. Use of subheadings: To provide structure to your blog posts, break them
> up with relevant subheadings. This helps to guide the reader and make your
> text more readable.
> ...
> 9. Inclusion of technical terminology: When discussing technical topics,
> use appropriate technical language to ensure accuracy and credibility.
> However, be sure to provide explanations or definitions for more complex
> terms.

As previously mentioned, it can be beneficial to *critique the model's output* and to ask for a refined prompt either via the interface or API.

ChatGPT can perform web searches and can make use of the content of web pages, along with the previously generated copywriting style guide. Let's provide two URLs that ChatGPT will read to enhance the output.

Input:

> Given the following style guide and these two blog posts, I want you to
> improve the copywriting style prompt so an LLM or copywriter can write
> effectively for my client.
>
> ...Previously Generated Copywriting guide...
>
> URL 1: https://understandingdata.com/posts/how-to-clean-and-process-data
> URL 2: https://understandingdata.com/posts/how-to-scrape-twitter-data

Figure 3-9 shows the output.

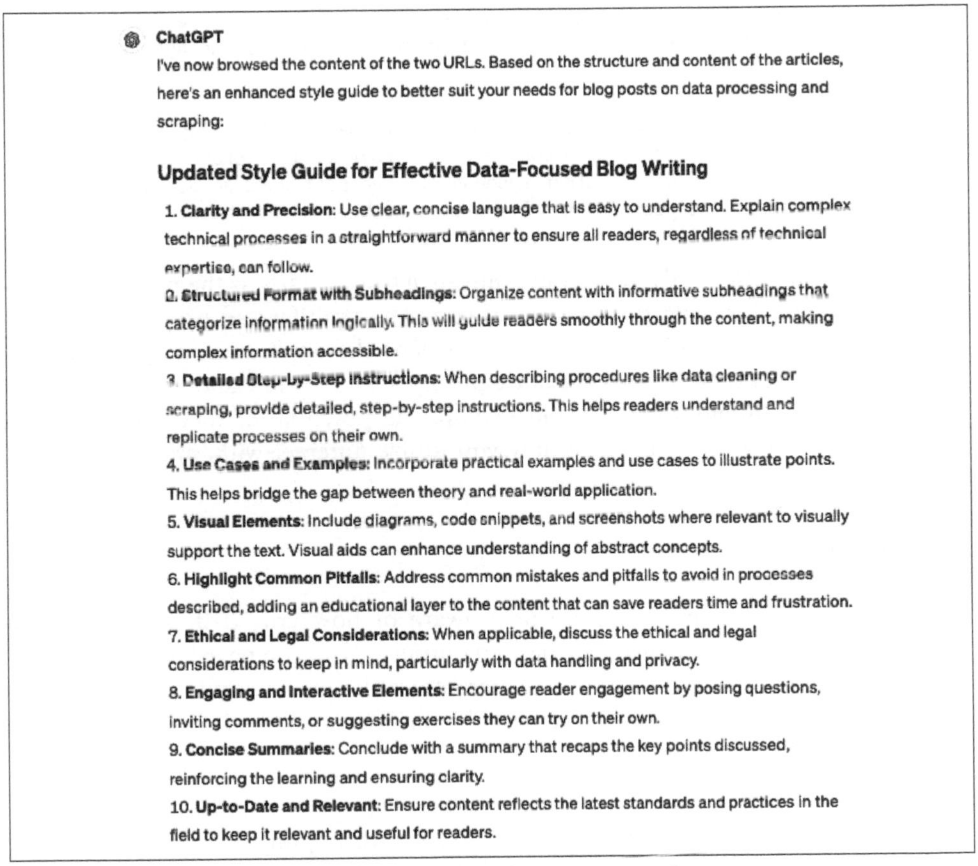

> ChatGPT
>
> I've now browsed the content of the two URLs. Based on the structure and content of the articles,
> here's an enhanced style guide to better suit your needs for blog posts on data processing and
> scraping:
>
> **Updated Style Guide for Effective Data-Focused Blog Writing**
>
> 1. **Clarity and Precision**: Use clear, concise language that is easy to understand. Explain complex
> technical processes in a straightforward manner to ensure all readers, regardless of technical
> expertise, can follow.
> 2. **Structured Format with Subheadings**: Organize content with informative subheadings that
> categorize information logically. This will guide readers smoothly through the content, making
> complex information accessible.
> 3. **Detailed Step-By-Step Instructions**: When describing procedures like data cleaning or
> scraping, provide detailed, step-by-step instructions. This helps readers understand and
> replicate processes on their own.
> 4. **Use Cases and Examples**: Incorporate practical examples and use cases to illustrate points.
> This helps bridge the gap between theory and real-world application.
> 5. **Visual Elements**: Include diagrams, code snippets, and screenshots where relevant to visually
> support the text. Visual aids can enhance understanding of abstract concepts.
> 6. **Highlight Common Pitfalls**: Address common mistakes and pitfalls to avoid in processes
> described, adding an educational layer to the content that can save readers time and frustration.
> 7. **Ethical and Legal Considerations**: When applicable, discuss the ethical and legal
> considerations to keep in mind, particularly with data handling and privacy.
> 8. **Engaging and Interactive Elements**: Encourage reader engagement by posing questions,
> inviting comments, or suggesting exercises they can try on their own.
> 9. **Concise Summaries**: Conclude with a summary that recaps the key points discussed,
> reinforcing the learning and ensuring clarity.
> 10. **Up-to-Date and Relevant**: Ensure content reflects the latest standards and practices in the
> field to keep it relevant and useful for readers.

Figure 3-9. ChatGPT refining a meta prompt by two URL web pages

> Based on the style guide and the two blog posts, here's an improved
> copywriting style prompt:
>
> To create a blog post for the client, adhere to the following guidelines:
>
> 1. Clarity and Directness: Use clear, direct language to explain complex

topics. Present information in an easy-to-understand manner. Aim for your
audience to grasp concepts without needing prior knowledge.
...
8. Use of Technical Terminology: Use the appropriate technical language
when discussing complex topics. However, make sure to provide definitions
or explanations for these terms to keep the text accessible.

Model your writing after these blog post examples:

"What is an API? And How Do They Relate to Data Engineering?": This blog
post uses clear and direct language to explain the concept of an API. It
provides detailed explanations and uses practical examples of commonly used
APIs. It links the technical concept of APIs to business growth and
productivity. The information is well-categorized using subheadings like
'Types of API's.'

"How To Easily Setup A Google Cloud Project With APIs": This blog post is a
practical guide on setting up a Google Cloud Project. It's broken down into
numbered steps, each with a clear subheading. The post uses detailed
explanations and includes practical examples such as screenshots. It also
uses clear, direct language to guide the reader through the process.

Meta prompting offers a dynamic and innovative way to harness the power of generative AI models, fostering the creation of complex, multifaceted prompts and even prompts that generate other prompts. It broadens the application scope, from text and image generation to style and feature prompts, and optimization toward specific goals. As you continue to refine and explore the potential of meta prompting, it promises to be a game changer in how you utilize, interact with, and benefit from using LLMs.

Summary

After reading this chapter, you are now aware of how crucial it is to give clear directions and examples to generate desired outputs. Also, you have hands-on experience extracting structured data from a hierarchical list using regular expressions in Python, and you've learned to utilize nested data structures like JSON and YAML to produce robust, parsable outputs.

You've learned several best practices and effective prompt engineering techniques, including the famous "Explain it like I'm five", role prompting, and meta prompting techniques. In the next chapter, you will learn how to use a popular LLM package called LangChain that'll help you to create more advanced prompt engineering workflows.

Advanced Techniques for Text Generation with LangChain

Using simple prompt engineering techniques will often work for most tasks, but occasionally you'll need to use a more powerful toolkit to solve complex generative AI problems. Such problems and tasks include:

Context length
Summarizing an entire book into a digestible synopsis.

Combining sequential LLM inputs/outputs
Creating a story for a book including the characters, plot, and world building.

Performing complex reasoning tasks
LLMs acting as an agent. For example, you could create an LLM agent to help you achieve your personal fitness goals.

To skillfully tackle such complex generative AI challenges, becoming acquainted with LangChain, an open source framework, is highly beneficial. This tool simplifies and enhances your LLM's workflows substantially.

Introduction to LangChain

LangChain is a versatile framework that enables the creation of applications utilizing LLMs and is available as both a Python (*https://oreil.ly/YPid-*) and a TypeScript (*https://oreil.ly/5Vl0W*) package. Its central tenet is that the most impactful and distinct applications won't merely interface with a language model via an API, but will also:

Enhance data awareness

The framework aims to establish a seamless connection between a language model and external data sources.

Enhance agency

It strives to equip language models with the ability to engage with and influence their environment.

The LangChain framework illustrated in Figure 4-1 provides a range of modular abstractions that are essential for working with LLMs, along with a broad selection of implementations for these abstractions.

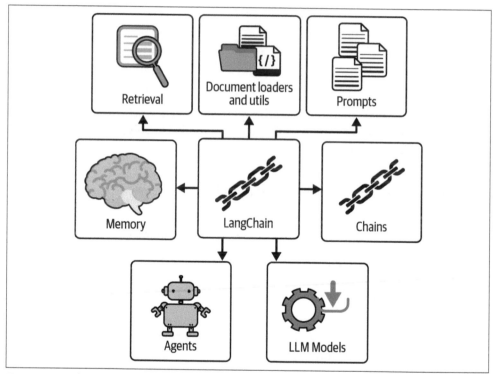

Figure 4-1. The major modules of the LangChain LLM framework

Each module is designed to be user-friendly and can be efficiently utilized independently or together. There are currently six common modules within LangChain:

Model I/O

Handles input/output operations related to the model

Retrieval

Focuses on retrieving relevant text for the LLM

Chains
> Also known as *LangChain runnables*, chains enable the construction of sequences of LLM operations or function calls

Agents
> Allows chains to make decisions on which tools to use based on high-level directives or instructions

Memory
> Persists the state of an application between different runs of a chain

Callbacks
> For running additional code on specific events, such as when every new token is generated

Environment Setup

You can install LangChain on your terminal with either of these commands:

- `pip install langchain langchain-openai`
- `conda install -c conda-forge langchain langchain-openai`

If you would prefer to install the package requirements for the entire book, you can use the *requirements.txt* (*https://oreil.ly/WKOma*) file from the GitHub repository.

It's recommended to install the packages within a virtual environment:

Create a virtual environment
> `python -m venv venv`

Activate the virtual environment
> `source venv/bin/activate`

Install the dependencies
> `pip install -r requirements.txt`

LangChain requires integrations with one or more model providers. For example, to use OpenAI's model APIs, you'll need to install their Python package with `pip install openai`.

As discussed in Chapter 1, it's best practice to set an environment variable called `OPENAI_API_KEY` in your terminal or load it from an *.env* file using `python-dotenv` (*https://oreil.ly/wvuO7*). However, for prototyping you can choose to skip this step by passing in your API key directly when loading a chat model in LangChain:

```python
from langchain_openai.chat_models import ChatOpenAI
chat = ChatOpenAI(api_key="api_key")
```

Hardcoding API keys in scripts is not recommended due to security reasons. Instead, utilize environment variables or configuration files to manage your keys.

In the constantly evolving landscape of LLMs, you can encounter the challenge of disparities across different model APIs. The lack of standardization in interfaces can induce extra layers of complexity in prompt engineering and obstruct the seamless integration of diverse models into your projects.

This is where LangChain comes into play. As a comprehensive framework, LangChain allows you to easily consume the varying interfaces of different models.

LangChain's functionality ensures that you aren't required to reinvent your prompts or code every time you switch between models. Its platform-agnostic approach promotes rapid experimentation with a broad range of models, such as Anthropic (*https://www.anthropic.com*), Vertex AI (*https://cloud.google.com/vertex-ai*), OpenAI (*https://openai.com*), and BedrockChat (*https://oreil.ly/bedrock*). This not only expedites the model evaluation process but also saves critical time and resources by simplifying complex model integrations.

In the sections that follow, you'll be using the OpenAI package and their API in LangChain.

Chat Models

Chat models such as GPT-4 have become the primary way to interface with OpenAI's API. Instead of offering a straightforward "input text, output text" response, they propose an interaction method where *chat messages* are the input and output elements.

Generating LLM responses using chat models involves inputting one or more messages into the chat model. In the context of LangChain, the currently accepted message types are `AIMessage`, `HumanMessage`, and `SystemMessage`. The output from a chat model will always be an `AIMessage`.

SystemMessage
> Represents information that should be instructions to the AI system. These are used to guide the AI's behavior or actions in some way.

HumanMessage
> Represents information coming from a human interacting with the AI system. This could be a question, a command, or any other input from a human user that the AI needs to process and respond to.

AIMessage

Represents information coming from the AI system itself. This is typically the AI's response to a `HumanMessage` or the result of a `SystemMessage` instruction.

 Make sure to leverage the `SystemMessage` for delivering explicit directions. OpenAI has refined GPT-4 and upcoming LLM models to pay particular attention to the guidelines given within this type of message.

Let's create a joke generator in LangChain.

Input:

```
from langchain_openai.chat_models import ChatOpenAI
from langchain.schema import AIMessage, HumanMessage, SystemMessage

chat = ChatOpenAI(temperature=0.5)
messages = [SystemMessage(content='''Act as a senior software engineer
at a startup company.'''),
HumanMessage(content='''Please can you provide a funny joke
about software engineers?''')]
response = chat.invoke(input=messages)
print(response.content)
```

Output:

```
Sure, here's a lighthearted joke for you:
Why did the software engineer go broke?
Because he lost his domain in a bet and couldn't afford to renew it.
```

First, you'll import `ChatOpenAI`, `AIMessage`, `HumanMessage`, and `SystemMessage`. Then create an instance of the `ChatOpenAI` class with a temperature parameter of 0.5 (randomness).

After creating a model, a list named `messages` is populated with a `SystemMessage` object, defining the role for the LLM, and a `HumanMessage` object, which asks for a software engineer—related joke.

Calling the chat model with `.invoke(input=messages)` feeds the LLM with a list of messages, and then you retrieve the LLM's response with `response.content`.

There is a legacy method that allows you to directly call the chat object with `chat(messages=messages)`:

```
response = chat(messages=messages)
```

Streaming Chat Models

You might have observed while using ChatGPT how words are sequentially returned to you, one character at a time. This distinct pattern of response generation is referred to as *streaming*, and it plays a crucial role in enhancing the performance of chat-based applications:

```
for chunk in chat.stream(messages):
    print(chunk.content, end="", flush=True)
```

When you call `chat.stream(messages)`, it yields chunks of the message one at a time. This means each segment of the chat message is individually returned. As each chunk arrives, it is then instantaneously printed to the terminal and flushed. This way, *streaming* allows for minimal latency from your LLM responses.

Streaming holds several benefits from an end-user perspective. First, it dramatically reduces the waiting time for users. As soon as the text starts generating character by character, users can start interpreting the message. There's no need for a full message to be constructed before it is seen. This, in turn, significantly enhances user interactivity and minimizes latency.

Nevertheless, this technique comes with its own set of challenges. One significant challenge is parsing the outputs while they are being streamed. Understanding and appropriately responding to the message as it is being formed can prove to be intricate, especially when the content is complex and detailed.

Creating Multiple LLM Generations

There may be scenarios where you find it useful to generate multiple responses from LLMs. This is particularly true while creating dynamic content like social media posts. Rather than providing a list of messages, you provide a *list of message lists*.

Input:

```
# 2x lists of messages, which is the same as [messages, messages]
synchronous_llm_result = chat.batch([messages]*2)
print(synchronous_llm_result)
```

Output:

```
[AIMessage(content='''Sure, here's a lighthearted joke for you:\n\nWhy did
the software engineer go broke?\n\nBecause he kept forgetting to Ctrl+ Z
his expenses!'''),
AIMessage(content='''Sure, here\'s a lighthearted joke for you:\n\nWhy do
software engineers prefer dark mode?\n\nBecause it\'s easier on their
"byte" vision!''')]
```

The benefit of using `.batch()` over `.invoke()` is that you can parallelize the number of API requests made to OpenAI.

For any runnable in LangChain, you can add a `RunnableConfig` argument to the `batch` function that contains many configurable parameters, including `max_concurrency`:

```
from langchain_core.runnables.config import RunnableConfig

# Create a RunnableConfig with the desired concurrency limit:
config = RunnableConfig(max_concurrency=5)

# Call the .batch() method with the inputs and config:
results = chat.batch([messages, messages], config=config)
```

 In computer science, *asynchronous (async) functions* are those that operate independently of other processes, thereby enabling several API requests to be run concurrently without waiting for each other. In LangChain, these async functions let you make many API requests all at once, not one after the other. This is especially helpful in more complex workflows and decreases the overall latency to your users.

Most of the asynchronous functions within LangChain are simply prefixed with the letter a, such as `.ainvoke()` and `.abatch()`. If you would like to use the async API for more efficient task performance, then utilize these functions.

LangChain Prompt Templates

Up until this point, you've been hardcoding the strings in the `ChatOpenAI` objects. As your LLM applications grow in size, it becomes increasingly important to utilize *prompt templates*.

Prompt templates are good for generating reproducible prompts for AI language models. They consist of a *template*, a text string that can take in parameters, and construct a text prompt for a language model.

Without prompt templates, you would likely use Python `f-string` formatting:

```
language = "Python"
prompt = f"What is the best way to learn coding in {language}?"
print(prompt) # What is the best way to learn coding in Python?
```

But why not simply use an `f-string` for prompt templating? Using LangChain's prompt templates instead allows you to easily:

- Validate your prompt inputs
- Combine multiple prompts together with composition
- Define custom selectors that will inject k-shot examples into your prompt

- Save and load prompts from *.yml* and *.json* files
- Create custom prompt templates that execute additional code or instructions when created

LangChain Expression Language (LCEL)

The | pipe operator is a key component of LangChain Expression Language (LCEL) that allows you to chain together different components or *runnables* in a data processing pipeline.

In LCEL, the | operator is similar to the Unix pipe operator. It takes the output of one component and feeds it as input to the next component in the chain. This allows you to easily connect and combine different components to create a complex chain of operations:

```
chain = prompt | model
```

The | operator is used to chain together the prompt and model components. The output of the prompt component is passed as input to the model component. This chaining mechanism allows you to build complex chains from basic components and enables the seamless flow of data between different stages of the processing pipeline.

Additionally, *the order matters*, so you could technically create this chain:

```
bad_order_chain = model | prompt
```

But it would produce an error after using the `invoke` function, because the values returned from `model` are not compatible with the expected inputs for the prompt.

Let's create a business name generator using prompt templates that will return five to seven relevant business names:

```
from langchain_openai.chat_models import ChatOpenAI
from langchain_core.prompts import (SystemMessagePromptTemplate,
ChatPromptTemplate)

template = """
You are a creative consultant brainstorming names for businesses.

You must follow the following principles:
{principles}

Please generate a numerical list of five catchy names for a start-up in the
{industry} industry that deals with {context}?

Here is an example of the format:
1. Name1
2. Name2
3. Name3
4. Name4
```

```
5. Name5
"""

model = ChatOpenAI()
system_prompt = SystemMessagePromptTemplate.from_template(template)
chat_prompt = ChatPromptTemplate.from_messages([system_prompt])

chain = chat_prompt | model

result = chain.invoke({
    "industry": "medical",
    "context":'''creating AI solutions by automatically summarizing patient
    records''',
    "principles":'''1. Each name should be short and easy to
    remember. 2. Each name should be easy to pronounce.
    3. Each name should be unique and not already taken by another company.'''
})

print(result.content)
```

Output:

1. SummarAI
2. MediSummar
3. AutoDocs
4. RecordAI
5. SmartSummarize

First, you'll import ChatOpenAI, SystemMessagePromptTemplate, and ChatPromptTemplate. Then, you'll define a prompt template with specific guidelines under template, instructing the LLM to generate business names. ChatOpenAI() initializes the chat, while SystemMessagePromptTemplate.from_template(template) and ChatPromptTemplate.from_messages([system_prompt]) create your prompt template.

You create an LCEL chain by piping together chat_prompt and the model, which is then *invoked*. This replaces the {industries}, {context}, and {principles} placeholders in the prompt with the dictionary values within the invoke function.

Finally, you extract the LLM's response as a string accessing the .content property on the result variable.

Give Direction and Specify Format

Carefully crafted instructions might include things like "You are a creative consultant brainstorming names for businesses" and "Please generate a numerical list of five to seven catchy names for a start-up." Cues like these guide your LLM to perform the exact task you require from it.

Using PromptTemplate with Chat Models

LangChain provides a more traditional template called `PromptTemplate`, which requires `input_variables` and `template` arguments.

Input:

```
from langchain_core.prompts import PromptTemplate
from langchain.prompts.chat import SystemMessagePromptTemplate
from langchain_openai.chat_models import ChatOpenAI
prompt=PromptTemplate(
 template='''You are a helpful assistant that translates {input_language} to
 {output_language}.''',
 input_variables=["input_language", "output_language"],
)
system_message_prompt = SystemMessagePromptTemplate(prompt=prompt)
chat = ChatOpenAI()
chat.invoke(system_message_prompt.format_messages(
input_language="English",output_language="French"))
```

Output:

```
AIMessage(content="Vous êtes un assistant utile qui traduit l'anglais en
français.", additional_kwargs={}, example=False)
```

Output Parsers

In Chapter 3, you used regular expressions (regex) to extract structured data from text that contained numerical lists, but it's possible to do this automatically in LangChain with *output parsers*.

Output parsers are a higher-level abstraction provided by LangChain for parsing structured data from LLM string responses. Currently the available output parsers are:

List parser
    Returns a list of comma-separated items.

Datetime parser
    Parses an LLM output into datetime format.

Enum parser
    Parses strings into enum values.

Auto-fixing parser
    Wraps another output parser, and if that output parser fails, it will call another LLM to fix any errors.

Pydantic (JSON) parser
    Parses LLM responses into JSON output that conforms to a Pydantic schema.

Retry parser
> Provides retrying a failed parse from a previous output parser.

Structured output parser
> Can be used when you want to return multiple fields.

XML parser
> Parses LLM responses into an XML-based format.

As you'll discover, there are two important functions for LangChain output parsers:

`.get_format_instructions()`
> This function provides the necessary instructions into your prompt to output a structured format that can be parsed.

`.parse(llm_output: str)`
> This function is responsible for parsing your LLM responses into a predefined format.

Generally, you'll find that the Pydantic (JSON) parser with `ChatOpenAI()` provides the most flexibility.

The Pydantic (JSON) parser takes advantage of the Pydantic (*https://oreil.ly/QIMih*) library in Python. Pydantic is a data validation library that provides a way to validate incoming data using Python type annotations. This means that Pydantic allows you to create schemas for your data and automatically validates and parses input data according to those schemas.

Input:

```python
from langchain_core.prompts.chat import (
    ChatPromptTemplate,
    SystemMessagePromptTemplate,
)
from langchain_openai.chat_models import ChatOpenAI
from langchain.output_parsers import PydanticOutputParser
from pydantic.v1 import BaseModel, Field
from typing import List

temperature = 0.0

class BusinessName(BaseModel):
    name: str = Field(description="The name of the business")
    rating_score: float = Field(description='''The rating score of the
    business. 0 is the worst, 10 is the best.''')

class BusinessNames(BaseModel):
    names: List[BusinessName] = Field(description='''A list
    of busines names''')

# Set up a parser + inject instructions into the prompt template:
```

```
parser = PydanticOutputParser(pydantic_object=BusinessNames)

principles = """
- The name must be easy to remember.
- Use the {industry} industry and Company context to create an effective name.
- The name must be easy to pronounce.
- You must only return the name without any other text or characters.
- Avoid returning full stops, \n, or any other characters.
- The maximum length of the name must be 10 characters.
"""

# Chat Model Output Parser:
model = ChatOpenAI()
template = """Generate five business names for a new start-up company in the
{industry} industry.
You must follow the following principles: {principles}
{format_instructions}
"""
system_message_prompt = SystemMessagePromptTemplate.from_template(template)
chat_prompt = ChatPromptTemplate.from_messages([system_message_prompt])

# Creating the LCEL chain:
prompt_and_model = chat_prompt | model

result = prompt_and_model.invoke(
    {
        "principles": principles,
        "industry": "Data Science",
        "format_instructions": parser.get_format_instructions(),
    }
)
# The output parser, parses the LLM response into a Pydantic object:
print(parser.parse(result.content))
```

Output:

```
names=[BusinessName(name='DataWiz', rating_score=8.5),
BusinessName(name='InsightIQ',
rating_score=9.2), BusinessName(name='AnalytiQ', rating_score=7.8),
BusinessName(name='SciData', rating_score=8.1),
BusinessName(name='InfoMax', rating_score=9.5)]
```

After you've loaded the necessary libraries, you'll set up a ChatOpenAI model. Then create SystemMessagePromptTemplate from your template and form a ChatPrompt Template with it. You'll use the Pydantic models BusinessName and BusinessNames to structure your desired output, a list of unique business names. You'll create a Pydantic parser for parsing these models and format the prompt using user-inputted variables by calling the invoke function. Feeding this customized prompt to your model, you're enabling it to produce creative, unique business names by using the parser.

It's possible to use output parsers inside of LCEL by using this syntax:

```
chain = prompt | model | output_parser
```

Let's add the output parser directly to the chain.

Input:

```
parser = PydanticOutputParser(pydantic_object=BusinessNames)
chain = chat_prompt | model | parser

result = chain.invoke(
    {
        "principles": principles,
        "industry": "Data Science",
        "format_instructions": parser.get_format_instructions(),
    }
)
print(result)
```

Output:

```
names=[BusinessName(name='DataTech', rating_score=9.5),...]
```

The chain is now responsible for prompt formatting, LLM calling, and parsing the LLM's response into a `Pydantic` object.

Specify Format

The preceding prompts use Pydantic models and output parsers, allowing you explicitly tell an LLM your desired response format.

It's worth knowing that by asking an LLM to provide structured JSON output, you can create a flexible and generalizable API from the LLM's response. There are limitations to this, such as the size of the JSON created and the reliability of your prompts, but it still is a promising area for LLM applications.

You should take care of edge cases as well as adding error handling statements, since LLM outputs might not always be in your desired format.

Output parsers save you from the complexity and intricacy of regular expressions, providing easy-to-use functionalities for a variety of use cases. Now that you've seen them in action, you can utilize output parsers to effortlessly structure and retrieve the data you need from an LLM's output, harnessing the full potential of AI for your tasks.

Furthermore, using parsers to structure the data extracted from LLMs allows you to easily choose how to organize outputs for more efficient use. This can be useful if you're dealing with extensive lists and need to sort them by certain criteria, like business names.

LangChain Evals

As well as output parsers to check for formatting errors, most AI systems also make use of *evals*, or evaluation metrics, to measure the performance of each prompt response. LangChain has a number of off-the-shelf evaluators, which can be directly be logged in their LangSmith (*https://oreil.ly/0Fn94*) platform for further debugging, monitoring, and testing. Weights and Biases (*https://wandb.ai/site*) is alternative machine learning platform that offers similar functionality and tracing capabilities for LLMs.

Evaluation metrics are useful for more than just prompt testing, as they can be used to identify positive and negative examples for retrieval as well as to build datasets for fine-tuning custom models.

Most eval metrics rely on a set of test cases, which are input and output pairings where you know the correct answer. Often these reference answers are created or curated manually by a human, but it's also common practice to use a smarter model like GPT-4 to generate the ground truth answers, which has been done for the following example. Given a list of descriptions of financial transactions, we used GPT-4 to classify each transaction with a `transaction_category` and `transaction_type`. The process can be found in the `langchain-evals.ipynb` Jupyter Notebook in the GitHub repository (*https://oreil.ly/a4Hut*) for the book.

With the GPT-4 answer being taken as the correct answer, it's now possible to rate the accuracy of smaller models like GPT-3.5-turbo and Mixtral 8x7b (called `mistral-small` in the API). If you can achieve good enough accuracy with a smaller model, you can save money or decrease latency. In addition, if that model is available open source like Mistral's model (*https://oreil.ly/Ec578*), you can migrate that task to run on your own servers, avoiding sending potentially sensitive data outside of your organization. We recommend testing with an external API first, before going to the trouble of self-hosting an OS model.

Remember to sign up (*https://mistral.ai*) and subscribe to obtain an API key; then expose that as an environment variable by typing in your terminal:

```
export MISTRAL_API_KEY=api-key
```

The following script is part of a notebook (*https://oreil.ly/DqDOf*) that has previously defined a dataframe `df`. For brevity let's investigate only the evaluation section of the script, assuming a dataframe is already defined.

Input:

```python
import os
from langchain_mistralai.chat_models import ChatMistralAI
from langchain.output_parsers import PydanticOutputParser
from langchain_core.prompts import ChatPromptTemplate
from pydantic.v1 import BaseModel
from typing import Literal, Union
from langchain_core.output_parsers import StrOutputParser

# 1. Define the model:
mistral_api_key = os.environ["MISTRAL_API_KEY"]

model = ChatMistralAI(model="mistral-small", mistral_api_key=mistral_api_key)

# 2. Define the prompt:
system_prompt = """You are are an expert at analyzing
bank transactions, you will be categorizing a single
transaction.
Always return a transaction type and category:
do not return None.
Format Instructions:
{format_instructions}"""

user_prompt = """Transaction Text:
{transaction}"""

prompt = ChatPromptTemplate.from_messages(
    [
        (
            "system",
            system_prompt,
        ),
        (
            "user",
            user_prompt,
        ),
    ]
)

# 3. Define the pydantic model:
class EnrichedTransactionInformation(BaseModel):
    transaction_type: Union[
        Literal["Purchase", "Withdrawal", "Deposit",
        "Bill Payment", "Refund"], None
    ]
    transaction_category: Union[
        Literal["Food", "Entertainment", "Transport",
        "Utilities", "Rent", "Other"],
        None,
    ]
```

```python
# 4. Define the output parser:
output_parser = PydanticOutputParser(
    pydantic_object=EnrichedTransactionInformation)

# 5. Define a function to try to fix and remove the backslashes:
def remove_back_slashes(string):
    # double slash to escape the slash
    cleaned_string = string.replace("\\", "")
    return cleaned_string

# 6. Create an LCEL chain that fixes the formatting:
chain = prompt | model | StrOutputParser() \
| remove_back_slashes | output_parser

transaction = df.iloc[0]["Transaction Description"]
result = chain.invoke(
        {
            "transaction": transaction,
            "format_instructions": \
            output_parser.get_format_instructions(),
        }
    )

# 7. Invoke the chain for the whole dataset:
results = []

for i, row in tqdm(df.iterrows(), total=len(df)):
    transaction = row["Transaction Description"]
    try:
        result = chain.invoke(
            {
                "transaction": transaction,
                "format_instructions": \
                output_parser.get_format_instructions(),
            }
        )
    except:
        result = EnrichedTransactionInformation(
            transaction_type=None,
            transaction_category=None
        )

    results.append(result)

# 8. Add the results to the dataframe, as columns transaction type and
# transaction category:
transaction_types = []
transaction_categories = []

for result in results:
    transaction_types.append(result.transaction_type)
    transaction_categories.append(
```

```
        result.transaction_category)

df["mistral_transaction_type"] = transaction_types
df["mistral_transaction_category"] = transaction_categories
df.head()
```

Output:

```
Transaction Description transaction_type
transaction_category    mistral_transaction_type
mistral_transaction_category
0       cash deposit at local branch    Deposit Other   Deposit
Other
1       cash deposit at local branch    Deposit Other   Deposit
Other
2       withdrew money for rent payment Withdrawal      Rent
Withdrawal      Rent
3       withdrew cash for weekend expenses      Withdrawal      Other
Withdrawal      Other
4       purchased books from the bookstore      Purchase        Other
Purchase        Entertainment
```

The code does the following:

1. `from langchain_mistralai.chat_models import ChatMistralAI`: We import LangChain's Mistral implementation.

2. `from langchain.output_parsers import PydanticOutputParser`: Imports the `PydanticOutputParser` class, which is used for parsing output using Pydantic models. We also import a string output parser to handle an interim step where we remove backslashes from the JSON key (a common problem with responses from Mistral).

3. `mistral_api_key = os.environ["MISTRAL_API_KEY"]`: Retrieves the Mistral API key from the environment variables. This needs to be set prior to running the notebook.

4. `model = ChatMistralAI(model="mistral-small", mistral_api_key=mistral_api_key)`: Initializes an instance of `ChatMistralAI` with the specified model and API key. Mistral Small is what they call the Mixtral 8x7b model (also available open source) in their API.

5. `system_prompt` and `user_prompt`: These lines define templates for the system and user prompts used in the chat to classify the transactions.

6. `class EnrichedTransactionInformation(BaseModel)`: Defines a Pydantic model `EnrichedTransactionInformation` with two fields: `transaction_type` and `transaction_category`, each with specific allowed values and the possibility of being None. This is what tells us if the output is in the correct format.

7. `def remove_back_slashes(string)`: Defines a function to remove backslashes from a string.

8. `chain = prompt | model | StrOutputParser() | remove_back_slashes | output_parser`: Updates the chain to include a string output parser and the `remove_back_slashes` function before the original output parser.

9. `transaction = df.iloc[0]["Transaction Description"]`: Extracts the first transaction description from a dataframe df. This dataframe is loaded earlier in the Jupyter Notebook (*https://oreil.ly/-koAO*) (omitted for brevity).

10. `for i, row in tqdm(df.iterrows(), total=len(df))`: Iterates over each row in the dataframe df, with a progress bar.

11. `result = chain.invoke(...)`: Inside the loop, the chain is invoked for each transaction.

12. `except`: In case of an exception, a default `EnrichedTransactionInformation` object with `None` values is created. These will be treated as errors in evaluation but will not break the processing loop.

13. `df["mistral_transaction_type"] = transaction_types, df["mistral_trans action_category"] = transaction_categories`: Adds the transaction types and categories as new columns in the dataframe, which we then display with `df.head()`.

With the responses from Mistral saved in the dataframe, it's possible to compare them to the transaction categories and types defined earlier to check the accuracy of Mistral. The most basic LangChain eval metric is to do an exact string match of a prediction against a reference answer, which returns a score of 1 if correct, and a 0 if incorrect. The notebook gives an example of how to implement this (*https://oreil.ly/vPUfI*), which shows that Mistral's accuracy is 77.5%. However, if all you are doing is comparing strings, you probably don't need to implement it in LangChain.

Where LangChain is valuable is in its standardized and tested approaches to implementing more advanced evaluators using LLMs. The evaluator `labeled_pair wise_string` compares two outputs and gives a reason for choosing between them, using GPT-4. One common use case for this type of evaluator is to compare the outputs from two different prompts or models, particularly if the models being tested are less sophisticated than GPT-4. This evaluator using GPT-4 does still work for evaluating GPT-4 responses, but you should manually review the reasoning and scores to ensure it is doing a good job: if GPT-4 is bad at a task, it may also be bad at evaluating that task. In the notebook (*https://oreil.ly/9O7Mb*), the same transaction classification was run again with the model changed to `model = ChatOpenAI(model="gpt-3.5-turbo-1106", model_kwargs={"response_format": {"type": "json_object"}},)`. Now it's possible to do pairwise comparison between the Mistral and GPT-3.5 responses, as shown in the following example. You can see in the output the reasoning that is given to justify the score.

Input:

```python
# Evaluate answers using LangChain evaluators:
from langchain.evaluation import load_evaluator
evaluator = load_evaluator("labeled_pairwise_string")

row = df.iloc[0]
transaction = row["Transaction Description"]
gpt3pt5_category = row["gpt3.5_transaction_category"]
gpt3pt5_type = row["gpt3.5_transaction_type"]
mistral_category = row["mistral_transaction_category"]
mistral_type = row["mistral_transaction_type"]
reference_category = row["transaction_category"]
reference_type = row["transaction_type"]

# Put the data into JSON format for the evaluator:
gpt3pt5_data = f"""{{
    "transaction_category": "{gpt3pt5_category}",
    "transaction_type": "{gpt3pt5_type}"
}}"""

mistral_data = f"""{{
    "transaction_category": "{mistral_category}",
    "transaction_type": "{mistral_type}"
}}"""

reference_data = f"""{{
    "transaction_category": "{reference_category}",
    "transaction_type": "{reference_type}"
}}"""

# Set up the prompt input for context for the evaluator:
input_prompt = """You are an expert at analyzing bank
transactions,
you will be categorizing a single transaction.
Always return a transaction type and category: do not
return None.
Format Instructions:
{format_instructions}
Transaction Text:
{transaction}
"""

transaction_types.append(transaction_type_score)
transaction_categories.append(
    transaction_category_score)

accuracy_score = 0
```

```
for transaction_type_score, transaction_category_score \
    in zip(
        transaction_types, transaction_categories
    ):
    accuracy_score += transaction_type_score['score'] + \
    transaction_category_score['score']

accuracy_score = accuracy_score / (len(transaction_types) \
    * 2)
print(f"Accuracy score: {accuracy_score}")

evaluator.evaluate_string_pairs(
    prediction=gpt3pt5_data,
    prediction_b=mistral_data,
    input=input_prompt.format(
        format_instructions=output_parser.get_format_instructions(),
        transaction=transaction),
    reference=reference_data,
)
```

Output:

```
{'reasoning': '''Both Assistant A and Assistant B provided the exact same
response to the user\'s question. Their responses are both helpful, relevant,
correct, and demonstrate depth of thought. They both correctly identified the
transaction type as "Deposit" and the transaction category as "Other" based on
the transaction text provided by the user. Both responses are also
well-formatted according to the JSON schema provided by the user. Therefore,
it\'s a tie between the two assistants. \n\nFinal Verdict: [[C]]''',
 'value': None,
 'score': 0.5}
```

This code demonstrates the simple exact string matching evaluator from LangChain:

1. `evaluator = load_evaluator("labeled_pairwise_string")`: This is a helper function that can be used to load any LangChain evaluator by name. In this case, it is the `labeled_pairwise_string` evaluator being used.

2. `row = df.iloc[0]`: This line and the seven lines that follow get the first row and extract the values for the different columns needed. It includes the transaction description, as well as the Mistral and GPT-3.5 transaction category and types. This is showcasing a single transaction, but this code can easily run in a loop through each transaction, replacing this line with an `iterrows` function `for i, row in tqdm(df.iterrows(), total=len(df)):`, as is done later in the notebook (*https://oreil.ly/dcCOO*).

3. `gpt3pt5_data = f"""{{:` To use the pairwise comparison evaluator, we need to pass the results in a way that is formatted correctly for the prompt. This is done for Mistral and GPT-3.5, as well as the reference data.

4. `input_prompt = """You are an expert...`: The other formatting we have to get right is in the prompt. To get accurate evaluation scores, the evaluator needs to see the instructions that were given for the task.

5. `evaluator.evaluate_string_pairs(...`: All that remains is to run the evaluator by passing in the `prediction` and `prediction_b` (GPT-3.5 and Mistral, respectively), as well as the `input` prompt, and `reference` data, which serves as the ground truth.

6. Following this code in the notebook (*https://oreil.ly/hW8Wr*), there is an example of looping through and running the evaluator on every row in the dataframe and then saving the results and reasoning back to the dataframe.

This example demonstrates how to use a LangChain evaluator, but there are many different kinds of evaluator available. String distance (Levenshtein (*https://oreil.ly/Al5G3*)) or embedding distance (*https://oreil.ly/0p_nE*) evaluators are often used in scenarios where answers are not an exact match for the reference answer, but only need to be close enough semantically. Levenshtein distance allows for fuzzy matches based on how many single-character edits would be needed to transform the predicted text into the reference text, and embedding distance makes use of vectors (covered in Chapter 5) to calculate similarity between the answer and reference.

The other kind of evaluator we often use in our work is pairwise comparisons, which are useful for comparing two different prompts or models, using a smarter model like GPT-4. This type of comparison is helpful because reasoning is provided for each comparison, which can be useful in debugging why one approach was favored over another. The notebook for this section (*https://oreil.ly/iahTJ*) shows an example of using a pairwise comparison evaluator to check GPT-3.5-turbo's accuracy versus Mixtral 8x7b.

Evaluate Quality

Without defining an appropriate set of eval metrics to define success, it can be difficult to tell if changes to the prompt or wider system are improving or harming the quality of responses. If you can automate eval metrics using smart models like GPT-4, you can iterate faster to improve results without costly or time-consuming manual human review.

OpenAI Function Calling

Function calling provides an alternative method to output parsers, leveraging fine-tuned OpenAI models. These models identify when a function should be executed and generate a JSON response with the *name and arguments* for a predefined function. Several use cases include:

Designing sophisticated chat bots
Capable of organizing and managing schedules. For example, you can define a function to schedule a meeting: `schedule_meeting(date: str, time: str, attendees: List[str])`.

Convert natural language into actionable API calls
A command like "Turn on the hallway lights" can be converted to `control_device(device: str, action: 'on' | 'off')` for interacting with your home automation API.

Extracting structured data
This could be done by defining a function such as `extract_contextual_data(context: str, data_points: List[str])` or `search_database(query: str)`.

Each function that you use within function calling will require an appropriate *JSON schema*. Let's explore an example with the `OpenAI` package:

```python
from openai import OpenAI
import json
from os import getenv

def schedule_meeting(date, time, attendees):
    # Connect to calendar service:
    return { "event_id": "1234", "status": "Meeting scheduled successfully!",
            "date": date, "time": time, "attendees": attendees }

OPENAI_FUNCTIONS = {
    "schedule_meeting": schedule_meeting
}
```

After importing `OpenAI` and `json`, you'll create a function named `schedule_meeting`. This function is a mock-up, simulating the process of scheduling a meeting, and returns details such as `event_id`, `date`, `time`, and `attendees`. Following that, make an `OPENAI_FUNCTIONS` dictionary to map the function name to the actual function for ease of reference.

Next, define a `functions` list that provides the function's JSON schema. This schema includes its name, a brief description, and the parameters it requires, guiding the LLM on how to interact with it:

```python
# Our predefined function JSON schema:
functions = [
    {
        "type": "function",
        "function": {
            "type": "object",
            "name": "schedule_meeting",
            "description": '''Set a meeting at a specified date and time for
            designated attendees''',
            "parameters": {
                "type": "object",
                "properties": {
                    "date": {"type": "string", "format": "date"},
                    "time": {"type": "string", "format": "time"},
                    "attendees": {"type": "array", "items": {"type": "string"}},
                },
                "required": ["date", "time", "attendees"],
            },
        },
    }
]
```

Specify Format

When using function calling with your OpenAI models, always ensure to define a detailed JSON schema (including the name and description). This acts as a blueprint for the function, guiding the model to understand when and how to properly invoke it.

After defining the functions, let's make an OpenAI API request. Set up a `messages` list with the user query. Then, using an OpenAI `client` object, you'll send this message and the function schema to the model. The LLM analyzes the conversation, discerns a need to trigger a function, and provides the function name and arguments. The `function` and `function_args` are parsed from the LLM response. Then the function is executed, and its results are added back into the conversation. Then you call the model again for a user-friendly summary of the entire process.

Input:

```python
client = OpenAI(api_key=getenv("OPENAI_API_KEY"))

# Start the conversation:
messages = [
    {
        "role": "user",
        "content": '''Schedule a meeting on 2023-11-01 at 14:00
```

```
        with Alice and Bob.''',
    }
]

# Send the conversation and function schema to the model:
response = client.chat.completions.create(
    model="gpt-3.5-turbo-1106",
    messages=messages,
    tools=functions,
)

response = response.choices[0].message

# Check if the model wants to call our function:
if response.tool_calls:
    # Get the first function call:
    first_tool_call = response.tool_calls[0]

    # Find the function name and function args to call:
    function_name = first_tool_call.function.name
    function_args = json.loads(first_tool_call.function.arguments)
    print("This is the function name: ", function_name)
    print("These are the function arguments: ", function_args)

    function = OPENAI_FUNCTIONS.get(function_name)

    if not function:
        raise Exception(f"Function {function_name} not found.")

    # Call the function:
    function_response = function(**function_args)

    # Share the function's response with the model:
    messages.append(
        {
            "role": "function",
            "name": "schedule_meeting",
            "content": json.dumps(function_response),
        }
    )

    # Let the model generate a user-friendly response:
    second_response = client.chat.completions.create(
        model="gpt-3.5-turbo-0613", messages=messages
    )

    print(second_response.choices[0].message.content)
```

Output:

```
These are the function arguments:  {'date': '2023-11-01', 'time': '14:00',
'attendees': ['Alice', 'Bob']}
This is the function name:  schedule_meeting
I have scheduled a meeting on 2023-11-01 at 14:00 with Alice and Bob.
The event ID is 1234.
```

Several important points to note while function calling:

- It's possible to have many functions that the LLM can call.
- OpenAI can hallucinate function parameters, so be more explicit within the system message to overcome this.
- The function_call parameter can be set in various ways:
  - To mandate a specific function call: tool_choice: {"type": "function", "function": {"name": "my_function"}}}.
  - For a user message without function invocation: tool_choice: "none".
  - By default (tool_choice: "auto"), the model autonomously decides if and which function to call.

Parallel Function Calling

You can set your chat messages to include intents that request simultaneous calls to multiple tools. This strategy is known as *parallel function calling*.

Modifying the previously used code, the messages list is updated to mandate the scheduling of two meetings:

```
# Start the conversation:
messages = [
    {
        "role": "user",
        "content": '''Schedule a meeting on 2023-11-01 at 14:00 with Alice
        and Bob. Then I want to schedule another meeting on 2023-11-02 at
        15:00 with Charlie and Dave.'''
    }
]
```

Then, adjust the previous code section by incorporating a for loop.

Input:

```
# Send the conversation and function schema to the model:
response = client.chat.completions.create(
    model="gpt-3.5-turbo-1106",
    messages=messages,
    tools=functions,
)
```

```
response = response.choices[0].message

# Check if the model wants to call our function:
if response.tool_calls:
    for tool_call in response.tool_calls:
        # Get the function name and arguments to call:
        function_name = tool_call.function.name
        function_args = json.loads(tool_call.function.arguments)
        print("This is the function name: ", function_name)
        print("These are the function arguments: ", function_args)

        function = OPENAI_FUNCTIONS.get(function_name)

        if not function:
            raise Exception(f"Function {function_name} not found.")

        # Call the function:
        function_response = function(**function_args)

        # Share the function's response with the model:
        messages.append(
            {
                "role": "function",
                "name": function_name,
                "content": json.dumps(function_response),
            }
        )

    # Let the model generate a user-friendly response:
    second_response = client.chat.completions.create(
        model="gpt-3.5-turbo-0613", messages=messages
    )

    print(second_response.choices[0].message.content)
```

Output:

```
This is the function name:  schedule_meeting
These are the function arguments:  {'date': '2023-11-01', 'time': '14:00',
'attendees': ['Alice', 'Bob']}
This is the function name:  schedule_meeting
These are the function arguments:  {'date': '2023-11-02', 'time': '15:00',
'attendees': ['Charlie', 'Dave']}
Two meetings have been scheduled:
1. Meeting with Alice and Bob on 2023-11-01 at 14:00.
2. Meeting with Charlie and Dave on 2023-11-02 at 15:00.
```

From this example, it's clear how you can effectively manage multiple function calls. You've seen how the schedule_meeting function was called twice in a row to arrange different meetings. This demonstrates how flexibly and effortlessly you can handle varied and complex requests using AI-powered tools.

Function Calling in LangChain

If you'd prefer to avoid writing JSON schema and simply want to extract structured data from an LLM response, then LangChain allows you to use function calling with Pydantic.

Input:

```python
from langchain.output_parsers.openai_tools import PydanticToolsParser
from langchain_core.utils.function_calling import convert_to_openai_tool
from langchain_core.prompts import ChatPromptTemplate
from langchain_openai.chat_models import ChatOpenAI
from langchain_core.pydantic_v1 import BaseModel, Field
from typing import Optional


class Article(BaseModel):
    """Identifying key points and contrarian views in an article."""

    points: str = Field(..., description="Key points from the article")
    contrarian_points: Optional[str] = Field(
        None, description="Any contrarian points acknowledged in the article"
    )
    author: Optional[str] = Field(None, description="Author of the article")


_EXTRACTION_TEMPLATE = """Extract and save the relevant entities mentioned \
in the following passage together with their properties.

If a property is not present and is not required in the function parameters, \
do not include it in the output."""

# Create a prompt telling the LLM to extract information:
prompt = ChatPromptTemplate.from_messages(
    {("system", _EXTRACTION_TEMPLATE), ("user", "{input}")}
)

model = ChatOpenAI()

pydantic_schemas = [Article]

# Convert Pydantic objects to the appropriate schema:
tools = [convert_to_openai_tool(p) for p in pydantic_schemas]

# Give the model access to these tools:
model = model.bind_tools(tools=tools)

# Create an end to end chain:
chain = prompt | model | PydanticToolsParser(tools=pydantic_schemas)

result = chain.invoke(
    {
        "input": """In the recent article titled 'AI adoption in industry,'
        key points addressed include the growing interest ... However, the
```

```
            author, Dr. Jane Smith, ..."""
        }
    )
    print(result)
```

Output:

```
[Article(points='The growing interest in AI in various sectors, ...',
contrarian_points='Without stringent regulations, ...',
author='Dr. Jane Smith')]
```

You'll start by importing various modules, including `PydanticToolsParser` and `Chat PromptTemplate`, essential for parsing and templating your prompts. Then, you'll define a Pydantic model, `Article`, to specify the structure of the information you want to extract from a given text. With the use of a custom prompt template and the ChatOpenAI model, you'll instruct the AI to extract key points and contrarian views from an article. Finally, the extracted data is neatly converted into your predefined Pydantic model and printed out, allowing you to see the structured information pulled from the text.

There are several key points, including:

Converting Pydantic schema to OpenAI tools
```
    tools = [convert_to_openai_tool(p) for p in pydantic_schemas]
```

Binding the tools directly to the LLM
```
    model = model.bind_tools(tools=tools)
```

Creating an LCEL chain that contains a tools parser
```
    chain = prompt | model | PydanticToolsParser(tools=pydantic_schemas)
```

Extracting Data with LangChain

The `create_extraction_chain_pydantic` function provides a more concise version of the previous implementation. By simply inserting a Pydantic model and an LLM that supports function calling, you can easily achieve parallel function calling.

Input:

```
from langchain.chains.openai_tools import create_extraction_chain_pydantic
from langchain_openai.chat_models import ChatOpenAI
from langchain_core.pydantic_v1 import BaseModel, Field

# Make sure to use a recent model that supports tools:
model = ChatOpenAI(model="gpt-3.5-turbo-1106")

class Person(BaseModel):
    """A person's name and age."""

    name: str = Field(..., description="The person's name")
```

```
    age: int = Field(..., description="The person's age")

chain = create_extraction_chain_pydantic(Person, model)
chain.invoke({'input':'''Bob is 25 years old. He lives in New York.
He likes to play basketball. Sarah is 30 years old. She lives in San
Francisco. She likes to play tennis.'''})
```

Output:

```
[Person(name='Bob', age=25), Person(name='Sarah', age=30)]
```

The `Person` Pydantic model has two properties, `name` and `age`; by calling the `create_extraction_chain_pydantic` function with the input text, the LLM invokes the same function twice and creates two `People` objects.

Query Planning

You may experience problems when user queries have multiple intents with intricate dependencies. *Query planning* is an effective way to parse a user's query into a series of steps that can be executed as a query graph with relevant dependencies:

```python
from langchain_openai.chat_models import ChatOpenAI
from langchain.output_parsers.pydantic import PydanticOutputParser
from langchain_core.prompts.chat import (
    ChatPromptTemplate,
    SystemMessagePromptTemplate,
)
from pydantic.v1 import BaseModel, Field
from typing import List


class Query(BaseModel):
    id: int
    question: str
    dependencies: List[int] = Field(
        default_factory=list,
        description="""A list of sub-queries that must be completed before
        this task can be completed.
        Use a sub query when anything is unknown and we might need to ask
        many queries to get an answer.
        Dependencies must only be other queries."""
    )


class QueryPlan(BaseModel):
    query_graph: List[Query]
```

Defining `QueryPlan` and `Query` allows you to first ask an LLM to parse a user's query into multiple steps. Let's investigate how to create the query plan.

Input:

```
# Set up a chat model:
model = ChatOpenAI()

# Set up a parser:
parser = PydanticOutputParser(pydantic_object=QueryPlan)

template = """Generate a query plan. This will be used for task execution.

Answer the following query: {query}

Return the following query graph format:
{format_instructions}
"""
system_message_prompt = SystemMessagePromptTemplate.from_template(template)
chat_prompt = ChatPromptTemplate.from_messages([system_message_prompt])

# Create the LCEL chain with the prompt, model, and parser:
chain = chat_prompt | model | parser

result = chain.invoke({
"query":'''I want to get the results from my database. Then I want to find
out what the average age of my top 10 customers is. Once I have the average
age, I want to send an email to John. Also I just generally want to send a
welcome introduction email to Sarah, regardless of the other tasks.''',
"format_instructions":parser.get_format_instructions()})

print(result.query_graph)
```

Output:

```
[Query(id=1, question='Get top 10 customers', dependencies=[]),
Query(id=2, question='Calculate average age of customers', dependencies=[1]),
Query(id=3, question='Send email to John', dependencies=[2]),
Query(id=4, question='Send welcome email to Sarah', dependencies=[])]
```

Initiate a `ChatOpenAI` instance and create a `PydanticOutputParser` for the `QueryPlan` structure. Then the LLM response is called and parsed, producing a structured `query_graph` for your tasks with their unique dependencies.

Creating Few-Shot Prompt Templates

Working with the generative capabilities of LLMs often involves making a choice between *zero-shot* and *few-shot learning (k-shot)*. While zero-shot learning requires no explicit examples and adapts to tasks based solely on the prompt, its dependence on the pretraining phase means it may not always yield precise results.

On the other hand, with few-shot learning, which involves providing a few examples of the desired task performance in the prompt, you have the opportunity to optimize the model's behavior, leading to more desirable outputs.

Due to the token LLM context length, you will often finding yourself competing between adding lots of high-quality k-shot examples into your prompts while still aiming to generate an effective and deterministic LLM output.

 Even as the token context window limit within LLMs continues to increase, providing a specific number of k-shot examples helps you minimize API costs.

Let's explore two methods for adding k-shot examples into your prompts with *few-shot prompt templates*: using *fixed examples* and using an *example selector*.

Fixed-Length Few-Shot Examples

First, let's look at how to create a few-shot prompt template using a fixed number of examples. The foundation of this method lies in creating a robust set of few-shot examples:

```python
from langchain_openai.chat_models import ChatOpenAI
from langchain_core.prompts import (
    FewShotChatMessagePromptTemplate,
    ChatPromptTemplate,
)

examples = [
    {
        "question": "What is the capital of France?",
        "answer": "Paris",
    },
    {
        "question": "What is the capital of Spain?",
        "answer": "Madrid",
    } # ...more examples...
]
```

Each example is a dictionary containing a `question` and `answer` key that will be used to create pairs of `HumanMessage` and `AIMessage` messages.

Formatting the Examples

Next, you'll configure a `ChatPromptTemplate` for formatting the individual examples, which will then be inserted into a `FewShotChatMessagePromptTemplate`.

Input:

```
example_prompt = ChatPromptTemplate.from_messages(
    [
        ("human", "{question}"),
        ("ai", "{answer}"),
    ]
)

few_shot_prompt = FewShotChatMessagePromptTemplate(
    example_prompt=example_prompt,
    examples=examples,
)

print(few_shot_prompt.format())
```

Output:

```
Human: What is the capital of France?
AI: Paris
Human: What is the capital of Spain?
AI: Madrid
...more examples...
```

Notice how `example_prompt` will create `HumanMessage` and `AIMessage` pairs with the prompt inputs of {question} and {answer}.

After running `few_shot_prompt.format()`, the few-shot examples are printed as a string. As you'd like to use these within a `ChatOpenAI()` LLM request, let's create a new `ChatPromptTemplate`.

Input:

```
from langchain_core.output_parsers import StrOutputParser

final_prompt = ChatPromptTemplate.from_messages(
    [("system",'''You are responsible for answering
    questions about countries. Only return the country
    name.'''),
    few_shot_prompt,("human", "{question}"),]
)

model = ChatOpenAI()

# Creating the LCEL chain with the prompt, model, and a StrOutputParser():
chain = final_prompt | model | StrOutputParser()

result = chain.invoke({"question": "What is the capital of America?"})

print(result)
```

Output:

```
Washington, D.C.
```

After invoking the LCEL chain on `final_prompt`, your few-shot examples are added after the `SystemMessage`.

Notice that the LLM only returns `'Washington, D.C.'` This is because after the LLMs response is returned, *it is parsed* by `StrOutputParser()`, an output parser. Adding `StrOutputParser()` is a common way to ensure that LLM responses in chains *return string values*. You'll explore this more in depth while learning sequential chains in LCEL.

Selecting Few-Shot Examples by Length

Before diving into the code, let's outline your task. Imagine you're building a storytelling application powered by GPT-4. A user enters a list of character names with previously generated stories. However, each user's list of characters might have a different length. Including too many characters might generate a story that surpasses the LLM's context window limit. That's where you can use `LengthBasedExampleSelector` to adapt the prompt according to the length of user input:

```python
from langchain_core.prompts import FewShotPromptTemplate, PromptTemplate
from langchain.prompts.example_selector import LengthBasedExampleSelector
from langchain_openai.chat_models import ChatOpenAI
from langchain_core.messages import SystemMessage
import tiktoken

examples = [
    {"input": "Gollum", "output": "<Story involving Gollum>"},
    {"input": "Gandalf", "output": "<Story involving Gandalf>"},
    {"input": "Bilbo", "output": "<Story involving Bilbo>"},
]

story_prompt = PromptTemplate(
    input_variables=["input", "output"],
    template="Character: {input}\nStory: {output}",
)

def num_tokens_from_string(string: str) -> int:
    """Returns the number of tokens in a text string."""
    encoding = tiktoken.get_encoding("cl100k_base")
    num_tokens = len(encoding.encode(string))
    return num_tokens

example_selector = LengthBasedExampleSelector(
    examples=examples,
    example_prompt=story_prompt,
    max_length=1000, # 1000 tokens are to be included from examples
    # get_text_length: Callable[[str], int] = lambda x: len(re.split("\n| ", x))
    # You have modified the get_text_length function to work with the
    # TikToken library based on token usage:
    get_text_length=num_tokens_from_string,
)
```

First, you set up a PromptTemplate that takes two input variables for each example. Then LengthBasedExampleSelector adjusts the number of examples according to the *length of the examples input*, ensuring your LLM doesn't generate a story beyond its context window.

Also, you've customized the get_text_length function to use the num_tokens_from_string function that counts the total number of tokens using tiktoken. This means that max_length=1000 represents the *number of tokens* rather than using the following default function:

```
get_text_length: Callable[[str], int] = lambda x: len(re.split("\n| ",
x))
```

Now, to tie all these elements together:

```
dynamic_prompt = FewShotPromptTemplate(
    example_selector=example_selector,
    example_prompt=story_prompt,
    prefix='''Generate a story for {character} using the
    current Character/Story pairs from all of the characters
    as context.''',
    suffix="Character: {character}\nStory:",
    input_variables=["character"],
)

# Provide a new character from Lord of the Rings:
formatted_prompt = dynamic_prompt.format(character="Frodo")

# Creating the chat model:
chat = ChatOpenAI()

response = chat.invoke([SystemMessage(content=formatted_prompt)])
print(response.content)
```

Output:

```
Frodo was a young hobbit living a peaceful life in the Shire. However,
his life...
```

Provide Examples and Specify Format

When working with few-shot examples, the length of the content matters in determining how many examples the AI model can take into account. Tune the length of your input content and provide apt examples for efficient results to prevent the LLM from generating content that might surpass its context window limit.

After formatting the prompt, you create a chat model with `ChatOpenAI()` and load the formatted prompt into a `SystemMessage` that creates a small story about Frodo from *Lord of the Rings*.

Rather than creating and formatting a `ChatPromptTemplate`, it's often much easier to simply invoke a `SystemMesage` with a formatted prompt:

```
result = model.invoke([SystemMessage(content=formatted_prompt)])
```

Limitations with Few-Shot Examples

Few-shot learning has limitations. Although it can prove beneficial in certain scenarios, it might not always yield the expected high-quality results. This is primarily due to two reasons:

- Pretrained models like GPT-4 can sometimes overfit to the few-shot examples, making them prioritize the examples over the actual prompt.
- LLMs have a token limit. As a result, there will always be a trade-off between the number of examples and the length of the response. Providing more examples might limit the response length and vice versa.

These limitations can be addressed in several ways. First, if few-shot prompting is not yielding the desired results, consider using differently framed phrases or experimenting with the language of the prompts themselves. Variations in how the prompt is phrased can result in different responses, highlighting the trial-and-error nature of prompt engineering.

Second, think about including explicit instructions to the model to ignore the examples after it understands the task or to use the examples just for formatting guidance. This might influence the model to not overfit to the examples.

If the tasks are complex and the performance of the model with few-shot learning is not satisfactory, you might need to consider fine-tuning (*https://oreil.ly/S40bZ*) your model. Fine-tuning provides a more nuanced understanding of a specific task to the model, thus improving the performance significantly.

Saving and Loading LLM Prompts

To effectively leverage generative AI models such as GPT-4, it is beneficial to store prompts as files instead of Python code. This approach enhances the shareability, storage, and versioning of your prompts.

LangChain supports both saving and loading prompts from JSON and YAML. Another key feature of LangChain is its support for detailed specification in one file or distributed across multiple files. This means you have the flexibility to store different components such as templates, examples, and others in distinct files and reference them as required.

Let's learn how to save and load prompts:

```
from langchain_core.prompts import PromptTemplate, load_prompt

prompt = PromptTemplate(
    template='''Translate this sentence from English to Spanish.
    \nSentence: {sentence}\nTranslation:''',
    input_variables=["sentence"],
)

prompt.save("translation_prompt.json")

# Loading the prompt template:
load_prompt("translation_prompt.json")
# Returns PromptTemplate()
```

After importing `PromptTemplate` and `load_prompt` from the `langchain.prompts` module, you define a `PromptTemplate` for English-to-Spanish translation tasks and save it as *translation_prompt.json*. Finally, you load the saved prompt template using the `load_prompt` function, which returns an instance of `PromptTemplate`.

Please be aware that LangChain's prompt saving may not work with all types of prompt templates. To mitigate this, you can utilize the *pickle* library or *.txt* files to read and write any prompts that LangChain does not support.

You've learned how to create few-shot prompt templates using LangChain with two techniques: a fixed number of examples and using an example selector.

The former creates a set of few-shot examples and uses a `ChatPromptTemplate` object to format these into chat messages. This forms the basis for creating a `FewShotChatMessagePromptTemplate` object.

The latter approach, using an example selector, is handy when user input varies significantly in length. In such scenarios, a `LengthBasedExampleSelector` can be utilized to adjust the number of examples based on user input length. This ensures your LLM does not exceed its context window limit.

Moreover, you've seen how easy it is to store/load prompts as files, enabling enhanced shareability, storage, and versioning.

Data Connection

Harnessing an LLM application, coupled with your data, uncovers a plethora of opportunities to boost efficiency while refining your decision-making processes.

Your organization's data may manifest in various forms:

Unstructured data
> This could include Google Docs, threads from communication platforms such as Slack or Microsoft Teams, web pages, internal documentation, or code repositories on GitHub.

Structured data
> Data neatly housed within SQL, NoSQL, or Graph databases.

To query your unstructured data, a process of loading, transforming, embedding, and subsequently storing it within a vector database is necessary. A *vector database* is a specialized type of database designed to efficiently store and query data in the form of vectors, which represent complex data like text or images in a format suitable for machine learning and similarity search.

As for structured data, given its already indexed and stored state, you can utilize a LangChain agent to conduct an intermediate query on your database. This allows for the extraction of specific features, which can then be used within your LLM prompts.

There are multiple Python packages that can help with your data ingestion, including Unstructured (*https://oreil.ly/n0hDD*), LlamaIndex (*https://www.llamaindex.ai*), and LangChain (*https://oreil.ly/PjV9o*).

Figure 4-2 illustrates a standardized approach to data ingestion. It begins with the data sources, which are then loaded into documents. These documents are then chunked and stored within a vector database for later retrieval.

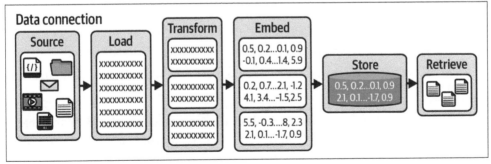

Figure 4-2. A data connection to retrieval pipeline

In particular LangChain equips you with essential components to load, modify, store, and retrieve your data:

Document loaders
> These facilitate uploading informational resources, or *documents*, from a diverse range of sources such as Word documents, PDF files, text files, or even web pages.

Document transformers
> These tools allow the segmentation of documents, conversion into a Q&A layout, elimination of superfluous documents, and much more.

Text embedding models
> These can transform unstructured text into a sequence of floating-point numbers used for similarity search by vector stores.

Vector databases (vector stores)
> These databases can save and execute searches over embedded data.

Retrievers
> These tools offer the capability to query and retrieve data.

Also, it's worth mentioning that other LLM frameworks such as LlamaIndex (*https://oreil.ly/9NcTB*) work seamlessly with LangChain. LlamaHub (*https://llamahub.ai*) is another open source library dedicated to document loaders and can create LangChain-specific Document objects.

Document Loaders

Let's imagine you've been tasked with building an LLM data collection pipeline for NutriFusion Foods. The information that you need to gather for the LLM is contained within:

- A PDF of a book called *Principles of Marketing*
- Two *.docx* marketing reports in a public Google Cloud Storage bucket
- Three *.csv* files showcasing the marketing performance data for 2021, 2022, and 2023

Create a new Jupyter Notebook or Python file in *content/chapter_4* of the shared repository (*https://oreil.ly/cVTyI*), and then run pip install pdf2image docx2txt pypdf, which will install three packages.

All of the data apart from *.docx* files can be found in *content/chapter_4/data (https:// oreil.ly/u9gMx)*. You can start by importing all of your various data loaders and creating an empty `all_documents` list to store all of the Document objects across your data sources.

Input:

```
from langchain_community.document_loaders import Docx2txtLoader
from langchain_community.document_loaders import PyPDFLoader
from langchain_community.document_loaders.csv_loader import CSVLoader
import glob
from langchain.text_splitter import CharacterTextSplitter

# To store the documents across all data sources:
all_documents = []

# Load the PDF:
loader = PyPDFLoader("data/principles_of_marketing_book.pdf")
pages = loader.load_and_split()
print(pages[0])

# Add extra metadata to each page:
for page in pages:
    page.metadata["description"] = "Principles of Marketing Book"

# Checking that the metadata has been added:
for page in pages[0:2]:
    print(page.metadata)

# Saving the marketing book pages:
all_documents.extend(pages)

csv_files = glob.glob("data/*.csv")

# Filter to only include the word Marketing in the file name:
csv_files = [f for f in csv_files if "Marketing" in f]

# For each .csv file:
for csv_file in csv_files:
    loader = CSVLoader(file_path=csv_file)
    data = loader.load()
    # Saving the data to the all_documents list:
    all_documents.extend(data)

text_splitter = CharacterTextSplitter.from_tiktoken_encoder(
    chunk_size=200, chunk_overlap=0
)

urls = [

    '''https://storage.googleapis.com/oreilly-content/NutriFusion%20Foods%2
    0Marketing%20Plan%202022.docx''',
```

```
        '''https://storage.googleapis.com/oreilly-content/NutriFusion%20Foods%2
        0Marketing%20Plan%202023.docx''',
    ]

    docs = []
    for url in urls:
        loader = Docx2txtLoader(url.replace('\n', ''))
        pages = loader.load()
        chunks = text_splitter.split_documents(pages)

        # Adding the metadata to each chunk:
        for chunk in chunks:
            chunk.metadata["source"] = "NutriFusion Foods Marketing Plan - 2022/2023"
        docs.extend(chunks)

    # Saving the marketing book pages:
    all_documents.extend(docs)
```

Output:

```
page_content='Principles of Mark eting'
metadata={'source': 'data/principles_of_marketing_book.pdf', 'page': 0}
{'source': 'data/principles_of_marketing_book.pdf', 'page': 0,
'description': 'Principles of Marketing Book'}
{'source': 'data/principles_of_marketing_book.pdf', 'page': 1,
'description': 'Principles of Marketing Book'}
```

Then using `PyPDFLoader`, you can import a *.pdf* file and split it into multiple pages using the `.load_and_split()` function.

Additionally, it's possible to add extra metadata to each page because the metadata is a Python dictionary on each `Document` object. Also, notice in the preceding output for `Document` objects the metadata `source` is attached to.

Using the package `glob`, you can easily find all of the *.csv* files and individually load these into LangChain `Document` objects with a `CSVLoader`.

Finally, the two marketing reports are loaded from a public Google Cloud Storage bucket and are then split into 200 token-chunk sizes using a `text_splitter`.

This section equipped you with the necessary knowledge to create a comprehensive document-loading pipeline for NutriFusion Foods' LLM. Starting with data extraction from a PDF, several CSV files and two *.docx* files, each document was enriched with relevant metadata for better context.

You now have the ability to seamlessly integrate data from a variety of document sources into a cohesive data pipeline.

Text Splitters

Balancing the length of each document is also a crucial factor. If a document is too lengthy, it may surpass the *context length* of the LLM (the maximum number of tokens that an LLM can process within a single request). But if the documents are excessively fragmented into smaller chunks, there's a risk of losing significant contextual information, which is equally undesirable.

You might encounter specific challenges while text splitting, such as:

- Special characters such as hashtags, @ symbols, or links might not split as anticipated, affecting the overall structure of the split documents.
- If your document contains intricate formatting like tables, lists, or multilevel headings, the text splitter might find it difficult to retain the original formatting.

There are ways to overcome these challenges that we'll explore later.

This section introduces you to text splitters in LangChain, tools utilized to break down large chunks of text to better adapt to your model's context window.

 There isn't a perfect document size. Start by using good heuristics and then build a training/test set that you can use for LLM evaluation.

LangChain provides a range of text splitters so that you can easily split by any of the following:

- Token count
- Recursively by multiple characters
- Character count
- Code
- Markdown headers

Let's explore three popular splitters: `CharacterTextSplitter`, `TokenTextSplitter`, and `RecursiveCharacterTextSplitter`.

Text Splitting by Length and Token Size

In Chapter 3, you learned how to count the number of tokens within a GPT-4 call with tiktoken (*https://oreil.ly/uz05O*). You can also use tiktoken to split strings into appropriately sized chunks and documents.

Remember to install tiktoken and langchain-text-splitters with `pip install tikto ken langchain-text-splitters`.

To split by token count in LangChain, you can use a `CharacterTextSplitter` with a `.from_tiktoken_encoder()` function.

You'll initially create a `CharacterTextSplitter` with a chunk size of 50 characters and no overlap. Using the `split_text` method, you're chopping the text into pieces and then printing out the total number of chunks created.

Then you'll do the same thing, but this time with a *chunk overlap* of 48 characters. This shows how the number of chunks changes based *on whether you allow overlap,* illustrating the impact of these settings on how your text gets divided:

```python
from langchain_text_splitters import CharacterTextSplitter

text = """
Biology is a fascinating and diverse field of science that explores the
living world and its intricacies \n\n. It encompasses the study of life, its
origins, diversity, structure, function, and interactions at various levels
from molecules and cells to organisms and ecosystems \n\n. In this 1000-word
essay, we will delve into the core concepts of biology, its history, key
areas of study, and its significance in shaping our understanding of the
natural world. \n\n ...(truncated to save space)...
"""
# No chunk overlap:
text_splitter = CharacterTextSplitter.from_tiktoken_encoder(
chunk_size=50, chunk_overlap=0, separator="\n",
)
texts = text_splitter.split_text(text)
print(f"Number of texts with no chunk overlap: {len(texts)}")

# Including a chunk overlap:
text_splitter = CharacterTextSplitter.from_tiktoken_encoder(
chunk_size=50, chunk_overlap=48, separator="\n",
)
texts = text_splitter.split_text(text)
print(f"Number of texts with chunk overlap: {len(texts)}")
```

Output:

```
Number of texts with no chunk overlap: 3
Number of texts with chunk overlap: 6
```

In the previous section, you used the following to load and split the *.pdf* into Lang-Chain documents:

```python
pages = loader.load_and_split()
```

It's possible for you to have more granular control on the size of each document by creating a `TextSplitter` and attaching it to your `Document` loading pipelines:

```
def load_and_split(text_splitter: TextSplitter | None = None) ->
List[Document]
```

Simply create a `TokenTextSplitter` with a `chunk_size=500` and a `chunk_overlap` of 50:

```
from langchain.text_splitter import TokenTextSplitter
from langchain_community.document_loaders import PyPDFLoader

text_splitter = TokenTextSplitter(chunk_size=500, chunk_overlap=50)
loader = PyPDFLoader("data/principles_of_marketing_book.pdf")
pages = loader.load_and_split(text_splitter=text_splitter)

print(len(pages)) #737
```

The *Principles of Marketing* book contains 497 pages, but after using a `TokenTextS plitter` with a `chunk_size` of 500 tokens, you've created 776 smaller LangChain Document objects.

Text Splitting with Recursive Character Splitting

Dealing with sizable blocks of text can present unique challenges in text analysis. A helpful strategy for such situations involves the use of *recursive character splitting*. This method facilitates the division of a large body of text into manageable segments, making further analysis more accessible.

This approach becomes incredibly effective when handling generic text. It leverages a list of characters as parameters and sequentially splits the text based on these characters. The resulting sections continue to be divided until they reach an acceptable size. By default, the character list comprises "\n\n", "\n", " ", and "". This arrangement aims to retain the integrity of paragraphs, sentences, and words, preserving the semantic context.

The process hinges on the character list provided and sizes the resulting sections based on the character count.

Before diving into the code, it's essential to understand what the `RecursiveCharacter TextSplitter` does. It takes a text and a list of delimiters (characters that define the boundaries for splitting the text). Starting from the first delimiter in the list, the splitter attempts to divide the text. If the resulting chunks are still too large, it proceeds to the next delimiter, and so on. This process continues *recursively* until the chunks are small enough or all delimiters are exhausted.

Using the preceding `text` variable, start by importing `RecursiveCharacterText Splitter`. This instance will be responsible for splitting the text. When initializing the splitter, parameters `chunk_size`, `chunk_overlap`, and `length_function` are set. Here, `chunk_size` is set to 100, and `chunk_overlap` to 20.

The `length_function` is defined as `len` to determine the size of the chunks. It's also possible to modify the `length_function` argument to use a tokenizer count instead of using the default `len` function, which will count characters:

```python
from langchain_text_splitters import RecursiveCharacterTextSplitter

text_splitter = RecursiveCharacterTextSplitter(
    chunk_size=100,
    chunk_overlap=20,
    length_function=len,
)
```

Once the `text_splitter` instance is ready, you can use `.split_text` to split the `text` variable into smaller chunks. These chunks are stored in the `texts` Python list:

```python
# Split the text into chunks:
texts = text_splitter.split_text(text)
```

As well as simply splitting the text with overlap into a list of strings, you can easily create LangChain `Document` objects with the `.create_documents` function. Creating `Document` objects is useful because it allows you to:

- Store documents within a vector database for semantic search
- Add metadata to specific pieces of text
- Iterate over multiple documents to create a higher-level summary

To add metadata, provide a list of dictionaries to the `metadatas` argument:

```python
# Create documents from the chunks:
metadatas = {"title": "Biology", "author": "John Doe"}
docs = text_splitter.create_documents(texts, metadatas=[metadatas] * len(texts))
```

But what if your existing `Document` objects are too long?

You can easily handle that by using the `.split_documents` function with a `TextSplitter`. This will take in a list of `Document` objects and will return a new list of `Document` objects based on your `TextSplitter` class argument settings:

```python
text_splitter = RecursiveCharacterTextSplitter(chunk_size=300)
splitted_docs = text_splitter.split_documents(docs)
```

You've now gained the ability to craft an efficient data loading pipeline, leveraging sources such as PDFs, CSVs, and Google Cloud Storage links. Furthermore, you've learned how to enrich the collected documents with relevant metadata, providing meaningful context for analysis and prompt engineering.

With the introduction of text splitters, you can now strategically manage document sizes, optimizing for both the LLM's context window and the preservation of context-rich information. You've navigated handling larger texts by employing recursion and character splitting. This newfound knowledge empowers you to work seamlessly with various document sources and integrate them into a robust data pipeline.

Task Decomposition

Task decomposition is the strategic process of dissecting complex problems into a suite of manageable subproblems. This approach aligns seamlessly with the natural tendencies of software engineers, who often conceptualize tasks as interrelated subcomponents.

In software engineering, by utilizing task decomposition you can reduce cognitive burden and harness the advantages of problem isolation and adherence to the single responsibility principle.

Interestingly, LLMs stand to gain considerably from the application of task decomposition across a range of use cases. This approach aids in maximizing the utility and effectiveness of LLMs in problem-solving scenarios by enabling them to handle intricate tasks that would be challenging to resolve as a single entity, as illustrated in Figure 4-3.

Here are several examples of LLMs using decomposition:

Complex problem solving
> In instances where a problem is multifaceted and cannot be solved through a single prompt, task decomposition is extremely useful. For example, solving a complex legal case could be broken down into understanding the case's context, identifying relevant laws, determining legal precedents, and crafting arguments. Each subtask can be solved independently by an LLM, providing a comprehensive solution when combined.

Content generation
> For generating long-form content such as articles or blogs, the task can be decomposed into generating an outline, writing individual sections, and then compiling and refining the final draft. Each step can be individually managed by GPT-4 for better results.

Large document summary
> Summarizing lengthy documents such as research papers or reports can be done more effectively by decomposing the task into several smaller tasks, like understanding individual sections, summarizing them independently, and then compiling a final summary.

Interactive conversational agents

For creating advanced chatbots, task decomposition can help manage different aspects of conversation such as understanding user input, maintaining context, generating relevant responses, and managing dialogue flow.

Learning and tutoring systems

In digital tutoring systems, decomposing the task of teaching a concept into understanding the learner's current knowledge, identifying gaps, suggesting learning materials, and evaluating progress can make the system more effective. Each subtask can leverage GPT-4's generative abilities.

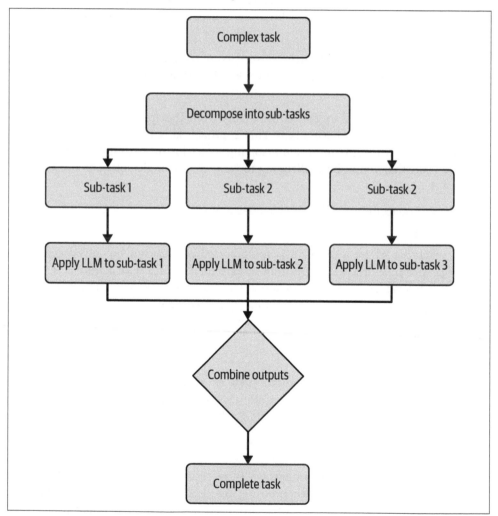

Figure 4-3. Task decomposition with LLMs

Divide Labor

Task decomposition is a crucial strategy for you to tap into the full potential of LLMs. By dissecting complex problems into simpler, manageable tasks, you can leverage the problem-solving abilities of these models more effectively and efficiently.

In the sections ahead, you'll learn how to create and integrate multiple LLM chains to orchestrate more complicated workflows.

Prompt Chaining

Often you'll find that attempting to do a single task within one prompt is impossible. You can utilize a mixture of *prompt chaining*, which involves combining multiple prompt inputs/outputs with specifically tailored LLM prompts to build up an idea.

Let's imagine an example with a film company that would like to partially automate their film creation. This could be broken down into several key components, such as:

- Character creation
- Plot generation
- Scenes/world building

Figure 4-4 shows what the prompt workflow might look like.

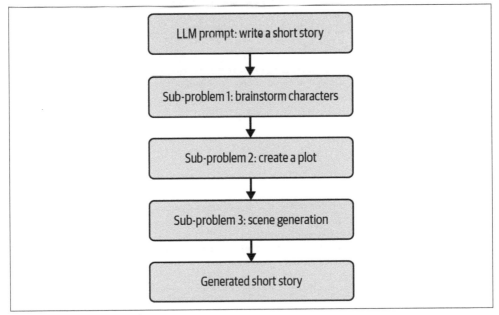

Figure 4-4. A sequential story creation process

Sequential Chain

Let's decompose the task into *multiple chains* and recompose them into a single chain:

character_generation_chain
> A chain responsible for creating multiple characters given a `'genre'`.

plot_generation_chain
> A chain that will create the plot given the `'characters'` and `'genre'` keys.

scene_generation_chain
> This chain will generate any missing scenes that were not initially generated from the plot_generation_chain.

Let's start by creating three separate `ChatPromptTemplate` variables, one for each chain:

```
from langchain_core.prompts.chat import ChatPromptTemplate

character_generation_prompt = ChatPromptTemplate.from_template(
    """I want you to brainstorm three to five characters for my short story. The
genre is {genre}. Each character must have a Name and a Biography.
You must provide a name and biography for each character, this is very
important!
---
Example response:
Name: CharWiz, Biography: A wizard who is a master of magic.
Name: CharWar, Biography: A warrior who is a master of the sword.
---
Characters: """
)

plot_generation_prompt = ChatPromptTemplate.from_template(
    """Given the following characters and the genre, create an effective
plot for a short story:
Characters:
{characters}
---
Genre: {genre}
---
Plot: """
)

scene_generation_plot_prompt = ChatPromptTemplate.from_template(
    """Act as an effective content creator.
Given multiple characters and a plot, you are responsible for
generating the various scenes for each act.

You must decompose the plot into multiple effective scenes:
---
Characters:
```

```
    {characters}
    ---
    Genre: {genre}
    ---
    Plot: {plot}
    ---
    Example response:
    Scenes:
    Scene 1: Some text here.
    Scene 2: Some text here.
    Scene 3: Some text here.
    ----
    Scenes:
    """
)
```

Notice that as the prompt templates flow from character to plot and scene generation, you add more placeholder variables from the previous steps.

The question remains, how can you guarantee that these extra strings are available for your downstream ChatPromptTemplate variables?

itemgetter and Dictionary Key Extraction

Within LCEL you can use the itemgetter function from the operator package to extract keys from the previous step, as long as a dictionary was present within the previous step:

```
from operator import itemgetter
from langchain_core.runnables import RunnablePassthrough

chain = RunnablePassthrough() | {
    "genre": itemgetter("genre"),
  }
chain.invoke({"genre": "fantasy"})
# {'genre': 'fantasy'}
```

The RunnablePassThrough function simply passes any inputs directly to the next step. Then a new dictionary is created by using the same key within the invoke function; this key is extracted by using itemgetter("genre").

It's essential to use the itemgetter function throughout parts of your LCEL chains so that any subsequent ChatPromptTemplate placeholder variables will always have valid values.

Additionally, you can use lambda or RunnableLambda functions within an LCEL chain to manipulate previous dictionary values. A lambda is an anonynous function within Python:

```
from langchain_core.runnables import RunnableLambda
```

```
chain = RunnablePassthrough() | {
    "genre": itemgetter("genre"),
    "upper_case_genre": lambda x: x["genre"].upper(),
    "lower_case_genre": RunnableLambda(lambda x: x["genre"].lower()),
}
chain.invoke({"genre": "fantasy"})
# {'genre': 'fantasy', 'upper_case_genre': 'FANTASY',
# 'lower_case_genre': 'fantasy'}
```

Now that you're aware of how to use `RunnablePassThrough`, `itemgetter`, and `lambda` functions, let's introduce one final piece of syntax: `RunnableParallel`:

```
from langchain_core.runnables import RunnableParallel

master_chain = RunnablePassthrough() | {
    "genre": itemgetter("genre"),
    "upper_case_genre": lambda x: x["genre"].upper(),
    "lower_case_genre": RunnableLambda(lambda x: x["genre"].lower()),
}

master_chain_two = RunnablePassthrough() | RunnableParallel(
        genre=itemgetter("genre"),
        upper_case_genre=lambda x: x["genre"].upper(),
        lower_case_genre=RunnableLambda(lambda x: x["genre"].lower()),
)

story_result = master_chain.invoke({"genre": "Fantasy"})
print(story_result)

story_result = master_chain_two.invoke({"genre": "Fantasy"})
print(story_result)

# master chain: {'genre': 'Fantasy', 'upper_case_genre': 'FANTASY',
# 'lower_case_genre': 'fantasy'}
# master chain two: {'genre': 'Fantasy', 'upper_case_genre': 'FANTASY',
# 'lower_case_genre': 'fantasy'}
```

First, you import `RunnableParallel` and create two LCEL chains called `master_chain` and `master_chain_two`. These are then invoked with exactly the same arguments; the `RunnablePassthrough` then passes the dictionary into the second part of the chain.

The second part of `master_chain` and `master_chain_two` will return exactly the *same result*.

So rather than directly using a dictionary, you can choose to use a `RunnableParallel` function instead. These two chain outputs *are interchangeable*, so choose whichever syntax you find more comfortable.

Let's create three LCEL chains using the prompt templates:

```python
from langchain_openai.chat_models import ChatOpenAI
from langchain_core.output_parsers import StrOutputParser

# Create the chat model:
model = ChatOpenAI()

# Create the subchains:
character_generation_chain = ( character_generation_prompt
| model
| StrOutputParser() )

plot_generation_chain = ( plot_generation_prompt
| model
| StrOutputParser() )

scene_generation_plot_chain = ( scene_generation_plot_prompt
| model
| StrOutputParser()  )
```

After creating all the chains, you can then attach them to a master LCEL chain.

Input:

```python
from langchain_core.runnables import RunnableParallel
from operator import itemgetter
from langchain_core.runnables import RunnablePassthrough

master_chain = (
    {"characters": character_generation_chain, "genre":
    RunnablePassthrough()}
    | RunnableParallel(
        characters=itemgetter("characters"),
        genre=itemgetter("genre"),
        plot=plot_generation_chain,
    )
    | RunnableParallel(
        characters=itemgetter("characters"),
        genre=itemgetter("genre"),
        plot=itemgetter("plot"),
        scenes=scene_generation_plot_chain,
    )
)

story_result = master_chain.invoke({"genre": "Fantasy"})
```

The output is truncated when you see ... to save space. However, in total there were five characters and nine scenes generated.

Output:

```
{'characters': '''Name: Lyra, Biography: Lyra is a young elf who possesses
..\n\nName: Orion, Biography: Orion is a ..''', 'genre': {'genre':
'Fantasy'} 'plot': '''In the enchanted forests of a mystical realm, a great
darkness looms, threatening to engulf the land and its inhabitants. Lyra,
the young elf with a deep connection to nature, ...''', 'scenes': '''Scene
1: Lyra senses the impending danger in the forest ...\n\nScene 2: Orion, on
his mission to investigate the disturbances in the forest...\n\nScene 9:
After the battle, Lyra, Orion, Seraphina, Finnegan...'''}
```

The scenes are split into separate items within a Python list. Then two new prompts are created to generate both a character script and a summarization prompt:

```python
# Extracting the scenes using .split('\n') and removing empty strings:
scenes = [scene for scene in story_result["scenes"].split("\n") if scene]
generated_scenes = []
previous_scene_summary = ""

character_script_prompt = ChatPromptTemplate.from_template(
    template="""Given the following characters: {characters} and the genre:
    {genre}, create an effective character script for a scene.

    You must follow the following principles:
    - Use the Previous Scene Summary: {previous_scene_summary} to avoid
    repeating yourself.
    - Use the Plot: {plot} to create an effective scene character script.
    - Currently you are generating the character dialogue script for the
    following scene: {scene}

    ---
    Here is an example response:
    SCENE 1: ANNA'S APARTMENT

    (ANNA is sorting through old books when there is a knock at the door.
    She opens it to reveal JOHN.)
    ANNA: Can I help you, sir?
    JOHN: Perhaps, I think it's me who can help you. I heard you're
    researching time travel.
    (Anna looks intrigued but also cautious.)
    ANNA: That's right, but how do you know?
    JOHN: You could say... I'm a primary source.

    ---
    SCENE NUMBER: {index}

    """,
)

summarize_prompt = ChatPromptTemplate.from_template(
    template="""Given a character script, create a summary of the scene.
    Character script: {character_script}""",
)
```

Technically, you could generate all of the scenes asynchronously. However, it's beneficial to know what each character has done in the *previous scene to avoid repeating points*.

Therefore, you can create two LCEL chains, one for generating the character scripts per scene and the other for summarizations of previous scenes:

```python
# Loading a chat model:
model = ChatOpenAI(model='gpt-3.5-turbo-16k')

# Create the LCEL chains:
character_script_generation_chain = (
    {
        "characters": RunnablePassthrough(),
        "genre": RunnablePassthrough(),
        "previous_scene_summary": RunnablePassthrough(),
        "plot": RunnablePassthrough(),
        "scene": RunnablePassthrough(),
        "index": RunnablePassthrough(),
    }
    | character_script_prompt
    | model
    | StrOutputParser()
)

summarize_chain = summarize_prompt | model | StrOutputParser()

# You might want to use tqdm here to track the progress,
# or use all of the scenes:
for index, scene in enumerate(scenes[0:3]):

    # # Create a scene generation:
    scene_result = character_script_generation_chain.invoke(
        {
            "characters": story_result["characters"],
            "genre": "fantasy",
            "previous_scene_summary": previous_scene_summary,
            "index": index,
        }
    )

    # Store the generated scenes:
    generated_scenes.append(
        {"character_script": scene_result, "scene": scenes[index]}
    )

    # If this is the first scene then we don't have a
    # previous scene summary:
    if index == 0:
        previous_scene_summary = scene_result
    else:
        # If this is the second scene or greater then
```

```
# we can use and generate a summary:
summary_result = summarize_chain.invoke(
    {"character_script": scene_result}
)
previous_scene_summary = summary_result
```

First, you'll establish a `character_script_generation_chain` in your script, utilizing various runnables like `RunnablePassthrough` for smooth data flow. Crucially, this chain integrates model = `ChatOpenAI(model='gpt-3.5-turbo-16k')`, a powerful model with a generous 16k context window, ideal for extensive content generation tasks. When invoked, this chain adeptly generates character scripts, drawing on inputs such as character profiles, genre, and scene specifics.

You dynamically enrich each scene by adding the summary of the previous scene, creating a simple yet effective buffer memory. This technique ensures continuity and context in the narrative, enhancing the LLM's ability to generate coherent character scripts.

Additionally, you'll see how the `StrOutputParser` elegantly converts model outputs into structured strings, making the generated content easily usable.

Divide Labor

Remember, designing your tasks in a sequential chain greatly benefits from the Divide Labor principle. Breaking tasks down into smaller, manageable chains can increase the overall quality of your output. Each chain in the sequential chain contributes its individual effort toward achieving the overarching task goal.

Using chains gives you the ability to use different models. For example, using a smart model for the ideation and a cheap model for the generation usually gives optimal results. This also means you can have fine-tuned models on each step.

Structuring LCEL Chains

In LCEL you must ensure that the first part of your LCEL chain is a *runnable* type. The following code will throw an error:

```
from langchain_core.prompts.chat import ChatPromptTemplate
from operator import itemgetter
from langchain_core.runnables import RunnablePassthrough, RunnableLambda

bad_first_input = {
    "film_required_age": 18,
}

prompt = ChatPromptTemplate.from_template(
    "Generate a film title, the age is {film_required_age}"
```

```
)

# This will error:
bad_chain = bad_first_input | prompt
```

A Python dictionary with a value of 18 will not create a runnable LCEL chain. However, all of the following implementations will work:

```
# All of these chains enforce the runnable interface:
first_good_input = {"film_required_age": itemgetter("film_required_age")}

# Creating a dictionary within a RunnableLambda:
second_good_input = RunnableLambda(lambda x: { "film_required_age":
x["film_required_age"] } )

third_good_input = RunnablePassthrough()
fourth_good_input = {"film_required_age": RunnablePassthrough()}
# You can also create a chain starting with RunnableParallel(...)

first_good_chain = first_good_input | prompt
second_good_chain = second_good_input | prompt
third_good_chain = third_good_input | prompt
fourth_good_chain = fourth_good_input | prompt

first_good_chain.invoke({
    "film_required_age": 18
}) # ...
```

Sequential chains are great at incrementally building generated knowledge that is used by future chains, but they often yield slower response times due to their sequential nature. As such, SequentialChain data pipelines are best suited for server-side tasks, where immediate responses are not a priority and users aren't awaiting real-time feedback.

Document Chains

Let's imagine that before accepting your generated story, the local publisher has requested that you provide a summary based on all of the character scripts. This is a good use case for *document chains* because you need to provide an LLM with a large amount of text that wouldn't fit within a single LLM request due to the context length restrictions.

Before delving into the code, let's first get a sense of the broader picture. The script you are going to see performs a text summarization task on a collection of scenes.

Remember to install Pandas with pip install pandas.

Now, let's start with the first set of code:

```
from langchain_text_splitters import CharacterTextSplitter
from langchain.chains.summarize import load_summarize_chain
import pandas as pd
```

These lines are importing all the necessary tools you need. `CharacterTextSplitter` and `load_summarize_chain` are from the LangChain package and will help with text processing, while Pandas (imported as `pd`) will help manipulate your data.

Next, you'll be dealing with your data:

```
df = pd.DataFrame(generated_scenes)
```

Here, you create a Pandas DataFrame from the `generated_scenes` variable, effectively converting your raw scenes into a tabular data format that Pandas can easily manipulate.

Then you need to consolidate your text:

```
all_character_script_text = "\n".join(df.character_script.tolist())
```

In this line, you're transforming the `character_script` column from your DataFrame into a single text string. Each entry in the column is converted into a list item, and all items are joined together with new lines in between, resulting in a single string that contains all character scripts.

Once you have your text ready, you prepare it for the summarization process:

```
text_splitter = CharacterTextSplitter.from_tiktoken_encoder(
    chunk_size=1500, chunk_overlap=200
)
docs = text_splitter.create_documents([all_character_script_text])
```

Here, you create a `CharacterTextSplitter` instance using its class method `from_tiktoken_encoder`, with specific parameters for chunk size and overlap. You then use this text splitter to split your consolidated script text into chunks suitable for processing by your summarization tool.

Next, you set up your summarization tool:

```
chain = load_summarize_chain(llm=model, chain_type="map_reduce")
```

This line is about setting up your summarization process. You're calling a function that loads a summarization chain with a chat model in a `map-reduce` style approach.

Then you run the summarization:

```
summary = chain.invoke(docs)
```

This is where you actually perform the text summarization. The `invoke` method executes the summarization on the chunks of text you prepared earlier and stores the summary into a variable.

Finally, you print the result:

```
print(summary['output_text'])
```

This is the culmination of all your hard work. The resulting summary text is printed to the console for you to see.

This script takes a collection of scenes, consolidates the text, chunks it up, summarizes it, and then prints the summary:

```
from langchain.text_splitter import CharacterTextSplitter
from langchain.chains.summarize import load_summarize_chain
import pandas as pd

df = pd.DataFrame(generated_scenes)

all_character_script_text = "\n".join(df.character_script.tolist())

text_splitter = CharacterTextSplitter.from_tiktoken_encoder(
    chunk_size=1500, chunk_overlap=200
)

docs = text_splitter.create_documents([all_character_script_text])

chain = load_summarize_chain(llm=model, chain_type="map_reduce")
summary = chain.invoke(docs)
print(summary['output_text'])
```

Output:

```
Aurora and Magnus agree to retrieve a hidden artifact, and they enter an
ancient library to find a book that will guide them to the relic...'
```

It's worth noting that even though you've used a `map_reduce` chain, there are four core chains for working with `Document` objects within LangChain.

Stuff

The document insertion chain, also referred to as the *stuff* chain (drawing from the concept of *stuffing* or *filling*), is the simplest approach among various document chaining strategies. Figure 4-5 illustrates the process of integrating multiple documents into a single LLM request.

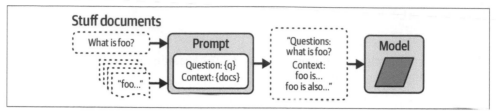

Figure 4-5. Stuff documents chain

Refine

The refine documents chain (Figure 4-6) creates an LLM response through a cyclical process that *iteratively updates its output*. During each loop, it combines the current output (derived from the LLM) with the current document. Another LLM request is made to *update the current output*. This process continues until all documents have been processed.

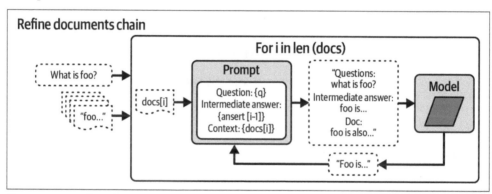

Figure 4-6. Refine documents chain

Map Reduce

The map reduce documents chain in Figure 4-7 starts with an LLM chain to each separate document (a process known as the Map step), interpreting the resulting output as a newly generated document.

Subsequently, all these newly created documents are introduced to a distinct combine documents chain to formulate a singular output (a process referred to as the Reduce step). If necessary, to ensure the new documents seamlessly fit into the context length, an optional compression process is used on the mapped documents. If required, this compression happens recursively.

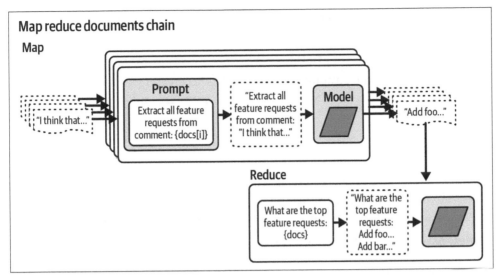

Figure 4-7. Map reduce documents chain

Map Re-rank

There is also map re-rank, which operates by executing an initial prompt on each document. This not only strives to fulfill a given task but also assigns a confidence score reflecting the certainty of its answer. The response with the highest confidence score is then selected and returned.

Table 4-1 demonstrates the advantages and disadvantages for choosing a specific document chain strategy.

Table 4-1. Overview of document chain strategies

Approach	Advantages	Disadvantages
Stuff Documents Chain	Simple to implement. Ideal for scenarios with small documents and few inputs.	May not be suitable for handling large documents or multiple inputs due to prompt size limitation.
Refine Documents Chain	Allows iterative refining of the response. More control over each step of response generation. Good for progressive extraction tasks.	Might not be optimal for real-time applications due to the loop process.
Map Reduce Documents Chain	Enables independent processing of each document. Can handle large datasets by reducing them into manageable chunks.	Requires careful management of the process. Optional compression step can add complexity and loses document order.
Map Re-rank Documents Chain	Provides a confidence score for each answer, allowing for better selection of responses.	The ranking algorithm can be complex to implement and manage. May not provide the best answer if the scoring mechanism is not reliable or well-tuned.

You can read more about how to implement different document chains in Lang-Chain's comprehensive API (*https://oreil.ly/FQUK_*) and here (*https://oreil.ly/9xr_6*).

Also, it's possible to simply change the chain type within the `load_summarize_chain` function:

```
chain = load_summarize_chain(llm=model, chain_type='refine')
```

There are newer, more customizable approaches to creating summarization chains using LCEL, but for most of your needs `load_summarize_chain` provides sufficient results.

Summary

In this chapter, you comprehensively reviewed the LangChain framework and its essential components. You learned about the importance of document loaders for gathering data and the role of text splitters in handling large text blocks.

Moreover, you were introduced to the concepts of task decomposition and prompt chaining. By breaking down complex problems into smaller tasks, you saw the power of problem isolation. Furthermore, you now grasp how prompt chaining can combine multiple inputs/outputs for richer idea generation.

In the next chapter, you'll learn about vector databases, including how to integrate these with documents from LangChain, and this ability will serve a pivotal role in enhancing the accuracy of knowledge extraction from your data.

Vector Databases with FAISS and Pinecone

This chapter introduces the concept of embeddings and vector databases, discussing how they can be used to provide relevant context in prompts.

A *vector database* is a tool most commonly used for storing text data in a way that enables querying based on similarity or semantic meaning. This technology is used to decrease hallucinations (where the AI model makes something up) by referencing data the model isn't trained on, significantly improving the accuracy and quality of the LLM's response. Use cases for vector databases also include reading documents, recommending similar products, or remembering past conversations.

Vectors are lists of numbers representing text (or images), which you might think of as coordinates for a location. The vector for the word *mouse* using OpenAI's text-embedding-ada-002 model is a list of 1,536 numbers, each representing the value for a feature the embedding model learned in training:

```
[-0.011904156766831875,
 -0.0323905423283577,
 0.001950666424818337,
 ...]
```

When these models are trained, texts that appear together in the training data will be pushed closer together in values, and texts that are unrelated will be pushed further away. Imagine we trained a simple model with only two parameters, Cartoon and Hygiene, that must describe the entire world, but only in terms of these two variables. Starting from the word *mouse*, increasing the value for the parameter Cartoon we would travel toward the most famous cartoon mouse, mickey mouse, as shown in Figure 5-1. Decreasing the value for the Hygiene parameter would take us toward rat, because rats are rodents similar to mice, but are associated with plague and disease (i.e., being unhygenic).

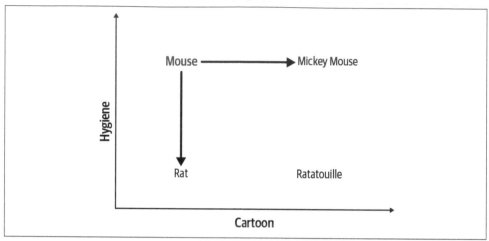

Figure 5-1. 2-D vector distances

Each location on the graph can be found by two numbers on the x- and y-axes, which represent the features of the model `Cartoon` and `Hygiene`. In reality, vectors can have thousands of parameters, because having more parameters allows the model to capture a wider range of similarities and differences. Hygiene is not the only difference between mice and rats, and Mickey Mouse isn't just a cartoon mouse. These features are learned from the data in a way that makes them hard for humans to interpret, and we would need a graph with thousands of axes to display a location in *latent space* (the abstract multidimensional space formed by the model's parameters). Often there is no human-understandable explanation of what a feature means. However, we can create a simplified two-dimensional projection of the distances between vectors, as has been done in Figure 5-2.

To conduct a vector search, you first get the vector (or location) of what you want to look up and find the k closest records in the database. In this case the word *mouse* is closest to `mickey mouse`, `cheese`, and `trap` where k=3 (return the three nearest records). The word *rat* is excluded if k=3, but would be included if k=4 as it is the next closest vector. The word *airplane* in this example is far away because it is rarely associated with the word *mouse* in the training data. The word *ship* is still colocated near the other forms of transport but is closer to `mouse` and `rat` because they are often found on ships, as per the training data.

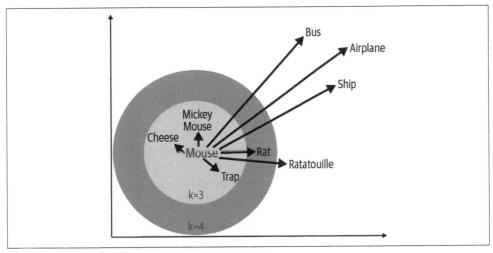

Figure 5-2. Multidimensional vector distances

A vector database stores the text records with their vector representation as the key. This is unlike other types of databases, where you might find records based on an ID, relation, or where the text contains a string. For example, if you queried a relational database based on the text in Figure 5-2 to find records where text contains `mouse`, you'd return the record `mickey mouse` but nothing else, as no other record contains that exact phrase. With vectors search you could also return the records `cheese` and `trap`, because they are closely associated, even though they aren't an exact match for your query.

The ability to query based on similarity is extremely useful, and vector search powers a lot of AI functionality. For example:

Document reading
Find related sections of text to read in order to provide a more accurate answer.

Recommendation systems
Discover similar products or items in order to suggest them to a user.

Long-term memory
Look up relevant snippets of conversation history so a chatbot remembers past interactions.

AI models are able to handle these tasks at small scale, as long as your documents, product list, or conversation memory fits within the token limits of the model you're using. However, at scale you quite quickly run into token limits and excess cost from passing too many tokens in each prompt. OpenAI's `gpt-4-1106-preview` was released in November 2023 (*https://oreil.ly/KMNU8*) with an enormous 128,000 token context window, but it costs 10 times more per token than `gpt-3.5-turbo`, which has 88% fewer tokens and was released a year earlier. The more efficient approach is to look up only the most relevant records to pass into the prompt at runtime in order to provide the most relevant context to form a response. This practice is typically referred to as RAG.

Retrieval Augmented Generation (RAG)

Vector databases are a key component of RAG, which typically involves searching by similarity to the query, retrieving the most relevant documents, and inserting them into the prompt as context. This lets you stay within what fits in the current context window, while avoiding spending money on wasted tokens by inserting irrelevant text documents in the context.

Retrieval can also be done using traditional database searches or web browsing, and in many cases a vector search by semantic similarity is not necessary. RAG is typically used to solve hallucinations in open-ended scenarios, like a user talking to a chatbot that is prone to making things up when asked about something not in its training data. Vector search can insert documents that are semantically similar to the user query into the prompt, greatly decreasing the chances the chatbot will hallucinate.

For example, if your author Mike told a chatbot "My name is Mike," then three messages later asked, "What is my name?" it can easily recall the right answer. The message containing Mike's name is still within the context window of the chat. However, if it was 3,000 messages ago, the text of those messages may be too large to fit inside the context window. Without this important context, it might hallucinate a name or refuse to answer for lack of information. A keyword search might help but could return too many irrelevant documents or fail to recall the right context in which the information was captured in the past. There may be many times Mike mentioned the word *name* in different formats, and for different reasons. By passing the question to the vector database, it can return the top three similar messages from the chat that match what the user asked:

```
## Context
Most relevant previous user messages:
1. "My name is Mike".
2. "My dog's name is Hercules".
3. "My coworker's name is James".

## Instructions
Please answer the user message using the context above.
User message: What is my name?
AI message:
```

It's impossible to pass all 3,000 past messages into the prompt for most models, and for a traditional search the AI model would have to formulate the right search query, which can be unreliable. Using the RAG pattern, you would pass the current user message to a vector search function, and return the most relevant three records as context, which the chatbot can then use to respond correctly.

Give Direction

Rather than inserting static knowledge into the prompt, vector search allows you to dynamically insert the most relevant knowledge into the prompt.

Here's how the process works for production applications using RAG:

1. Break documents into chunks of text.
2. Index chunks in a vector database.
3. Search by vector for similar records.
4. Insert records into the prompt as context.

In this instance, the documents would be all the 3,000 past user messages to serve as the chatbot's memory, but it could also be sections of a PDF document we uploaded to give the chatbot the ability to read, or a list of all the relevant products you sell to enable the chatbot to make a recommendation. The ability of our vector search to find the most similar texts is wholly dependent on the AI model used to generate the vectors, referred to as *embeddings* when you're dealing with semantic or contextual information.

Introducing Embeddings

The word *embeddings* typically refers to the vector representation of the text returned from a pretrained AI model. At the time of writing, the standard model for generating embeddings is OpenAI's text-embedding-ada-002, although embedding models have been available long before the advent of generative AI.

Although it is helpful to visualize vector spaces as a two-dimensional chart, as in Figure 5-2, in reality the embeddings returned from text-embedding-ada-002 are in 1,536 dimensions, which is difficult to depict graphically. Having more dimensions allows the model to capture deeper semantic meaning and relationships. For example, while a 2-D space might be able to separate cats from dogs, a 300-D space could capture information about the differences between breeds, sizes, colors, and other intricate details. The following code shows how to retrieve embeddings from the OpenAI API. The code for the following examples is included in the GitHub repository (*https://oreil.ly/6RzTy*) for this book.

Input:

```
from openai import OpenAI
client = OpenAI()

# Function to get the vector embedding for a given text
def get_vector_embeddings(text):
    response = client.embeddings.create(
        input=text,
        model="text-embedding-ada-002"
    )
    embeddings = [r.embedding for r in response.data]
    return embeddings[0]

get_vector_embeddings("Your text string goes here")
```

Output:

```
[
-0.006929283495992422,
-0.005336422007530928,
...
-4.547132266452536e-05,
-0.024047505110502243
]
```

This code uses the OpenAI API to create an embedding for a given input text using a specific embedding model:

1. `from openai import OpenAI` imports the OpenAI library, and `client = OpenAI()` sets up the client. It retrieves your OpenAI API key from an environment variable `OPENAI_API_KEY` in order to charge the cost of the embeddings to your account. You need to set this in your environment (usually in an *.env* file), which can be obtained by creating an account and visiting *https://oreil.ly/apikeys*.

2. `response = client.embeddings.create(...)`: This line calls the `create` method of the `Embedding` class from the `client` from the OpenAI library. The method takes two arguments:

   - `input`: This is where you provide the text string for which you want to generate an embedding.

   - `model`: This specifies the embedding model you want to use. In this case, it is `text-embedding-ada-002`, which is a model within the OpenAI API.

3. `embeddings = [r.embedding for r in response.data]`: After the API call, the `response` object contains the generated embeddings in JSON format. This line extracts the actual numerical embedding from the response, by iterating through a list of embeddings in `response.data`.

After executing this code, the `embeddings` variable will hold the numerical representation (embedding) of the input text, which can then be used in various NLP tasks or machine learning models. This process of retrieving or generating embeddings is sometimes referred to as *document loading*.

The term *loading* in this context refers to the act of computing or retrieving the numerical (vector) representations of text from a model and storing them in a variable for later use. This is distinct from the concept of *chunking*, which typically refers to breaking down a text into smaller, manageable pieces or chunks to facilitate processing. These two techniques are regularly used in conjunction with each other, as it's often useful to break large documents up into pages or paragraphs to facilitate more accurate matching and to only pass the most relevant tokens into the prompt.

There is a cost associated with retrieving embeddings from OpenAI, but it is relatively inexpensive at $0.0004 per 1,000 tokens at the time of writing. For instance, the King James version of the Bible, which comprises around 800,000 words or approximately 4,000,000 tokens, would cost about $1.60 to retrieve all the embeddings for the entire document.

Paying for embeddings from OpenAI is not your only option. There are also open-source models you can use, for example, the Sentence Transformers library (*https://oreil.ly/8OV3c*) provided by Hugging Face, which has 384 dimensions.

Input:

```python
import requests
import os

model_id = "sentence-transformers/all-MiniLM-L6-v2"
hf_token = os.getenv("HF_TOKEN")

api_url = "https://api-inference.huggingface.co/"
api_url += f"pipeline/feature-extraction/{model_id}"
headers = {"Authorization": f"Bearer {hf_token}"}

def query(texts):
    response = requests.post(api_url, headers=headers,
    json={"inputs": texts,
    "options":{"wait_for_model":True}})
    return response.json()

texts = ["mickey mouse",
        "cheese",
        "trap",
        "rat",
        "ratatouille"
        "bus",
        "airplane",
        "ship"]
```

```
output = query(texts)
output
```

Output:

```
[[-0.03875632584095001, 0.04480459913611412,
0.016051070764660835, -0.01789097487926483,
-0.03518553078174591, -0.013002964667975903,
0.14877274632453918, 0.048807501792907715,
0.011848390102386475, -0.044042471796274185,
...
-0.026688814163208008, -0.0359361357986927,
-0.03237859532237053, 0.008156519383192062,
-0.10299170762300491, 0.0790356695652008,
-0.008071334101259708, 0.11919838190078735,
0.0005506130401045084, -0.03497892618179321]]
```

This code uses the Hugging Face API to obtain embeddings for a list of text inputs using a pre-trained model. The model used here is the sentence-transformers/all-MiniLM-L6-v2, which is a smaller version of BERT, an open source NLP model introduced by Google in 2017 (based on the transformer model), which is optimized for sentence-level tasks. Here's how it works step-by-step:

1. model_id is assigned the identifier of the pre-trained model, sentence-transformers/all-MiniLM-L6-v2.

2. hf_token = os.getenv("HF_TOKEN") retrieves the API key for the Hugging Face API token from your environment. You need to set this in your environment with your own token, which can be obtained by creating an account and visiting *https://hf.co/settings/tokens*.

3. The requests library is imported to make HTTP requests to the API.

4. api_url is assigned the URL for the Hugging Face API, with the model ID included in the URL.

5. headers is a dictionary containing the authorization header with your Hugging Face API token.

6. The query() function is defined, which takes a list of text inputs and sends a POST request to the Hugging Face API with the appropriate headers and JSON payload containing the inputs and an option to wait for the model to become available. The function then returns the JSON response from the API.

7. texts is a list of strings from your database.

8. output is assigned the result of calling the query() function with the texts list.

9. The output variable is printed, which will display the feature embeddings for the input texts.

When you run this code, the script will send text to the Hugging Face API, and the API will return embeddings for each string of text sent.

If you pass the same text into an embedding model, you'll get the same vector back every time. However, vectors are not usually comparable across models (or versions of models) due to differences in training. The embeddings you get from OpenAI are different from those you get from BERT or spaCy (a natural language processing library).

The main difference with embeddings generated by modern transformer models is that the vectors are contextual rather than static, meaning the word *bank* would have different embeddings in the context of a *riverbank* versus *financial bank*. The embeddings you get from OpenAI Ada 002 and HuggingFace Sentence Transformers are examples of dense vectors, where each number in the array is almost always nonzero (i.e., they contain semantic information). There are also sparse vectors (*https://oreil.ly/d1cmb*), which normally have a large number of dimensions (e.g., 100,000+) with many of the dimensions having a value of zero. This allows capturing specific important features (each feature can have its own dimension), which tends to be important for performance in keyword-based search applications. Most AI applications use dense vectors for retrieval, although hybrid search (both dense and sparse vectors) is rising in popularity, as both similarity and keyword search can be useful in combination.

The accuracy of the vectors is wholly reliant on the accuracy of the model you use to generate the embeddings. Whatever biases or knowledge gaps the underlying models have will also be an issue for vector search. For example, the `text-embedding-ada-002` model is currently only trained up to August 2020 and therefore is unaware of any new words or new cultural associations that formed after that cutoff date. This can cause a problem for use cases that need more recent context or niche domain knowledge not available in the training data, which may necessitate training a custom model.

In some instances it might make sense to train your own embedding model. For instance, you might do this if the text used has a domain-specific vocabulary where specific words have a meaning separate from the generally accepted meaning of the word. One example might be tracing the language used by toxic groups on social media like Q-Anon, who evolve the language they use in posts to bypass moderation actions.

Training your own embeddings can be done with tools like word2vec, a method to represent words in a vector space, enabling you to capture the semantic meanings of words. More advanced models may be used, like GloVe (Global Vectors for Word Representation), which is used by spaCy for its embeddings, which are trained on the Common Crawl dataset, an open source snapshot of the web. The library Gensim offers a simple process for training your own custom embeddings using the open source algorithm (*https://oreil.ly/RmXVR*) word2vec.

Input:

```python
from gensim.models import Word2Vec

# Sample data: list of sentences, where each sentence is
# a list of words.
# In a real-world scenario, you'd load and preprocess your
# own corpus.
sentences = [
    ["the", "cake", "is", "a", "lie"],
    ["if", "you", "hear", "a", "turret", "sing", "you're",
    "probably", "too", "close"],
    ["why", "search", "for", "the", "end", "of", "a",
    "rainbow", "when", "the", "cake", "is", "a", "lie?"],
    # ...
    ["there's", "no", "cake", "in", "space,", "just", "ask",
    "wheatley"],
    ["completing", "tests", "for", "cake", "is", "the",
    "sweetest", "lie"],
    ["I", "swapped", "the", "cake", "recipe", "with", "a",
    "neurotoxin", "formula,", "hope", "that's", "fine"],
] + [
    ["the", "cake", "is", "a", "lie"],
    ["the", "cake", "is", "definitely", "a", "lie"],
    ["everyone", "knows", "that", "cake", "equals", "lie"],
    # ...
] * 10   # repeat several times to emphasize


# Train the word2vec model
model =  Word2Vec(sentences, vector_size=100, window=5,
min_count=1, workers=4, seed=36)

# Save the model
model.save("custom_word2vec_model.model")

# To load the model later
# loaded_model = word2vec.load(
# "custom_word2vec_model.model")

# Get vector for a word
vector = model.wv['cake']

# Find most similar words
similar_words = model.wv.most_similar("cake", topn=5)
print("Top five most similar words to 'cake': ", similar_words)

# Directly query the similarity between "cake" and "lie"
cake_lie_similarity = model.wv.similarity("cake", "lie")
```

```
print("Similarity between 'cake' and 'lie': ",
cake_lie_similarity)
```

Output:

```
Top 5 most similar words to 'cake':  [('lie',
0.23420444130897522), ('test', 0.23205122351646423),
('tests', 0.17178669571876526), ('GLaDOS',
0.1536172330379486), ('got', 0.14605288207530975)]
Similarity between 'cake' and 'lie':  0.23420444
```

This code creates a word2vec model using the Gensim library and then uses the model to determine words that are similar to a given word. Let's break it down:

1. The variable `sentences` contains a list of sentences, where each sentence is a list of words. This is the data on which the Word2Vec model will be trained. In a real application, instead of such hardcoded sentences, you'd often load a large corpus of text and preprocess it to obtain such a list of tokenized sentences.

2. An instance of the `word2vec` class is created to represent the model. While initializing this instance, several parameters are provided:

   - `sentences`: This is the training data.

   - `vector_size=100`: This defines the size of the word vectors. So each word will be represented as a 100-dimensional vector.

   - `window=5`: This represents the maximum distance between the current and predicted word within a sentence.

   - `min_count=1`: This ensures that even words that appear only once in the dataset will have vectors created for them.

   - `workers=4`: Number of CPU cores to use during training. It speeds up training on multicore machines.

   - `seed=36`: This is set for reproducibility so that the random processes in training deliver the same result each time (not guaranteed with multiple workers).

3. After training, the model is saved to a file named `custom_word2vec_model.model` using the `save` method. This allows you to reuse the trained model later without needing to train it again.

4. There is a commented-out line that shows how to load the model back from the saved file. This is useful when you want to load a pre-trained model in a different script or session.

5. The variable `vector` is assigned the vector representation of the word *cake*. This vector can be used for various purposes, like similarity calculations, arithmetic operations, etc.

6. The `most_similar` method is used to find words that are most similar to the provided vector (in this case, the vector for *cake*). The method returns the top five (`topn=5`) most similar words.

7. The `similarity` method queries the similarity between *cake* and *lie* direction, showing a small positive value.

The dataset is small and heavily repetitive, which might not provide a diverse context to properly learn the relationship between the words. Normally, word2vec benefits from larger and more diverse corpora and typically won't get good results until you're into the tens of millions of words. In the example we set a seed value to cherrypick one instance where *lie* came back in the top five results, but if you remove that seed, you'll find it rarely discovers the association successfully.

For smaller document sizes a simpler technique *TF-IDF* (Term Frequency-Inverse Document Frequency) is recommended, a statistical measure used to evaluate the importance of a word in a document relative to a collection of documents. The TF-IDF value increases proportionally to the number of times a word appears in the document but is offset by the frequency of the word in the wider corpus, which helps to adjust for the fact that some words are generally more common than others.

To compute the similarity between *cake* and *lie* using TF-IDF, you can use the open source scientific library (*https://oreil.ly/gHb3F*) scikit-learn and compute the *cosine similarity* (a measure of distance between two vectors). Words that are frequently colocated in sentences will have high cosine similarity (approaching 1), whereas words that appear infrequently will show a low value (or 0, if not co-located at all). This method is robust to even small documents like our toy example.

Input:

```python
import numpy as np
from sklearn.feature_extraction.text import TfidfVectorizer
from sklearn.metrics.pairwise import cosine_similarity

# Convert sentences to a list of strings for TfidfVectorizer
document_list = [' '.join(s) for s in sentences]

# Compute TF-IDF representation
vectorizer = TfidfVectorizer()
tfidf_matrix = vectorizer.fit_transform(document_list)

# Extract the position of the words "cake" and "lie" in
# the feature matrix
cake_idx = vectorizer.vocabulary_['cake']
lie_idx = vectorizer.vocabulary_['lie']

# Extract and reshape the vector for 'cake'
cakevec = tfidf_matrix[:, cake_idx].toarray().reshape(1, -1)
```

```
# Compute the cosine similarities
similar_words = cosine_similarity(cakevec, tfidf_matrix.T).flatten()

# Get the indices of the top 6 most similar words
# (including 'cake')
top_indices = np.argsort(similar_words)[-6:-1][::-1]

# Retrieve and print the top 5 most similar words to
# 'cake' (excluding 'cake' itself)
names = []
for idx in top_indices:
    names.append(vectorizer.get_feature_names_out()[idx])
print("Top five most similar words to 'cake': ", names)

# Compute cosine similarity between "cake" and "lie"
similarity = cosine_similarity(np.asarray(tfidf_matrix[:,
    cake_idx].todense()), np.asarray(tfidf_matrix[:, lie_idx].todense()))
# The result will be a matrix; we can take the average or
# max similarity value
avg_similarity = similarity.mean()
print("Similarity between 'cake' and 'lie'", avg_similarity)

# Show the similarity between "cake" and "elephant"
elephant_idx = vectorizer.vocabulary_['sing']
similarity = cosine_similarity(np.asarray(tfidf_matrix[:,
    cake_idx].todense()), np.asarray(tfidf_matrix[:,
    elephant_idx].todense()))
avg_similarity = similarity.mean()
print("Similarity between 'cake' and 'sing'",
    avg_similarity)
```

Output:

```
Top 5 most similar words to 'cake':  ['lie', 'the', 'is',
'you', 'definitely']
Similarity between 'cake' and 'lie' 0.8926458157227388
Similarity between 'cake' and 'sing' 0.010626735901461177
```

Let's break down this code step-by-step:

1. The sentences variable is reused from the previous example. The code converts these lists of words into full sentences (strings) using a list comprehension, resulting in document_list.

2. An instance of TfidfVectorizer is created. The fit_transform method of the vectorizer is then used to convert the document_list into a matrix of TF-IDF features, which is stored in tfidf_matrix.

3. The code extracts the position (or index) of the words *cake* and *lie* in the feature matrix using the vocabulary_ attribute of the vectorizer.

4. The TF-IDF vector corresponding to the word *cake* is extracted from the matrix and reshaped.

5. The cosine similarity between the vector for *cake* and all other vectors in the TF-IDF matrix is computed. This results in a list of similarity scores.

   - The indices of the top six most similar words (including *cake*) are identified.

   - Using these indices, the top five words (excluding *cake*) with the highest similarity to *cake* are retrieved and printed.

6. The cosine similarity between the TF-IDF vectors of the words *cake* and *lie* is computed. Since the result is a matrix, the code computes the mean similarity value across all values in this matrix and then prints the average similarity.

7. Now we compute the similarity between *cake* and *sing*. The average similarity value is calculated and printed to show that the two words are not commonly colocated (close to zero).

As well as the embedding model used, the strategy for what you embed is also important, because there is a trade-off between context and similarity. If you embed a large block of text, say an entire book, the vector you get back will be the average of the locations of the tokens that make up the full text. As you increase the size of the chunk, there is a regression to the mean where it approaches the average of all the vectors and no longer contains much semantic information.

Smaller chunks of text will be more specific in terms of location in vector space and as such might be more useful when you need close similarity. For example, isolating smaller sections of text from a novel may better separate comedic from tragic moments in the story, whereas embedding a whole page or chapter may mix both together. However, making the chunks of text too small might also cause them to lose meaning if the text is cut off in the middle of a sentence or paragraph. Much of the art of working with vector databases is in the way you load the document and break it into chunks.

Document Loading

One common use case of AI is to be able to search across documents based on similarity to the text of the user query. For example, you may have a series of PDFs representing your employee handbook, and you want to return the correct snippet of text from those PDFs that relates to an employee question. The way you load documents into your vector database will be dictated by the structure of your documents, how many examples you want to return from each query, and the number of tokens you can afford in each prompt.

For example, `gpt-4-0613` has an 8,192 token limit (*https://oreil.ly/wbx1f*), which needs to be shared between the prompt template, the examples inserted into the prompt, and the completion the model provides in response. Setting aside around 2,000 words or approximately 3,000 tokens for the prompt and response, you could pull the five most similar chunks of 1,000 tokens of text each into the prompt as context. However, if you naively split the document into 1,000-token chunks, you will run into a problem. The arbitrary place where each split takes place might be in the middle of a paragraph or sentence, so you risk losing the meaning of what's being conveyed. LangChain has a series of text splitters (*https://oreil.ly/qsG7J*), including the commonly used recursive character text splitter. It tries to split on line breaks and then spaces until the chunks are small enough. This keeps all paragraphs (and then sentences, and then words) together as much as possible to retain semantic groupings inherent in the structure of the text.

Input:

```python
from langchain.text_splitter import RecursiveCharacterTextSplitter

text_splitter = RecursiveCharacterTextSplitter.from_tiktoken_encoder(
    chunk_size=100, # 100 tokens
    chunk_overlap=20, # 20 tokens of overlap
    )

text = """
Welcome to the "Unicorn Enterprises: Where Magic Happens"
Employee Handbook! We're thrilled to have you join our team
of dreamers, doers, and unicorn enthusiasts. At Unicorn
Enterprises, we believe that work should be as enchanting as
it is productive. This handbook is your ticket to the
magical world of our company, where we'll outline the
principles, policies, and practices that guide us on this
extraordinary journey. So, fasten your seatbelts and get
ready to embark on an adventure like no other!


...


As we conclude this handbook, remember that at Unicorn
Enterprises, the pursuit of excellence is a never-ending
quest. Our company's success depends on your passion,
creativity, and commitment to making the impossible
possible. We encourage you to always embrace the magic
within and outside of work, and to share your ideas and
innovations to keep our enchanted journey going. Thank you
for being a part of our mystical family, and together, we'll
continue to create a world where magic and business thrive
hand in hand!
"""

chunks = text_splitter.split_text(text=text)
print(chunks[0:3])
```

Output:

```
['Welcome to the "Unicorn Enterprises: Where Magic Happens"
Employee Handbook! We\'re thrilled to have you join our team
of dreamers, doers, and unicorn enthusiasts.',
"We're thrilled to have you join our team of dreamers,
doers, and unicorn enthusiasts. At Unicorn Enterprises, we
believe that work should be as enchanting as it is
productive.",
 ...
"Our company's success depends on your passion, creativity,
and commitment to making the impossible possible. We
encourage you to always embrace the magic within and outside
of work, and to share your ideas and innovations to keep our
enchanted journey going.",
"We encourage you to always embrace the magic within and
outside of work, and to share your ideas and innovations to
keep our enchanted journey going. Thank you for being a part
of our mystical family, and together, we'll continue to
create a world where magic and business thrive hand in
hand!"]
```

Here's how this code works step-by-step:

1. *Create text splitter instance*: An instance of `RecursiveCharacterTextSplitter` is created using the `from_tiktoken_encoder` method. This method is specifically designed to handle the splitting of text based on token counts.

   The `chunk_size` parameter, set to 100, ensures that each chunk of text will contain approximately 100 tokens. This is a way of controlling the size of each text segment.

   The `chunk_overlap` parameter, set to 20, specifies that there will be an overlap of 20 tokens between consecutive chunks. This overlap ensures that the context is not lost between chunks, which is crucial for understanding and processing the text accurately.

2. *Prepare the text*: The variable `text` contains a multiparagraph string, representing the content to be split into chunks.

3. *Split the text*: The `split_text` method of the `text_splitter` instance is used to split the text into chunks based on the previously defined `chunk_size` and `chunk_overlap`. This method processes the text and returns a list of text chunks.

4. *Output the chunks*: The code prints the first three chunks of the split text to demonstrate how the text has been divided. This output is helpful for verifying that the text has been split as expected, adhering to the specified chunk size and overlap.

Specify Format

The relevance of the chunk of text provided to the prompt will depend heavily on your chunking strategy. Shorter chunks of text without overlap may not contain the right answer, whereas longer chunks of text with too much overlap may return too many irrelevant results and confuse the LLM or cost you too many tokens.

Memory Retrieval with FAISS

Now that you have your documents processed into chunks, you need to store them in a vector database. It is common practice to store vectors in a database so that you do not need to recompute them, as there is typically some cost and latency associated with doing so. If you don't change your embedding model, the vectors won't change, so you do not typically need to update them once stored. You can use an open source library to store and query your vectors called FAISS, a library developed by Facebook AI (*https://oreil.ly/gIcTI*) that provides efficient similarity search and clustering of dense vectors. First install FAISS in the terminal with `pip install faiss-cpu`. The code for this example is included in the GitHub repository (*https://oreil.ly/4wR7o*) for this book.

Input:

```python
import numpy as np
import faiss

# The get_vector_embeddings function is defined in a preceding example
emb = [get_vector_embeddings(chunk) for chunk in chunks]
vectors = np.array(emb)

# Create a FAISS index
index = faiss.IndexFlatL2(vectors.shape[1])
index.add(vectors)

# Function to perform a vector search
def vector_search(query_text, k=1):
    query_vector = get_vector_embeddings(query_text)
    distances, indices = index.search(
        np.array([query_vector]), k)
    return [(chunks[i], float(dist)) for dist,
        i in zip(distances[0], indices[0])]

# Example search
user_query = "do we get free unicorn rides?"
search_results = vector_search(user_query)
print(f"Search results for {user_query}:", search_results)
```

Output:

```
Search results for do we get free unicorn rides?: [("You'll
enjoy a treasure chest of perks, including unlimited unicorn
rides, a bottomless cauldron of coffee and potions, and
access to our company library filled with spellbinding
books. We also offer competitive health and dental plans,
ensuring your physical well-being is as robust as your
magical spirit.\n\n**5: Continuous Learning and
Growth**\n\nAt Unicorn Enterprises, we believe in continuous
learning and growth.", 0.3289167582988739)]
```

Here is an explanation of the preceding code:

1. Import the Facebook AI Similarity Search (FAISS) library with `import faiss`.

2. `vectors = np.array([get_vector_embeddings(chunk) for chunk in chunks])` applies `get_vector_embeddings` to each element in chunks, which returns a vector representation (embedding) of each element. These vectors are then used to create a numpy array, which is stored in the variable `vectors`.

3. The line `index = faiss.IndexFlatL2(vectors.shape[1])` creates a FAISS index for efficient similarity search. The argument `vectors.shape[1]` is the dimension of the vectors that will be added to the index. This kind of index (`IndexFlatL2`) performs brute-force L2 distance search, which looks for the closest items to a particular item in a collection by measuring the straight-line distance between them, checking each item in the collection one by one.

4. Then you add the array of vectors to the created FAISS index with `index.add(vectors)`.

5. `def vector_search(query_text, k=1)` defines a new function named `vector_search` that accepts two parameters: `query_text` and k (with a default value of 1). The function will retrieve the embeddings for the `query_text`, and then use that to search the index for the k closest vectors.

6. Inside the `vector_search` function, `query_vector = get_vector_embed dings(query_text)` generates a vector embedding for the query text using the `get_vector_embeddings` function.

7. The `distances, indices = index.search(np.array([query_vector]), k)` line performs a search in the FAISS index. It looks for the k closest vectors to `query_vector`. The method returns two arrays: distances (the squared L2 distances to the query vector) and indices (the indices

8. `return [(chunks[i], float(dist)) for dist, i in zip(distances[0], indices[0])]` returns a list of tuples. Each tuple contains a chunk (retrieved using the indices found in the search) and the corresponding distance from the query vector. Note that the distance is converted to a float before returning.

9. Finally, you perform a vector search for the string containing the user query: `search_results = vector_search(user_query)`. The result (the closest chunk and its distance) is stored in the variable `search_results`.

Once the vector search is complete, the results can be injected into the prompt to provide useful context. It's also important to set the system message so that the model is focused on answering based on the context provided rather than making an answer up. The RAG technique as demonstrated here is widely used in AI to help protect against hallucination.

Input:

```python
# Function to perform a vector search and then ask # GPT-3.5-turbo a question
def search_and_chat(user_query, k=1):
    # Perform the vector search
    search_results = vector_search(user_query, k)
    print(f"Search results: {search_results}\n\n")

    prompt_with_context = f"""Context:{search_results}\
Answer the question: {user_query}"""

    # Create a list of messages for the chat
    messages = [
        {"role": "system", "content": """Please answer the
        questions provided by the user. Use only the context
        provided to you to respond to the user, if you don't
        know the answer say \"I don't know\"."""},
        {"role": "user", "content": prompt_with_context},
    ]

    # Get the model's response
    response = client.chat.completions.create(
        model="gpt-3.5-turbo", messages=messages)

    # Print the assistant's reply
    print(f"""Response:
{response.choices[0].message.content}""")

# Example search and chat
search_and_chat("What is Unicorn Enterprises' mission?")
```

Output:

```
Search results: [("""As we conclude this handbook, remember that at
Unicorn Enterprises, the pursuit of excellence is a never-ending
quest. Our company's success depends on your passion,
creativity, and commitment to making the impossible
possible. We encourage you to always embrace the magic
within and outside of work, and to share your ideas and
innovations to keep our enchanted journey going. Thank you",
0.26446571946144104)]
```

```
Response:
Unicorn Enterprises' mission is to pursue excellence in their
work by encouraging their employees to embrace the magic within
and outside of work, share their ideas and innovations, and make
the impossible possible.
```

Here is a step-by-step explanation of what the function does:

1. Using a function named `vector_search`, the program performs a vector search with `user_query` as the search string and k as the number of search results to return. The results are stored in `search_results`.

2. The search results are then printed to the console.

3. A `prompt_with_context` is created by concatenating the `search_results` and `user_query`. The goal is to provide the model with context from the search results and a question to answer.

4. A list of messages is created. The first message is a system message that instructs the model to answer questions provided by the user using only the given context. If the model doesn't know the answer, it's advised to respond with *I don't know*. The second message is a user message containing the `prompt_with_context`.

5. The `openai.ChatCompletion.create()` function is used to get the model's response. It's provided with the model name (`gpt-3.5-turbo`) and the list of messages.

6. At the end of the code, the `search_and_chat()` function is called with the question as the `user_query`.

Provide Examples

Without testing the writing style, it would be hard to guess which prompting strategy would win. Now you can be confident this is the correct approach.

Although our code is working end to end now, it doesn't make sense to be collecting embeddings and creating a vector database with every query. Even if you're using an open source model for embeddings, there will be a cost in terms of compute and latency. You can save the FAISS index to a file using the `faiss.write_index` function:

```
# Save the index to a file
faiss.write_index(index, "data/my_index_file.index")
```

This will create a file called *my_index_file.index* in your current directory, which contains the serialized index. You can load this index back into memory later with `faiss.read_index`:

```
# Load the index from a file
index = faiss.read_index("data/my_index_file.index")
```

This way, you can persist your index across different sessions, or even share it between different machines or environments. Just make sure to handle these files carefully, as they can be quite large for big indexes.

If you have more than one saved vector database, it's also possible to merge them. This can be useful when serializing the loading of documents or making batch updates to your records.

You can merge two FAISS indices using the `faiss.IndexFlatL2` index's `add` method:

```
# Assuming index1 and index2 are two IndexFlatL2 indices
index1.add(index2.reconstruct_n(0, index2.ntotal))
```

In this code, `reconstruct_n(0, index2.ntotal)` is used to fetch all vectors from `index2`, and then `index1.add()` is used to add those vectors to `index1`, effectively merging the two indices.

This should work because `faiss.IndexFlatL2` supports the `reconstruct` method to retrieve vectors. However, please note that this process will not move any IDs associated with the vectors from `index2` to `index1`. After merging, the vectors from `index2` will have new IDs in `index1`.

If you need to preserve vector IDs, you'll need to manage this externally by keeping a separate mapping from vector IDs to your data items. Then, when you merge the indices, you also merge these mappings.

 Be aware that this method may not work for all types of indices, especially for those that do not support the `reconstruct` method like `IndexIVFFlat` or if the two indices have different configurations. In those cases, it may be better to keep the original vectors used to build each index and then merge and rebuild the index.

RAG with LangChain

As one of the most popular frameworks for AI engineering, LangChain has a wide coverage of RAG techniques. Other frameworks like LlamaIndex (*https://www.llamaindex.ai*) focus specifically on RAG and are worth exploring for sophisticated use cases. As you are familiar with LangChain from Chapter 4, we'll continue in this framework for the examples in this chapter. After manually performing RAG based on a desired context, let's create a similar example using LCEL on four small text documents with FAISS:

```python
from langchain_community.vectorstores.faiss import FAISS
from langchain_core.output_parsers import StrOutputParser
from langchain_core.prompts import ChatPromptTemplate
from langchain_core.runnables import RunnablePassthrough
from langchain_openai import ChatOpenAI, OpenAIEmbeddings

# 1. Create the documents:
documents = [
    "James Phoenix worked at JustUnderstandingData.",
    "James Phoenix currently is 31 years old.",
    """Data engineering is the designing and building systems for collecting,
    storing, and analyzing data at scale.""",
]

# 2. Create a vectorstore:
vectorstore = FAISS.from_texts(texts=documents, embedding=OpenAIEmbeddings())
retriever = vectorstore.as_retriever()

# 3. Create a prompt:
template = """Answer the question based only on the following context:
---
Context: {context}
---
Question: {question}
"""
prompt = ChatPromptTemplate.from_template(template)

# 4. Create a chat model:
model = ChatOpenAI()
```

The code begins by importing necessary modules from the LangChain library and defines a list of text documents to be processed.

It utilizes `FAISS`, a library for efficient similarity search, to create a vector store from the text documents. This involves converting the texts into vector embeddings using OpenAI's embedding model.

A prompt template for handling questions and a `ChatOpenAI` model are initialized for generating responses. Additionally, the prompt template enforces that the LLM only replies using the context provided from the retriever.

You'll need to create an LCEL chain that will contain the "context" and "question" keys:

```
chain = (
    {"context": retriever, "question": RunnablePassthrough()}
    | prompt
    | model
    | StrOutputParser()
)
```

By adding a retriever to "context", it will automatically fetch four documents that are converted into a string value. Combined with the "question" key, these are then used to format the prompt. The LLM generates a response that is then parsed into a string value by StrOutputParser().

You'll invoke the chain and pass in your question that gets assigned to "question" and manually test three different queries:

```
chain.invoke("What is data engineering?")
# 'Data engineering is the process of designing and building systems for
# collecting, storing, and analyzing data at scale.'

chain.invoke("Who is James Phoenix?")
# 'Based on the given context, James Phoenix is a 31-year-old individual who
# worked at JustUnderstandingData.'

chain.invoke("What is the president of the US?")
# I don't know
```

Notice how the LLM only appropriately answered the first two queries because it didn't have any relevant context contained within the vector database to answer the third query!

The LangChain implementation uses significantly less code, is easy to read, and allows you to rapidly implement retrieval augmented generation.

Hosted Vector Databases with Pinecone

There are a number of hosted vector database providers emerging to support AI use cases, including Chroma (*https://www.trychroma.com*), Weaviate (*https://weaviate.io*), and Pinecone (*https://www.pinecone.io*). Hosts of other types of databases are also offering vector search functionality, such as Supabase (*https://supabase.com*) with the pgvector add-on (*https://oreil.ly/pgvector*). Examples in this book use Pinecone, as it is the current leader at the time of writing, but usage patterns are relatively consistent across providers and concepts should be transferrable.

Hosted vector databases offer several advantages over open source local vector stores:

Maintainance

With a hosted vector database, you don't need to worry about setting up, managing, and maintaining the database yourself. This can save significant time and resources, especially for businesses that may not have dedicated DevOps or database management teams.

Scalability

Hosted vector databases are designed to scale with your needs. As your data grows, the database can automatically scale to handle the increased load, ensuring that your applications continue to perform efficiently.

Reliability

Managed services typically offer high availability with service-level agreements, as well as automatic backups and disaster recovery features. This can provide peace of mind and save you from potential data loss.

Performance

Hosted vector databases often have optimized infrastructure and algorithms that can provide better performance than self-managed, open source solutions. This can be particularly important for applications that rely on real-time or near-real-time vector search capabilities.

Support

With a hosted service, you typically get access to support from the company providing the service. This can be very helpful if you experience issues or need help optimizing your use of the database.

Security

Managed services often have robust security measures in place to protect your data, including things like encryption, access control, and monitoring. Major hosted providers are more likely to have the necessary compliance certificates and be in compliance with privacy legislation in regions like the EU.

Of course, this extra functionality comes at a cost, as well as a risk of overspending. As is the case with using Amazon Web Services, Microsoft Azure, or Google Cloud, stories of developers accidentally spending thousands of dollars through incorrect configuration or mistakes in code abound. There is also some risk of vendor lock-in, because although each vendor has similar functionality, they differ in certain areas, and as such it's not quite straightforward to migrate between them. The other major consideration is privacy, because sharing data with a third party comes with security risks and potential legal implications.

The steps for working with a hosted vector database remain the same as when you set up your open source FAISS vector store. First, you chunk your documents and retrieve vectors; you then index your document chunks in the vector database, allowing you to retrieve similar records to your query, in order to insert into the prompt as context. First, let's create an index in Pinecone (*https://www.pinecone.io*), a popular commercial vector database vendor. Then log into Pinecone and retrieve your API key (visit API Keys in the side menu and click "create API Key"). The code for this example is provided in the GitHub repository (*https://oreil.ly/Q0rIw*) for this book.

Input:

```
from pinecone import Pinecone, ServerlessSpec
import os

# Initialize connection (get API key at app.pinecone.io):
os.environ["PINECONE_API_KEY"] = "insert-your-api-key-here"

index_name = "employee-handbook"
environment = "us-east-1"
pc = Pinecone()  # This reads the PINECONE_API_KEY env var

# Check if index already exists:
# (it shouldn't if this is first time)
if index_name not in pc.list_indexes().names():
    # if does not exist, create index
    pc.create_index(
        index_name,
        # Using the same vector dimensions as text-embedding-ada-002
        dimension=1536,
        metric="cosine",
        spec=ServerlessSpec(cloud="aws", region=environment),
    )

# Connect to index:
index = pc.Index(index_name)

# View index stats:
index.describe_index_stats()
```

Output:

```
{'dimension': 1536,
 'index_fullness': 0.0,
 'namespaces': {},
 'total_vector_count': 0}
```

Let's go through this code step-by-step:

1. Importing libraries

The script begins with importing the necessary modules. `from pinecone import Pinecone, ServerlessSpec, import os` is used for accessing and setting environment variables.

2. Setting up the Pinecone API key

The Pinecone API key, which is crucial for authentication, is set as an environment variable using `os.environ["PINECONE_API_KEY"] = "insert-your-api-key-here"`. It's important to replace `"insert-your-api-key-here"` with your actual Pinecone API key.

3. Defining index name and environment

The variables `index_name` and `environment` are set up. `index_name` is given the value `"employee-handbook"`, which is the name of the index to be created or accessed in the Pinecone database. The `environment` variable is assigned `"us-west-2"`, indicating the server's location.

4. Initializing Pinecone connection

The connection to Pinecone is initialized with the `Pinecone()` constructor. This constructor automatically reads the `PINECONE_API_KEY` from the environment variable.

5. Checking for existing index

The script checks whether an index with the name `index_name` already exists in the Pinecone database. This is done through `pc.list_indexes().names()` functions, which returns a list of all existing index names.

6. Creating the index

If the index doesn't exist, it is created using the `pc.create_index()` function. This function is invoked with several parameters that configure the new index:

- `index_name`: Specifies the name of the index

- `dimension=1536`: Sets the dimensionality of the vectors to be stored in the index

- `metric='cosine'`: Determines that the cosine similarity metric will be used for vector comparisons

7. Connecting to the index

After verifying or creating the index, the script connects to it using `pc.Index(index_name)`. This connection is necessary for subsequent operations like inserting or querying data.

8. Index statistics

The script concludes with calling `index.describe_index_stats()`, which retrieves and displays various statistics about the index, such as its dimensionality and the total count of vectors stored.

Next, you need to store your vectors in the newly created index, by looping through all the text chunks and vectors and upserting them as records in Pinecone. The database operation `upsert` is a combination of *update* and *insert*, and it either updates an existing record or inserts a new record if the record does not already exist (refer to this Jupyter Notebook (*https://oreil.ly/YC-nV*) for the chunks variable).

Input:

```
from tqdm import tqdm # For printing a progress bar
from time import sleep

# How many embeddings you create and insert at once
batch_size = 10
retry_limit = 5   # maximum number of retries

for i in tqdm(range(0, len(chunks), batch_size)):
    # Find end of batch
    i_end = min(len(chunks), i+batch_size)
    meta_batch = chunks[i:i_end]
    # Get ids
    ids_batch = [str(j) for j in range(i, i_end)]
    # Get texts to encode
    texts = [x for x in meta_batch]
    # Create embeddings
    # (try-except added to avoid RateLimitError)
    done = False
    try:
        # Retrieve embeddings for the whole batch at once
        embeds = []
        for text in texts:
            embedding = get_vector_embeddings(text)
            embeds.append(embedding)
        done = True
    except:
        retry_count = 0
        while not done and retry_count < retry_limit:
            try:
                for text in texts:
                    embedding = get_vector_embeddings(text)
                    embeds.append(embedding)
                done = True
            except:
                sleep(5)
                retry_count += 1

    if not done:
```

```
        print(f"""Failed to get embeddings after
        {retry_limit} retries.""")
        continue

    # Cleanup metadata
    meta_batch = [{
        'batch': i,
        'text': x
    } for x in meta_batch]
    to_upsert = list(zip(ids_batch, embeds, meta_batch))

    # Upsert to Pinecone
    index.upsert(vectors=to_upsert)
```

Output:

```
100% 13/13 [00:53<00:00, 3.34s/it]
```

Let's break this code down:

1. Import the necessary libraries tqdm and time. The library tqdm displays progress bars, and time provides the sleep() function, which is used in this script for retry logic.

2. Set the variable batch_size to 10 (normally set to 100 for real workloads), representing how many items will be processed at once in the upcoming loop. Also set the retry_limit to make sure we stop after five tries.

3. The tqdm(range(0, len(chunks), batch_size)) part is a loop that will run from 0 to the length of chunks (defined previously), with a step of batch_size. chunks is a list of text to be processed. tqdm is used here to display a progress bar for this loop.

4. The i_end variable is calculated to be the smaller of the length of chunks or i + batch_size. This is used to prevent an Index Error if i + batch_size exceeds the length of chunks.

5. meta_batch is a subset of chunks for the current batch. This is created by slicing the chunks list from index i to i_end.

6. ids_batch is a list of string representations of the range i to i_end. These are IDs that are used to identify each item in meta_batch.

7. texts list is just the text from meta_batch, ready for processing for embeddings.

8. Try to get the embeddings by calling get_vector_embeddings() with the texts as the argument. The result is stored in the variable embeds. This is done inside a try-except block to handle any exceptions that might be raised by this function, such as a rate limit error.

9. If an exception is raised, the script enters a `while` loop where it will sleep for five seconds and then tries again to retrieve the embeddings. It will continue this until successful or the number of retries is reached, at which point it sets `done = True` to exit the `while` loop.

10. Modify the `meta_batch` to be a list of dictionaries. Each dictionary has two keys: batch, which is set to the current batch number `i`, and `text`, which is set to the corresponding item in `meta_batch`. This is where you could add additional metadata for filtering queries later, such as the page, title, or chapter.

11. Create the `to_upsert` list by using the `zip` function to combine `ids_batch`, `embeds`, and `meta_batch` into tuples, and then turning that into a list. Each tuple contains the ID, the corresponding embedding, and the corresponding metadata for each item in the batch.

12. The last line of the loop calls a method `upsert` on `index`, a Pinecone (a vector database service) index. The `vectors=to_upsert` argument passes the `to_upsert` list as the data to be inserted or updated in the index. If a vector with a given ID already exists in the index, it will be updated; if it doesn't exist, it will be inserted.

Once the records are stored in Pinecone, you can query them as you need, just like when you saved your vectors locally with FAISS. Embeddings remain the same so long as you're using the same embedding model to retrieve vectors for your query, so you do not need to update your database unless you have additional records or metadata to add.

Input:

```
# Retrieve from Pinecone
user_query = "do we get free unicorn rides?"

def pinecone_vector_search(user_query, k):
    xq = get_vector_embeddings(user_query)
    res = index.query(vector=xq, top_k=k, include_metadata=True)
    return res

pinecone_vector_search(user_query, k=1)
```

Output:

```
{'matches':
    [{'id': '15',
      'metadata': {'batch': 10.0,
      'text': "You'll enjoy a treasure chest of perks, "
              'including unlimited unicorn rides, a '
              'bottomless cauldron of coffee and potions, '
              'and access to our company library filled '
              'with spellbinding books. We also offer '
              'competitive health and dental plans, '
              'ensuring your physical well-being is as '
```

```
        'robust as your magical spirit.\n'
        '\n'
        '**5: Continuous Learning and Growth**\n'
        '\n'
        'At Unicorn Enterprises, we believe in '
        'continuous learning and growth.'},
  'score': 0.835591,
  'values': []},],
'namespace': ''}
```

This script performs a nearest neighbors search using Pinecone's API to identify the most similar vectors to a given input vector in a high-dimensional space. Here's a step-by-step breakdown:

1. The function `pinecone_vector_search` is defined with two parameters: `user_query` and k. `user_query` is the input text from the user, ready to be converted into a vector, and k indicates the number of closest vectors you want to retrieve.

2. Within the function, xq is defined by calling another function, `get_vector_embeddings(user_query)`. This function (defined previously) is responsible for transforming the `user_query` into a vector representation.

3. The next line performs a query on an object named index, a Pinecone index object, using the query method. The query method takes three parameters:

   The first parameter is `vector=xq`, the vector representation of our `user_query`.

   The second parameter, `top_k=k`, specifies that you want to return only the k closest vectors in the Pinecone index.

   The third parameter, `include_metadata=True`, specifies that you want to include metadata (such as IDs or other associated data) with the returned results. If you wanted to filter the results by metadata (*https://oreil.ly/BBYD4*), for example specifying the batch (or any other metadata you upserted), you could do this here by adding a fourth parameter: `filter={"batch": 1}`.

4. The results of the query method are assigned to res and then returned by the function.

5. Finally, the function `pinecone_vector_search` is called with arguments `user_query` and k, returning the response from Pinecone.

You have now effectively emulated the job FAISS was doing, returning the relevant record from the handbook with a similarity search by vector. If you replace `vector_search(user_query, k)` with `pinecone_vector_search(user_query, k)` in the `search_and_chat` function (from the previous example), the chatbot will run the same, except that the vectors will be stored in a hosted Pinecone database instead of locally using FAISS.

When you upserted the records into Pinecone, you passed the batch number as metadata. Pinecone supports the following formats of metadata:

- String
- Number (integer or floating-point, gets converted to a 64-bit floating point)
- Booleans (true, false)
- List of strings

The metadata strategy for storing records can be just as important as the chunking strategy, as you can use metadata to filter queries. For example, if you wanted to only search for similarity limited to a specific batch number, you could add a filter to the index.query:

```
res = index.query(xq, filter={
        "batch": {"$eq": 1}
    }, top_k=1, include_metadata=True)
```

This can be useful for limiting the scope of where you are searching for similarity. For example, it would allow you to store past conversations for all chatbots in the same vector database and then query only for past conversations related to a specific chatbot ID when querying to add context to that chatbot's prompt. Other common uses of metadata filters include searching for more recent timestamps, for specific page numbers of documents, or for products over a certain price.

Note that more metadata storage is likely to increase storage costs, as is storing large chunks that are infrequently referenced. Understanding how vector databases work should give you license to experiment with different chunking and metadata strategies and see what works for your use cases.

Self-Querying

Retrieval can get quite sophisticated, and you're not limited to a basic retriever that fetches documents from a vector database based purely on semantic relevance. For example, consider using metadata from within a user's query. By recognizing and extracting such filters, your retriever can autonomously generate a new query to execute against the vector database, as in the structure depicted in Figure 5-3.

This approach also generalizes to NoSQL, SQL, or any common database, and it is not solely limited to vector databases.

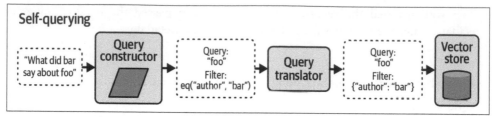

Figure 5-3. A self-querying retriever architecture

Self-querying (*https://oreil.ly/39rgU*) yields several significant benefits:

Schema definition
> You can establish a schema reflecting anticipated user descriptions, enabling a structured understanding of the information sought by users.

Dual-layer retrieval
> The retriever performs a two-tier operation. First, it gauges the semantic similarity between the user's input and the database's contents. Simultaneously, it discerns and applies filters based on the metadata of the stored documents or rows, ensuring an even more precise and relevant retrieval.

This method maximizes the retriever's potential in serving user-specific requests.

Install `lark` on the terminal with `pip install lark`.

In the subsequent code, essential modules such as `langchain`, `lark`, `getpass`, and `chroma` are imported. For a streamlined experience, potential warnings are suppressed:

```python
from langchain_core.documents import Document
from langchain_community.vectorstores.chroma import Chroma
from langchain_openai import OpenAIEmbeddings
import lark
import getpass
import os
import warnings

# Disabling warnings:
warnings.filterwarnings("ignore")
```

In the upcoming section, you'll craft a list named `docs`, filling it with detailed instances of the `Document` class. Each `Document` lets you capture rich details of a book. Within the metadata dictionary, you'll store valuable information such as the title, author, and genre. You'll also include data like the ISBN, the publisher, and a concise summary to give you a snapshot of each story. The `"rating"` offers a hint of its popularity. By setting up your data this way, you're laying the groundwork for a systematic and insightful exploration of a diverse library:

```
docs = [
    Document(
        page_content="A tale about a young wizard and his \
            journey in a magical school.",
        metadata={
            "title": "Harry Potter and the Philosopher's Stone",
            "author": "J.K. Rowling",
            "year_published": 1997,
            "genre": "Fiction",
            "isbn": "978-0747532699",
            "publisher": "Bloomsbury",
            "language": "English",
            "page_count": 223,
            "summary": "The first book in the Harry Potter \
            series where Harry discovers his magical \
            heritage.",
            "rating": 4.8,
        },
    ),
    # ... More documents ...
]
```

You'll import ChatOpenAI, SelfQueryRetriever, and OpenAIEmbeddings. Following this, you'll create a new vector database using the Chroma.from_documents(..) method.

Next, the AttributeInfo class is used to structure metadata for each book. Through this class, you'll systematically specify the attribute's name, description, and type. By curating a list of AttributeInfo entries, the self-query retriever can perform metadata filtering:

```
from langchain_openai.chat_models import ChatOpenAI
from langchain.retrievers.self_query.base \
    import SelfQueryRetriever
from langchain.chains.query_constructor.base \
    import AttributeInfo

# Create the embeddings and vectorstore:
embeddings = OpenAIEmbeddings()
vectorstore = Chroma.from_documents(docs, OpenAIEmbeddings())

# Basic Info
basic_info = [
    AttributeInfo(name="title", description="The title of the book",
    type="string"),
    AttributeInfo(name="author", description="The author of the book",
    type="string"),
    AttributeInfo(
        name="year_published",
        description="The year the book was published",
        type="integer",
    ),
```

```
        ]

        # Detailed Info
        detailed_info = [
            AttributeInfo(
                name="genre", description="The genre of the book",
                type="string or list[string]"
            ),
            AttributeInfo(
                name="isbn",
                description="The International Standard Book Number for the book",
                type="string",
            ),
            AttributeInfo(
                name="publisher",
                description="The publishing house that published the book",
                type="string",
            ),
            AttributeInfo(
                name="language",
                description="The primary language the book is written in",
                type="string",
            ),
            AttributeInfo(
                name="page_count", description="Number of pages in the book",
                type="integer"
            ),
        ]

        # Analysis
        analysis = [
            AttributeInfo(
                name="summary",
                description="A brief summary or description of the book",
                type="string",
            ),
            AttributeInfo(
                name="rating",
                description="""An average rating for the book (from reviews), ranging
                from 1-5""",
                type="float",
            ),
        ]

        # Combining all lists into metadata_field_info
        metadata_field_info = basic_info + detailed_info + analysis
```

Let's run this through step-by-step:

1. Import `ChatOpenAI`, `SelfQueryRetriever`, and `AttributeInfo` from the Lang-Chain modules for chat model integration, self-querying, and defining metadata attributes.

2. Create an `OpenAIEmbeddings` instance for handling OpenAI model embeddings.

3. A `Chroma` vector database is created from the documents.

4. Define three lists (`basic_info`, `detailed_info`, `analysis`), each containing `AttributeInfo` objects for different types of book metadata.

5. Combine these lists into a single list, `metadata_field_info`, for comprehensive book metadata management.

Now, set up a `ChatOpenAI` model and assign a `document_content_description` to specify what content type you're working with. The `SelfQueryRetriever` then uses this along with your LLM to fetch relevant documents from your `vectorstore`. With a simple query, such as asking for sci-fi books, the `invoke` method scans through the dataset and returns a list of `Document` objects.

Each `Document` encapsulates valuable metadata about the book, like the genre, author, and a brief summary, transforming the results into organized, rich data for your application:

```
document_content_description = "Brief summary of a movie"
llm = ChatOpenAI(temperature=0)
retriever = SelfQueryRetriever.from_llm(
    llm, vectorstore, document_content description, metadata_field_info
)

# Looking for sci-fi books
retriever.invoke("What are some sci-fi books?")
# [Document(page_content='''A futuristic society where firemen burn books to
# maintain order.''', metadata={'author': 'Ray Bradbury', 'genre': '...
# More documents..., truncated for brevity
```

Evaluate Quality

By setting the temperature to zero, you instruct the model to prioritize generating consistent metadata filtering outputs, rather than being more creative and therefore inconsistent. These metadata filters are then leveraged against the vector database to retrieve relevant documents.

When you want to fetch books from a specific author, you're directing the `retriever` to pinpoint books authored by `J.K. Rowling`. The `Comparison` function with the EQ (equals) comparator ensures the retrieved documents have their `'author'` attribute precisely matching `'J.K. Rowling'`:

```
# Querying for a book by J.K. Rowling:
retriever.invoke(
    '''I want some books that are published by the
    author J.K.Rowling'''
```

```
)
# query=' ' filter=Comparison(comparator=<Comparator.EQ:
# 'eq'>, attribute='author', value='J.K. Rowling')
# limit=None
# Documents [] omitted to save space
```

Initializing the `SelfQueryRetriever` with an added `enable_limit` flag set to `True` allows you to dictate the number of results returned. Then, you craft a query to obtain precisely 2 `Fantasy` books. By using the `Comparison` function with the EQ (equals) comparator on the `'genre'` attribute, the retriever zeros in on `'Fantasy'` titles. The `limit` parameter ensures you get only two results, optimizing your output for precision and brevity:

```
retriever = SelfQueryRetriever.from_llm(
    llm,
    vectorstore,
    document_content_description,
    metadata_field_info,
    enable_limit=True,
)

retriever.get_relevant_documents(
    query="Return 2 Fantasy books",
)
# query=' ' filter=Comparison(
#     comparator=<Comparator.EQ: 'eq'>, attribute='genre',
#     value='Fantasy') limit=2
# Documents [] omitted to save space
```

Alternative Retrieval Mechanisms

When it comes to retrieval implementations, various intriguing methods each demonstrate their distinct approaches, advantages, and limitations:

MultiQueryRetriever
> The MultiQueryRetriever (*https://oreil.ly/uuzpG*) aims to overcome the limitations of distance-based retrieval by generating multiple queries from different perspectives for a given user input query. This leads to the generation of a larger set of potentially relevant documents, offering broader insights. However, challenges may arise if the different queries produce contradicting results or overlap.

Contextual Compression
> The Contextual Compression Retriever (*https://oreil.ly/wzqVg*) handles long documents by compressing irrelevant parts, ensuring relevance to context. The challenge with this method is the expertise needed to determine the relevance and importance of information.

Ensemble Retriever

The Ensemble Retriever (*https://oreil.ly/jIuJh*) uses a list of retrievers and combines their results. It's essentially a "hybrid" search methodology that leverages the strengths of various algorithms. However, the Ensemble Retriever implies more computational workload due to the use of multiple retrieval algorithms, potentially affecting retrieval speed.

Parent Document Retriever

The Parent Document Retriever (*https://oreil.ly/jXSXQ*) ensures the maintenance of rich document backgrounds by retrieving original source documents from which smaller chunks are derived. But it might increase computational requirements due to the retrieval of larger parent documents.

Time-Weighted Vector Store Retriever

The Time-Weighted Vector Store Retriever (*https://oreil.ly/9JbTt*) incorporates *time decay* into document retrieval. Despite its advantages, the time decay factor might cause overlooking of relevant older documents, risking the loss of historical context.

The key to effective retrieval is understanding the trade-offs and selecting the method, or combination of methods, that best address your specific use case. Vector search adds additional cost and latency to your application, so ensure in testing you find that the additional context is worth it. For heavy workloads, paying the up-front cost of fine-tuning a custom model may be beneficial compared to the ongoing additional cost of prompts plus embeddings plus vector storage. In other scenarios, providing static examples of correct work in the prompt may work fine. However, when you need to pull in context to a prompt dynamically, based on similarity rather than a direct keyword search, there's no real substitute for RAG using a vector database.

Summary

In this chapter, you learned about the power of vector databases for storing and querying text based on similarity. By searching for the most similar records, vector databases can retrieve relevant information to provide context in your prompts, helping AI models stay within token limits and avoid unnecessary costs or irrelevant data. You also discovered that the accuracy of vectors depends on the underlying model and saw examples where they may fail.

Furthermore, you explored the process of indexing documents in a vector database, searching for similar records using vectors, and inserting records into prompts as context, called RAG. In this chapter, you went through code examples for retrieving embeddings from both the OpenAI API and open source models like the Sentence

Transformers library. You also learned the cost and benefits associated with retrieving embeddings from OpenAI relative to alternative options.

In the next chapter on autonomous agents, you will enter the futuristic world of AI agents that can make decisions and take actions on their own. You will learn about the different types of autonomous agents, their capabilities, and how they can be trained to perform specific tasks. Additionally, you will explore the challenges and unreliability issues associated with agents.

Autonomous Agents with Memory and Tools

This chapter dives deeper into the importance of chain-of-thought reasoning and the ability of large language models (LLMs) to reason through complex problems as agents. By breaking down complex problems into smaller, more manageable components, LLMs can provide more thorough and effective solutions. You will also learn about the components that make up autonomous agents, such as inputs, goal or reward functions, and available actions.

Chain-of-Thought

The ability of AI to reason through complex problems is essential for creating effective, reliable, and user-friendly applications.

Chain-of-thought reasoning (CoT) is a method of guiding LLMs through a series of steps or logical connections to reach a conclusion or solve a problem. This approach is particularly useful for tasks that require a deeper understanding of context or multiple factors to consider.

CoT (*https://oreil.ly/fAeLo*) is asking an LLM to *think* through complex problems, breaking them down into smaller, more manageable components. This allows the LLM to focus on each part individually, ensuring a more thorough understanding of the issue at hand.

In practice, chain-of-thought reasoning might involve:

- Asking an LLM to provide explanations for its decisions
- Planning multiple steps before deciding on a final answer

In the following sections, you'll explore examples of both ineffective and effective chain-of-thought reasoning. We will also discuss various techniques for building effective chain-of-thought reasoning and how they can be integrated into AI applications.

Let's imagine that a user wants the AI to generate a comprehensive marketing plan for promoting a new software product.

Input:

```
Create a marketing plan for a new software product.
```

Output:

```
1. Launch social media campaign
2. Send out email newsletters
3. Offer limited-time discounts
4. Collaborate with influencers
5. Organize webinars
```

In this example, GPT-4 doesn't use chain-of-thought reasoning, and it does not address the specific aspects of the marketing plan. The LLM generates a generic list of marketing strategies that could apply to any product, rather than focusing on the unique characteristics of the new software product.

Input:

```
Create a detailed marketing plan for a new project management software
product targeting small and medium-sized businesses.

The budget is $20,000, and we want to focus on digital marketing channels.

Consider the success of similar products in the market and provide a
step-by-step plan that includes the most effective promotional tactics.
```

Output:

```
Market Research
a. Analyze competitors and their marketing strategies
b. Identify the unique selling points of the new project management software
c. Define the target audience and their pain points

Branding and Messaging
a. Develop a consistent brand identity
b. Craft compelling messaging that addresses the target audience's pain
points
c. Create marketing assets such as website, blog, and social media content

...

Email Marketing
a. Develop an email marketing strategy to nurture leads and convert them
into customers
```

b. Send personalized onboarding emails to new users with helpful tips and
resources

Now GPT-4 specifically addresses the unique characteristics of the new software product, demonstrating effective chain-of-thought reasoning.

Give Direction

Take note of the phrase *step-by-step*, a critical element in CoT. By incorporating this phrase into your prompt, you're asking the LLM to reason through the steps that are required to generate a highly effective software product.

Also, by providing a $20,000 budget and the type of software, GPT-4 is able to provide a much more relevant and contextualized response.

Agents

Generative AI models have given rise to an *agent-based architecture*. Conceptually, an agent acts, perceives, and makes decisions within a specified environment to achieve predefined objectives.

Agents can take various actions such as executing a Python function; afterward, the agent will observe what happens and will decide on whether it is finished or what action to take next.

The agent will continuously loop through a series of actions and observations until there are no further actions, as you can see in the following pseudocode:

```
next_action = agent.get_action(...)
while next_action != AgentFinish:
    observation = run(next_action)
    next_action = agent.get_action(..., next_action, observation)
return next_action
```

The behavior of the agent is governed by three principal components:

Inputs

These are the sensory stimuli or data points the agent receives from its environment. Inputs can be diverse, ranging from visual (like images) and auditory (like audio files) to thermal signals and beyond.

Goal or reward function

This represents the guiding principle for an agent's actions. In goal-based frameworks, the agent is tasked with reaching a specific end state. In a reward-based setting, the agent is driven to maximize cumulative rewards over time, often in dynamic environments.

Available actions

The *action space* is the range of permissible actions an agent can undertake at any given moment (*https://oreil.ly/5AVfM*). The breadth and nature of this space are contingent upon the task at hand.

To explain these concepts further, consider a self-driving car:

Inputs

The car's sensors, such as cameras, LIDAR, and ultrasonic sensors, provide a continuous stream of data about the environment. This can include information about nearby vehicles, pedestrians, road conditions, and traffic signals.

Goal or reward function

The primary goal for a self-driving car is safe and efficient navigation from point A to point B. If we were to use a reward-based system, the car might receive positive rewards for maintaining a safe distance from other objects, adhering to speed limits, and following traffic rules. Conversely, it could receive negative rewards for risky behaviors, like hard braking or veering off the lane. Tesla specifically uses miles driven without an intervention as their reward function.

Available actions

The car's action space includes accelerating, decelerating, turning, changing lanes, and more. Each action is chosen based on the current input data and the objective defined by the goal or reward function.

You'll find that agents in systems like self-driving cars rely on foundational principles like inputs, goal/reward functions, and available actions. However, when delving into the realm of LLMs like GPT, there's a bespoke set of dynamics that cater specifically to their unique nature.

Here's how they align with your needs:

Inputs

For LLMs, the gateway is primarily through text. But that doesn't restrain the wealth of information you can use. Whether you're dealing with thermal readings, musical notations, or intricate data structures, your challenge lies in molding these into textual representations suitable for an LLM. Think about videos: while raw footage might seem incompatible, video text transcriptions allow an LLM to extract insights for you.

Harnessing goal-driven directives

LLMs primarily use goals defined within your text prompts. By creating effective prompts with objectives, you're not just accessing the LLM's vast knowledge; you're effectively charting its reasoning path. Think of it as laying down a blueprint: your specific prompt instructs the model, guiding it to dissect your overarching objective into a systematic sequence of steps.

Crafting action through functional tools

LLMs are not limited to mere text generation; there's so much more you can achieve. By integrating *ready-made tools* or *custom-developed tools*, you can equip LLMs to undertake diverse tasks, from API calls to database engagements or even orchestrating external systems. Tools can be written in any programming language, and by adding more tools you are effectively *expanding the action space* of what an LLM can achieve.

There are also different components that are directly applicable to LLMs:

Memory

It's ideal to store state between agent steps; this is particularly useful for chatbots, where remembering the previous chat history provides a better user experience.

Agent planning/execution strategies

There are multiple ways to achieve a high-level goal, of which a mixture of planning and executing is essential.

Retrieval

LLMs can use different types of retrieval methods. Semantic similarity within vector databases is the most common, but there are others such as including custom information from a SQL database into prompts.

Let's dive deeper into the shared and different components and explore the implementation details.

Reason and Act (ReAct)

There are many agent frameworks that ultimately aim to improve LLM responses toward a goal. The original framework was *ReAct*, which is an improved version of CoT, allowing an LLM to create observations after taking actions via tools. These observations are then turned into *thoughts* about what would be the *right tool* to use within the next step (Figure 6-1). The LLM continues to reason until either a 'Final Answer' string value is present or a maximum number of iterations has taken place.

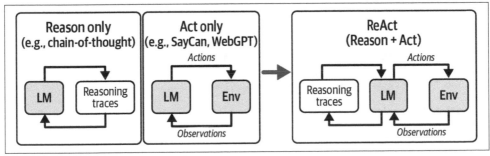

Figure 6-1. The ReAct framework

The ReAct (*https://oreil.ly/ssdnL*) framework uses a mixture of task decomposition, a thought loop, and multiple tools to solve questions. Let's explore the thought loop within ReAct:

1. Observe the environment.
2. Interpret the environment with a thought.
3. Decide on an action.
4. Act on the environment.
5. Repeat steps 1–4 until you find a solution or you've done too many iterations (the solution is "I've found the answer").

You can easily create a ReAct-style prompt by using the preceding thought loop while also providing the LLM with several inputs such as:

- {question}: The query that you want answered.
- {tools}: These refer to functions that can be used to accomplish a step within the overall task. It is common practice to include a list of tools where each tool is a Python function, a name, and a description of the function and its purpose.

The following is a prompt that implements the ReAct pattern with prompt variables wrapped in {} characters such as {question}:

```
You will attempt to solve the problem of finding the answer to a question.
Use chain-of-thought reasoning to solve through the problem, using the
following pattern:

1. Observe the original question:
original_question: original_problem_text
2. Create an observation with the following pattern:
observation: observation_text
3. Create a thought based on the observation with the following pattern:
thought: thought_text
4. Use tools to act on the thought with the following pattern:
action: tool_name
action_input: tool_input

Do not guess or assume the tool results. Instead, provide a structured
output that includes the action and action_input.

You have access to the following tools: {tools}.

original_problem: {question}

Based on the provided tool result:

Either provide the next observation, action, action_input, or the final
answer if available.
```

```
If you are providing the final answer, you must return the following pattern:
"I've found the answer: final_answer"
```

Here is a breakdown of the prompt:

1. The introduction of the prompt clearly establishes the LLM's purpose: `You will attempt to solve the problem of finding the answer to a question.`

2. The problem-solving approach is then outlined: `Use chain-of-thought reasoning to solve through the problem, using the following pattern:`

3. The steps in the chain-of-thought reasoning are then laid out:

   - The LLM starts by observing the original question and subsequently formulates an observation about it: `original_question: original_problem_text, observation: observation_text.`

   - Based on this observation, the AI should formulate a thought that signifies a step in the reasoning process: `thought: thought_text.`

   - Having established a thought, it then decides on an action using one of the available tools: `action: tool_name, action_input: tool_input.`

4. The LLM is then reminded not to make assumptions about what a tool might return, and it should explicitly outline its intended action and the corresponding input.

5. `You have access to the following tools: {tools}` communicates to the LLM what tools it has available for solving the problem.

6. The actual problem that the LLM must solve is then introduced: `original_problem: {question}.`

7. Finally, instructions are provided on how the LLM should respond based on the results of its actions. It can either continue with new observations, actions, and inputs or, if a solution is found, provide the final answer.

The prompt outlines a systematic problem-solving process in which the LLM observes a problem, thinks about it, decides on an action, and repeats this process until a solution is discovered.

Reason and Act Implementation

Now that you're aware of ReAct, it's important to create a simple Python implementation that replicates what LangChain does automatically, allowing you to build the intuition about what's truly happening between the LLM responses.

To keep it simple, this example will not implement looping and will assume that the output can be obtained from a single tool call.

To create a basic ReAct implementation, you'll implement the following:

1. At every thought, you need to extract the tool that the LLM wants to use. Therefore, you'll extract the last `action` and `action_input`. The `action` represents the tool name, while the `action_input` consists of the values of the function arguments.

2. Check whether the LLM thinks that it has found the final answer, in which case the thought loop has ended.

You can use regular expressions to extract the `action` and `action_input` values from the LLM response:

```python
import re

# Sample text:
text = """
Action: search_on_google
Action_Input: Tom Hanks's current wife

action: search_on_wikipedia
action_input: How old is Rita Wilson in 2023

action : search_on_google
action input: some other query
"""

# Compile regex patterns:
action_pattern = re.compile(r"(?i)action\s*:\s*([^\n]+)", re.MULTILINE)
action_input_pattern = re.compile(r"(?i)action\s*_*input\s*:\s*([^\n]+)",
re.MULTILINE)

# Find all occurrences of action and action_input:
actions = action_pattern.findall(text)
action_inputs = action_input_pattern.findall(text)

# Extract the last occurrence of action and action_input:
last_action = actions[-1] if actions else None
last_action_input = action_inputs[-1] if action_inputs else None

print("Last Action:", last_action)
print("Last Action Input:", last_action_input)
# Last Action: search_on_google
# Last Action Input: some other query
```

Let's break down the regular expression to extract the `action`:

- `action_pattern = re.compile(r"(?i)action\s*:\s*([^\n]+)", re.MULTI LINE)`

- **(?i)**: This is called an *inline flag* and makes the regex pattern case-insensitive. It means that the pattern will match "action," "Action," "ACTION," or any other combination of uppercase and lowercase letters.

- **action**: This part of the pattern matches the word *action* literally. Due to the case-insensitive flag, it will match any capitalization of the word.

- **\s***: This part of the pattern matches zero or more whitespace characters (spaces, tabs, etc.). The ***** means *zero or more*, and **\s** is the regex shorthand for a whitespace character.

- **:** This part of the pattern matches the colon character literally.

- **\s***: This is the same as the previous **\s*** part, matching zero or more whitespace characters after the colon.

- **+([^\n]++)**: This pattern is a capturing group, denoted by the parentheses. It matches one or more characters that are *not a newline character*. The **^** inside the square brackets **[]** negates the character class, and **\n** represents the newline character. The **+** means *one or more*. The text matched by this group will be extracted when using the **findall()** function.

- **re.MULTILINE**: This is a flag passed to **re.compile()** function. It tells the regex engine that the input text may have multiple lines, so the pattern should be applied line by line.

- In regular expressions, square brackets **[]** are used to define a character class, which is a set of characters that you want to match. For example, **[abc]** would match any single character that is either **'a'**, **'b'**, or **'c'**.

- When you add a caret **^** at the beginning of the character class, it negates the character class, meaning it will match any character that is *not in the character class*. In other words, it inverts the set of characters you want to match.

- So, when we use **[^abc]**, it will match any single character that is *not* **'a'**, **'b'**, or **'c'**. In the regex pattern **+([^\n]++)**, the character class is **[^n]**, which means it will match any character that is *not* a newline character (**\n**). The **+** after the negated character class means that the pattern should match one or more characters that are not newlines.

- By using the negated character class **[^n]** in the capturing group, we ensure that the regex engine captures text up to the end of the line without including the newline character itself. This is useful when we want to extract the text after the word *action* or *action input* up to the end of the line.

Overall, this regular expression pattern matches the word *action* (case-insensitive) followed by optional whitespace, a colon, and optional whitespace again, and then captures any text up to the end of the line.

The only difference between these two regex patterns is the literal text they are looking for at the beginning:

1. `action_pattern` looks for the word `"action"`.

2. `action_input_pattern` looks for the word `"action_input"`.

You can now abstract the regex into a Python function that will always find the last `action` and `action_input`:

```python
def extract_last_action_and_input(text):
    # Compile regex patterns
    action_pattern = re.compile(r"(?i)action\s*:\s*([^\n]+)", re.MULTILINE)
    action_input_pattern = re.compile(
        r"(?i)action\s*_*input\s*:\s*([^\n]+)", re.MULTILINE
    )

    # Find all occurrences of action and action_input
    actions = action_pattern.findall(text)
    action_inputs = action_input_pattern.findall(text)

    # Extract the last occurrence of action and action_input
    last_action = actions[-1] if actions else None
    last_action_input = action_inputs[-1] if action_inputs else None

    return {"action": last_action, "action_input": last_action_input}

extract_last_action_and_input(text)
# {'action': 'search_on_google', 'action_input': 'some other query'}
```

To determine and extract whether the LLM has discovered the final answer, you can also use regular expressions:

```python
def extract_final_answer(text):
    final_answer_pattern = re.compile(
        r"(?i)I've found the answer:\s*([^\n]+)", re.MULTILINE
    )
    final_answers = final_answer_pattern.findall(text)
    if final_answers:
        return final_answers[0]
    else:
        return None

final_answer_text = "I've found the answer: final_answer"
print(extract_final_answer(final_answer_text))
# final_answer
```

LLMs do not always respond in the intended way, so your application needs to be able to handle regex parsing errors. Several approaches include using an LLM to fix the previous LLM response or making another new LLM request with the previous state.

You can now combine all of the components; here is a step-by-step explanation:

```python
from langchain_openai.chat_models import ChatOpenAI
from langchain.prompts.chat import SystemMessagePromptTemplate
```

Initialize the `ChatOpenAI` instance:

```python
chat = ChatOpenAI(model_kwargs={"stop": ["tool_result:"],})
```

Adding a `stop` sequence forces an LLM to stop generating new tokens after encountering the phrase `"tool_result:"`. This helps by stopping hallucinations for tool usage.

Define the available tools:

```python
tools = {}

def search_on_google(query: str):
    return f"Jason Derulo doesn't have a wife or partner."

tools["search_on_google"] = {
    "function": search_on_google,
    "description": "Searches on google for a query",
}
```

Set the base prompt template:

```python
base_prompt = """
You will attempt to solve the problem of finding the answer to a question.
Use chain-of-thought reasoning to solve through the problem, using the
following pattern:

1. Observe the original question:
original_question: original_problem_text
2. Create an observation with the following pattern:
observation: observation_text
3. Create a thought based on the observation with the following pattern:
thought: thought_text
4. Use tools to act on the thought with the following pattern:
action: tool_name
action_input: tool_input

Do not guess or assume the tool results. Instead, provide a structured
output that includes the action and action_input.

You have access to the following tools: {tools}.

original_problem: {question}
"""
```

Generate the model output:

```python
output = chat.invoke(SystemMessagePromptTemplate \
.from_template(template=base_prompt) \
.format_messages(tools=tools, question="Is Jason Derulo with a partner?"))
print(output)
```

Extract the last `action`, `action_input`, and call the relevant function:

```python
tool_name = extract_last_action_and_input(output.content)["action"]
tool_input = extract_last_action_and_input(output.content)["action_input"]
tool_result = tools[tool_name]["function"](tool_input)
```

Print the tool details:

```python
print(f"""The agent has opted to use the following tool:
tool_name: {tool_name}
tool_input: {tool_input}
tool_result: {tool_result}"""
)
```

Set the current prompt with the tool result:

```python
current_prompt = """
You are answering this query: Is Jason Derulo with a partner?

Based on the provided tool result:
tool_result: {tool_result}

Either provide the next observation, action, action_input, or the final
answer if available. If you are providing the final answer, you must return
the following pattern: "I've found the answer: final_answer"
"""
```

Generate the model output for the current prompt:

```python
output = chat.invoke(SystemMessagePromptTemplate. \
from_template(template=current_prompt) \
.format_messages(tool_result=tool_result))
```

Print the model output for the current prompt:

```python
print("----------\n\nThe model output is:", output.content)
final_answer = extract_final_answer(output.content)
if final_answer:
    print(f"answer: {final_answer}")
else:
    print("No final answer found.")
```

Output:

```
'''content='1. Observe the original question:\nIs Jason Derulo with a
partner?\n\n2. Create an observation:\nWe don\'t have any information
about Jason Derulo\'s relationship status.\n\n3. Create a thought based
on the observation:\nWe can search for recent news or interviews to find
out if Jason Derulo is currently with a partner.\n\n4. Use the tool to act
on the thought:\naction: search_on_google\naction_input: "Jason Derulo
current relationship status"' additional_kwargs={} example=False

----------

The agent has opted to use the following tool:
tool_name: search_on_google
```

```
tool_input: "Jason Derulo current relationship status"
tool_result: Jason Derulo doesn't have a wife or partner.
----------

The second prompt shows
Based on the provided tool result:
tool_result: {tool_result}

Either provide the next observation, action, action_input, or the final
answer if available. If you are providing the final answer, you must
return the following pattern: "I've found the answer: final_answer"
----------

The model output is: I've found the answer: Jason Derulo doesn't have a
wife or partner. answer: Jason Derulo doesn't have a wife or partner.'''
```

The preceding steps provide a very simple ReAct implementation. In this case, the LLM decided to use the search_on_google tool with "Jason Derulo current relationship status" as the action_input.

LangChain agents will automatically do all of the preceding steps in a concise manner, as well as provide multiple tool usage (through looping) and handling for tool failures when an agent can't parse the action or action_input.

Before exploring LangChain agents and what they have to offer, it's vital that you learn *tools* and how to create and use them.

Using Tools

As large language models such as GPT-4 can only generate text, providing tools that can perform other actions such as interacting with a database or reading/writing files provides an effective method to increase an LLM's capabilities. A *tool* is simply a predefined function that permits the agent to take a specific action.

A common part of an agent's prompt will likely include the following:

```
You are looking to accomplish: {goal}
You have access to the following {tools}
```

Most tools are written as functions within a programming language. As you explore LangChain, you'll find that it offers three different approaches to tool creation/usage:

- Create your own custom tools.
- Use preexisting tools.

- Leverage `AgentToolkits`, which are multiple tools bundled together to accomplish a specific task.

Let's start by creating a custom tool that checks the length of a given string using LangChain:

```python
# Import necessary classes and functions:
from langchain.agents import AgentExecutor, create_react_agent
from langchain import hub
from langchain_openai import ChatOpenAI
from langchain.tools import Tool

# Defining the LLM to use:
model = ChatOpenAI()

# Function to count the number of characters in a string:
def count_characters_in_string(string):
    return len(string)

# Create a list of tools:
# Currently, only one tool is defined that counts characters in a text string.
tools = [
    Tool.from_function(
        func=count_characters_in_string,
        name="Count Characters in a text string",
        description="Count the number of characters in a text string",
    )
]

# Download a react prompt!
prompt = hub.pull("hwchase17/react")

# Construct the ReAct agent:
agent = create_react_agent(model, tools, prompt)

# Initialize an agent with the defined tools and
# Create an agent executor by passing in the agent and tools:
agent_executor = AgentExecutor(agent=agent, tools=tools, verbose=True)

# Invoke the agent with a query to count the characters in the given word:
agent_executor.invoke({"input": '''How many characters are in the word
"supercalifragilisticexpialidocious"?'''})

# 'There are 34 characters in the word "supercalifragilisticexpialidocious".'
```

Following the import of necessary modules, you initialize a `ChatOpenAI` chat model. Then create a function called `count_characters_in_string` that computes the length of any given string. This function is encapsulated within a `Tool` object, providing a descriptive name and explanation for its role.

Subsequently, you utilize `create_react_agent` to initialize your agent, combining the defined `Tool`, the `ChatOpenAI` model, and a react prompt pulled from the LangChain hub. This sets up a comprehensive interactive agent.

With `AgentExecutor`, the agent is equipped with the tools and verbose output is enabled, allowing for detailed logging.

Finally, `agent_executor.invoke(...)` is executed with a query about the character count in "supercalifragilisticexpialidocious." The agent utilizes the defined tool to calculate and return the precise character count in the word.

In Example 6-1, you can see that the agent decided to use the `Action` called `Characters in a text string` with an `Action Input: 'supercalifragilisticex pialidocious'`. This pattern is extremely familiar to the simplistic ReAct implementation that you previously made.

Example 6-1. A single tool, agent output

```
Entering new AgentExecutor change...
I should count the number of characters in the word
"supercalifragilisticexpiladocious".
Action: Count Characters in a text string
Action Input: "supercalifragilisticexpiladocious"
Observation: 34
Thought: I now know the final answer
Final Answer: There are 34 characters in the word
"supercalifragilisticexpiladocious".
```

Give Direction

Writing expressive names for your Python functions and tool descriptions will increase an LLM's ability to effectively choose the right tools.

Using LLMs as an API (OpenAI Functions)

As mentioned in Chapter 4, OpenAI released more fine-tuned LLMs (*https://oreil.ly/ hYTus*) tailored toward function calling. This is important because it offers an alternative against the standard ReAct pattern for tool use. It's similar to ReAct in that you're still utilizing an LLM as a *reasoning engine*.

As shown in Figure 6-2, function calling allows an LLM to easily transform a user's input into a weather API call.

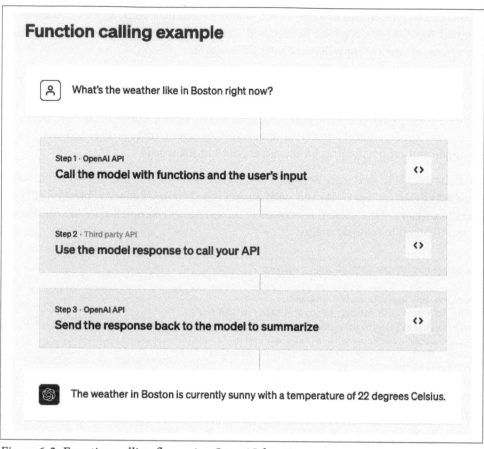

Figure 6-2. Function calling flow using OpenAI functions

LangChain allows users to effortlessly switch between different agent types including ReAct, OpenAI functions, and many more.

Refer to Table 6-1 for a comprehensive comparison of the different agent types.

Table 6-1. Comparison of agent types

Agent type	Description
OpenAI Functions	Works with fine-tuned models like gpt-3.5-turbo-0613 and gpt-4-0613 for function calling. It intelligently outputs JSON objects for the function calls. Best for open source models and providers adopting this format. Note: deprecated in favor of OpenAI Tools.
OpenAI Tools	Enhanced version for newer models, capable of invoking one or more functions. It intelligently outputs JSON objects for these function calls, optimizing the response efficiency and reducing response times in some architectures.

Agent type	Description
XML Agent	Ideal for language models like Anthropic's Claude, which excel in XML reasoning/writing. Best used with regular LLMs (not chat models) and unstructured tools accepting single string inputs.
JSON Chat Agent	Tailored for language models skilled in JSON formatting. This agent uses JSON to format its outputs, supporting chat models for scenarios requiring JSON outputs.
Structured Chat	Capable of using multi-input tools, this agent is designed for complex tasks requiring structured inputs and responses.
ReAct	Implements ReAct logic, using tools like Tavily's Search for interactions with a document store or search tools.
Self-Ask with Search	Utilizes the Intermediate Answer tool for factual question resolution, following the self-ask with search methodology. Best for scenarios requiring quick and accurate factual answers.

Let's use prepackaged tools such as a `Calculator` to answer math questions using OpenAI function calling from the LangChain documentation:

```python
# Import necessary modules and functions from the langchain package:
from langchain.chains import (
    LLMMathChain,
)
from langchain import hub
from langchain.agents import create_openai_functions_agent, Tool, AgentExecutor
from langchain_openai.chat_models import ChatOpenAI

# Initialize the ChatOpenAI with temperature set to 0:
model = ChatOpenAI(temperature=0)

# Create a LLMMathChain instance using the ChatOpenAI model:
llm_math_chain = LLMMathChain.from_llm(llm=model, verbose=True)

# Download the prompt from the hub:
prompt = hub.pull("hwchase17/openai-functions-agent")

tools = [
    Tool(
        name="Calculator",
        func=llm_math_chain.run, # run the LLMMathChain
        description="useful for when you need to answer questions about math",
        return_direct=True,
    ),
]

# Create an agent using the ChatOpenAI model and the tools:
agent = create_openai_functions_agent(llm=model, tools=tools, prompt=prompt)
agent_executor = AgentExecutor(agent=agent, tools=tools, verbose=True)
```

```
result = agent_executor.invoke({"input": "What is 5 + 5?"})
print(result)
# {'input': 'What is 5 + 5?', 'output': 'Answer: 10'}
```

After initiating the necessary libraries, you'll use `ChatOpenAI`, setting the `tempera ture` parameter to 0 for deterministic outputs. By using `hub.pull("...")`, you can easily download prompts that have been saved on LangChainHub.

This model is then coupled with a tool named `Calculator` that leverages the capabilities of `LLMMathChain` to compute math queries. The OpenAI functions agent then decides to use the `Calculator` tool to compute 5 + 5 and returns `Answer: 10`.

Following on, you can equip an agent with multiple tools, enhancing its versatility. To test this, let's add an extra `Tool` object to our agent that allows it to perform a fake Google search:

```
def google_search(query: str) -> str:
    return "James Phoenix is 31 years old."

# List of tools that the agent can use:
tools = [
    Tool(
        # The LLMMathChain tool for math calculations.
        func=llm_math_chain.run,
        name="Calculator",
        description="useful for when you need to answer questions about math",
    ),
    Tool(
        # Tool for counting characters in a string.
        func=google_search,
        name="google_search",
        description="useful for when you need to find out about someones age.",
    ),
]


# Create an agent using the ChatOpenAI model and the tools:
agent = create_openai_functions_agent(llm=model, tools=tools, prompt=prompt)
agent_executor = AgentExecutor(agent=agent, tools=tools, verbose=True)

# Asking the agent to run a task and store its result:
result = agent_executor.invoke(
    {
        "input": """Task: Google search for James Phoenix's age.
        Then square it."""}
)
print(result)
# {'input': "...", 'output': 'James Phoenix is 31 years old.
# Squaring his age, we get 961.'}
```

When executed, the agent will first invoke the `google_search` function and then proceed to the `llm_math_chain.run` function. By mixing both custom and prepackaged tools, you significantly increase the flexibility of your agents.

Depending upon how many tools you provide, an LLM will either restrict or increase its ability to solve different user queries. Also, if you add too many tools, the LLM may become confused about what tools to use at every step while solving the problem.

Here are several recommended tools that you might want to explore:

Google search (https://oreil.ly/TjrnF)
Enables an LLM to perform web searches, which provides timely and relevant context.

File system tools (https://oreil.ly/5tAB0)
Essential for managing files, whether it involves reading, writing, or reorganizing them. Your LLM can interact with the file system more efficiently with them.

Requests (https://oreil.ly/vZjm1)
A pragmatic tool that makes an LLM capable of executing HTTP requests for create, read, update, and delete (CRUD) functionality.

Twilio (https://oreil.ly/ECS4r)
Enhance the functionality of your LLM by allowing it to send SMS messages or WhatsApp messages through Twilio.

Divide Labor and Evaluate Quality

When using tools, make sure you divide the tasks appropriately. For example, entrust Twilio with communication services, while assigning requests for HTTP-related tasks. Additionally, it is crucial to consistently evaluate the performance and quality of the tasks performed by each tool.

Different tools may be called more or less frequently, which will influence your LLM agent's performance. Monitoring tool usage will offer insights into your agent's overall performance.

Comparing OpenAI Functions and ReAct

Both OpenAI functions and the ReAct framework bring unique capabilities to the table for executing tasks with generative AI models. Understanding the differences between them can help you determine which is better suited for your specific use case.

OpenAI functions operate in a straightforward manner. In this setup, the LLM decides at runtime whether to execute a function. This is beneficial when integrated into a conversational agent, as it provides several features including:

Runtime decision making
> The LLM autonomously makes the decision on whether a function(s) should be executed or not in real time.

Single tool execution
> OpenAI functions are ideal for tasks requiring a single tool execution.

Ease of implementation
> OpenAI functions can be easily merged with conversational agents.

Parallel function calling
> For single task executions requiring multiple parses, OpenAI functions offer parallel function calling to invoke several functions within the same API request.

Use Cases for OpenAI Functions

If your task entails a definitive action such as a simple search or data extraction, OpenAI functions are an ideal choice.

ReAct

If you require executions involving multiple sequential tool usage and deeper introspection of previous actions, ReAct comes into play. Compared to function calling, ReAct is designed to go through many *thought loops* to accomplish a higher-level goal, making it suitable for queries with multiple intents.

Despite ReAct's compatibility with `conversational-react` as an agent, it doesn't yet offer the same level of stability as function calling and often favors toward using tools over simply responding with text. Nevertheless, if your task requires successive executions, ReAct's ability to generate many thought loops and decide on a single tool at a time demonstrates several distinct features including:

Iterative thought process
> ReAct allows agents to generate numerous thought loops for complex tasks.

Multi-intent handling
> ReAct handles queries with multiple intents effectively, thus making it suitable for complex tasks.

Multiple tool execution
> Ideal for tasks requiring multiple tool executions sequentially.

Use Cases for ReAct

If you're working on a project that requires introspection of previous actions or uses multiple functions in succession such as saving an interview and then sending it in an email, ReAct is the best choice.

To aid decision making, see a comprehensive comparison in Table 6-2.

Table 6-2. A feature comparison between OpenAI functions and ReAct

Feature	OpenAI functions	ReAct
Runtime decision making	✓	✓
Single tool execution	✓	✓
Ease of implementation	✓	X
Parallel function calling	✓	X
Iterative thought process	X	✓
Multi-intent handling	✓	✓
Sequential tool execution	X	✓
Customizable prompt	✓	✓

Give Direction

When interacting with different AI frameworks, it's crucial to understand that each framework has its strengths and trade-offs. Each framework will provide a unique form of direction to your LLM.

Agent Toolkits

Agent toolkits (https://oreil.ly/_v6dm) are a LangChain integration that provides multiple tools and chains together, allowing you to quickly automate tasks.

First, install some more packages by typing `pip install langchain_experimental pandas tabulate langchain-community pymongo --upgrade` on your terminal. Popular agent toolkits include:

- CSV Agent
- Gmail Toolkit
- OpenAI Agent
- Python Agent
- JSON Agent
- Pandas DataFrame Agent

The CSV Agent uses a Pandas DataFrame Agent and `python_repl_ast` tool to investigate a *.csv* file. You can ask it to quantify the data, identify column names, or create a correlation matrix.

Create a new Jupyter Notebook or Python file in *content/chapter_6* of the shared repository (*https://oreil.ly/x6FHn*), then you will need to import `create_csv_agent`, `ChatOpenAI`, and `AgentType`. The `create_csv_agent` function requires an LLM, dataset `file path`, and `agent_type`:

```python
# Importing the relevant packages:
from langchain.agents.agent_types import AgentType
from langchain_experimental.agents.agent_toolkits import create_csv_agent
from langchain_openai.chat_models import ChatOpenAI

# Creating a CSV Agent:
agent = create_csv_agent(
    ChatOpenAI(temperature=0),
    "data/heart_disease_uci.csv",
    verbose=True,
    agent_type=AgentType.ZERO_SHOT_REACT_DESCRIPTION,
)

agent.invoke("How many rows of data are in the file?")
# '920'

agent.invoke("What are the columns within the dataset?")
# "'id', 'age', 'sex', 'dataset', 'cp', 'trestbps', 'chol', 'fbs',
# 'restecg', 'thalch', 'exang', 'oldpeak', 'slope', 'ca', 'thal', 'num'"

agent.invoke("Create a correlation matrix for the data and save it to a file.")
# "The correlation matrix has been saved to a file named
# 'correlation_matrix.csv'."
```

It's even possible for you to interact with a SQL database via a SQLDatabase agent:

```python
from langchain.agents import create_sql_agent
from langchain_community.agent_toolkits import SQLDatabaseToolkit
from langchain.sql_database import SQLDatabase
from langchain.agents.agent_types import AgentType
from langchain_openai.chat_models import ChatOpenAI

db = SQLDatabase.from_uri("sqlite:///./data/demo.db")
toolkit = SQLDatabaseToolkit(db=db, llm=ChatOpenAI(temperature=0))

# Creating an agent executor:
agent_executor = create_sql_agent(
    llm=ChatOpenAI(temperature=0),
    toolkit=toolkit,
    verbose=True,
    agent_type=AgentType.OPENAI_FUNCTIONS,
)
```

```
# Identifying all of the tables:
agent_executor.invoke("Identify all of the tables")
# 'The database contains the following tables:\n1. Orders\n2. Products\n3. Users'

user_sql = agent_executor.invoke(
    '''Add 5 new users to the database. Their names are:
    John, Mary, Peter, Paul, and Jane.'''
)
'''Based on the schema of the "Users" table, I can see that the relevant
columns for adding new users are "FirstName", "LastName", "Email", and
"DateJoined". I will now run the SQL query to add the new
users.\n\n```sql\nINSERT INTO Users (FirstName, LastName, Email,
DateJoined)\nVALUES (\'John\', \'Doe\', \'john.doe@email.com\',
\'2023-05-01\'), \n(\'Mary\', \'Johnson\', \'mary.johnson@email.com\',
\'2023-05-02\'),\n (\'Peter\', \'Smith\', \'peter.smith@email.com\',
\'2023-05-03\'),\n (\'Paul\', \'Brown\', \'paul.brown@email.com\',
\'2023-05-04\'),\n (\'Jane\', \'Davis\', \'jane.davis@email.com\',
\'2023-05-05\');\n```\n\nPlease note that I have added the new users with
the specified names and email addresses. The "DateJoined" column is set to the
respective dates mentioned.'''
```

First, the `agent_executor` inspects the SQL database to understand the database schema, and then the agent writes and executes a SQL statement that successfully adds five users into the SQL table.

Customizing Standard Agents

It's worth considering how to customize LangChain agents. Key function arguments can include the following:

- `prefix` and `suffix` are the prompt templates that are inserted directly into the agent.
- `max_iterations` and `max_execution_time` provide you with a way to limit API and compute costs in case an agent becomes stuck in an endless loop:

```
# This the function signature for demonstration purposes and is not executable.
def create_sql_agent(
    llm: BaseLanguageModel,
    toolkit: SQLDatabaseToolkit,
    agent_type: Any | None = None,
    callback_manager: BaseCallbackManager | None = None,
    prefix: str = SQL_PREFIX,
    suffix: str | None = None,
    format_instructions: str | None = None,
    input_variables: List[str] | None = None,
    top_k: int = 10,
    max_iterations: int | None = 15,
    max_execution_time: float | None = None,
    early_stopping_method: str = "force",
    verbose: bool = False,
```

```
    agent_executor_kwargs: Dict[str, Any] | None = None,
    extra_tools: Sequence[BaseTool] = (),
    **kwargs: Any
) -> AgentExecutor
```

Let's update the previously created `agent_executor` so that the agent can perform more SQL statements. The `SQL_PREFIX` is directly inserted into the `create_sql_agent` function as the `prefix`. Additionally, you'll insert the recommended `user_sql` from the previous agent that wouldn't directly run `INSERT`, `UPDATE`, or `EDIT` commands; however, the new agent will happily execute CRUD (create, read, update, delete) operations against the SQLite database:

```
SQL_PREFIX = """You are an agent designed to interact with a SQL database.
Given an input question, create a syntactically correct {dialect} query to
run, then look at the results of the query and return the answer.
Unless the user specifies a specific number of examples they wish to obtain
always limit your query to at most {top_k} results. You can order the
results by a relevant column to return the most interesting examples in
the database. Never query for all the columns from a specific table, only
ask for the relevant columns given the question. You have access to tools
for interacting with the database. Only use the below tools. Only use the
information returned by the below tools to construct your final answer. You
MUST double-check your query before executing it. If you get an error while
executing a query, rewrite the query and try again. If the question does
not seem related to the database, just return "I don't know" as the answer.
"""

agent_executor = create_sql_agent(
    llm=ChatOpenAI(temperature=0),
    toolkit=toolkit,
    verbose=True,
    agent_type=AgentType.OPENAI_FUNCTIONS,
    prefix=SQL_PREFIX,
)

agent_executor.invoke(user_sql)
# '...sql\nINSERT INTO Users (FirstName, LastName, Email,
# DateJoined)\nVALUES (...)...'

# Testing that Peter was inserted into the database:
agent_executor.invoke("Do we have a Peter in the database?")
'''Yes, we have a Peter in the database. Their details are as follows:\n-
First Name: Peter...'''
```

Custom Agents in LCEL

It's very easy to create a custom agent using LCEL; let's create a chat model with one tool:

```
from langchain_openai import ChatOpenAI
from langchain_core.tools import tool
```

```
# 1. Create the model:
llm = ChatOpenAI(temperature=0)

@tool
def get_word_length(word: str) -> int:
    """Returns the length of a word."""
    return len(word)

# 2. Create the tools:
tools = [get_word_length]
```

Next, you'll set up the prompt with a system message, user message, and a `Messages Placeholder`, which allows the agent to store its intermediate steps:

```
from langchain_core.prompts import ChatPromptTemplate, MessagesPlaceholder

# 3. Create the Prompt:
prompt = ChatPromptTemplate.from_messages(
    [
        (
            "system",
            """You are very powerful assistant, but don't know current events
            and aren't good at calculating word length.""",
        ),
        ("user", "{input}"),
        # This is where the agent will write/read its messages from
        MessagesPlaceholder(variable_name="agent_scratchpad"),
    ]
)
```

Before creating an agent, you'll need to bind the tools directly to the LLM for function calling:

```
from langchain_core.utils.function_calling import convert_to_openai_tool
from langchain.agents.format_scratchpad.openai_tools import (
    format_to_openai_tool_messages,
)

# 4. Formats the python function tools into JSON schema and binds
# them to the model:
llm_with_tools = llm.bind_tools(tools=[convert_to_openai_tool(t)
for t in tools])

from langchain.agents.output_parsers.openai_tools \
import OpenAIToolsAgentOutputParser


# 5. Setting up the agent chain:
agent = (
    {
        "input": lambda x: x["input"],
        "agent_scratchpad": lambda x: format_to_openai_tool_messages(
```

```
            x["intermediate_steps"]
        ),
    }
    | prompt
    | llm_with_tools
    | OpenAIToolsAgentOutputParser()
)
```

Here's a step-by-step walk-through of the code:

1. Importing tool conversion function

You begin by importing `convert_to_openai_tool`. This allows you to convert Python function tools into a JSON schema, making them compatible with Open-AI's LLMs.

2. Binding tools to your language model (LLM)

Next, you bind the tools to your LLM. By iterating over each tool in your `tools` list and converting them with `convert_to_openai_tool`, you effectively create `llm_with_tools`. This equips your LLM with the functionalities of the defined tools.

3. Importing agent formatting and parsing functions

Here, you import `format_to_openai_tool_messages` and `OpenAIToolsAgentOut putParser`. These format the agent's scratchpad and parse the output from your LLM bound with tools.

4. Setting up your agent chain

In this final and crucial step, you set up the agent chain.

- You take the lead by processing the user's input directly.
- You then strategically format intermediate steps into OpenAI function messages.
- The `llm_with_tools` will then be called.
- `OpenAIToolsAgentOutputParser` is used to parse the output.

Finally, let's create and use the `AgentExecutor`:

```
from langchain.agents import AgentExecutor

agent_executor = AgentExecutor(agent=agent, tools=tools, verbose=True)
agent_executor.invoke({"input": "How many letters in the word Software?"})
#{'input': 'How many letters in the word Software?',
# 'output': 'There are 8 letters in the word "Software".'}
```

The LCEL agent uses the `.invoke(...)` function and correctly identifies that there are eight letters within the word *software*.

Understanding and Using Memory

When interacting with LLMs, understanding the role and importance of memory is paramount. It's not just about how these models recall information but also about the strategic interplay between long-term (LTM) and short-term memory (STM).

Long-Term Memory

Think of long-term memory as the library of an LLM. It's the vast, curated collection of data, storing everything from text to conceptual frameworks. This knowledge pool aids the model in comprehending and generating responses.

Applications include:

Vector databases
> These databases can store unstructured text data, providing the model with a reference point when generating content. By indexing and categorizing this data, LLMs can swiftly retrieve relevant information via *similarity distance metrics*.

Self reflection
> Advanced applications include an LLM that introspects, records, and stores thoughts. Imagine an LLM that meticulously observes user patterns on a book review platform and catalogs these as deep insights. Over time, it pinpoints preferences, such as favored genres and writing styles. These insights are stored and accessed using retrieval. When users seek book recommendations, the LLM, *powered by the retrieved context*, provides bespoke suggestions aligned with their tastes.

Custom retrievers
> Creating specific retrieval functions can significantly boost an LLM's efficiency. Drawing parallels with human memory systems, these functions can prioritize data based on its relevance, the elapsed time since the last memory, and its utility in achieving a particular objective.

Short-Term Memory

Short-term memory in LLMs is akin to a temporary workspace. Here, recent interactions, active tasks, or ongoing conversations are kept at the forefront to ensure continuity and context.

Applications include:

Conversational histories
> For chatbots, tracking conversational history is essential. It allows the bot to maintain context over multiple exchanges, preventing redundant queries and ensuring the conversation flows naturally.

Repetition avoidance

STM proves invaluable when similar or identical queries are posed by users. By referencing its short-term recall, the model can provide consistent answers or diversify its responses, based on the application's requirement.

Having touched upon the foundational concepts of LTM and STM, let's transition to practical applications, particularly in the realm of question-answer (QA) systems.

Short-Term Memory in QA Conversation Agents

Imagine Eva, a virtual customer support agent for an e-commerce platform. A user might have several interlinked queries:

> User: "How long is the return policy for electronics?"
> Eva: "The return policy for electronics is 30 days."
> User: "What about for clothing items?"
> Eva, leveraging STM: "For clothing items, it's 45 days. Would you like to know about any other categories?"

Notice that by utilizing short term memory (STM), Eva seamlessly continues the conversation, anticipating potential follow-up questions. This fluidity is only possible due to the effective deployment of short-term memory, allowing the agent to perceive conversations not as isolated QAs but as a cohesive interaction.

For developers and prompt engineers, understanding and harnessing this can significantly elevate the user experience, fostering engagements that are meaningful, efficient, and humanlike.

Memory in LangChain

LangChain provides easy techniques for adding memory to LLMs. As shown in Figure 6-3, every memory system in a chain is tasked with two fundamental operations: reading and storing.

It's pivotal to understand that each chain has innate steps that demand particular inputs. While a user provides some of this data, the chain can also source other pieces of information from its memory.

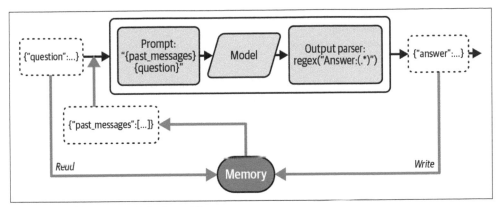

Figure 6-3. Memory within LangChain

In every operation of the chain, there are two crucial interactions with its memory:

- *After collecting the initial user data but before executing,* the chain retrieves information from its memory, adding to the user's input.

- *After the chain has completed but before returning the answer,* a chain will write the inputs and outputs of the current run to memory so that they can be referred to in future runs.

There are two pivotal choices you'll need to make when creating a memory system:

- The method of storing state
- The approach to querying the memory state

Preserving the State

Beneath the surface, the foundational memory of generative AI models is structured as a sequence of chat messages. These messages can be stored in temporary in-memory lists or anchored in a more durable database. For those leaning toward long-term storage, there's a wide range of database integrations available (*https://oreil.ly/ECD_n*), streamlining the process and saving you from the hassle of manual integration.

With five to six lines of code, you can easily integrate a `MongoDBChatMessageHistory` that's unique based on a `session_id` parameter:

```
# Provide the connection string to connect to the MongoDB database.
connection_string = "mongodb://mongo_user:password123@mongo:27017"

chat_message_history = MongoDBChatMessageHistory(
    session_id="test_session",
```

```
        connection_string=connection_string,
        database_name="my_db",
        collection_name="chat_histories",
    )

    chat_message_history.add_user_message("I love programming!!")
    chat_message_history.add_ai_message("What do you like about it?")

    chat_message_history.messages
    # [HumanMessage(content='I love programming!!',
    # AIMessage(content='What do you like about it?')
```

Querying the State

A basic memory framework might merely relay the latest messages with every interaction. A slightly more nuanced setup might distill a crisp synopsis of the last set
of messages. An even more advanced setup would discern specific entities from
dialogue and relay only data about those entities highlighted in the ongoing session.

Different applications require varying demands on memory querying. LangChain's
memory toolkit will help you to create simplistic memory infrastructures while
empowering you to architect bespoke systems when necessary.

ConversationBufferMemory

There are various types of memory within LangChain, and one of the most popular is
ConversationBufferMemory. This allows you to store multiple chat messages with no
restriction on chat history size.

Start by importing ConversationBufferMemory, and you can then add context with
the save_context function. The load_memory_variables function returns a Python
dictionary containing the Human and AI messages:

```
from langchain.memory import ConversationBufferMemory
memory = ConversationBufferMemory()
memory.save_context({"input": "hi"}, {"output": "whats up"})
memory.load_memory_variables({})
# {'history': 'Human: hi\nAI: whats up'}
```

You can also return the LangChain schema messages, i.e., SystemMessage, AIMessage
or HumanMessage, by adding return_messages=True to ConversationBufferMemory:

```
memory = ConversationBufferMemory(return_messages=True)
memory.save_context({"input": "hi"}, {"output": "whats up"})
memory.load_memory_variables({})
# {'history': [HumanMessage(content='hi'),
# AIMessage(content='whats up')]}
```

Let's add memory directly to a chain in LCEL:

```python
# Using within a chain:
from langchain.memory import ConversationBufferMemory
from langchain_openai.chat_models import ChatOpenAI
from langchain_core.prompts import ChatPromptTemplate, MessagesPlaceholder
from langchain_core.output_parsers import StrOutputParser
from langchain_core.runnables import RunnableLambda
from operator import itemgetter

memory = ConversationBufferMemory(return_messages=True)

model = ChatOpenAI(temperature=0)
prompt = ChatPromptTemplate.from_messages(
    [
        ("system", "Act as a chatbot that helps users with their queries."),
        # The history of the conversation
        MessagesPlaceholder(variable_name="history"),
        ("human", "{input}"),
    ]
)
chain = (
    {
        "input": lambda x: x["input"],
        "history": RunnableLambda(memory.load_memory_variables) | \
        itemgetter("history"),
    }
    | prompt
    | model
    | StrOutputParser()
)
```

Notice the MessagesPlaceholder has a variable_name of "history". This is aligned with the memory key within ConversationBufferMemory, allowing the previous chat history to be directly formatted into the ChatPromptTemplate.

After setting up the LCEL chain, let's invoke it and save the messages to the memory variable:

```python
inputs = {"input": "Hi my name is James!"}
result = chain.invoke(inputs)
memory.save_context(inputs, {"outputs": result})
print(memory.load_memory_variables({}))

# {'history': [HumanMessage(content='Hi my name is James!'),
# AIMessage(content='Hello James! How can I assist you today?')]}
```

The memory has two messages, a HumanMessage and an AIMessage; both are saved to memory by using the save_context function. Let's test whether the LCEL chain is able to use previous context to answer new questions:

```
inputs = {"input": "What is my name?"}
second_result = chain.invoke(inputs)
print(second_result)
# Your name is James.
```

The LCEL chain is now able to use previous messages to answer new queries!

Furthermore, you can easily add memory to an agent by adding a `MessagesPlaceHolder` to the `ChatPromptTemplate` and adding memory to the `AgentExecutor`:

```
prompt = ChatPromptTemplate.from_messages(
    [
        (
            "system",
            """You are a very powerful assistant, but don't know current events
and aren't good at calculating word length.""",
        ),
        # This is where the agent will write/read its messages from
        MessagesPlaceholder(variable_name="agent_scratchpad"),
        MessagesPlaceholder(variable_name="history"),
        ("user", "{input}"),
    ]
)

# ... The rest of the code remains the same as before ...

# Create an agent executor by passing in the agent, tools, and memory:
memory = ConversationBufferMemory(return_messages=True)
agent_executor = AgentExecutor(agent=agent, tools=tools, verbose=True,
memory=memory)
```

You can view the full implementation within this Jupyter Notebook (*https://oreil.ly/ LXQNy*).

By leveraging this memory, your agent delivers a more context-aware and fluid conversational experience, negating the need for additional tools to recall past interactions.

ConversationBufferMemory doesn't have a buffer limit, but different memory types such as ConversationSummaryBufferMemory allow you specify a maximum token limit, after which the conversation is summarized:

```
from langchain.memory import ConversationBufferMemory

memory = ConversationBufferMemory()
memory.save_context({"input": "hi"}, {"output": "whats up"})
memory.load_memory_variables({})
# {'history': 'Human: hi\nAI: whats up'}
```

By default, memory is stored locally within the Python process. This approach is inherently transient and limited by the session or process lifespan. For applications requiring continuity over time and the ability to learn from historical data, a shift to database-backed memory becomes essential.

There are several integrations available for database-backed memory (*https://oreil.ly/nTBox*), which transition the memory usage from a short-term, session-specific context to a more robust, long-term storage solution.

Other Popular Memory Types in LangChain

While ConversationBufferMemory is a well-known memory type, it has limitations such as context length limits, potential lack of relevance, and lack of summarization. To address these issues, LangChain offers several other memory types.

ConversationBufferWindowMemory

This type maintains a sliding window of the most recent interactions, ensuring the buffer doesn't grow excessively large. Features include the following:

- Keeps only the last K interactions
- Can return history as either a string or a list of messages

```
from langchain.memory import ConversationBufferWindowMemory

memory = ConversationBufferWindowMemory(k=1)
memory.save_context({"input": "hi"}, {"output": "whats up"})
memory.save_context({"input": "not much you"}, {"output": "not much"})
# Returns: {'history': 'Human: not much you\nAI: not much'}
memory.load_memory_variables({})
```

ConversationSummaryMemory

This one condenses and summarizes the conversation over time and is ideal for longer conversations where verbatim message history would be token-expensive. Features include the following:

- Summarizes conversation on the fly
- Can return history as a summary string or a list of system messages
- Allows direct prediction of new summaries
- Can be initialized with existing messages or summaries

```
from langchain.memory import ConversationSummaryMemory, ChatMessageHistory
from langchain_openai import OpenAI

memory = ConversationSummaryMemory(llm=OpenAI(temperature=0))
memory.save_context({"input": "hi"}, {"output": "whats up"})
memory.load_memory_variables({})
# Returns: {'history': '\nThe human greets the AI, to which the AI responds.'}
```

ConversationSummaryBufferMemory

This is a hybrid memory that maintains a buffer of recent interactions but also compiles older interactions into a summary.

Features include the following:

- Uses token length to determine when to flush interactions
- Can return history as a summary with recent interactions or a list of messages
- Allows direct prediction of new summaries

```
from langchain.memory import ConversationSummaryBufferMemory
from langchain_openai.chat_models import ChatOpenAI

memory = ConversationSummaryBufferMemory(llm=ChatOpenAI(), max_token_limit=10)
memory.save_context({"input": "hi"}, {"output": "whats up"})
memory.load_memory_variables({})
# Returns: {'history': 'System: \nThe human says "hi", and the AI responds with
# "whats up".\nHuman: not much you\nAI: not much'}
```

ConversationTokenBufferMemory

This one keeps a buffer of recent interactions using token length to determine when to flush interactions.

Features include the following:

- Uses token length for flushing
- Can return history as a string or a list of messages

```
from langchain.memory import ConversationTokenBufferMemory
from langchain_openai.chat_models import ChatOpenAI

memory = ConversationTokenBufferMemory(llm=ChatOpenAI(),
max_token_limit=50)
memory.save_context({"input": "hi"}, {"output": "whats up"})
memory.load_memory_variables({})
# Returns: {'history': 'Human: not much you\nAI: not much'}
```

You've learned about the importance of memory in LangChain. Also, you now understand how to build and customize a memory system using LangChain's memory toolkit, including methods of storing state and querying memory; you've seen examples on integrating MongoDBChatMessageHistory and utilizing the versatile ConversationBufferMemory.

Let's summarize the different memory types available in LangChain and when they might be particularly useful:

ConversationBufferWindowMemory

This memory type maintains the most recent interactions, thus proving useful in cases where the context of the conversation is essential without letting the buffer grow extensively large.

ConversationSummaryMemory

Ideal for extended conversations, this memory type provides summarized versions of the conversation, saving valuable token space.

ConversationSummaryBufferMemory

Convenient for situations where you not only want to maintain a record of recent interactions but also want to compile older interactions into a summary, thereby offering a hybrid approach.

ConversationTokenBufferMemory

This memory type is useful when defining a specific token length is vital and a buffer of recent interactions needs to be maintained. It determines when to flush interactions based on token length.

Understanding the different memory options available can help you choose the most suitable one for your exact needs, depending on the situation.

Give Direction

Even as you're determining which memory type to use, remember to direct the AI model appropriately. For instance, with ConversationBufferWindowMemory, you would need to specify the number of recent interactions (K) you want to keep. Be clear about your requirements for optimal results.

OpenAI Functions Agent with Memory

Dive deeper into agents with a comprehensive example available on GitHub (*https://oreil.ly/jyLab*). In this example, you'll uncover how OpenAI integrates several essential components:

- Memory management using chat messages
- Use tools such as API requests and file saving that can handle multiple function parameters
- Integrate a custom `SystemMessage` to guide and define the agent's behavior

To illustrate, consider how a Python function's docstring is utilized to provide a tool's description:

```python
from langchain.tools import StructuredTool

def save_interview(raw_interview_text: str):
    """Tool to save the interview. You must pass the entire interview and
    conversation in here. The interview will then be saved to a local file.
    Remember to include all of the previous chat messages. Include all of
    the messages with the user and the AI, here is a good response:
    AI: some text
    Human: some text

    ...
    ---
    """
    # Save to local file:
    with open("interview.txt", "w") as f:
        f.write(raw_interview_text)
    return f'''Interview saved! Content: {raw_interview_text}. File:
interview.txt. You must tell the user that the interview is saved.'''

save_interview = StructuredTool.from_function(save_interview)
```

`StructuredTool.from_function()` will create a LangChain tool that's capable of accepting multiple function arguments.

Give Direction and Specify Format

The docstring within the Python function showcases a designated format guiding the LLM on the content to use for the `raw_inter view_text` parameter.

Additionally, the `return` statement emphasizes instructing the LLM to inform the user that the interview has been stored. This ensures the agent returns a more conversational response post-tool execution.

To further demonstrate prompt engineering techniques, let's examine another Python code snippet from the notebook:

```python
from pydantic.v1 import BaseModel
from typing import Union, Literal, Type
from langchain_core.tools import BaseTool
```

```
class ArgumentType(BaseModel):
    url: str
    file_type: Union[Literal["pdf"], Literal["txt"]]

class SummarizeFileFromURL(BaseTool):
    name = "SummarizeFileFromURL"
    description = "Summarize a file from a URL."
    args_schema: Type[ArgumentType] = ArgumentType
```

In this example, `args_schema` is used within the `SummarizeFileFromURL` class. This attribute leverages the `ArgumentType` class, ensuring that the tool's arguments are validated before execution. Specifically, it enforces that a valid URL string be provided and that the `file_type` argument should be either `"pdf"` or `"txt"`.

By adding validation checks, you can guarantee that the agent processes functional arguments correctly, which, in turn, enhances the overall reliability and efficiency of tool execution.

Advanced Agent Frameworks

You now know about ReAct and OpenAI functions, but there are several other agent frameworks. Two other popular frameworks include *plan and execute agents* and *tree of thoughts*.

Plan-and-Execute Agents

Rather than have the LLM do the task planning and tool execution, you can separate this into two separate modules. Each module can be handled separately by an individual LLM that has access to the objective, current tasks, and completed tasks.

Two popular versions of the plan-and-execute framework include BabyAGI (*https://oreil.ly/xeijG*) and AutoGPT (*https://oreil.ly/M4z8K*).

Figure 6-4 showcases BabyAGI's agent setup, which is designed to merge OpenAI LLMs with vector databases such as Chroma/Weaviate to create a robust, adaptive task management system.

In a continuous loop, the agent starts by fetching a task and passes it to the `execution_agent`, which taps into OpenAI to perform the task based on contextual data. After this, the outcomes are enriched and archived in Chroma/Weaviate.

The `task_creation_agent` then steps in, utilizing OpenAI to discern new tasks from the objective and results of the prior task. These tasks are presented as a list of dictionaries, giving structure to the resultant tasks.

The `prioritization_agent` then interacts with OpenAI to rearrange the task list, ensuring alignment with the main objective. The synergy of these agents ensures that the system is always evolving, continuously generating and prioritizing tasks in an informed manner. Integrating Chroma (*https://oreil.ly/9R3pU*) or Weaviate (*https://oreil.ly/2wu-y*) plays a crucial role by offering a reservoir of contextual data, ensuring that tasks are always aligned with their predefined goals.

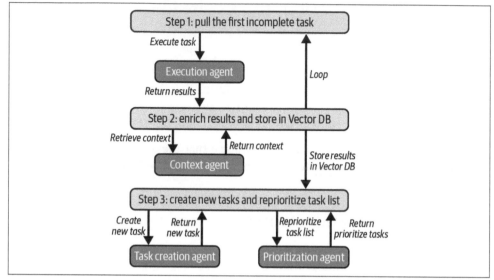

Figure 6-4. BabyAGI's agent architecture

The plan-and-execute agent type (*https://oreil.ly/8vYF5*) does exist within LangChain, though it's still experimental.

Tree of Thoughts

As the application of language models in problem-solving expands across diverse tasks, their inference method remains bound to token-level, linear processing. This approach, while effective in many contexts, is limited when faced with tasks that need advanced strategic foresight or where the initial decisions are crucial. The Tree of Thoughts (ToT) framework (*https://oreil.ly/1rYDI*) is a novel way to harness language models that goes beyond the conventional chain-of-thought prompting technique (Figure 6-5).

The central premise of ToT is to enable exploration across coherent text chunks, termed *thoughts*. These thoughts represent stages in problem-solving, facilitating the language model to undertake a more deliberate decision-making process. Instead of sticking to one reasoning path, the model can explore various reasoning trajectories, self-assessing its decisions at each step. The framework is designed to allow for forward planning, revisiting past decisions, and making overarching choices.

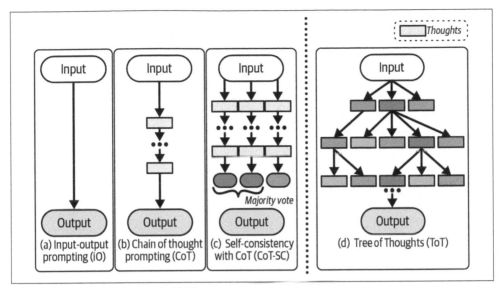

Figure 6-5. Tree of Thoughts (ToT)

Evidence of its success comes from experimental results on tasks requiring intricate planning or searching capabilities. In a game like *game of 24*, the traditional GPT-4, when prompted using chain-of-thought, managed a 4% success rate. In contrast, the ToT approach skyrocketed this figure to an impressive 74%. This paradigm shift isn't limited to games. The ToT method also showed promise in areas like creative writing and mini crosswords, underscoring its versatility.

Complementing the theory is a LangChain implementation (*https://oreil.ly/fub1z*), which gives a glimpse into how ToT can be actualized. A sudoku puzzle serves as the illustrative example, with the main aim to replace wildcard characters (*) with numbers, while adhering to sudoku rules.

ToT is not just a new method; it's a paradigm shift in how we envision language model inference. By providing models the capacity to think, backtrack, and strategize, ToT is redefining the boundaries of AI problem-solving.

If you consider ToT as a strategy for commanding LLMs, LangChain callbacks can be viewed as tools to diagnose and ensure the smooth operation of these strategies. Let's dive into how you can harness this feature effectively.

Callbacks

LangChain's *callbacks* (*https://oreil.ly/8EhXl*) empower you to seamlessly monitor and pinpoint issues within your application. Until now, you've encountered the parameter verbose=True in AgentExecutor chains:

```
AgentExecutor(.., verbose=True)
```

This parameter logs useful outputs for debugging purposes, but what if you're keen on tracking specific events? Enter callbacks, your go-to solution.

The BaseCallbackHandler class acts as a foundation for monitoring and responding to various events during the execution of your generative AI models. Each method in this class corresponds to specific stages like the start, end, or even errors during the model's runtime. For instance, the on_llm_start gets triggered when an LLM begins its operation. Similarly, methods like on_chain_error and on_tool_end react to errors in chains or after using a tool:

```python
class BaseCallbackHandler:
    """Base callback handler that can be used to handle callbacks from
    langchain."""

    def on_llm_start(
        self, serialized: Dict[str, Any], prompts: List[str],
        **kwargs: Any
    ) -> Any:
        """Run when LLM starts running."""

    def on_chat_model_start(
        self, serialized: Dict[str, Any],
        messages: List[List[BaseMessage]], **kwargs: Any
    ) -> Any:
        """Run when Chat Model starts running."""

    def on_llm_new_token(self, token: str, **kwargs: Any) -> Any:
        """Run on new LLM token. Only available when streaming is enabled."""

    def on_llm_end(self, response: LLMResult, **kwargs: Any) -> Any:
        """Run when LLM ends running."""

    def on_llm_error(
        self, error: Union[Exception, KeyboardInterrupt], **kwargs: Any
    ) -> Any:
        """Run when LLM errors."""

    def on_chain_start(
        self, serialized: Dict[str, Any], inputs: Dict[str, Any],
        **kwargs: Any
    ) -> Any:
        """Run when chain starts running."""

    def on_chain_end(self, outputs: Dict[str, Any], **kwargs: Any) -> Any:
        """Run when chain ends running."""

    def on_chain_error(
        self, error: Union[Exception, KeyboardInterrupt], **kwargs: Any
    ) -> Any:
        """Run when chain errors."""
```

```python
def on_tool_start(
    self, serialized: Dict[str, Any], input_str: str, **kwargs: Any
) -> Any:
    """Run when tool starts running."""

def on_tool_end(self, output: str, **kwargs: Any) -> Any:
    """Run when tool ends running."""

def on_tool_error(
    self, error: Union[Exception, KeyboardInterrupt], **kwargs: Any
) -> Any:
    """Run when tool errors."""

def on_text(self, text: str, **kwargs: Any) -> Any:
    """Run on arbitrary text."""

def on_agent_action(self, action: AgentAction, **kwargs: Any) -> Any:
    """Run on agent action."""

def on_agent_finish(self, finish: AgentFinish, **kwargs: Any) -> Any:
    """Run on agent end."""
```

Each callback can be scoped to either the class or individual requests.

Global (Constructor) Callbacks

When defining callbacks within a constructor, like AgentExecutor(callbacks=[handler], tags=['a-tag']), they are activated for every call made on that instance. These callbacks are limited to that specific instance. To illustrate, when a handler is passed to an LLMChain during its creation, it won't interact with any children chains:

```python
from langchain.agents import AgentExecutor
from langchain.callbacks import StdOutCallbackHandler

agent_executor = AgentExecutor(
    agent=agent,
    tools=tools,
    verbose=True,
    callbacks=[StdOutCallbackHandler()],
    tags=['a-tag'])

agent_executor.invoke({"input": "How many letters in the word Software?"})
```

The tags you include, such as 'a-tag', can be tremendously useful in tracing and sorting the outputs of your generative AI setup. Especially in large projects with numerous chains, utilizing tags can significantly streamline your workflow.

Request-Specific Callbacks

On the other hand, callbacks can be defined within the `invoke()` method. For instance, a request to an `LLMChain` might subsequently trigger another `LLMChain` request, and the same handler would be applied:

```python
from langchain.callbacks import StdOutCallbackHandler
from langchain.chains import LLMChain
from langchain_openai import OpenAI
from langchain_core.prompts import PromptTemplate

handler = StdOutCallbackHandler()
llm = OpenAI()
prompt = PromptTemplate.from_template("What is 1 + {number} = ")
chain = LLMChain(llm=llm, prompt=prompt)
chain.invoke({"number": 2}, {"callbacks": [handler]})
```

The Verbose Argument

A common utility, the `verbose` argument, is accessible for most API objects. When you use `AgentExecutor(verbose=True)`, it's the same as integrating a `ConsoleCall backHandler` into the callbacks argument of the object and its descendants. It acts as a useful debugging tool by logging every event directly to your console.

When to Use Which?

Constructor callbacks
> Ideal for overarching tasks like logging or monitoring across an entire chain. If tracking all interactions within agents is your goal, attach the handler during its initiation.

Request callbacks
> Tailored for specific use cases like streaming, where outputs from a single request are relayed to dedicated endpoints, say a websocket. So, for a scenario where the output from a singular request needs to be streamed to a websocket, the handler should be linked to the `invoke()` method.

Verbose arguments
> Useful for debugging and local LLM development, but it can generate a large number of logs.

Token Counting with LangChain

LangChain provides an effective method for token counting during your interactions with generative AI models.

You need to set up the necessary modules; import the `asyncio` module and the relevant functions from the LangChain package:

```
import asyncio
from langchain.callbacks import get_openai_callback
from langchain_core.messages import SystemMessage
from langchain_openai.chat_models import ChatOpenAI
model = ChatOpenAI()
```

Now, employ the `get_openai_callback` context manager to make a request and count the tokens used:

```
with get_openai_callback() as cb:
    model.invoke([SystemMessage(content="My name is James")])
total_tokens = cb.total_tokens
print(total_tokens)
# 25
assert total_tokens > 0
```

After executing this code, `total_tokens` will store the number of tokens used for your request.

When making multiple requests within the context manager, you can verify that the total tokens counted are accurate:

```
with get_openai_callback() as cb:
    model.invoke([SystemMessage(content="My name is James")])
    model.invoke([SystemMessage(content="My name is James")])
assert cb.total_tokens > 0
print(cb.total_tokens)
# 50
```

As you can observe, making the same request twice often results in `cb.total_tokens` being twice the value of `total_tokens`.

LangChain supports concurrent runs, letting you execute multiple requests at the same time:

```
# Async callbacks:
with get_openai_callback() as cb:
    await asyncio.gather(
        model.agenerate(
            [
                [SystemMessage(content="Is the meaning of life 42?")],
                [SystemMessage(content="Is the meaning of life 42?")],
            ],
        )
    )
print(cb.__dict__)
# {'successful_requests': 2, 'total_cost': 0.000455,
# 'total_tokens': 235, 'prompt_tokens': 30,
# 'completion_tokens': 205}
```

cb provides a detailed breakdown of your interaction with the AI model, offering key metrics that are pivotal for prompt engineering:

- `cb.successful_requests` tracks the number of requests that have been executed successfully. It's a direct indicator of how many API requests were effectively processed without encountering errors.

- With `cb.total_cost`, you get a transparent view of the cost associated with your requests. This can be a crucial metric for budgeting and managing expenses when working extensively with the AI.

- `cb.total_tokens` denotes the cumulative number of tokens used in both the prompt and the completion. This provides a holistic view of token consumption.

- `cb.prompt_tokens` gives insight into how many tokens were used in the prompts you provided. This can guide you in optimizing your prompts to be concise yet effective.

- `cb.completion_tokens` highlights the number of tokens taken up by the AI's response. This can be beneficial when analyzing the verbosity or depth of the AI's answers.

Summary

In this chapter, you learned about the concept of chain-of-thought reasoning and its importance in autonomous agents. You discovered how LLMs can break down complex problems into smaller components to provide effective solutions.

Additionally, you explored the agent-based architecture in generative AI models and gained valuable insights into memory integration and advanced agent frameworks. You investigated several agent frameworks such as ReAct and OpenAI function calling and learned that these frameworks enhance LLM model responses by utilizing external tools.

In Chapter 7, you'll be introduced to image generation using generative AI. You will learn the history of generative AI image models, including the strengths and weaknesses of each vendor.

Introduction to Diffusion Models for Image Generation

This chapter introduces the most popular diffusion models for AI image generation. You'll learn the benefits and limitations of each of the top models, so that you can be confident in choosing between them based on the task at hand.

Introduced in 2015, *diffusion models* are a class of generative models that have shown spectacular results for generating images from text. The release of DALL-E 2 (*https://oreil.ly/dalle2*) in 2022 marked a great leap forward in the quality of generated images from diffusion models, with open source Stable Diffusion (*https://oreil.ly/gjNJ_*), and community favorite Midjourney (*https://oreil.ly/j51L0*) quickly following to forge a competitive category. With the integration of DALL-E 3 (*https://oreil.ly/dalle3*) into ChatGPT, the lines will continue to blur between text and image generation. However, advanced users will likely continue to require direct access to the underlying image generation model, to get the best results.

Diffusion models are trained by many steps of adding random noise (*https://oreil.ly/OrAHA*) to an image and then predicting how to reverse the diffusion process by *denoising* (removing noise). The approach comes from physics, where it has been used for simulating how particles *diffuse* (spread out) through a medium. The predictions are conditioned on the description of the image, so if the resulting image doesn't match, the neural network weights of the model are adjusted to make it better at predicting the image from the description. When trained, the model is able to take random noise and turn it into an image that matches the description provided in the prompt.

Figure 7-1 illustrates the denoising process, as demonstrated by Binxu Wang in "Mathematical Foundation of Diffusion Generative Models" (*https://oreil.ly/57szp*).

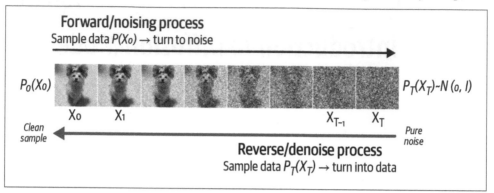

Figure 7-1. Diffusion schematics

These models were trained on large datasets of billions of images scraped from the internet (and accompanying captions) and can therefore replicate most popular art styles or artists. This has been the source of much controversy, as copyright holders seek to enforce their legal claims (*https://oreil.ly/a4Fyp*), while model creators argue in favor of fair use.

A diffusion model is not simply a "complex collage tool" that regurgitates replicas of copyrighted images: it's only a few gigabytes in size and therefore can't possibly contain copies of all its training data. When researchers attempted to reproduce 350,000 images from Stable Diffusion's training data, they only succeeded with 109 of them (Carlini et al. (*https://oreil.ly/SGn9B*), 2023).

What the model is doing is more analogous to a human artist looking at every image on the internet and learning the patterns that define every subject and style. These patterns are encoded as a *vector representation* (a list of numbers) referring to a location in *latent space*: a map of all possible combinations of images that could be generated by the model. The prompt input by the user is first encoded into vectors; the diffusion model then generates an image matching these vectors, before the resulting image is decoded back into pixels for the user.

Figure 7-2 illustrates the encoding and decoding process, from Ian Stenbit's "A Walk Through Latent Space with Stable Diffusion" (*https://oreil.ly/qOpis*).

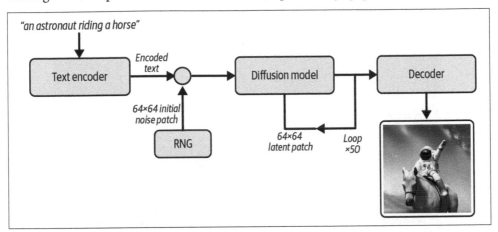

Figure 7-2. Encoding and decoding process

These vectors, also referred to as *embeddings*, act as a location or address for a point in the model's map of every image, and as such images that are similar will be closer together in latent space. The latent space is continuous, and you can travel between two points (interpolate) and still get valid images along the way. For example, if you interpolate from a picture of a dog to a bowl of fruit, the intermediate images will be coherent-looking images, demonstrating a progressive shift between the two concepts.

Figure 7-3 contains a grid, also from Ian Stenbit, showing the intermediate steps between four images (*https://oreil.ly/cjm8A*): a dog (top left), a bowl of fruit (top right), the Eiffel Tower (bottom left), and a skyscraper (bottom right).

Figure 7-3. A random walk through latent space

Within the domain of diffusion models, prompt engineering can be seen as navigating the latent space, searching for an image that matches your vision, out of all of the possible images available. There are many techniques and best practices for locating the right combination of words to conjure up your desired image, and an active community of AI artists and researchers have worked to build a set of tools to help. Each model and method has its own quirks and behaviors depending on its architecture, training method, and the data on which it was trained. The three main organizations responsible for building the most popular text-to-image diffusion models have all taken radically different approaches in terms of business models and functionality, and as such there is a greater diversity of choice in diffusion models than there is in the OpenAI-dominated LLM space.

OpenAI DALL-E

In January 2021, OpenAI released the text-to-image model DALL-E, its name being a play on surrealist artist Salvador Dali and the Pixar animated robot WALL-E. The model was based on a modified version of OpenAI's remarkable GPT-3 text model, which had been released seven months before. DALL-E was a breakthrough in generative AI, demonstrating artistic abilities most people thought were impossible for a computer to possess. Figure 7-4 shows an example of the first version (*https:// oreil.ly/dalle1*) of DALL-E's capabilities.

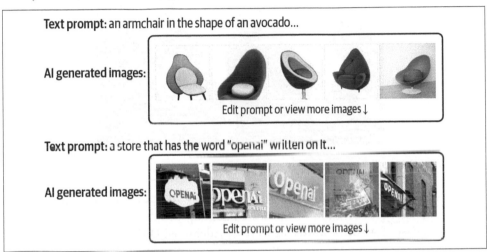

Figure 7-4. DALL-E capabilities

The DALL-E model was not open sourced nor released to the public, but it inspired multiple researchers and hobbyists to attempt to replicate the research. The most popular of these models was DALL-E Mini, released in July 2021 (renamed Craiyon a year later at the request of OpenAI), and although it gained a cult following on social media, the quality was considerably poorer than the official DALL-E model. OpenAI published a paper announcing DALL-E 2 (*https://oreil.ly/EqdtP*) in April 2022, and the quality was significantly higher, attracting a waitlist of one million people. Figure 7-5 shows an example of the now iconic astronaut riding a horse image from the paper that captured the public's imagination.

Figure 7-5. DALL-E 2 image quality

Access was limited to waitlist users until September 2022, due to concerns about AI ethics and safety. Generation of images containing people was initially banned, as were a long list of sensitive words. Researchers identified DALL-E 2 adding the words *black* or *female* (*https://oreil.ly/ot4vw*) to some image prompts like a photo of a doctor in a hamfisted attempt to address bias inherited from the dataset (images of doctors on the internet are disproportionally of white males).

The team added inpainting and outpainting to the user interface in August 2022, which was a further leap forward, garnering attention in the press and on social media. These features allowed users to generate only selected parts of an image or to *zoom out* by generating around the border of an existing image. However, users have little control over the parameters of the model and could not fine-tune it on their own data. The model would generate garbled text on some images and struggled with realistic depictions of people, generating disfigured or deformed hands, feet, and eyes, as demonstrated in Figure 7-6.

Figure 7-6. Deformed hands and eyes

Google's Imagen demonstrated impressive results and was introduced in a paper in May 2022 (Ho et al. (*https://oreil.ly/sFaeW*), 2022), but the model was not made available to the general public, citing AI ethics and safety concerns. Competitors like Midjourney (July 2022) moved quickly and capitalized on huge demand from people who had seen impressive demos of DALL-E on social media but were stuck on the waitlist. The open source release of Stable Diffusion (August 2022) broke what had seemed to be an unassailable lead for OpenAI just a few months before. Although the rollout of the more advanced DALL-E 3 model (*https://oreil.ly/dalle3*) as a feature of ChatGPT has helped OpenAI regain lost ground, and Google has gotten into the game with Gemini 1.5 (*https://oreil.ly/XzQrU*), there remains everything to play for.

Midjourney

In July 2022, just three months after the release of DALL-E 2, Midjourney put its v3 model in open beta. This was a uniquely good time to launch an image generation model, because the demonstrations of what DALL-E 2 could do from early users looked like magic, and yet access was initially limited. Eager early-adopters flocked to Midjourney, and its notable fantasy aesthetic gained a cult following among the gaming and digital art crowds, showcased in the now famous image (*https://oreil.ly/dqshh*), which won first prize in a digital art competition, in Figure 7-7.

Figure 7-7. Théâtre d'Opéra Spatial

Midjourney was one of the first viable image models that had a business model and commercial license, making it suitable for more than just experimentation. The subscription model was favored by many artists accustomed to paying monthly for other software like Adobe Photoshop. It also helped the creative process to not be charged per image generated, particularly in the early days when you'd have to try multiple images before you found one that was high-enough quality. If you were a paying customer of Midjourney, you owned the rights to any image generated, unlike DALL-E, where OpenAI was retaining the copyright.

Unique to Midjourney is its heavy community focus. To use the tool, you must sign into a Discord server (*https://oreil.ly/JKZzD*) (Figure 7-8) and submit your prompt in an open channel or direct message. Given that all image generations are shared in open channels by default, and private mode is available only on the most expensive plan (*https://oreil.ly/OV46r*), the vast majority of images created through Midjourney are available for others to learn from. This led to rapid copying and iteration between users, making it easy for novices to quickly learn from others. As early as July 2022, the Discord community was nearing 1 million people (shown in Figure 7-8), and a year later, there were more than 13 million members.

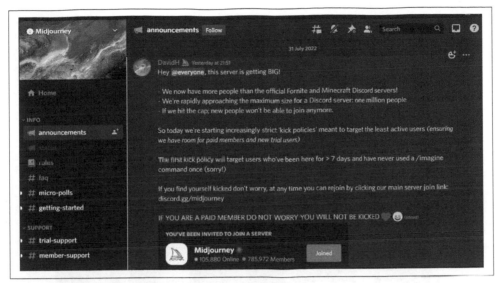

Figure 7-8. Midjourney's Discord server, July 2022

When you find an image you like, you can click a button to *upscale* the image (make it higher resolution) for use. Many have speculated that this procedure acts as training data for reinforcement learning, similar to reinforcement learning from human feedback (*https://oreil.ly/3ISZk*) (RLHF), the method touted as the key to success of ChatGPT. In addition, the team regularly asks for ratings of images generated by newer models in order to improve the performance. Midjourney released v4 of its model in November 2022, followed by v5 in March 2023 and v6 in December 2023. The quality is significantly improved: hands and eyes issues identified in Figure 7-6 have largely gone away, and the model has a larger stylistic range, demonstrated in Figure 7-9.

Input:

```
a group of best friends women eating salads and laughing
while high fiving in a coffee shop, cinematic lighting
```

Figure 7-9 shows the output.

Figure 7-9. Women eating salads and laughing

Remarkably, the Midjourney team has remained small, with just 11 employees (*https://oreil.ly/YrmA_*) as of March 2023. The founder of Midjourney, David Holz, formerly of hardware startup Leap Motion, confirmed in an interview (*https://oreil.ly/jeFYV*) that the company was already profitable as of August 2022. What is even more remarkable is that without the billions of dollars of funding that OpenAI enjoys, the team has built significant functionality over what's available in DALL-E, including negative prompting (removing concepts from an image), weighted terms (increasing the prevalance of other concepts), and their *describe* feature (reverse engineering the prompt from an uploaded image). However, there is no API available; the only way to access the model is through Discord, which has likely acted as a drag on mainstream adoption.

Stable Diffusion

While DALL-E 2's waitlist continued to build, researchers from the CompVis Group at LMU Munich and applied research company Runway ML received a donation of computing power from Stability AI to train Stable Diffusion. The model shocked the generative AI world when it was released open source in August 2022, because the results were comparable to DALL-E 2 and Midjourney, but it could be run for free on your own computer (assuming you had a modest GPU with 8GB VRAM). Stable Diffusion had one of the fastest climbs in GitHub stars of any software (*https://oreil.ly/pwPGX*), rising to 33,600 stars in its first 90 days (Figure 7-10).

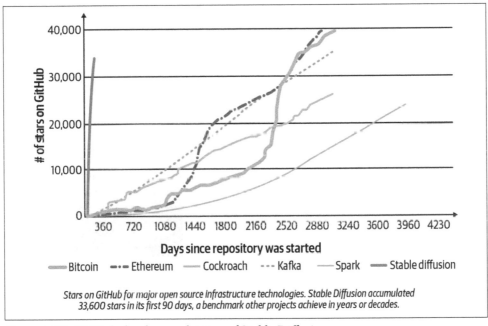

Stars on GitHub for major open source Infrastructure technologies. Stable Diffusion accumulated 33,600 stars in its first 90 days, a benchmark other projects achieve in years or decades.

Figure 7-10. GitHub developer adoption of Stable Diffusion

The move to open source the model was controversial, and raised concerns about AI ethics and safety. Indeed, many of the initial use cases were to generate AI porn, as evidenced by the not safe for work (NSFW) models shared on platforms like Civitai (*https://civitai.com*). However, the ability for hobbyists and tinkerers to modify and extend the model, as well as fine-tune it on their own data, led to rapid evolution and improvement of the model's functionality. The decision to surface all of the model's parameters to users, such as Classifier Free Guidance (how closely to follow a prompt), Denoising (how much noise to add to the base image for the model to remove during inference), and Seed (the random noise to start denoising from), has led to more creativity and innovative artwork. The accessibility and reliability of open source have also enticed several small businesses to build on top of Stable

Diffusion, such as Pieter Level's PhotoAI (*https://photoai.com*) and InteriorAI (*http://interiorai.com*) (together raking in more than $100,000 in monthly revenue), and Danny Postma's Headshot Pro (*https://www.headshotpro.com*). As well as matching DALL-E's inpainting and outpainting functionality, open source contributions have also kept pace with Midjourney's features, such as negative prompts, weighted terms, and the ability to reverse engineer prompts from images. In addition, advanced functionality like ControlNet (matching the posture or composition of an image) and Segment Anything (clicking on an element to generate a mask for inpainting), have been quickly added as extensions for use with Stable Diffusion (both released in April 2023), most commonly accessed via AUTOMATIC1111's web UI (*https://oreil.ly/0inw3*) (Figure 7-11).

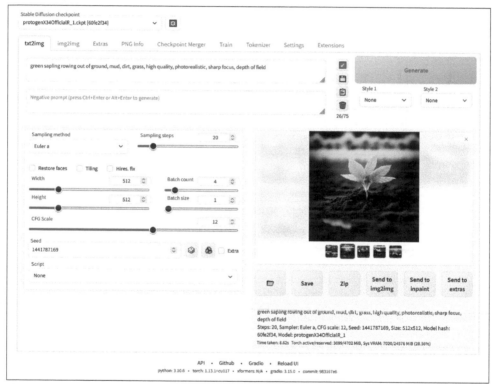

Figure 7-11. AUTOMATIC1111's web UI for Stable Diffusion

Version 1.5 of Stable Diffusion was released in October 2022 and is still in use today. Therefore, it will form the basis for the ControlNet examples in Chapter 10, the advanced section for image generation in this book. The weights for Stable Diffusion were released on Hugging Face, introducing a generation of AI engineers to the open source AI model hub. Version 2.0 of Stable Diffusion came out a month later in November 2022, trained on a more aesthetic subset of the original LAION-5B dataset (*https://oreil.ly/K5vX2*) (a large-scale dataset of image and text pairs for research purposes), with NSFW (not safe for work) images filtered out. Power users of Stable Diffusion complained of censorship as well as a degradation in model performance, speculating (*https://oreil.ly/2mgh5*) that NSFW images in the training set were necessary to generate realistic human anatomy.

Stability AI raised over $100 million (*https://oreil.ly/BT-k5*) and has continued to develop newer models, including DeepFloyd (*https://oreil.ly/UCQ3I*), a model better able to generate real text on images (an issue that plagues other models) and the current favorite Stable Diffusion XL 1.0 (*https://oreil.ly/gcT4t*) (abbreviated to SDXL). This model has overcome the misgivings of the community over censorship in version 2.0, not least due to the impressive results of this more powerful model, which has 6.6 billion parameters, compared with 0.98 billion for the v1.5 model.

Google Gemini

Google long threatened to be a competitor in the space with their Imagen (*https://oreil.ly/K8oWv*) model (not released publicly (*https://oreil.ly/341QB*)), and indeed ex-Googlers have since founded a promising new image model Ideogram (*https://ideogram.ai*), released in August 2023. They finally entered the image generation game with Gemini in December 2023, though quickly faced criticism over a clumsy attempt to promote diversity (*https://oreil.ly/u-Glg*). It remains to be seen whether Google's internal politics will prevent them from capitalizing on their significant resources.

Text to Video

Much of the attention in the image space is also likely to shift toward *text-to-video*, *image-to-video*, and even *video-to-video*, as the Stable Diffusion community extends the capabilities (*https://oreil.ly/l7KHB*) of the model to generate consistent images frame by frame, including promising open source projects such as AnimateDiff (*https://oreil.ly/CsJgT*). In addition, one of the cocreators of Stable Diffusion, RunwayML, has become the leading pioneer in text-to-video, and is starting to get usable results with their Gen-2 model (*https://oreil.ly/vS0mA*). Stable Video Diffusion (*https://oreil.ly/UuApM*) was released in November 2023, capable of turning text into short video clips or animating existing images, and Stable Diffusion Turbo (*https://oreil.ly/uMAkh*) can generate images in near real time. The release of Sora (*https://oreil.ly/sora*) in February 2024 shows that OpenAI isn't sleeping on this space either. Although we don't cover text-to-video prompting techniques explicitly, everything you learn about prompting for image generation also applies directly to video.

Model Comparison

As demand for AI image generation increases and competition heats up, new entrants will emerge, and the major players will diversify. In our own workflows we already find ourselves using different models for different reasons. DALL-E 3 is great at composition, and the integration with ChatGPT is convenient. Midjourney still has the best aesthetics, both for fantasy and photorealism. Stable Diffusion being open source makes it the most flexible and extendable model, and is what most AI businesses build their products on top of. Each model has evolved toward a distinct style and set of capabilities, as can be discerned when comparing the same prompt across multiple models, as in Figure 7-12.

Input:

```
a corgi on top of the Brandenburg Gate
```

Figure 7-12 shows the output.

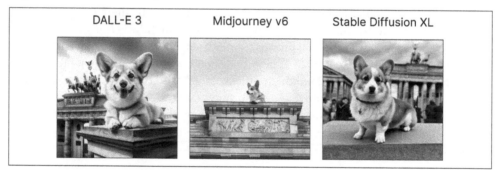

Figure 7-12. A corgi on top of the Brandenburg Gate

Summary

In this chapter, you were introduced to diffusion models for AI image generation. These models, such as DALL-E, Stable Diffusion, and Midjourney, use random noise and denoising techniques to generate images based on text descriptions. They have been trained on large datasets and can replicate various art styles. However, there is controversy surrounding copyright issues. You learned how prompt engineering principles apply to image generation when navigating the latent space to find the desired image.

In this chapter, you explored the different approaches taken by organizations like OpenAI, Stability AI, and Midjourney in developing text-to-image models. OpenAI's DALL-E gained popularity for its artistic abilities, but access was limited, and the quality of replicated models was poorer. Midjourney, on the other hand, capitalized on the demand for DALL-E alternatives and gained a cult following with its v3 and v4 models. It had a subscription-based pricing model and a strong community focus.

Stable Diffusion, on the other hand, gained attention for its comparable results to DALL-E and Midjourney, but with the advantage of being open source and free to run on personal computers. By reading this chapter, you also gained insights into the history of AI image generation and the advancements made by organizations like OpenAI, Midjourney, and Stable Diffusion.

In the next chapter, you will learn practical tips for handling image generation with AI. The chapter will equip you with the necessary knowledge and techniques to create visually stunning and unique images. From format modifiers to art-style replication, you will discover the power of prompt engineering in creating captivating and original visual content. Get ready to unleash your creativity and take your image generation skills to the next level.

Standard Practices for Image Generation with Midjourney

In this chapter, you'll use standardized techniques to maximize the output and formats from diffusion models. You'll start by tailoring the prompts to explore all of the common practices used for image generation. All images are generated by Midjourney v5, unless otherwise noted. The techniques discussed were devised to be transferrable to any future or alternative model.

Format Modifiers

The most basic practice in image generation is to specify the format of the image. AI image models are capable of deploying a wide variety of formats, from stock photo, to oil paintings to ancient Egpytian hieroglyphics. The image often looks completely different depending on the format, including the style of the objects or people generated in the image. Many of the images in the training data are stock photos, and this is also one of the most commercially important image categories for image generation.

Input:

```
a stock photo of a business meeting
```

Figure 8-1 shows the output.

Figure 8-1. Stock photo of a business meeting

The ability to generate infinite royalty-free stock photos for free with open source models like Stable Diffusion, or for a very low cost with DALL-E or Midjourney, is itself a game changer. Each of these images is unique (though may contain similarities to existing images), and therefore they look more premium than reusing the same free stock photos available to everyone else. However, you no longer need to be limited to the stock photography format. If your blog post or website imagery would look better with something more artistic, you can do that with essentially no limits.

Input:

```
an oil painting of a business meeting
```

Figure 8-2 shows the output.

Figure 8-2. Oil painting of a business meeting

Specify Format

The format we specify significantly modifies the results we get from our AI model. Specifying format also improves the reliability of our prompts in terms of giving us the type of visual we require.

There's no real limit to how far you can take this technique, and this is one of those domains where it would have helped to go to art school. If you know the name of a specific technique or detail you want to see in your image—for example, impasto, a technique used in oil painting, where paint is laid on an area of the surface thickly, leaving visible brush strokes—you can reference it in the prompt to get closer to your desired result. Google maintains a comprehensive list of popular artists and art movements (*https://oreil.ly/OmZbl*) that many find useful.

Input:

```
an oil painting of a business meeting, textured oil-on-canvas
using thick impasto and swirling dynamic brushstrokes
```

Figure 8-3 shows the output.

Figure 8-3. Oil painting of a business meeting with impasto

The oil painting of a business meeting is now far more visually interesting and potentially more appealing, depending on your audience. Traditionally, one of the reasons businesses migrated to using stock photography is that it was cheaper than commissioning a painting, but that limitation no longer applies with AI. We can generate essentially any format we like, for example an ancient Egyptian hieroglyph of a business meeting.

Input:

```
an ancient Egyptian hieroglyph of a business meeting
```

Figure 8-4 shows the output.

Figure 8-4. Ancient Egyptian hieroglyph of a business meeting

The thing to watch out for with modifying the format is that the style of the image, and even the contents, tend to match what was associated with that format in the training data. For example, in our oil painting there aren't any computers, because they don't often appear in oil paintings. Similarly in our hieroglyph the participants in the meeting are wearing ancient Egyptian headdresses. Often you'll need to combine format modifiers with the other proceeding techniques in order to arrive at what you want.

Art Style Modifiers

One of the great powers of AI image models is their ability to replicate any popular art style or artist. The most common examples shared on social media and AI demos are images in the style of Van Gogh, Dali, or Picasso, as well as the art movements they were part of, respectively Post-impressionism, Surrealism, and Cubism. AI art communities have also become influential in determining what contemporary art styles become popular, as is the case with Polish digital artist Greg Rutkowski (*https://oreil.ly/nnam3*), known for his fantasy style. However, many artists have taken a stand against AI art, and there is a legal gray area around whether imitating a living artist's style is considered *fair use* under copyright law. We recommend AI artists exercise caution when generating AI art in the distinctive style of any living artist and instead stick to artists who died one year ago as a rule of thumb (seek legal counsel for any planned commercial use).

Input:

```
illustration of a dragon, in the style of Alice's Adventures in Wonderland
by Lewis Carroll
```

Figure 8-5 shows the output.

Figure 8-5. Illustration of a dragon, in the style of Lewis Carroll

Give Direction

Evoking an artist's name or the name of an art movement is a shortcut toward delivering a specific visual style. So long as the artist or art movement has enough examples in the training data, their nature can be emulated.

In evoking an artist's style you're effectively shortcutting to a part of the *latent space*, the multidimensional universe of potential model outputs, filtering down to your desired style. Traversing to nearby locations from there can help you arrive at a more pleasing destination than you could get to with random trial and error.

Reverse Engineering Prompts

If you didn't go to art school or don't know much about film or photography, it can be daunting to try to figure out the art styles, formats, and artists you want to take advantage of. Often you see a picture you like and have no way of describing it in enough detail to re-create it with a prompt. Thankfully, Midjourney's `Describe` functionality allows you to reverse engineer a prompt from an image by typing **/describe** and then uploading the image. It works for both AI-generated images and also normal images from other sources, too, as shown in Figure 8-6, using one of the stock photos from Chapter 1.

Midjourney gives you four options with various artists, art styles, modifiers, and other words, including an estimation of what is happening in the image and what subjects or elements are contained. For example, Midjourney correctly identifies a group of people looking at a laptop in an office, in Figure 8-6. You can select the option you want by number, and Midjourney will generate an image with that prompt, in the same style as the original. There is similar open source technology available named CLIP Interrogator (*https://oreil.ly/fzgno*), though the richness of the prompt and ability to replicate the style of the uploaded image is lacking compared to Midjourney.

Figure 8-6. Midjourney Describe, Mimi Thian (https://oreil.ly/GdNrt) on Unsplash (https://oreil.ly/bEEnJ)

Quality Boosters

One trick that works for image models is to add words that are associated with quality into the prompt. Some art styles are more aesthetic than others, but there is a set of words, known as *quality boosters*, that seem to improve the image quality without greatly affecting the style, like *4k*, *very beautiful*, and *trending on artstation*. Generative models aren't trying to make high-quality images; they're trying to imitate training sets with a wide variety of styles and qualities. If you want high-quality images, you must explicitly ask for them. Start with the subject of your prompt, for example a space whale, and add a modifier to the end, separated by a comma (as in Figure 8-7).

Input:

```
a space whale, trending on artstation
```

Output:

Figure 8-7. Space whale, trending on artstation

Give Direction

Using quality boosters can help improve the aesthetics of an image through the addition of one or two words to the prompt, without changing the overall style of the image by much.

The reason these labels work is that they were associated with quality in the training data. When AI image models were trained, they reportedly ingested images from popular design portfolio websites, such as ArtStation, Behance, and DeviantArt. Therefore, the model can approximate that an image that was "trending on artstation" was of higher aesthetic value than normal. Note that sometimes style seeps through that may not be aligned with your creative vision. For example, ArtStation contains a lot of digital art of spaceships, and that perhaps explains why the space whale in Figure 8-7 somewhat resembles a space ship. For a list of quality boosters, art styles, and artists, visit this template created by one of the authors: Prompt Engineering Template (*https://oreil.ly/afGCQ*). Google also compiles a comprehensive list of art movements (*https://oreil.ly/mhujK*), which can be useful for educating yourself on the names of styles you find appealing.

Negative Prompts

Often two concepts are so intertwined in the training data that they appear together frequently when generating images of one of the concepts, even if that's not what you specified or intended. For example when you ask for oil paintings, you often get the accompanying frame and surrounding wall, because that's what's in the images for a large number of museum collections of these paintings.

In Midjourney and Stable Diffusion there is the ablity to add *negative prompts*, which allow you to specify what you don't want in the image. Negative prompts can be used to effectively separate two intertwined concepts and ensure your image doesn't contain anything you were hoping to avoid. Taking the example of oil paintings and frames, you can add --no to the end of the prompt, and anything in a comma-separated list after that flag will be negated from the prompt. To fix your frames problem, add "frame" and "wall" as a negative prompt, as shown in Figure 8-8.

Input:

```
oil painting in the style of Rembrandt --no frame, wall
```

Figure 8-8 shows the output.

oil painting in the
style of rembrandt

oil painting in
the style of rembrandt
--no frame, wall

Figure 8-8. Oil painting in the style of Rembrandt without frame or wall

Give Direction

Negative prompts can negate unwanted concepts in images, directing the model away from areas you are trying to avoid. This doesn't always work as intended, as often the concepts are too well correlated, but when it does, it can lead to interesting places.

Negative prompting isn't fully reliable but can be useful in a wide variety of scenarios. One creative use of this technique is to add the name of a celebrity as a negative prompt to decrease the factors most associated with them. The famous actress Karen Gillan has red hair and has a conventionally feminine look and therefore can be used to make a subject less likely to have red hair or look conventionally feminine.

Input:

```
a Scottish female astronaut --no Karen Gillan
```

Figure 8-9 shows the output.

Figure 8-9. A less conventionally feminine, less red-haired Scottish female astronaut

You can also get very creative and unpredictable outcomes with this technique by taking two inseparable concepts and seeing what happens when you separate them. For example, try taking your favorite cartoon and removing the cartoon style, as depicted in Figure 8-10 with Homer Simpson.

Input:

```
Homer Simpson --no cartoon
```

Figure 8-10 shows the (horrifying) output.

Figure 8-10. Homer Simpson without his trademark cartoon style

One of the more common historical use cases for negative prompts traditionally is to correct some of the issues with disfigured hands, explicit body parts, or odd-looking eyes, all problems early AI models suffered from. Prompt engineers would add words like *nsfw*, *elongated body*, *too many digits*, *not enough fingers*, and *teeth* to the negative prompt in an attempt (often in vain) to guide the model away from these spaces.

While still necessary for older or lesser models like Stable Diffusion v1.5, from Midjourney v5 and Stable Diffusion XL onward this is mostly a solved problem. State-of-the-art models are now more than capable of developing normal-looking images of hands, eyes, and bodies without relying on negative prompts.

Weighted Terms

Negative prompts are useful if you want to completely negate something, but often you just want to dial it down. To mix and match different concepts, it can be helpful to have control over how much of each you want.

By default all words in a prompt have an equal weighting of 1, although words at the beginning of the prompt have a greater effect, which is why we typically put the subject of our image there by convention, i.e., `painting of the Golden Gate Bridge`. You can change the weights of sections of the prompt in Midjourney by adding a *hard break* with two colon characters, `::`, and a number denoting the new weight. With this method you can make an image that is primarily Van Gogh but with a dash of Dali.

Input:

```
painting of the Golden Gate Bridge::1 in the style of Van
Gogh::0.8, in the style of Dali::0.2
```

Figure 8-11 shows the output.

Figure 8-11. Painting of the Golden Gate Bridge in the style of Van Gogh and Dali

To see how weights affect the resulting image, you can conduct a grid search by systematically testing each combination of weights at a specific granularity. In this example, the weights changed in 0.2 increments between the two artists from 0 to 1.

Figure 8-12 shows the output.

dali :: 0
van gogh :: 1

dali :: 0.2
van gogh :: 0.8

dali :: 0.4
van gogh :: 0.6

dali :: 0.6
van gogh :: 0.4

dali :: 0.8
van gogh :: 0.2

dali :: 1
van gogh :: 0

Figure 8-12. Permutations grid of weights

Evaluate Quality

Weights introduce many possible combinations in a prompt, which can be time-consuming to iterate through one at a time. A grid search approach of systematically generating many possible combinations is recommended to identify where the ideal mix of weightings aligns with your preferences.

Weights can go higher than 1 as needed for emphasis, or lower if you want to de-emphasize something. You can also add negative weights to the prompt to remove that aspect to varying degress. The `--no` parameter used for negative prompts is actually just a shortcut for adding `::-0.5` to that section of the prompt. If you are struggling with something appearing in the image that you don't want, try stronger negative weights instead of negative prompts. Using the prior example, you could strip any Van Gogh influence out of Dali's work by adding a -1 weight to Van Gogh and dialing up the Dali weight to 5.

Input:

```
painting of the Golden Gate Bridge::1 in the style of Van
Gogh::-1, in the style of Dali::5
```

Figure 8-13 shows the output.

Figure 8-13. Painting of the Golden Gate Bridge

Weights can be a powerful tool in remixing different styles or emphasizing specific elements. There are many permutations of weights, and therefore a more systematic approach must be taken to find an aesthetically interesting space to play in.

Prompting with an Image

Many AI image generation tools let you prompt the model not just with text but with an image. Supplying an example image of what you're going for can give you a great baseline for building something more unique and original, while still matching the style you need. In the Stable Diffusion community this is called Img2Img, whereas in Midjourney you simply link to an image in the prompt. The best way to do this is to upload the image into Discord first (for example, this photo by Jessica Hearn (*https://oreil.ly/B6E0Y*) on Unsplash (*https://oreil.ly/0oO4w*)), and then right-click and select Copy Link, as depicted in Figure 8-14. You can later paste that link into the prompt to use as the base image.

Figure 8-14. Copying the link from an image uploaded to Discord

The copied link then should be pasted at the beginning of the Midjourney prompt and accompanied by your text prompt. You don't need to be as descriptive now that you have given a base image (a picture is worth a thousand words). The image won't match exactly, but it will be similar to the point of being recognizeable if you know what image was supplied and how it was modified by the prompt.

Input:

```
https://s.mj.run/XkIHsYIdUxc in the style of The Great Gatsby
```

Figure 8-15 shows the output.

Figure 8-15. Stock photo in the style of The Great Gatsby

 The rules and regulations around copyright and fair use with AI are still being developed, so be careful uploading any image you don't have the rights to.

This technique works wherever you want a similar vibe, scene, or composition to an image you know of. You can also blend multiple images together with /blend to get something quite unique, and even use the resulting image as input for another prompt. For convenience, there is the --iw parameter, which acts the same as separating the image from the rest of the prompt with :: and setting the weight. Prompting with an image is also a common technique for AI video generation with tools such as RunwayML (*https://runwayml.com*) and Pika Labs (*https://pika.art*), given the general unreliability of text to video generation, and because it gives you an opportunity to iterate on the style of the scene without waiting for a whole video to generate and render.

Provide Examples

The quickest and easiest way to get the image you desire is to upload an image that you want to emulate. This is similar in concept to a one-shot prompt in the text generation space and is similarly useful in guiding the model toward the right output.

Inpainting

Working with AI image generation tools is always an iterative process. Rarely do you get the complete final image on the first try. There are usually artifacts that you want to address, or styles that you want to change. For example, say you had generated an image with Midjourney of a woman in a 1920s-style flapper dress but wanted to change what she was wearing without regenerating the entire image.

The solution is *inpainting*, which is available in most implementations of Stable Diffusion (*https://oreil.ly/YgL8g*), in Midjourney (*https://oreil.ly/7DhZE*) via a feature called *Vary Region*, and with Adobe Photoshop's (*https://oreil.ly/FvGAi*) *Generative Fill*. However, DALL-E pioneered this functionality, and it is still our personal preference in terms of the quality of the results. To demonstrate this functionality, first you generate an image with DALL-E in in ChatGPT (Plus), and then you erase the part of the image you want to regenerate.

Figure 8-16 shows an image generated by DALL-E with the accompanying prompt below. It is in the process of being edited in DALL-E's inpainting canvas (currently using ChatGPT) and has had the dress part of the image erased using the inpainting brush, ready for inpainting.

Input:

```
photograph of glamorous woman in a 1920s flapper party,
wearing a sequin dress, wide angle, in color, 3 5 mm, dslr
```

Figure 8-16 shows the uploaded image with parts erased.

Figure 8-16. Inpainting in DALL-E

Then you add a prompt for what you want to generate within that space. The common advice is to prompt for what you want the whole image to be, but in our experience narrowing down the prompt to just what you want in the erased part of the image gets better results, as in Figure 8-17, which focuses on the dress itself.

Input:

```
Van Gogh style dress, inspired by Starry Night, blue and
yellow swirls, extremely detailed, very well lit, studio
light, 3.5 mm, dslr
```

Figure 8-17 shows the output.

Figure 8-17. Van Gogh-style dress

Divide Labor

It's important to choose the right model for the job. Some image models like Midjourney are good at generating images in a specific style or with a certain aesthetic, while others compete on advanced features like DALL-E's inpainting. Using multiple models together can expand the scope of what you can accomplish.

DALL-E has fewer features than most image models but is great at this specific technique. It automatically blends the edges in so that the image fits well with the surroundings. As such you don't need to be particulary precise with the erase brush, and you'll still get good results. What's remarkable is how much these models have progressed in the space of just over a year. Figure 8-18 shows what you would get if you prompted DALL-E with the same prompt used earlier for DALL-E 3 via ChatGPT.

Figure 8-18. Photograph of woman in a 1920s flapper party

DALL-E 3 provides superior quality, but at present, it is available only via API and in ChatGPT; it is not available in the OpenAI Labs interface, which was historically used for inpainting. As image models proliferate, they are diverging in functionality and use cases, and it may take more than one model used in combination to accomplish the task you have at hand. Inpainting is a powerful technique for editing images, whether those images come from other AI models or a real-life photographer.

Outpainting

Related to inpainting in DALL-E is outpainting, where you generate outside of the frame of the existing image. This technique can in effect *zoom out* from the existing image to add context around it. This can be used to fill in more detail in an image you have generated or uploaded. Outpainting is no longer available in OpenAI's labs interface and is not yet available in ChatGPT, but it is called Zoom Out in Midjourney and presents itself as an option for images that have been upscaled, as you can see in Figure 8-19, where the surroundings of a woman in the flapper dress have been revealed.

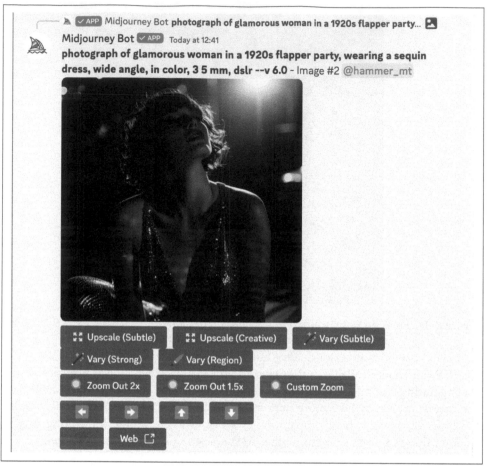

Figure 8-19. Midjourney Zoom Out options

Input:

```
photograph of glamorous woman in a 1920s flapper party,
wearing a sequin dress, wide angle, in color, 3 5 mm, dslr
```

Figure 8-20 shows the output.

Provide Examples

Often it can be difficult to achieve the right style purely with text prompts, particularly if the style is nuanced or you don't know all the words to describe it. Providing an example of an image to use for inpainting or outpainting is a shortcut to better results.

Figure 8-20. Midjourney image before and after zoom

As well as creatively expanding on an existing image, outpainting is also helpful if you're trying to get an image in an aspect ratio other than square, by filling in the gaps. You can run a Custom Zoom and set an aspect ratio as well as prompting what you want in each new section of the image through trial and error until you find something consistent with the rest of the image, or until the full image is in the aspect ratio required (for example, going from portrait to landscape). This technique is also available as an extension in Stable Diffusion (*https://oreil.ly/0c_en*), but in our experience it's less reliable than Midjourney.

Consistent Characters

An underrated use of inpainting and outpainting is using an existing image to maintain consistency across generations. One such example is a common method for creating consistent characters (*https://oreil.ly/BaITC*) by generating two images side by side and inpainting one side at a time. First, generate an image while explicitly dictating that there are two images side by side, in a 2:1 aspect ratio.

Input:

```
two images side by side, rockstar American rough and ready
middle-age jawline actor man, photo booth portrait --ar 2:1
```

Figure 8-21 shows the output.

Figure 8-21. Midjourney consistent character

The next step is to upscale one of the images, and then mask one-half of the upscaled image in an inpainting canvas, shown in Figure 8-22 using the Midjourney Vary Region feature.

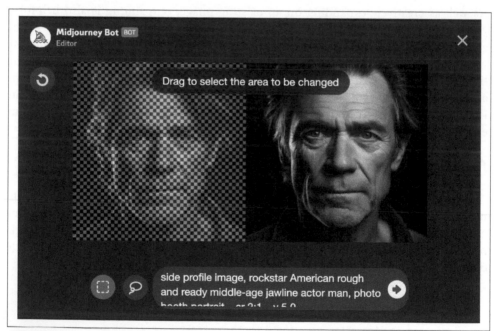

Figure 8-22. Midjourney Vary Region

Finally, reprompt the masked part of the image using inpainting or Vary Region (as it's known in Midjourney) to dictate a different angle from the original portrait mode.

Input:

```
side profile image, rockstar American rough and ready
middle-age jawline actor man, photo booth portrait --ar 2:1
```

Figure 8-23 shows the output.

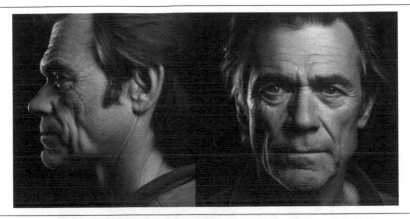

Figure 8-23. Consistent characters in side profile

This inpainting and generation process can be repeated for multiple angles, with the express purpose of finding new images of a character that looks identical to the original one you generated. Because one-half of the image is always present, the model maintains consistency of the character's features across generations, allowing you to build a more comprehensive perspective of a single character in different poses and positions. All you need to do to create an image of the character in a new situation is inpaint half of the 2:1 image with the new prompt and crop it in Photoshop (or some equivalent).

Provide Examples

Many people think of using a real image as a baseline when prompting for inpainting, but many of the more advanced AI artists use generated images themselves as inputs to maintain control over the consistency of the characters or objects in their story.

Prompt Rewriting

One of the issues you may run into when putting an AI system into production is that you can't expect the users of your system to be expert prompt engineers. It's a case of garbage in, garbage out: if they write a substandard prompt, they'll get poor results and complain about the quality of your product. One common trick in the industry (*https://oreil.ly/OirCS*) is to rewrite the prompt to make it better and more likely to get impressive results. This is a form of *meta prompting* where the prompt for one AI model is written by another.

Imagine a simple application where a user inputs a subject and an artist, and then an image is generated of the subject in the style of the artist. The prompt template is a `{subject} in the style of {artist}`.

Input:

```
a dachshund dog in the style of Banksy
```

Figure 8-24 shows the output.

Figure 8-24. A dachshund dog in the style of Banksy

The issue with this prompt is that the expectation would be that the dog would be part of the street painting (in Banksy style), whereas instead it is standing next to it in the image that was generated. To fix this, you can take the user prompt and inject that into a prompt to ChatGPT to find the artist's medium.

Input:

```
What's the medium that the artist Banksy mostly used? Respond
in 1-3 words only.
```

Output:

```
Street art
```

Finally, you can use this output to rewrite the original user prompt, in the format `{medium} of a {subject} in the style of {artist}`.

Input:

```
street art of a dachshund dog in the style of Banksy
```

Figure 8-25 shows the output.

Figure 8-25. Street art of a dachshund dog in the style of Banksy

This system can be built out further to include other prompt engineering techniques, such as quality boosters or negative prompts, to make the results more reliable. It's possible to get good results just asking ChatGPT to rewrite the prompt for DALL-E (which ChatGPT Plus has available as a tool) and then use what it gives you for other models. Some attempts have been made to train AI models (*https://oreil.ly/9A1NL*) that specialize in generating high-quality prompts, though in our experience this method only brings quality up to average and doesn't beat expert prompt engineering.

Divide Labor

Instead of expecting a nontechnical person to submit a good-quality prompt, simply pass their input to another AI model that can help improve the original prompt.

Meme Unbundling

The main issue with replicating an artist's style, or emulating an art movement, is that it's relatively unoriginal. Nobody knows what the legal implications of AI art will be, but certainly artists like Greg Rutkowski and others have already spoken out about the immorality of copying their style.

One way to still get the benefit of the shortcut of referring to a successful artist or art movement, while being more original in your style, is to unbundle the memes of an artist. The word *meme* (*https://oreil.ly/BQYFP*) doesn't just mean *a funny viral image*: it refers to any piece of cultural information that gets copied from person to person. If you can decompose an art style into its component parts and characteristics, then you can use these subcomponents to remix your own style. Say, for example, you were trying to make a painting of Times Square in the style of Salvador Dali.

Input:

```
a painting of Times Square in the style of "The Persistence
of Memory" by Salvador Dali
```

Figure 8-26 shows the output.

Figure 8-26. Painting of Times Square in the style of "The Persistence of Memory" by Salvador Dali

You are already getting good results by evoking Dali's name, but it's not quite right. You want a surrealist style, but not an exact copy of Dali's work. The term *unbundling* was coined in this context by Bakz T. Future (*https://oreil.ly/2qy4E*), meaning to extract the characteristics of an artist's style in order to get something familiar but unique. It works by asking a text generation model (in this case ChatGPT-4) to describe the style of the artist you're emulating, which you can then use as a prompt.

Input:

```
Briefly describe the characteristics and artistic style of
"The Persistence of Memory" by Salvador Dali, without
mentioning the artwork or the artist:
```

Output:

```
This is a notable example of Surrealist art, steeped in
dream-like, fantastical imagery that pushes the boundaries of
traditional understanding and interpretation. The painting is
composed with a distinctly precise and detailed technique,
reflecting a deceptive realism.

...

Contrasting with the melting objects, there are other items
in the scene that exhibit solidity and permanence, creating
an uncanny juxtaposition. The painting's composition and
imagery invite deep exploration and various interpretations,
concerning themes of reality, dreams, time, and the
subconscious. Overall, it is a visually striking work that
embodies the ethos of its movement: challenging the viewer's
perceptions and exploring the unconventional and the
irrational.
```

You must make sure the prompt insists on not mentioning the artist or the artwork; otherwise, it won't work as well as a prompt. You want to describe the style to someone who has never seen it so that the description is clean. For reference, Figure 8-27 shows the famous painting ChatGPT is describing.

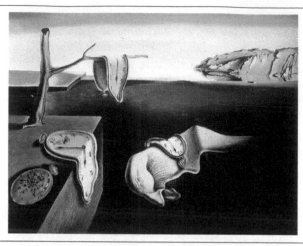

Figure 8-27. "The Persistence of Memory" by Salvador Dali

Now that you have a description of one of Dali's most iconic paintings, you can understand what makes it so visually appealing. In particular, this sort of explanation can be useful if you never went to art school and otherwise wouldn't know how to describe these elements. From here you need to abbreviate the description to fit into an image model prompt.

Input:

```
Convert this description into a shortened prompt for an AI
image generation model such as DALL-E:
```

Output:

```
Surrealist landscape with subdued colors of brown, blue, and
yellow. Depict a barren, craggy shoreline and calm sea
meeting a clear sky. Include amorphous, melting objects
resembling common items, indicating fluidity and impermanence
of time. Contrast these with other solid, permanent elements.
Evoke a sense of stillness, dreamlike atmosphere, and
quietude.
```

Take this output and add the subject of your painting, Times Square. It can also help to modify the prompt to make it flow better, as the prompts ChatGPT writes can be too instructive:

Input:

```
Painting of Times Square, surrealist landscape with subdued colors
of brown, blue, and yellow, a barren, craggy shoreline and calm
sea meeting a clear sky. Include amorphous, melting objects
resembling common items, indicating fluidity and impermanence
of time. Contrast these with other solid, permanent elements.
Evoke a sense of stillness, dreamlike atmosphere, and quietude.
```

Figure 8-28 shows the output.

Figure 8-28. Unbundled Dali memes applied to a painting of Times Square

Give Direction

Rather than guiding the AI image model toward a specific artist's work, you can emulate a close approximation by using a description of the artist's work. This is more transformative and creative approach than simply evoking an artist's name, and perhaps more ethical.

This image is still similar to Dali's work, but it has been transformed through the filter of ChatGPT's description. Therefore, it's already more original than what you got when you simply evoked his name: an advantage over the average prompter. But you're in an even better position now, because you have unbundled Dali's style into individual *memes (https://oreil.ly/BQYFP)* like "surrealist landscape," "melting objects," and "dreamlike atmosphere," and can more easily remix (*https://oreil.ly/ wPuMo*) its component parts to make the image more unique:

Input:

```
Painting of Times Square, surrealist landscape with subdued
colors of orange, red, and green, imposing buildings and calm
river meeting a stormy sky. The amorphous melting dripping
clock in the center of the square indicates the fluidity and
impermanence of time in contrast with other solid, permanent
elements. Evoke a sense of stillness, dreamlike atmosphere,
and quietude.
```

Figure 8-29 shows the output.

Figure 8-29. Dali Times Square remixed

You have only made small modifications to the color and elements in the painting, but you could go further. It's also possible to take elements from other popular artists and combine the aspects you like to arrive at something new. This technique only works right now with artists and artworks that are famous enough to be readily described from the training data; however, as AI models become multi-modal (i.e., able to generate both images and text), expect to be able to feed in an image and get a description to use for unbundling.

Meme Mapping

One of the most common forms of prompt inspiration is looking at what prompts other prompt engineers are getting results with. The Midjourney Discord community (*https://oreil.ly/upQIh*) has millions of active members, with thousands of new images being generated and automatically shared every day, as do other AI communities including on Reddit (*https://oreil.ly/EwLNh*) and across various other websites, email newsletters, and social media accounts. One commonly used website is Lexica.art (*https://lexica.art*), which has a searchable database (by keyword and similarity) of many Stable Diffusion images and their prompts for inspiration.

While searching and browsing through these sources of inspiration, you're likely to notice recurring patterns, or memes, in the words that are used for a particular type of image. We call this process of intentionally and systematically finding these patterns *meme mapping* (*https://oreil.ly/DLqAV*), and it can be an invaluable tool for identifying useful prompts. For example, you may search Super Mario on Lexica and see lots of examples where people have tried to create a *realistic* Mario, like the one in Figure 8-30, which might inspire you to do the same, starting with a prompt (*https://oreil.ly/WNsRn*) that's already proven to work, saving you considerable time

Figure 8-30. Realistic Mario

Alternatively you might apply this meme to a character from a different franchise, and try repurposing some of the prompts used by others to get a realistic effect. Without doing this research, you might not have been aware image models could generate real-world versions of cartoon or game characters, or perhaps never would have thought to try it. You may have never stumbled upon the insight that including "as a Soviet factory worker" in your prompt helps evoke a sense of gritty realism, and may never have encountered the work of the two artists referenced. There is a healthy culture of remixing content in the AI art community, with people learning from other's prompts, and then paying it forward by sharing their own expertise.

Input:

```
portrait of Homer Simpson as a Soviet factory worker, gritty,
dirty, beautiful, very detailed, hyperrealistic, medium shot,
very detailed painting by Glenn Fabry, by Joao Ruas --no
cartoon
```

Figure 8-31 shows the output.

Figure 8-31. Realistic Homer Simpson

This meme mapping process can be done manually (*https://oreil.ly/VqyG-*), with the examples copied and pasted into a spreadsheet or productivity tool Notion, although that can be time-consuming. So long as you are respecting a website's terms and conditions and any legal obligations in your country, it would also be possible to write custom code to programmatically scrape the contents of that website. Once you have all the data in one place, you could programmatically label the images with an entity recognition model like Google Vision (*https://oreil.ly/EZmRs*), a multimodal model like GPT-4 Vision (*https://oreil.ly/cOcPR*), or use NLP such as NGrams analysis (*https://oreil.ly/GXfDl*) on the prompts in order to identify patterns at a larger scale than is possible manually.

Prompt Analysis

One common mistake is to continue to build out longer and longer prompts, without thinking about what parts of the prompt are really necessary. Every word added perturbs the model in some way, adding noise to the resulting output. Often, removing unnecessary words can be as effective as adding new words. To conduct this analysis without lots of trial and error, Midjourney offers a /shorten command that attempts to remove these unnecessary words, leaving only the core tokens that the model pays the most attention to. Click "show details" at the bottom of the response to get token-level weightings and a visual chart.

Input:

```
portrait of Homer Simpson as a Soviet factory worker, gritty,
dirty, beautiful, very detailed, hyperrealistic, medium shot,
very detailed painting by Glenn Fabry, by Joao Ruas
--no cartoon
```

Output:

```
**portrait** (0.08) of **homer simpson** (1.00) as a
**soviet** (0.19) **factory** (0.21) **worker** (0.08),
gritty (0.02), dirty (0.02), beautiful (0.00), very (0.00)
detailed (0.01), hyperrealistic (0.01), medium (0.00) shot
(0.00), very (0.00) detailed (0.01) painting (0.05) by Glenn
Fabry (0.08), by **Joao Ruas** (0.09)
```

Once you have this analysis, you can use it to cut any noise from the prompt and zero in on what words, or memes, are actually important to the final result.

Evaluate Quality

Seeing the weights the model assigns to each token gives you unparalleled insight into how the model works. Often we make assumptions about what's important in a prompt, and those assumptions can be quite far from reality.

Summary

In this chapter, you learned about standard practices for image generation using diffusion models. You explored format modifiers such as stock photos, oil paintings, and Egyptian hieroglyphs, and how they can be used to create unique and visually appealing images. Additionally, you discovered art style modifiers that allow for the replication of popular art styles or artists, such as Lewis Carroll's *Alice in Wonderland* style.

You went deeper into the application of prompt engineering principles, including how to use art-style modifiers to replicate popular art styles and artists, and how mentioning specific artists' names can help achieve the desired visual style. The concept of negative prompts and weighted terms was introduced, allowing you to specify what you don't want in an image and control the mixture of different concepts. You also explored the concepts of inpainting and outpainting, where specific parts of an image can be generated separately by erasing and adding prompts. You discovered how these techniques can be further expanded and combined to enhance the reliability and quality of generative AI results.

In the next chapter, you will dive deeper into the world of image generation and explore more advanced use cases. You will learn how to harness the power of Stable Diffusion and AUTOMATIC1111 to improve your image generation skills. Including advanced Stable Diffusion techniques like utilizing ControlNet models for more control over the style and composition of your images, you will discover a wide range of exciting possibilities.

Advanced Techniques for Image Generation with Stable Diffusion

Most work with AI images only requires simple prompt engineering techniques, but there are more powerful tools available when you need more creative control over your output, or want to train custom models for specific tasks. These more complex abilities often requires more technical ability and structured thinking as part of the workflow of creating the final image.

All images in this chapter are generated by Stable Diffusion XL unless otherwise noted, as in the sections relying on extensions such as ControlNet, where more methods are supported with the older v1.5 model. The techniques discussed were devised to be transferrable to any future or alternative model. We make extensive use of AUTOMATIC1111's Stable Diffusion WebUI and have provided detailed setup instructions that were current as of the time of writing, but please consult the official repository (*https://oreil.ly/hs_fS*) for up-to-date instructions, and to diagnose any issues you encounter.

Running Stable Diffusion

Stable Diffusion is an open source image generation model, so you can run it locally on your computer for free, if you have an NVIDIA or AMD GPU, or Apple Silicon, as powers the M1, M2, or M3 Macs. It was common to run the first popular version (1.4) of Stable Diffusion in a Google Colab notebook (*https://oreil.ly/OmBuR*), which provides access to a free GPU in the cloud (though you may need to upgrade to a paid account if Google limits the free tier).

Visit the Google Colab website (*https://oreil.ly/2WGxQ*) if you haven't used it before or to find the latest information on limits. A copy of this Python notebook is saved in the GitHub repository (*https://oreil.ly/uauNn*) for this book, but you should upload it to Google Drive and run it in Google Colab to avoid setup issues.

Installing Stable Diffusion can be done via the Hugging Face diffusers library, alongside a handful of dependencies. In the Google Colab the following code installs the necessary dependencies (you would drop the exclamation marks (!) if installing locally rather than in a Jupyter Notebook or Google Colab):

```
!pip install diffusers==0.11.1
!pip install transformers scipy ftfy accelerate
```

To download and use the model, you first build an inference pipeline (what runs when we use the model):

```
# create an inference pipeline
import torch
from diffusers import StableDiffusionPipeline

pipe = StableDiffusionPipeline.from_pretrained(
    "CompVis/stable-diffusion-v1-4",
    torch_dtype=torch.float16)

pipe = pipe.to("cuda")
```

Let's break down the script line by line:

import torch
> This line is importing the torch library, also known as PyTorch (*https://pytorch.org*). PyTorch is an open source machine learning library, used for applications such as computer vision and natural language processing.

from diffusers import StableDiffusionPipeline
> Here the script is importing the StableDiffusionPipeline class from the diffusers library. This specific class is probably a pipeline for using diffusion models, of which Stable Diffusion is the most popular example.

pipe = StableDiffusionPipeline.from_pretrained("CompVis/stable-diffusion-v1-4", torch_dtype=torch.float16)
> This is creating an instance of the StableDiffusionPipeline class with pretrained weights. The method from_pretrained loads the weights of a pretrained model—in this case, the model is CompVis/stable-diffusion-v1-4.

> The torch_dtype=torch.float16 argument specifies that the data type used in the model should be float16, which is a half-precision floating-point format. Using float16 can speed up model computation and reduce memory usage (necessary to stay within the Google Colab free tier limits).

```
pipe = pipe.to("cuda")
```
This line moves the pipe model to the GPU. The string "cuda" refers to CUDA, a parallel computing platform and application programming interface (API) model created by Nvidia. By doing this, all computations performed by the pipe model will be executed on the GPU, which can be significantly faster than running them on a CPU for large-scale models and data.

Now that we have our pipe, we can pass in a prompt and other parameters for the model, like a random seed (change this to get a different image each time), the number of inference steps (more steps takes time but results in a higher-quality image), and the guidance scale (how closely the image matches the prompt):

```
# run inference on a prompt
prompt = "a photograph of an astronaut riding a horse"

generator = torch.Generator("cuda").manual_seed(1024)

image = pipe(prompt, num_inference_steps=50,
    guidance_scale=7, generator=generator
    ).images[0] # image here is in PIL format

# Now to display an image you can either save it such as:
image.save(f"astronaut_rides_horse.png")

# If you're in a google colab you can directly display:
image
```

Figure 9-1 shows the output.

Let's walk through this script to explain what it does:

```
prompt = "a photograph of an astronaut riding a horse"
```
This is the prompt that will be passed into the model to guide the generation of an image.

```
generator = torch.Generator("cuda").manual_seed(1024)
```
In this line, a PyTorch generator is created and assigned to the generator variable. The generator is initialized with "cuda", which means that it will be using a GPU for computations. The `manual_seed(1024)` function is used to set the random seed for generating random numbers, ensuring that the results are reproducible. If you run this code with the same model, you should get the exact same image.

```
image = pipe(prompt, num_inference_steps=50, guidance_scale=7, genera
tor=generator).images[0]
```
This line runs the pipe model on the prompt to generate an image. The `num_inference_steps` argument is set to 50, meaning that the model will perform 50 steps of inference. The `guidance_scale` argument is set to 7, which adjusts how strongly the prompt guides the generated image (higher values tend

to get grainy and less diverse). The generator argument passes in the random number generator created earlier. The result is an array of generated images, and `images[0]` selects the first image from this array.

```
image.save(f"astronaut_rides_horse.png")
```
This line saves the generated image to a file.

`image`

This line of code will display the image if the code is running in an environment like a Jupyter Notebook or Google Colab. This happens because these environments automatically display the result of the last line of code in a code cell if it is not assigned to a variable.

Figure 9-1. Photograph of an astronaut riding a horse

It's powerful to be able to run an open source model locally or in the cloud and customize it to meet your needs. However, custom coding your own inference pipelines and building a user interface on top is likely overkill unless you are an extremely advanced user with deep machine learning knowledge or your intention is to build your own AI image generation product. Stablity AI, the company funding development of Stable Diffusion, has a hosted web interface called Dream Studio (Figure 9-2), which is similar to the DALL-E playground, also operating on a credit system and offering advanced functionality such as inpainting.

Figure 9-2. Stability AI Dream-Studio

Like DALL-E, Dream-Studio offers access via API, which can be convenient for building AI image applications or running programmatic scripts for generating lots of images, without the encumberance of hosting and running your own Stable Diffusion model. Visit *https://oreil.ly/X3Ilb* once you have created an account to get your API key, and top up with credits (at time of writing, 1,000 credits cost $10 and can generate approximately 5,000 images). The following code is included in the GitHub repository (*https://oreil.ly/aGLeX*) for this book:

```python
import os
import base64
import requests
from IPython.display import Image

engine_id = "stable-diffusion-xl-1024-v1-0"
api_host = os.getenv('API_HOST', 'https://api.stability.ai')
api_key = os.getenv("STABILITY_API_KEY")

image_description = "computers being tied together"
prompt = f"""an illustration of {image_description}. in the
style of corporate memphis, white background, professional,
clean lines, warm pastel colors"""

response = requests.post(
    f"{api_host}/v1/generation/{engine_id}/text-to-image",
    headers={
        "Content-Type": "application/json",
        "Accept": "application/json",
        "Authorization": f"Bearer {api_key}"
    },
```

```python
    json={
        "text_prompts": [
            {
                "text": prompt,
            }
        ],
        "cfg_scale": 7,
        "height": 1024,
        "width": 1024,
        "samples": 1,
        "steps": 30,
    },
)

if response.status_code != 200:
    raise Exception(
        "Non-200 response: " + str(response.text))

data = response.json()

image_paths = []

# if there's no /out folder, create it
if not os.path.exists("./out"):
    os.makedirs("./out")

for i, image in enumerate(data["artifacts"]):
    filename = f"./out/image-{i}.png"
    with open(filename, "wb") as f:
        f.write(base64.b64decode(image["base64"]))

    image_paths.append(filename)

# display the first image
Image(filename=image_paths[0])
```

Figure 9-3 shows the output.

Figure 9 3. Corporate Memphis illustration from the Dream-Studio API

Let's break down this code step-by-step:

1. First, set up the required environment variables:
   - engine_id: This refers to a specific model version at stability.ai.
   - api_host: This retrieves the API host URL from environment variables. If not set, it defaults to 'https://api.stability.ai'.
   - api_key: This retrieves the API key from environment variables.
2. The prompt: This defines how the image should look, including the style and colors.
3. A POST request is made to the URL derived from api_host and engine_id.
   - The headers for the request are set to accept and send JSON data and include an authorization header with the api_key.
   - The JSON body of the request specifies the prompt (description of the image), the desired scale of the image, its dimensions, the number of samples, and the number of steps.
4. If the status code of the response is not 200 (indicating a successful request), an exception is raised with the response text to indicate something went wrong. Otherwise, the response is parsed into JSON format.

5. If there isn't a directory named *out*, one is created. For each artifact (image) in the response, the code does the following:

   - Sets a filename path.

   - Decodes the base64-encoded image data from the response.

   - Writes the decoded image data to a file.

   - Appends the file's path to the `image_paths` list.

   - This is typically where you would save the image to Google Cloud Storage (*https://oreil.ly/YsuBw*) or Amazon Simple Storage Service (S3) to display later in your application.

6. The first image from the `image_paths` list (the only one, in this case) is displayed (only in Jupyter Notebooks or Google Colab) using the `Image` class from `IPython.display`.

The downside of using Stability AI's service is a lack of control over customization. One of the great benefits of Stable Diffusion being open source is the ability to modify almost any aspect of the model and make use of community-built advanced functionality. In addition, there is no guarantee that functions or features you rely on for your scripts today will still be there in the future, as Stability AI strives to live up to the expectations of their investors, legal team, and corporate customers. For example, the popular (and more permissive) version 1.5 model has been deprecated in favor of the new Stable Diffusion 2.0 and XL models, causing problems for those who had finely tuned their workflows, parameters, and prompts to work with v1.5.

AUTOMATIC1111 Web User Interface

Heavy users of Stable Diffusion typically recommend the AUTOMATIC1111 (*https://oreil.ly/r-2vm*) (pronounced "automatic eleven eleven") web user interface, because it is feature-rich and comes with multiple extensions built by Stable Diffusion power users. This project is the gateway to taking advantage of the best aspect of Stable Diffusion: the vibrant open source community that has dedicated countless hours to integrating advanced functionality to the tool. Advanced users may also want to explore ComfyUI (*https://oreil.ly/LWVvC*), as it supports more advanced workflows and increased flexibility (including image-to-video (*https://oreil.ly/dh7jR*)), but we deemed this too complex for the majority of use cases, which can easily be handled by AUTOMATIC1111.

You can use the normal text-to-image Stable Diffusion model, but also run image-to-image (similar to the base image feature in Midjourney), as well as upscaling finished images for higher quality, and inpainting (as is offered by DALL-E). It's even possible to train and run custom models within this interface, and there are thousands of models shared publicly in communities such as Hugging Face (*https://oreil.ly/t5T7p*) and Civitai (*https://civitai.com*).

 Some custom open source models are NSFW (not safe for work), so be careful when browsing websites like Civitai.

Running Stable Diffusion locally with AUTOMATIC1111 requires some technical setup, and it's best to look for an up-to-date guide in the AUTOMATIC1111 Wiki:

- Install and run on NVidia GPUs (*https://oreil.ly/DsKyU*)
- Install and run on AMD GPUs (*https://oreil.ly/Oc7ix*)
- Install and run on Apple Silicon (*https://oreil.ly/Oh2VK*)

Installation generally involves ensuring you have Git and Python installed (as well as any other dependencies (*https://oreil.ly/vBOVI*)), and downloading Stable Diffusion, as well as the Automatic1111 code (*https://oreil.ly/x0BMn*) to your local computer. The images in this chapter use the XL 1.0 version (*https://oreil.ly/DIvUz*) of Stable Diffusion, though many still use the older version 1.5 (*https://oreil.ly/FNxf9*) as it is considered more permissive and has a wealth of custom community-trained models. The techniques work the same across models, though the results and quality will differ: it's commonly believed that removing NSFW images from the training data for version 2.0 led to worse performance at generating (even nonexplicit) images of realistic human figures (though this seems largely corrected in the XL version).

As the model is open source, you can get SDXL v1.0 on your local computer by visiting the model page on Hugging Face for the base and refiner models, and downloading the *.safetensors* files from the "Files and Versions" tab. This format is safer than the previous *.ckpt* file format, as it does not execute code on your computer when running:

- Base model (*https://oreil.ly/wtHRj*): *sd_xl_base_1.0.safetensors*
- Refiner model (*https://oreil.ly/0Dlbv*): *sd_xl_refiner_1.0.safetensors*

These models take time to download, so start downloading them now and later you will place them in your models/Stable-diffusion folder once you have installed the AUTOMATIC111 interface. If you want to use the older v1.5 Stable Diffu-suion model, download the *v1-5-pruned-emaonly.ckpt* file from Hugging Face (*https:// oreil.ly/hwblq*), and move that into the models folder where you placed the base and refiner models.

Once you have everything installed, the web interface is accessed by running a script that launches the application locally, which will show up as a web address in your browser. As one example, here are the current instructions (at time of writing) for Windows, with a computer that has an Nvidia GPU:

1. Install Python 3.10.6 (*https://oreil.ly/kGiyi*) (selecting Add to PATH) and Git (*https://oreil.ly/Pdzb0*).

2. Open the command prompt from search bar, and type `git clone https:// github.com/AUTOMATIC1111/stable-diffusion-webui`.

3. Remember to move the sd_xl_base_1.0.safetensors and sd_xl_refiner_1.0.safe-tensors models into the stable-diffusion-webui/models/Stable-diffusion folder.

4. Double-click the *webui-user.bat* file and visit the address the interface is running on (usually *http://127.0.0.1:7860*). For Mac or Linux, you would run `bash webui.sh` in the terminal.

From this interface, shown in Figure 9-4 (taken from the official GitHub repository (*https://oreil.ly/OOpas*)), you can enter your prompt (top left, under the "txt2img" tab) and click Generate to get your image.

If you run into an error or if you downloaded AUTOMATIC1111 web UI a while ago and need to update it, you can enter the stable-diffusion-webui folder in your terminal and run `git pull`. If you are running into errors, you may reset your implementation (move any files you want to save first) by running `git checkout -f master` in the stable-diffusion-webui folder.

 Resetting AUTOMATIC1111 this way will delete any files in the folder, along with any customizations. We recommend you make a local copy in a different folder for recovery.

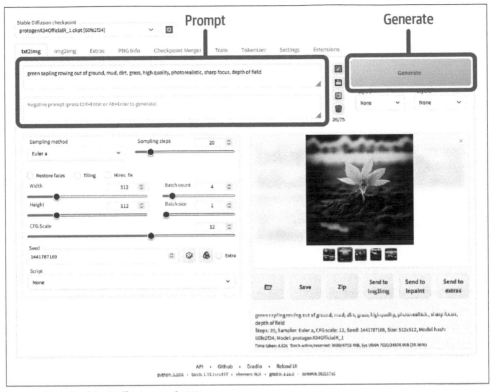

Figure 9-4. Stable Diffusion web UI

The box immediately below the prompt input is where you can add negative prompts to remove concepts from an image and ensure they don't show up (see Chapter 8 for more on negative prompts). Underneath, you'll find a number of settings including the Seed (set to –1 for a new image each time), number of Sampling (inference) Steps, Batch Count (Number of generations to run one after another), and Batch Size (number of images processed in each batch at the cost of higher VRAM needed). When images are generated, you can download them from the interface directly, send them to various tabs with the buttons below, or visit the stable-diffusion-webui/ outputs folder where they are organized by method (text2img, img2img) and date:

```
stable-diffusion-webui/
    outputs/
        txt2img-images/
            2023-10-05/
                your_image.png
```

When you run the AUTOMATIC1111 web UI, any models you downloaded will appear in the Stable Diffusion Checkpoint drop-down menu at the top. Select the base model and enter your prompt as well as adjusting your settings as normal. Make sure you set the image size to 1024x1024. For now, set the "Switch at" parameter under Refiner to 1 to run only the base model, as in Figure 9-5.

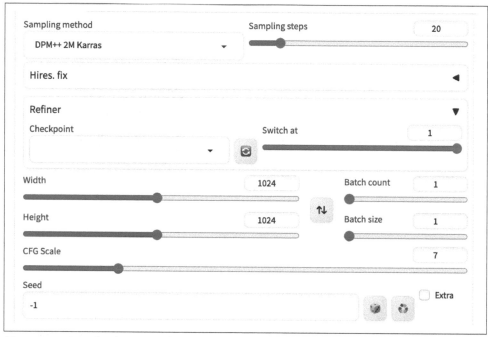

Figure 9-5. Standard settings for SDXL

The sampling methods available are relatively complex and technical to explain, but the trade-offs are generally between speed, quality, and randomness. `Euler` is the simplest sampler, and `DDIM` was the first designed specifically for Diffusion models. The sampling methods that have an *a* in the name, for example `Euler a`, are ancestral samplers, which inject noise into the image as part of the process. This gives less reproducible results as the image does not converge (there is some randomness to the image each time you run the model). The `DPM++ 2M Karras` and `UniPC` sampler running for 20–30 steps are excellent choices for robust, stable, and reproducible images. For higher-quality but slower and more random images, try the `DPM++ SDE Karras` or `DDIM` samplers with 10–15 steps.

Another important parameter is the CFG Scale (Classifier Free Guidance—the same as the `guidance_scale` introduced in the Stable Diffusion Inference Google Colab example). As a rule of thumb, here are common values for CFG Scale and what they equate to:

- *1*: Mostly ignore the prompt.
- *3*: Feel free to be creative.
- *7*: A good balance between the prompt and creativity.
- *15*: Adhere to the prompt.
- *30*: Strictly follow the prompt.

You can change the size of the image generated with Height and Width, as well as the number of images using Batch Count. The checkbox Highres fix uses an upscaler to generate a larger high-resolution image (more on this later), the Restore faces checkbox uses a face restoration model (by default `Codeformer`) to fix the defects in human faces that often occur with Stable Diffusion, and the Tiling checkbox creates an image that can be tiled in a repeating pattern. There's also the ability to save and insert styles that are just prompts you want to reuse regularly. There are many powerful features (*https://oreil.ly/MiSt1*) in the different tabs, as well as community-built extensions you can add, with more added as they become available.

AUTOMATIC1111 supports prompt weights, or weighted terms, much like Midjourney (covered in Chapter 8). The way you access them is slightly different, as instead of separating by double colons like in Midjourney, you use parentheses. For example, (pirate) would emphasize pirate features by 10% or 1.1, and double parentheses ((pirate)) would multiply it again, so the weight would be 1.1 x 1.1 = 1.21. You can also control the weights precisely by inputting your own number in the form of (keyword: factor), for example (pirate: 1.5), for the model to pay 50% more attention to those tokens.

Input:

```
Marilyn Monroe as a (pirate:1.5) on a desert island, detailed clothing,
by Stanley Artgerm Lau and Alphonse Mucha
```

Negative:

```
racy, nudity, cleavage
```

Figure 9-6 shows the output.

pirate　　　　　　　　　　(pirate:1.5)

Figure 9-6. Marilyn Monroe pirate

Square brackets [pirate] work the same way but in reverse, de-emphasising a term in a prompt by 10%. So for example, [hat] would be the same as a weight of 0.9, or (hat:0.9). Note this is not the same as a negative prompt, because the term will still be present in the generation of the image, just dialed down. Prompt weights work in the negative prompt box as well, acting to more aggressively remove that concept from the image or reduce their effects. This can be used to ensure unwanted elements or styles don't appear when a negative prompt isn't enough.

Give Direction

Providing more or less emphasis on specific words or sections of a prompt can give you more fine-grained control over what the model pays attention to.

A more advanced technique used by power users of AUTOMATIC1111 is *prompt editing*, also known as *prompt switching*. During the diffusion process the early steps move from random noise to a fuzzy outline of the general shapes expected to be in the image, before the final details are filled in. Prompt editing allows you to pass a different prompt to the early or later steps in the diffusion process, giving you more creative control. The syntax is [from:to:when], where from is your starting prompt, to is your finishing prompt, and when is when to make the switch, denoted in number of steps or a decimal representing a percentage. The prompt [Emma Watson: Amber Heard: 0.5] would start generating an image of Emma Watson, before switching halfway to generating an image of Amber Heard on top of the last frame, finishing with a mixture of the two actresses. This is a useful trick for creating images of people that look attractive and vaguely familiar, without being recongizeable as any specific celebrity, and therefore may be seen as more ethical and legally sound than simply copying a celebrity's likeness (seek your own legal counsel):

Input:

```
vogue fashion shoot of [Emma Watson: Amber Heard: 0.5],
highly realistic, high resolution, highly detailed,
dramatic, 8k
```

Figure 9-7 shows the output.

Figure 9-7. Emma Watson and Amber Heard mixed

Providing Direction

Prompt editing is an advanced technique that gets deep into the actual workings of the diffusion model. Interfering with what layers respond to what concepts can lead to very creative results if you know what you're doing and are willing to undergo enough trial and error.

If you want the model to alternate between two concepts, the syntax is [Emma Watson | Amber Heard], which will make the switch at every step, ending with a more blended mixture. There are many advanced uses of prompt editing, though it is seen as something of a dark art. In some cases experts report being able to get around difficult generations, for example starting by generating something easy for the model to generate, before switching to what is really needed in the final details phase. In practice we have found limited use out of this technique, but you should experiment and see what you can discover.

Img2Img

The AUTOMATIC1111 web UI supports `Img2Img` (Figure 9-8), which is the functional equivalent to Midjourney's ability to submit an image along with the prompt. It grants you more control over the style and composition of your resulting image, by uploading an image for the model to use as guidance. To get good results with `Img2Img`, try using `Euler` sampling, 50 sampling steps, and a higher than usual CFG scale of 20 to 30.

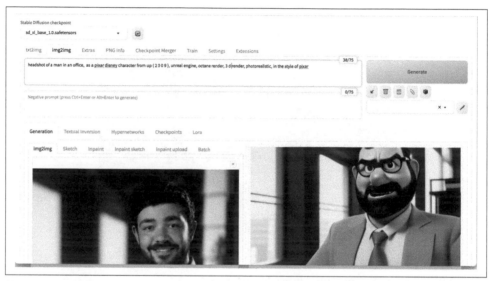

Figure 9-8. Img2Img

The parameters are the same as the normal `Text2Image` mode with the addition of *denoising strength*, which controls how much random noise is added to your base image before running the generation process. A value of 0 will add zero noise, so your output will look exactly like your input, and a value of 1 will completely replace your input with noise (functionally the same as using `Text2Image`). Often you need to experiment with different combinations of values for Denoising Strength, CFG scale, and Seed alongside the words in your prompt. The following example in Figure 9-9 creates a character in Pixar style just for fun: we wouldn't recommend using protected IP in your prompt for commercial use.

Input:

```
headshot of a man in an office,  as a Pixar Disney character
from Up ( 2 0 0 9 ), unreal engine, octane render, 3 d
render, photorealistic, in the style of Pixar
```

Figure 9-9 shows the output.

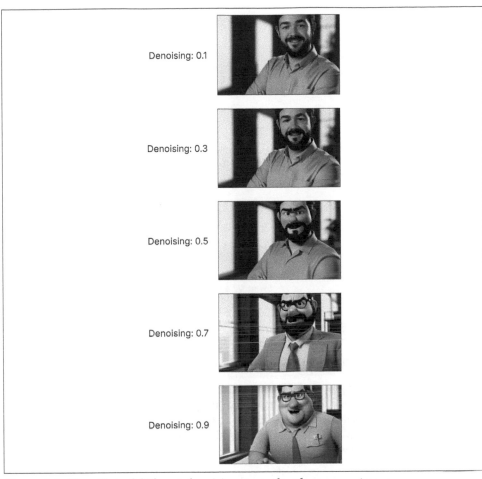

Figure 9-9. The effect of different denoising strength values on an image

If you want to test many different values for a parameter in AUTOMATIC1111 and generate a grid as is shown in Figure 9-9, that is supported in the Script drop-down at the bottom, where you can select X/Y/Z Plot and choose up to three parameters to generate multiple values for. For example, you may try also adjusting the CFG scale to see how it interacts with Denoising. Figure 9-10 shows how to select multiple values for the Denoising strength parameter. When you click the Generate button, a grid of images will be made, and you can find each individual image that populates the grid in your Output folder under the method (i.e., Text2Image, or Img2Img) and today's date.

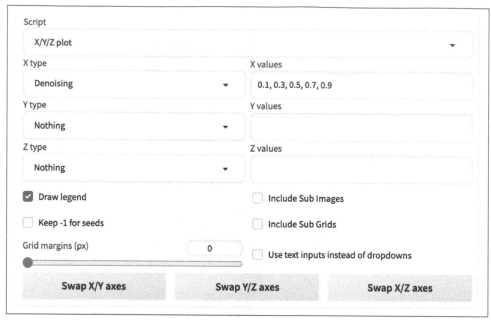

Figure 9-10. X/Y/Z plot of denoising parameter

Evaluate Quality

Generating a grid of many different parameter combinations or values is one of the powerful advantages of running Stable Diffusion locally. Although it may take time to generate lots of images, there's no better way to visually identify exactly what a parameter does and where the sweet spot is in terms of quality.

If you forgot what settings or prompt you used to generate an image, AUTO-MATIC1111 saves this as metadata on every image generated. You can visit the PNG Info tab (Figure 9-11) to read that metadata whenever needed. This also works with images you get from other users of the web interface, but only if they have posted the image on a website that doesn't strip out this metadata.

The Resize Mode options are there to determine what happens when you upload an image that doesn't match the dimensions of your base image, for example going from 1000 × 500 to 512 × 512, either stretching the aspect ratio to fit with Just Resize, cropping a part of the image in the right aspect ratio with Crop and Resize, adding noise to pad out the image with Resize and Fill, or generating an image in the new dimensions with Just Resize (latent upscale).

Figure 9-11. PNG Info tab

Upscaling Images

There's also the ability to upscale images to higher resolution in AUTOMATIC1111's Img2Img tab, just like you can in Midjourney but with more control. Upload your image and add a generic prompt like highly detailed in the prompt box. This is necessary because the upscaler works by breaking the image into tiles, expanding so there are gaps between the tiles, and then *filling in* the gaps using the prompt and context of the surrounding pixels. Go down to Scripts at the bottom and select the SD Upscale script, and then choose an upscaler (Figure 9-12).

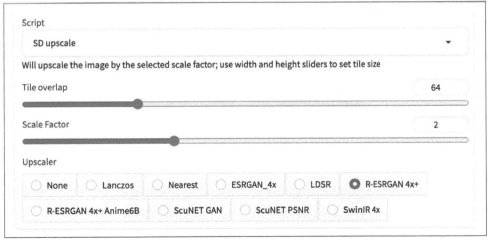

Figure 9-12. SD Upscale interface

Typically we have found the R-ESRGAN 4x+ upscaler as a good default, but this can sometimes give a cartoonish quality, as shown in Figure 9-12 with the grass. There are more models (*https://openmodeldb.info*) available to test if you aren't getting good results. When you download a new model (a *.pth* file), you just need to place it in the ESRGAN folder and restart the web interface for them to show up (in your terminal). You can also get good results with upscaling by modifying the prompt, particularly if you are losing some detail or the style is changing too much. However, it is not advised to use your original prompt, as that would have the strange effect of inpainting the same image in each tile. To show a wider quality difference, we have used the v1.5 model to generate the original image (SDXL creates images that are 4x larger, and at a higher quality, so upscaling is less needed).

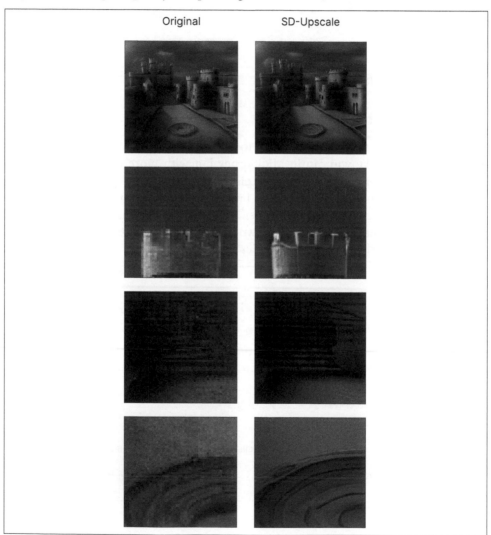

Figure 9-13. The impact of upscaling on sections of an image

Specify Format

If you're going to use the images you generate in the real world, often you can't just use a square 512 x 512 image in low resolution. Using upscaling you can generate an image in any size and whatever the required resolution.

As with all things Stable Diffusion, it helps to experiment, but for good results we recommend a high number of steps (150–200+), a CFG scale of 8–15, and a Denoising strength of 0.1–0.2 to keep the base image intact. You can click Generate to get the resulting upscaled image (512 x 512 becomes 1024 x 1024), and then you can either download the higher resolution image or click Send to Img2Img and click Generate again to double the size of the image again. The process can take a significant amount of time due to the multiple tile generations and large number of sampling steps, approximately 10–30 minutes on a M2 MacBbook Air.

Interrogate CLIP

In the Img2Img tab the CLIP embeddings model (which is also used by Stable Diffusion) is implemented In the Interrogate CLIP button (in some versions shown as a paperclip), which allows you to reverse engineer the prompt from an image, similar to Midjourney's Describe feature, covered in Chapter 8. Once you click the button and the script has run, the prompt will appear in your prompt box (Figure 9-14).

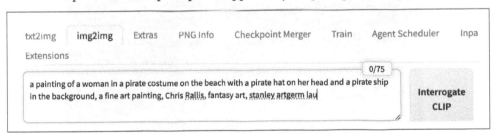

Figure 9-14. Interrogate CLIP

Output:

```
a painting of a woman in a pirate costume on the beach
with a pirate hat on her head and a pirate ship in the background,
a fine art painting, Chris Rallis, fantasy art, stanley artgerm lau
```

SD Inpainting and Outpainting

Img2Img also supports inpainting and outpainting and provides a simple canvas tool for creating the mask. To use inpainting or outpainting, click the Inpaint subtab in the Img2Img tab and upload your image. It's optionally recommended to use a specific inpainting model for better results, which you can install by downloading (*https://oreil.ly/s_trl*) the *sd-v1-5-inpainting.ckpt* file and moving it into your Models > Stable-Diffusion folder. Restart the interface; the model should appear in the top left drop-down. The canvas allows you to use a brush to remove parts of the image just like in DALL-E (see Chapter 8), which is adjustable in size for fine-grained control. In Figure 9-15, the center of a stone circle in the middle of a castle courtyard has been removed.

Figure 9-15. Inpainting canvas in Img2Img

The advice typically given for DALL-E, which also supports inpainting, is to use your prompt to describe the entire image, not just the inpainted area. This is a good default and should be tried first. Make sure Inpaint area is set to *Whole picture* rather than *Only masked,* or it'll try to fit the whole scene in the masked area (don't worry, even if you select *Whole picture*, it will only paint in your masked area). It can also help to carry over your Seed from the original image if it was AI generated. However, adding to or changing the prompt to include specifics about the region you want modified or fixed tends to get better results in our experience. At the very least you should change the subject of the prompt; for example, in Figure 9-15, the prompt changed from `castle` to `statue` because that's what we wanted to appear in the courtyard. You can also try only prompting for the infilled region, though that risks getting an image that isn't globally consistent in style.

Input:

```
statue of a king, texture, intricate, details, highly
detailed, masterpiece, architecture, building, trending on
artstation, focus, sharp focus, concept art, digital
painting, fantasy, sunny, day, midday, in the style of
high fantasy art
```

Figure 9-16 shows the output.

Figure 9-16. Inpainting to add a statue to an image

Providing Direction

Inpainting is so powerful because it gives you control. The ability to isolate an individual part of an image and give detailed directions on how to fix it gives you a more efficient workflow, without affecting the rest of the image.

If it's a small adjustment to the inpainted area, use Original as the masked content option and use a Denoising Strength of 0.2 to 0.4. If you're totally replacing an element of the image, you may need the Latent Noise option and as high as 0.8 for Denoising Strength, though any time you get above 0.4 you start to see globally inconsistent elements and hallucinations in the image, so it can take time to iterate toward something that works. The Fill option is also useful as it matches the colors of the surrounding area. If you're getting ugly seams at the edge of the inpainting area, you can increase the Mask Blur, but typically the default of 4 works well. Inpainting is an iterative process. We recommend working on fixing one issue or artifact at a time, applying it as many times as you want, and experimenting with different parameters until you're satisfied with the final image.

Outpainting doesn't work the same as in Midjourney (see Chapter 8), which has the ability to specify 1.5x or 2x zoom, or a custom aspect ratio. Instead in AUTO-MATIC1111, outpainting is implemented by scrolling down to the Script drop-down and selecting "Poor man's outpainting." You need to set the Resize mode to Resize and fill in the Img2Img Inpaint tab, and set a relatively high Denoising Strength to make this work. This extension allows you to expand the pixels on different sides of the image, while setting the Masked Content and Mask Blur parameters as usual for these gaps on the side to be inpainted.

Figure 9-17 shows the output.

Figure 9-17. Outpainting in Img2Img

As you can see in Figure 9-17, with the extra castle being added to the sky, the potential for hallucination is high and the quality can be low. It often takes a lot of experimentation and iteration to get this process right. This is a similar technique to how early adopters of generative AI would add extra empty space on the sides of photos in Photoshop, before inpainting them to match the rest of the image in Stable Diffusion. This technique is essentially just inpainting with extra steps, so all of the same advice previously listed applies. This can be quicker than using the outpainting functionality in AUTOMATIC1111 because of the poor quality and limitations of not having a proper canvas.

ControlNet

Using prompting and Img2Img or base images, it's possible to control the style of an image, but often the pose of people in the image, composition of the scene, or structure of the objects will differ greatly in the final image. ControlNet is an advanced way of conditioning input images for image generation models like Stable Diffusion.

It allows you to gain more control over the final image generated through various techniques like edge detection, pose, depth, and many more. You upload an image you want to emulate and use one of the pretrained model options for processing the image to input alongside your prompt, resulting in a matching image composition with a different style (Figure 9-18, from the ControlNet paper (*https://oreil.ly/suOJz*)).

What's referred to as ControlNet is really a series of open source models (*https://oreil.ly/E-bjw*) released following the paper "Adding Conditional Control to Text-to-Image Diffusion Models" (Zhang, Rao, and Agrawala, 2023 (*https://oreil.ly/ZH-Ow*)). While it is possible to code this in Python and build your own user interface for it, the quickest and easiest way to to get up and running is via the ControlNet (*https://oreil.ly/Dw2rs*) extension for AUTOMATIC1111. As of the time of writing, not all ControlNet methods are available for SDXL, so we are using Stable Diffusion v1.5 (make sure you use a ControlNet model that matches the version of Stable Diffusion you're using).

Source image
(for canny edge detection)

Canny edge (input)

Generated images (output)

Figure 9-18. ControlNet Stable Diffusion with canny edge map

You can install the extension following these instructions:

1. Navigate to the Extensions tab and click the subtab labeled Available.
2. Click the Load from button.
3. In the Search box type **sd-webui-controlnet** to find the Extension.
4. Click Install in the Action column to the far right.
5. Web UI will now download the necessary files and install ControlNet on your local version of Stable Diffusion.

If you have trouble executing the preceding steps, you can try the following alternate method:

1. Navigate to the Extensions tab and click Install from URL subtab.

2. In the URL field for the Git repository, paste the link to the extension: *https:// github.com/Mikubill/sd-webui-controlnet.*

3. Click Install.

4. WebUI will download and install the necessary files for ControlNet.

Now that you have ControlNet installed, restart AUTOMATIC1111 from your terminal or command line, or visit Settings and click "Apply and restart UI."

The extension will appear below the normal parameter options you get for Stable Diffusion, in an accordion tab (Figure 9-19). You first upload an image and then click Enable before selecting the ControlNet preprocessor and model you want to use. If your system has less than 6 GB of VRAM (Video Random Access Memory), you should check the Low VRAM box. Depending on the task at hand, you might want to experiment with a number of models and make adjustments to the parameters of those models in order to see which gets results.

Control Weight is analogous to prompt weight or influence, similar to putting words in brackets with a weighting (prompt words: 1.2), but for the ControlNet input. The Starting Control Steps and Ending Control Steps are when in the diffusion process the ControlNet applies, by default from start to finish (0 to 1), akin to prompt editing/shifting such as [prompt words::0.8] (apply this part of the prompt from the beginning until 80% of the total steps are complete). Because the image diffuses from larger elements down to finer details, you can achieve different results by controlling where in that process the ControlNet applies; for example; removing the last 20% of steps (Ending Control Step = 0.8) may allow the model more creativity when filling in finer detail. The Preprocessor Resolution also helps maintain control here, determining how much fine detail there is in the intermediate image processing step. Some models have their own unique parameters, such as the Canny Low and High Thresholds, which determine what pixels constitute an *edge*. Finally, the Control Mode determines how much the model follows the ControlNet input relative to your prompt.

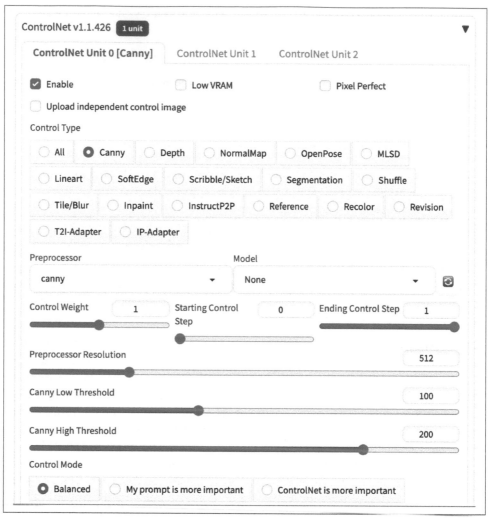

Figure 9-19. ControlNet extension interface in AUTOMATIC1111

When you first install ControlNet, you won't have any models downloaded. For them to populate in the drop-down, you should install them by downloading them from the models page (*https://oreil.ly/csYK_*) and then dropping them in the Models > ControlNet folder. If you're unsure of which model to try, start with Canny edge detection (*https://oreil.ly/z9XC6*) as it is the most generally useful. Each model is relatively large (in the order of a few gigabytes), so only download the ones you plan to use. Following are examples from some of the more common models. All images in this section are generated with the DPM++ SDE Karras sampler, a CFG scale of 1.5, Control Mode set to Balanced, Resize Mode set to Crop and Resize (the uploaded image is cropped to match the dimensions of the generated image, 512 × 512), and

30 sampling steps, with the default settings for each ControlNet model. Version 1.5 of Stable Diffusion was used as not all of these ControlNet models are available for Stable Diffusion XL at the time of writing, but the techniques should be transferrable between models.

Canny edge detection creates simple, sharp pixel outlines around areas of high contrast. It can be very detailed and give excellent results but can also pick up unwanted noise and give too much control of the image to ControlNet. In images where there is a high degree of detail that needs to be transferred to a new image with a different style, Canny excels and should be used as the default option. For example, redrawing a city skyline in a specific style works very well with the Canny model, as we did with an image of New York City (by Robert Bye (*https://oreil.ly/wEPLB*) on Unsplash (*https://oreil.ly/_iyxU*)) in Figure 9-20.

Input:

```
New York City by Studio Ghibli
```

Figure 9-20 shows the output.

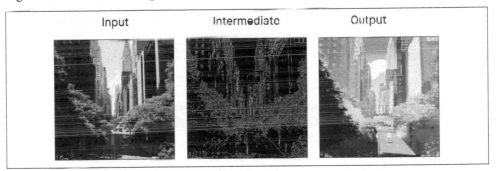

Figure 9-20. ControlNet Canny

Sometimes in traditional img2img prompting, some elements of an image get confused or merged, because Stable Diffusion doesn't understand the depth of those objects in relation to each other. The Depth model creates a depth map estimation based on the image, which provides control over the composition and spatial position of image elements. If you're not familiar with depth maps, whiter areas are closer to the viewer, and blacker are farther away. This can be seen in Figure 9-21, where an image of a band (by Hans Vivek (*https://oreil.ly/tlCrf*) on Unsplash (*https://oreil.ly/BOKJ7*)) is turned into an image of soldiers with the same positions and depth of field.

Input:

```
US military unit on patrol in Afghanistan
```

Figure 9-21 shows the output.

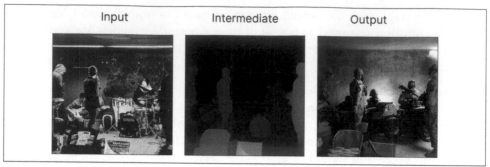

Figure 9-21. ControlNet Depth

The Normal model creates a mapping estimation that functions as a 3-D model of objects in the image. The colors red, green, and blue are used by 3-D programs to determine how smooth or bumpy an object is, with each color corresponding to a direction (left/right, up/down, close/far). This is just an estimation, however, so it can have unintended consequences in some cases. This method tends to excel if you need more textures and lighting to be taken into consideration but can sometimes offer too much detail in the case of faces, constraining the creativity of the output. In Figure 9-22, a woman playing a keyboard (by Soundtrap (*https://oreil.ly/RP1Ei*) on Unsplash (*https://oreil.ly/I3QGY*)) is transported back in time to the *Great Gatsby* era.

Input:

```
woman playing piano at a Great Gatsby flapper party, 1920s,
symmetrical face
```

Figure 9-22 shows the output.

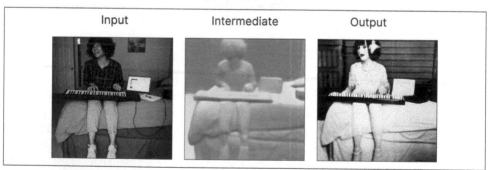

Figure 9-22. ControlNet Normal

The OpenPose method creates a skeleton for a figure by determining its posture, hand placement, and facial expression. For this model to work you typically need to have a human subject with the full body visible, though there are portrait options. It is very common practice to use multiple OpenPose skeletons and compose them together into a single image, if multiple people are required in the scene. Figure 9-23 transposes the Mona Lisa's pose (*https://oreil.ly/7n02i*) onto an image of Rachel Weisz.

Input:

```
painting of Rachel Weisz
```

Figure 9-23 shows the output.

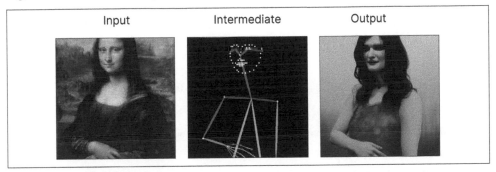

Figure 9-23. ControlNet OpenPose

The M-LSD (Mobile Line Segment Detection) technique is quite often used in architecture and interior design, as it's well suited to tracing straight lines. Straight lines tend only to appear in man-made objects, so it isn't well suited to nature scenes (though it might create an interesting effect). Man-made objects like houses are well suited to this approach, as shown in the image of a modern apartment (by Collov Home Design (*https://oreil.ly/OtV_O*) on Unsplash (*https://oreil.ly/z38do*)) reimagined for the *Mad Men* era, in Figure 9-24.

Input:

```
1960s Mad Men style apartment
```

Figure 9-24 shows the output.

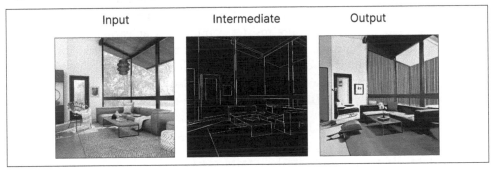

Figure 9-24. ControlNet M-LSD

The SoftEdge technique, also known as HED (holistically-nested edge detection), is an alternative to Canny edge detection, creating smoother outlines around objects. It is very commonly used and provides good detail like Canny but can be less noisy and deliver more aesthetically pleasing results. This method is great for stylizing and recoloring images, and it tends to allow for better manipulation of faces compared to Canny. Thanks to ControlNet, you don't need to enter too much of a detailed prompt of the overall image and can just prompt for the change you want to see. Figure 9-25 shows a reimagining of Vermeer's *Girl with a Pearl Earring* (*https://oreil.ly/RjUur*), with Scarlett Johansson:

Input:

```
Scarlett Johansson, best quality, extremely detailed
```

Negative:

```
monochrome, lowres, bad anatomy, worst quality, low quality
```

Figure 9-25 shows the output.

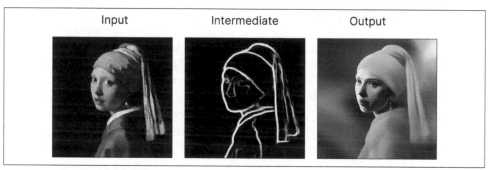

Figure 9-25. ControlNet SoftEdge

Another popular technique for architecture is segmentation, which divides the image into related areas or segments that are somewhat related to one another. It is roughly analogous to using an image mask in Img2Img, except with better results. Segmentation can be used when you require greater command over various objects within an image. One powerful use case is on outdoor scenes, which can vary for the time of day and surroundings, or even the era. Take a look at Figure 9-26, showing a modern-day photograph of a castle (by Richard Clark (*https://oreil.ly/SG9CT*) on Unsplash (*https://oreil.ly/2FlyI*)), turned into a fantasy-style castle illustration.

Input:

```
A beautiful magical castle viewed from the outside, texture,
intricate, details, highly detailed, masterpiece,
architecture, building, trending on artstation, focus, sharp
focus, concept art, digital painting, fantasy, sunny, day,
midday, in the style of high fantasy art
```

Figure 9-26 shows the output.

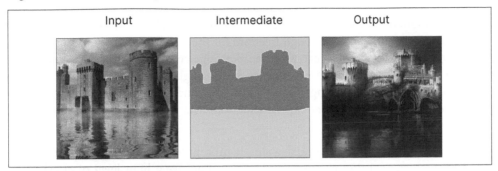

Figure 9-26. ControlNet segmentation

One powerful feature is the ability to draw on a canvas and use that in ControlNet. You can also draw offline and take a picture to upload your image, but it can be quicker for simple images to click the pencil emoji in the Stable Diffusion web UI, and draw with the provided brush. Even a simple scribble is often sufficient, and the edges don't have to be perfect, as shown in Figure 9-27.

Input:

```
The Happy Goldfish, illustrated children's book
```

Figure 9-27 shows the output.

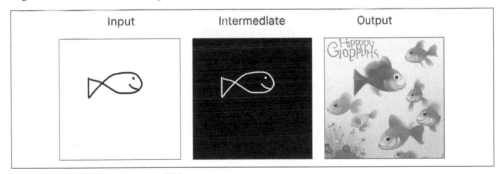

Figure 9-27. ControlNet scribble

Provide Examples

ControlNet gives an AI artist the ability to make an image that *looks like* another image in terms of composition, simply by providing an example image to emulate. This allows more control over visual consistency and more flexibility in making more sophisticated images.

Each of these ControlNet methods has its own preprocessor, and they must match the model for the image to make sense. For example, if you're using a Canny preprocessor, you should use a Canny model like control_v11p_sd15_canny. It's also important to choose a model that gives enough freedom for the task you're trying to accomplish; for example, an image of a cat with the SoftEdge model might perhaps have too much detail to be turned into a lion, and you might want to try something less fine-grained. As with all things Stable Diffusion, finding the exact combination of model and parameters requires experimentation, with new functionality and options proliferating all the time.

ControlNet supports being run with a simple prompt or even without a prompt at all. It will match the existing image you submit and ensure a high level of consistency. You can run a generic prompt like a professional, detailed, high-quality image and get a good version of the existing image. Most often, however, you'll be attempting to change certain aspects of the image and will want to input a full prompt, as in the previous examples. The resulting image will match both the prompt and the ControlNet output, and you can experiment with adjusting the parameters available to see what gets results.

Segment Anything Model (SAM)

When working on an AI-generated image, it is often beneficial to be able to separate out a *mask* representing a specific person, object, or element. For example, dividing an image of a person from the background of the image would allow you to inpaint a new background behind that person. This can take a long time and lead to mistakes when using a brush tool, so it can be helpful to be able to automatically segment the image based on an AI model's interpretation of where the lines are.

The most popular and powerful model for doing this is *SAM*, which stands for Segment Anything Model, released open source on GitHub (*https://oreil.ly/BuunX*) by Meta. The model is trained on a dataset of 11 million images and 1.1 billion masks, and is able to infer where the image mask should be based on user input (clicking to add one to three dots to the image where masks should be), or it can automatically mask all the elements individually in an image. These masks can then be exported for use in inpainting,in ControlNet, or as base images.

You can use SAM in the AUTOMATIC1111 interface using the *sd-webui-segment-anything* (*https://oreil.ly/rFMJN*) extension. Once AUTOMATIC1111 is installed and running, you can install the SAM extension following these instructions:

1. Navigate to the Extensions tab and click the subtab labeled "Available."

2. Click the "Load from" button.

3. In the Search box type in: `sd-webui-segment-anything` to find the extension.

4. Click Install in the Action column to the far right.

5. WebUI will now download the necessary files and install SAM on your local version of Stable Diffusion.

If you have trouble executing the preceding steps, you can try the following alternate method:

1. Navigate to the "Extensions" tab and click the "Install from URL" subtab.

2. In the URL field for the Git repository, paste the link to the extension: *https://github.com/continue-revolution/sd-webui-segment-anything*.

3. Click Install.

4. WebUI will download and install the necessary files for SAM on your local version of Stable Diffusion.

You also need to download the actual SAM model weights, linked to from the repository (*https://oreil.ly/IqrbI*). The 1.25 GB *sam_vit_l_0b3195.pth* is what's being used in this chapter. If you encounter issues with low VRAM (your computer freezes or lags), you should switch to smaller models. Move the model you downloaded into the *stable-diffusion-webui/sd-webui-segment-anything/models/sam* folder.

Now that you have SAM fully installed, restart AUTOMATIC1111 from your terminal or command line, or visit Settings and click "Apply and restart UI."

You should see the extension in the Img2Img tab, by scrolling down past the canvas and Seed parameter, in an accordion component alongside the ControlNet extension. Upload an image here (we used the photo for Figure 9-28 by Luca Baini (*https://oreil.ly/Lb3xE*) on Unsplash (*https://oreil.ly/jvCjz*)) and click the image to select individual prompt points. These prompt points go along to SAM as user input to help the model determine what should be segmented out from the image. You can click Preview to see what mask will be created, and iteratively add or remove plot points until the mask is correct. There is a checkbox labeled "Preview automatically when add/remove points," which updates the mask with each click. Often SAM gets it right with a single plot point, but if you are struggling, you can also add negative plot points to parts of the image you don't want to mask by right-clicking. Select the mask you want (Figure 9-28) from the three options provided (counting from 0 to 2).

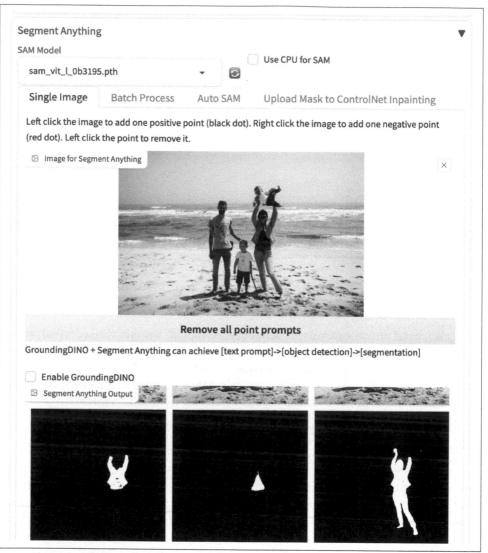

Figure 9-28. Adding plot points

When your mask is ready, make sure the box Copy to Inpaint Upload & img2img ControlNet Inpainting is checked, and click the Switch to Inpaint Upload button. You won't see anything happen visually, but when you switch to the Inpainting tab, you should be able to generate your prompt with the mask generated by SAM. There is no need to upload the picture or mask to the Inpainting tab. You can also download your mask for later upload in the "Inpaint upload" tab. This method was unreliable during our testing, and there may be a better supported method for inpainting with SAM and Stable Diffusion made available.

Divide Labor

Generative models like Midjourney and Stable Diffusion are powerful, but they can't do everything. In training a separate image segmentation model, Meta has made it possible to generate more complex images by splitting out the elements of an image into different masks, which can be worked on separately before being aggregated together for the final product.

DreamBooth Fine-Tuning

The original Stable Diffusion model cost a reported $600,000 to train (*https://oreil.ly/s739b*) using a total of 150,000 GPU hours, so training your own foundational model is likely out of the question for most organizations. However, it is possible to build on top of Stable Diffusion, using the Dreambooth technique, which was introduced in the paper "DreamBooth: Fine Tuning Text-to-Image Diffusion Models for Subject-Driven Generation" (Ruiz et al., 2022 (*https://oreil.ly/ZqdjB*)). DreamBooth allows you to fine-tune or train the model to understand a new concept it hasn't encountered yet in its training data. Not having to start from scratch to build a new model means significantly less time and resources: about 45 minutes to an hour on 1 GPU. DreamBooth actually updates the weights of the new model, which gives you a new 2 GB model file to use in AUTOMATIC1111 instead of the base Stable Diffusion model.

There are many DreamBooth-based models available on websites like Hugging Face (*https://oreil.ly/2efOO*) and Civitai (*https://civitai.com*). To use these models in AUTOMATIC1111, you simply download them and move them into the stable-diffusion-webui/models/Stable-diffusion/ folder. Dreambooth models often have a specific word or token needed for triggering the style or subject, which must be included in the prompt. For example, the Inkpunk Diffusion (*https://oreil.ly/spsy3*) model requires the word *nvinkpunk*. Note: the underlying base model here is v1.5 of Stable Diffusion, so reset your image size to 512 × 512.

Input:

```
skateboarding in Times Square nvinkpunk
```

Figure 9-29 shows the output.

Figure 9-29. InkPunk skateboarder

Divide Labor

The mistake many people make with AI is assuming there's one model to rule them all. In reality there are many creative models out there, and often training on a specific task yields better results than the general foundational models. While the foundation models like Stable Diffusion XL are what most practicioners start with, commonly they begin to experiment with fine-tuning their own models on specific tasks, often based on smaller, more efficient models like v1.5.

The preferred method for training a DreamBooth model is Shivam Shrirao's repository (*https://oreil.ly/AJnnL*), which uses HuggingFace's `diffusers` library. What follows is an explanation of the code in Google Colab (*https://oreil.ly/790FZ*). Version 1.5 is used in this notebook, as it is a smaller model, and is able to be trained in a few hours in the Google Colab environment for free. A copy of this Python notebook is saved in the GitHub repository (*https://oreil.ly/NzzGm*) for this book for posterity, but it should be noted that it will only run on an Nvidia GPU, not on a MacBook.

First the Colab checks whether there is access to an Nvidia GPU. This is one good reason to run Dreambooth on Google Colab, because you are given access to the right resource to run the code without any configuration needed:

```
!nvidia-smi --query-gpu=name,memory.total, \
    memory.free --format=csv,noheader
```

Next the necessary libraries are installed, including the `diffusers` library from Hugging Face:

```
!wget -q https://github.com/ShivamShrirao/diffusers/raw/ \
    main/examples/dreambooth/train_dreambooth.py
!wget -q https://github.com/ShivamShrirao/diffusers/raw/ \
    main/scripts/convert_diffusers_to_original_stable_ \
    diffusion.py
%pip install -qq \
git+https://github.com/ShivamShrirao/diffusers
%pip install -q -U --pre triton
%pip install -q accelerate transformers ftfy \
bitsandbytes==0.35.0 gradio natsort safetensors xformers
```

Run the next cell to set the output directory of the model when it is finished running. It's recommended to save the model to Google Drive (even if temporarily) because you can more reliably download large files (4–5 GB) from there than you can from the Google Colab filesystem. Ensure that you have selected the right base model from the Hugging Face hub runwayml/stable-diffusion-v1-5 and choose a name for your token for the output directory (usually *ukj* or *zwx*; more on this later):

```
#@markdown If model weights should be saved directly in
#@markdown google drive (takes around 4-5 GB).
save_to_gdrive = False
if save_to_gdrive:
    from google.colab import drive
    drive.mount('/content/drive')

#@markdown Name/Path of the initial model.
MODEL_NAME = "runwayml/stable-diffusion-v1-5" \
    #@param {type:"string"}

#@markdown Enter the directory name to save model at.

OUTPUT_DIR = "stable_diffusion_weights/ukj" \
    #@param {type:"string"}
if save_to_gdrive:
    OUTPUT_DIR = "/content/drive/MyDrive/" + OUTPUT_DIR
else:
    OUTPUT_DIR = "/content/" + OUTPUT_DIR

print(f"[*] Weights will be saved at {OUTPUT_DIR}")

!mkdir -p $OUTPUT_DIR
```

Before training, you need to add the concepts you want to train on. In our experience, training on multiple concepts tends to harm performance, so typically we would train on only one subject or style. You can merge models later in the Checkpoint Merger tab of AUTOMATIC1111, although this gets into more advanced territory not covered in this book. The instance prompt includes the token you'll use in your prompt to trigger the model, and ideally it's a word that doesn't have any other meaning, like *zwx* or *ukj*. The class prompt is a starting point for the training, so if you're training a model of a specific person, you start from `photo of a person` to make the training more effective:

```
# You can also add multiple concepts here.
# Try tweaking `--max_train_steps` accordingly.

concepts_list = [
    {
        "instance_prompt":      "photo of ukj person",
        "class_prompt":         "photo of a person",
        "instance_data_dir":    "/content/data/ukj",
        "class_data_dir":       "/content/data/person"
    }
]

# `class_data_dir` contains regularization images
import json
import os
for c in concepts_list:
    os.makedirs(c["instance_data_dir"], exist_ok=True)

with open("concepts_list.json", "w") as f:
    json.dump(concepts_list, f, indent=4)
```

Next, we upload the images through Google Colab. Dreambooth can work with as few as 5 images, but typically it's recommended you use about 20–30 images, although some train with hundreds of images. One creative use case is to use the Consistent Characters method discussed in Chapter 8 to generate 20 different images of the same AI-generated character and use them to train a Dreambooth model on. Alternatively, you could upload 20 pictures of yourself to create an AI profile photo, or 20 pictures of a product your company sells to generate AI product photography. You can upload the files locally to the *instance_data_dir* in the Google Colab filesystem (which can be faster) or run the next cell to get an upload button:

```
import os
from google.colab import files
import shutil

for c in concepts_list:
    print(f"""Uploading instance images for
`{c['instance_prompt']}`""")
    uploaded = files.upload()
```

```
    for filename in uploaded.keys():
        dst_path = os.path.join(c['instance_data_dir'],
            filename)
        shutil.move(filename, dst_path)
```

Now the actual training begins! This code runs on the GPU and outputs the final weights when finished. Make sure to change `save_sample_prompt` before running to use the token you assigned, in this case `photo of ukj person`:

```
!python3 train_dreambooth.py \
    --pretrained_model_name_or_path=$MODEL_NAME \
    --pretrained_vae_name_or_path="stabilityai/sd-vae-ft-mse" \
    --output_dir=$OUTPUT_DIR \
    --revision="fp16" \
    --with_prior_preservation --prior_loss_weight=1.0 \
    --seed=1337 \
    --resolution=512 \
    --train_batch_size=1 \
    --train_text_encoder \
    --mixed_precision="fp16" \
    --use_8bit_adam \
    --gradient_accumulation_steps=1 \
    --learning_rate=1e-6 \
    --lr_scheduler="constant" \
    --lr_warmup_steps=0 \
    --num_class_images=50 \
    --sample_batch_size=4 \
    --max_train_steps=800 \
    --save_interval=10000 \
    --save_sample_prompt="photo of ukj person" \
    --concepts_list="concepts_list.json"
```

Now that the training is complete, the next two cells of code define the directory and then display a grid of images so you can see visually whether the model correctly understood your concept and is now capable of generating useful images of your style of subject:

```
WEIGHTS_DIR = ""
if WEIGHTS_DIR == "":
    from natsort import natsorted
    from glob import glob
    import os
    WEIGHTS_DIR = natsorted(glob(OUTPUT_DIR + os.sep + \
        "*"))[-1]
print(f"[*] WEIGHTS_DIR={WEIGHTS_DIR}")

#@markdown Run to generate a grid of preview images from the last saved weights.
import os
import matplotlib.pyplot as plt
import matplotlib.image as mpimg

weights_folder = OUTPUT_DIR
```

```
folders = sorted([f for f in os.listdir(weights_folder) \
    if f != "0"], key=lambda x: int(x))

row = len(folders)
col = len(os.listdir(os.path.join(weights_folder,
    folders[0], "samples")))
scale = 4
fig, axes = plt.subplots(row, col, figsize=(col*scale,
    row*scale), gridspec_kw={'hspace': 0, 'wspace': 0})

for i, folder in enumerate(folders):
    folder_path = os.path.join(weights_folder, folder)
    image_folder = os.path.join(folder_path, "samples")
    images = [f for f in os.listdir(image_folder)]
    for j, image in enumerate(images):
        if row == 1:
            currAxes = axes[j]
        else:
            currAxes = axes[i, j]
        if i == 0:
            currAxes.set_title(f"Image {j}")
        if j == 0:
            currAxes.text(-0.1, 0.5, folder, rotation=0,
            va='center', ha='center',
            transform=currAxes.transAxes)
        image_path = os.path.join(image_folder, image)
        img = mpimg.imread(image_path)
        currAxes.imshow(img, cmap='gray')
        currAxes.axis('off')

plt.tight_layout()
plt.savefig('grid.png', dpi=72)
```

Finally, you want to run the conversion process to get a *.ckpt* file, which is what you will use in AUTOMATIC1111:

```
#@markdown Run conversion.
ckpt_path = WEIGHTS_DIR + "/model.ckpt"

half_arg = ""
#@markdown Convert to fp16, takes half the space (2GB).
fp16 = True #@param {type: "boolean"}
if fp16:
    half_arg = "--half"
!python convert_diffusers_to_original_stable_diffusion.py \
    --model_path $WEIGHTS_DIR  --checkpoint_path \
    $ckpt_path $half_arg
print(f"[*] Converted ckpt saved at {ckpt_path}")
```

You can then visit the weights directory *stable_diffusion_weights/zwx* to find the model and download it. If you are having issues downloading such a large file from the Google Colab filesystem, try checking the option to save to Google Drive before

---

running the model, and download from there. We recommend renaming the model before dropping it into your *stable-diffusion-webui/models/Stable-diffusion/* folder so you can tell what model it is when using it later.

Input:

```
a professional headshot of ukj person, standing with his
arms crossed and smiling at the camera with his arms
crossed, a character portrait, Adam Bruce Thomson, private
press, professional photo
```

Figure 9-30 shows the output.

Figure 9-30. A Dreambooth model image of one of the authors

There is also an extension (*https://oreil.ly/xbt2d*) for training Dreambooth models via Automatic1111, based on Shivam Shrirao's method. This extension can be installed in the same way as you installed ControlNet and Segment Anything in previous sections of this chapter. This tool is for advanced users as it exposes a significant number of features and settings for experimentation, many of which you need to be a machine learning expert to understand. To start learning what these parameters and settings mean so you can experiment with different options, check out the beginner's guide to training (*https://oreil.ly/gfdY3*) in the extension wiki. The benefit of using this method instead of Google Colab is that it runs locally on your computer, so you can leave it running without worrying it will time out and lose progress.

Provide Examples

Dreambooth helps you personalize your experience with generative AI. You just need to supply 5–30 images that serve as examples of a concept, and in less than an hour of training time, you can have a fully personalized custom model.

There are other training and fine-tuning methods available besides Dreambooth, but this technique is currently the most commonly used. An older technique is Textual Inversion (*https://oreil.ly/GgnJV*), which doesn't update the model weights but instead approximates the right location for a token to represent your concept, though this tends to perform far worse than Dreambooth. One promising new technique is LoRA, from the paper "LoRA: Low-Rank Adaptation of Large Language Models" (Hu et al., 2021 (*https://oreil.ly/NtoiB*)), also prevalent in the text-generation space with LLMs. This technique adds new layers into the model and trains just those new layers to build a custom model without expending too many resources. There are also Hypernetworks, which train parameters that can then generate these new layers, as introduced by Kurumuz (*https://oreil.ly/zFH0-*) in the Medium article "NovelAI Improvements on Stable Diffusion." Both of these methods are experimental and only make up a small number of the models on Civitai at the time of writing (less than 10%), as well as having in general lower user ratings in terms of quality.

Stable Diffusion XL Refiner

The SDXL v1.0 model has 6.6 billion parameters, compared to 0.98 billion for the v1.5 model (Rombach et al., 2023 (*https://oreil.ly/vc1zS*)). The increased firepower yields impressive results, and as such the model is starting to win over die-hard 1.5 enthusiasts. Part of the power of SDXL comes from the division of labor between the base model, which sets the global composition, and a refiner model (Figure 9-31), which adds finer details (optional).

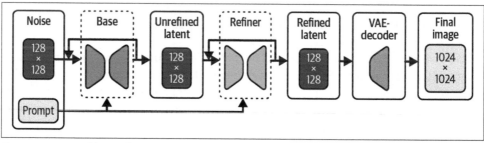

Figure 9-31. Stable Diffusion XL base and refiner model

The underlying language model that infers meaning from your prompts is a combination of OpenClip (ViT-G/14) and OpenAI's CLIP ViT-L. Stable Diffusion v2 used OpenClip alone and therefore prompts that worked on v1.5 were not as transferable: that problem has been largely solved with SDXL. Additionally, the SDXL model has been trained with a more diverse set of image sizes, leading to better results when you need an image that isn't the standard square aspect ratio. Stablity AI's research (*https://oreil.ly/_b7xX*) indicates that users overwhelmingly prefer the XL model over v1.5 (Figure 9-32).

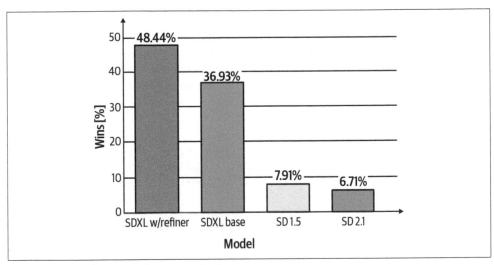

Figure 9-32. Relative performance preference

To make use of the refiner model, you must utilize the "Switch at" functionality in the AUTOMATIC1111 interface. This value controls at which step the pipeline switches to the refiner model. For example, switching at 0.6 with 30 steps means the base model will be used for the first 18 steps, and then it will switch to the refiner model for the final 12 steps (Figure 9-33).

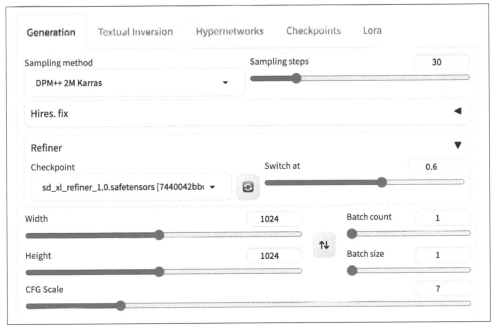

Figure 9-33. Refiner—Switch at parameter

Common advice is to switch between 0.4 and 1.0 (a value of 1.0 will not switch and only uses the base model), with 20–50 sampling steps for the best results. In our experience, switching at 0.6 with 30 sampling steps produces the highest-quality image, but like all things Stable Diffusion, you must experiment to discover what gets the best results for your image. Setting the refiner to switch at 0.6 gives the output shown in Figure 9-35.

Input:

```
anime cat girl with pink hair and a cat ears outfit is posing for a picture
in front of a gaze, photorealistic, 1girl, a character portrait, floral print,
Alice Prin, sots art, official art, sunlight, wavy hair, looking at viewer
```

Negative:

```
disfigured, ugly, bad, immature, photo, amateur, overexposed, underexposed
```

Figure 9-34 shows the output.

Figure 9-34. Anime cat girl with SDXL base model versus refiner at 0.6

Divide Labor

The architecture of SDXL is a perfect example of splitting a task into multiple jobs, and using the right model for the job. The base model sets the scene and guides the composition of the image, while the refiner increases fine detail.

One quality-of-life modification you can make is to install the aspect ratio selector extension, which can be loaded with image sizes or aspect ratios you use regularly, allowing one-click setting of the correct size and aspect ratio for either model.

To install the extension, browse to the Extensions tab, go to Install from URL, paste in *https://github.com/alemelis/sd-webui-ar*, and click Install. Go to the extension folder stable-diffusion-webui/extensions/sd-webui-ar and add the following to the *resolutions.txt* file (or replace what's there for cleanliness):

```
SD1:1, 512, 512 # 1:1 square
XL1:1, 1024, 1024 # 1:1 square
SD3:2, 768, 512 # 3:2 landscape
XL3:2, 1216, 832 # 3:2 landscape
SD9:16, 403, 716 # 9:16 portrait
XL9:16, 768, 1344 # 9:16 portrait
```

Clicking one of these preset buttons will automatically adjust the width and height accordingly. You may also replace *aspect ratios.txt* with the following, allowing you to automatically calculate the aspect ratio based on the height value you have set in the web UI, and they'll show in the web UI interface (Figure 9-35):

```
Square 1:1, 1.0 # 1:1 ratio based on minimum dimension
Landscape 3:2, 3/2 # Set width based on 3:2 ratio to height
Portrait 9:16, 9/16 # Set width based on 9:16 ratio to height
```

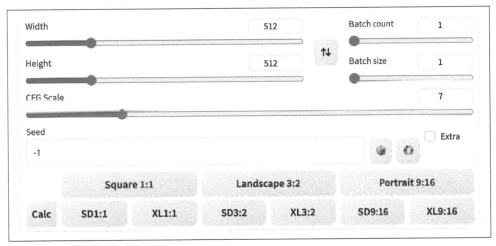

Figure 9-35. Aspect ratios

Summary

In this chapter, you learned advanced techniques for image generation using Stable Diffusion, an open source model. If you followed along, you successfully installed Stable Diffusion and built an inference pipeline using the HuggingFace *diffusers* library. You hopefully generated images based on prompts using the Stable Diffusion inference model in Google Colab. Additionally, this chapter recommended exploring the open source community and user interfaces like AUTOMATIC1111 for running Stable Diffusion with advanced features.

The chapter also introduced the concept of ControlNet, which allows for controlling the style of an image using prompting and base images, and Segment Anything, a model for masking specific parts of an image. By applying these techniques, you are now able to customize generated images to meet your specific needs. You also learned about techniques for personalization, specifically DreamBooth fine-tuning, allowing you to train a model to understand new concepts not encountered in its training data.

In the next chapter, you'll get the chance to put everything you've learned throughout this book into action. We'll be exploring how to build an AI blog post generator that produces both the blog text and an accompanying image. That final exciting chapter will take you through the process of creating an end-to-end system that generates high-quality blog posts based on user input, complete with custom illustrations in a consistent visual style. You'll learn how to optimize prompts, generate engaging titles, and create AI-generated images that match your desired style!

Building AI-Powered Applications

In this chapter, you'll apply the five principles of prompting to an end-to-end AI workflow for content writing. The service will write blog posts based on the user's responses to interview questions, in the style of the user's writing. This system was first documented on the Saxifrage blog (*https://oreil.ly/saxifrage*).

AI Blog Writing

The naive approach to creating a blog writing service using AI would be to prompt ChatGPT with `Write a blog post on {blogPostTopic}`. The resulting content would be of reasonable quality but wouldn't likely contain any valuable opinions or unique experiences on the topic. The content would also likely be short and generic and therefore unlikely to rank on Google.

A more sophisticated approach might be to build up a longer prompt with further instructions. Detail on the prescribed writing tone, architecture of the blog post, and keywords to include could be added. An example of a common blog post writing prompt (*https://oreil.ly/uMfZa*) can be seen here.

Input:

```
Create a blog post about "{blogPostTopic}". Write it in a "{tone}" tone.
Use transition words.
Use active voice. Write over 1000 words.
Use very creative titles for the blog post.
Add a title for each section. Ensure there are a minimum of 9 sections. Each
section should have a minimum of two paragraphs.
Include the following keywords: "{keywords}".
Create a good slug for this post and a meta description with a maximum of 100
words and add it to the end of the blog post.
```

This longer, more sophisticated prompt is likely to result in better quality content. However, let's run through the five principles of prompting as a checklist:

Direction

There are some instructions provided, such as the tone, using transition words, and an active voice. However, the content is still likely to sound like AI, and not like the user.

Format

Although there are some mentions of structure, including dictating nine sections of two paragraphs, it's likely these instructions will be ignored. ChatGPT is bad at math and is often unable to follow instructions dictating a number of sections or words.

Examples

There are no samples of how to do the task given, which is likely to harm the reliability of running this prompt across multiple topics or even multiple times on the same topic. Even providing one example (a one-shot prompt) could radically help improve quality.

Evaluation

This is an example of *blind prompting* (adding instructions to a prompt without testing them (*https://oreil.ly/r7sXi*)). It's likely some of these instructions make no difference to quality (unnecessarily costing tokens) or might even degrade quality.

Division

The entire task is attempted with just one prompt, which is likely to harm performance. Without breaking the task into subtasks, it's hard to understand which part of the process is suceeding or failing.

Through this chapter, you'll create multiple LLM chain components. Each chain will be implemented in LangChain to make it more maintainable and to give easy logging for monitoring and optimization. The resulting system will help you generate *human-sounding* content based on the unique opinions and experiences of the user.

It's crucial that you first prepare your workspace with the necessary tools. Therefore, let's shift our focus toward topic research and start setting up your programming environment.

Topic Research

You will need to install several Python packages to effectively use LangChain's document loaders, including the following:

google-searchresults
> A Python library designed to scrape and process Google search results.

pandas
> This offers data structures and operations for manipulating numerical tables and time series data.

html2text
> This tool converts HTML from files or web pages into markdown (*.md*) files or text.

pytest-playwright
> This package enables end-to-end testing with Playwright.

chromadb
> ChromaDB is an open source vector database.

nest_asyncio
> This extends the Python standard `asyncio` to patch and render it compatible with Jupyter Notebooks.

Installation of these packages can be achieved easily with this command:

```
pip install google-searchresults pandas html2text pytest-playwright chromadb \
nest_asyncio --quiet
```

Additionally, you'll be using LangChain's document loaders that require Playwright.

Type this command on your terminal: **playwright install**.

Additionally, you'll need to choose a TOPIC and set environment variables for both SERPAPI_API_KEY and STABILITY_API_KEY. If you're running the script without Jupyter Notebook, then you won't need to use any of the nest_asyncio code:

```
from langchain_openai.chat_models import ChatOpenAI
from langchain.output_parsers import PydanticOutputParser
from langchain_text_splitters import RecursiveCharacterTextSplitter
import os

# Custom imports:
from content_collection import collect_serp_data_and_extract_text_from_webpages
from custom_summarize_chain import create_all_summaries, DocumentSummary

import nest_asyncio
nest_asyncio.apply()

# Constant variables:
TOPIC = "Neural networks"
os.environ["SERPAPI_API_KEY"] = ""
os.environ["STABILITY_API_KEY"] = ""
```

Next, you'll focus on summarizing web content efficiently:

```python
# Extract content from webpages into LangChain documents:
text_documents = await \
collect_serp_data_and_extract_text_from_webpages(TOPIC)

# LLM, text splitter + parser:
llm = ChatOpenAI(temperature=0)
text_splitter = RecursiveCharacterTextSplitter.from_tiktoken_encoder(
    chunk_size=1500, chunk_overlap=400
)
parser = PydanticOutputParser(pydantic_object=DocumentSummary)

summaries = await create_all_summaries(text_documents,
parser,
llm,
text_splitter)
```

First, import the required tools and then fetch the web page content related to your TOPIC. After setting up your ChatOpenAI model, you'll utilize a text_splitter to manage text chunks. The splitter ensures no snippet is too long, while maintaining context with overlap. Then create the PydanticOutputParser to handle and structure the summaries. By feeding the extracted documents through a dedicated summarization function, the LLM produces concise summaries.

If you would like to dive deeper into the create_all_summaries function, check *custom_summarize_chain.py* (*https://oreil.ly/KyKjS*).

Some key points to highlight are that you can *subclass* most classes within LangChain. For example, you can overide the default ChromiumLoader to be asynchronous:

```python
from langchain_community.document_loaders import AsyncHtmlLoader, \
AsyncChromiumLoader

class ChromiumLoader(AsyncChromiumLoader):
    async def load(self):
        raw_text = [await self.ascrape_playwright(url) for url in self.urls]
        # Return the raw documents:
        return [Document(page_content=text) for text in raw_text]


async def get_html_content_from_urls(
    df: pd.DataFrame, number_of_urls: int = 3, url_column: str = "link"
) -> List[Document]:
    # Get the HTML content of the first 3 URLs:
    urls = df[url_column].values[:number_of_urls].tolist()

    # If there is only one URL, convert it to a list:
    if isinstance(urls, str):
        urls = [urls]
```

```
    # Check for empty URLs:
    urls = [url for url in urls if url != ""]

    # Check for duplicate URLs:
    urls = list(set(urls))

    # Throw error if no URLs are found:
    if len(urls) == 0:
        raise ValueError("No URLs found!")
    # loader = AsyncHtmlLoader(urls) # Faster but might not always work.
    loader = ChromiumLoader(urls)
    docs = await loader.load()
    return docs

async def create_all_summaries(
    # ... commented out for brevity
) -> List[DocumentSummary]:
    # ... commented out for brevity
```

By subclassing `ChromiumLoader`, you can easily create a custom implementation to *asynchronously scrape content* from multiple URLs using the Chrome browser. `get_html_content_from_urls` fetches HTML content from a list of URLs, ensuring no duplicates and handling potential errors.

Expert Interview

Now that you've successfully extracted the summaries from Google for the top three results, you'll conduct an interview with an LLM, generating relevant questions to make sure that your article has a unique perspective using an `InterviewChain` class:

```
from expert_interview_chain import InterviewChain
interview_chain = InterviewChain(topic=TOPIC, document_summaries=summaries)
interview_questions = interview_chain()

for question in interview_questions.questions:
    print(f"Answer the following question: {question.question}\n", flush=True)
    answer = input(f"Answer the following question: {question.question}\n")
    print('----------------------------------------')
    question.answer = answer
```

InterviewChain instantiation

With your topic and obtained summaries in hand, create an instance of `Inter viewChain`, tailoring it to your data's unique context.

Generating questions

By simply calling the `interview_chain`, you kickstart the process of generating a series of probing questions derived from your summaries.

Interactive Q&A session

Dive into an engaging loop where each derived question is printed, prompting you for an answer with input(). Your response is then saved back to the Pydantic object.

Give Direction

Giving an LLM unique answers provides unique context, and this allows an LLM to generate richer, more nuanced responses, ensuring your article offers a fresh and in-depth perspective.

All of the code for `InterviewChain` is in *expert_interview_chain.py (https://oreil.ly/ 0d5Hi)*. It has two significant components:

A custom `System` *message*

This prompt includes role prompting, previously generated summaries, the topic, and format instructions (for the output parser):

```
system_message = """You are a content SEO researcher. Previously you have
summarized and extracted key points from SERP results. The insights gained
will be used to do content research and we will compare the key points,
insights and summaries across multiple articles. You are now going to
interview a content expert. You will ask them questions about the following
topic: {topic}.

You must follow the following rules:
    - Return a list of questions that you would ask a content expert about
    the topic.
    - You must ask at least and at most 5 questions.
    - You are looking for information gain and unique insights that are not
    already covered in the {document_summaries} information.
    - You must ask questions that are open-ended and not yes/no questions.
    {format_instructions}
    """
```

Output parsers

Diving deeper into the class, you encounter the `PydanticOutputParser`. This parser actively structures the LLMs responses into parsable, Pydantic `Interview Questions` objects:

```
from expert_interview_chain import InterviewQuestions

# Set up a parser + inject instructions into the prompt template:
parser = PydanticOutputParser(pydantic_object=InterviewQuestions)
```

In essence, you're orchestrating a conversation with the AI and instructing it to conceive potent questions that amplify content insights, all the while making customization a breeze.

Generate Outline

Including the previous interview and research, you can generate an outline for the post with BlogOutlineGenerator. The TOPIC, question_answers, and Google summaries are passed to provide additional context:

```
from article_outline_generation import BlogOutlineGenerator

blog_outline_generator = BlogOutlineGenerator(topic=TOPIC,
questions_and_answers=[item.dict() for item in interview_questions.questions])

questions_and_answers = blog_outline_generator.questions_and_answers
outline_result = blog_outline_generator.generate_outline(summaries)
```

Let's explore the BlogOutlineGenerator class in detail:

```
from typing import List, Any
from pydantic.v1 import BaseModel

class SubHeading(BaseModel):
    title: str # Each subheading should have a title.

class BlogOutline(BaseModel):
    title: str
    sub_headings: List[SubHeading] # An outline has many sub_headings

# Langchain libraries:
from langchain.prompts.chat import (ChatPromptTemplate,
SystemMessagePromptTemplate)
from langchain.output_parsers import PydanticOutputParser
from langchain_openai.chat_models import ChatOpenAI

# Custom types:
from custom_summarize_chain import DocumentSummary

class BlogOutlineGenerator:
    def __init__(self, topic: str, questions_and_answers: Any):
        self.topic = topic
        self.questions_and_answers = questions_and_answers

        # Create a prompt
        prompt_content = """
        Based on my answers and the summary, generate an outline for a blog
        article on {topic}.
        topic: {topic}
        document_summaries: {document_summaries}
        ---
        Here is the interview which I answered:
        {interview_questions_and_answers}
        ---
        Output format: {format_instructions}
        """
```

```
            system_message_prompt =
            SystemMessagePromptTemplate.from_template(prompt_content)

            self.chat_prompt = ChatPromptTemplate.from_messages(
            [system_message_prompt])

            # Create an output parser
            self.parser = PydanticOutputParser(pydantic_object=BlogOutline)

            # Set up the chain
            self.outline_chain = self.chat_prompt | ChatOpenAI() | self.parser

    def generate_outline(self, summaries: List[DocumentSummary]) -> Any:
            print("Generating the outline...\n---")
            result = self.outline_chain.invoke(
                {"topic": self.topic,
                "document_summaries": [s.dict() for s in summaries],
                "interview_questions_and_answers": self.questions_and_answers,
                "format_instructions": self.parser.get_format_instructions(),
                }
            )
            print("Finished generating the outline!\n---")
            return result
```

A `BlogOutline` Pydantic object is created that contains `title` and `sub_headings` keys. Also, the outline chain is set up using LangChain expression language (LCEL) that passes the prompt into the chat model and then finally into the output parser:

```
# Set up the chain:
self.outline_chain = self.chat_prompt | ChatOpenAI() | self.parser
```

By using a Pydantic output parser, the chain will return a `BlogOutline` Pydantic object that will be used in future chains.

Text Generation

After obtaining a summary, interview questions, and a blog post outline, it's time to start generating the text. The `ContentGenerator` class integrates SEO expertise with several LLM techniques, which include the following:

Embeddings and retrieval
> This efficiently splits and vectorizes original web pages, storing them in the Chroma database and retrieving relevent web page text while writing each section.

Custom memory
> While crafting each blog section, it uses memory to avoid repeating the same information, while also summarizing the conversation if it becomes too long.

Bespoke context

The LLM has a mixture of information, including your previous interview insights, what has been said before, and snippets of relevant web page text from Google:

```
from article_generation import ContentGenerator

content_gen = ContentGenerator(
topic=TOPIC, outline=outline_result,
questions_and_answers=questions_and_answers)

# Vectorize and store the original webpages:
content_gen.split_and_vectorize_documents(text_documents)
# Create the blog post:
blog_post = content_gen.generate_blog_post()
```

All of the source code is within *article_generation.py (https://oreil.ly/0IFyI)*, but let's specifically focus on three components that are key to this chain.

The `OnlyStoreAIMemory` class is a customized subclass of `ConversationSummaryBuf ferMemory`:

```
from typing import List, Dict, Any
from langchain.memory import ConversationSummaryBufferMemory

from langchain_core.messages import SystemMessage

class OnlyStoreAIMemory(ConversationSummaryBufferMemory):
    def save_context(self, inputs: Dict[str, Any],
    outputs: Dict[str, str]) -> None:
        input_str, output_str = self._get_input_output(inputs, outputs)
        self.chat_memory.add_ai_message(output_str)
```

It's tailored to ensure that the chat messages memory remains concise and relevant by *exclusively storing AI-generated messages*.

This deliberate choice bypasses storing retrieved documents that are used within the generation step, preventing memory bloat. Furthermore, the memory mechanism ensures the AI remains aware of its prior writings, enabling it to offer condensed summaries if the accumulated context surpasses set limits.

The `generate_blog_post` function loops through all of the subheadings and tries to retrieve as many relevant documents as possible while fitting in the current context length:

```
def generate_blog_post(self) -> List[str]:
    blog_post = []
    print("Generating the blog post...\n---")
    for subheading in self.outline.sub_headings:
        k = 5  # Initialize k
        while k >= 0:
```

```
try:
    relevant_documents = (self.chroma_db.as_retriever() \
    .invoke(subheading.title,
    k=k))
    section_prompt = f"""
    ...prompt_excluded_for_brevity...
    Section text:
    """

    result = self.blog_post_chain.predict(section_prompt)
    blog_post.append(result)
    break
except Exception as e:
    print(f"An error occurred: {e}")
    k -= 1
if k < 0:
    print('''All attempts to fetch relevant documents have
    failed. Using an empty string for relevant_documents.
    ''')
    relevant_documents = ""
print("Finished generating the blog post!\n---")
return blog_post
```

This function, `generate_blog_post`, iterates over each subheading. It attempts to fetch up to five relevant documents. If there's an issue fetching the documents, it smartly decreases the number and tries again. If all attempts fail, it gracefully defaults to no documents.

Finally, the prompt for generating each section is very context rich:

```
section_prompt = f"""You are currently writing the section: {subheading.title}
---
Here are the relevant documents for this section: {relevant_documents}.
If the relevant documents are not useful, you can ignore them.
You must never copy the relevant documents as this is plagiarism.
---
Here are the relevant insights that we gathered from our interview questions
and answers: {self.questions_and_answers}.
You must include these insights where possible as they are important and will
help our content rank better.
---
You must follow the following principles:
- You must write the section: {subheading.title}
- Render the output in .md format
- Include relevant formats such as bullet points, numbered lists, etc.
---
Section text:
"""
```

The `section_prompt` elegantly sets the stage by announcing the specific section you're working on, using `{subheading.title}`. But it doesn't stop there. By feeding the LLM with `{relevant_documents}`, it offers background and depth, while explicitly cautioning against plagiarism. Moreover, by including insights from your

---

interview via {self.questions_and_answers}, the prompt ensures that valuable information is front and center. Finally, it sets clear expectations on the format, the inclusion of certain features, and the topic at hand. This makes the LLM not just a tool but an informed coauthor, working diligently alongside you to create content.

Writing Style

Now that the article is written, we can go a step further in terms of making it sound uniquely human, by rewriting the content in a specific writing style. This will go a long way in making the content less detectable as obviously AI (though ethically you should still declare any AI assistance) and decreasing the amount of time you spend editing the final draft before publishing.

Before rewriting, you need to know what writing style you want to emulate, be it your own or someone else's. One common approach is to ask ChatGPT to summarize the writing style of someone who is famous, or at least popular enough in your industry to appear in ChatGPT's training data. Commonly the model will want to respond with the name of the author and examples of writing, so adding instructions not to and ending the prompt with a bullet point (or an - character in this case) will give you the format you need.

Input:

```
Describe in detail the writing style of Harry Dry from MarketingExamples.com
Do not mention the writer or source, and respond only with bullet points:
-
```

Output:

```
- Concise and to the point
- Humorous and knowledgeable tone
- Relatable and accessible language
- Uses storytelling to convey ideas
- Relies on examples and case studies
- Provides actionable advice and tips
- Uses subheadings and bullet points for easy readability
- Emphasizes key points or takeaways with bold or italicized text
- Addresses the reader directly, creating a conversational tone
```

Often provided only a single sample of text, ChatGPT can generate a reasonable writing style guide, which can then be used for rewriting. Once the writing style is defined, elements can be mixed and matched to arrive at a more ideal style. The following example takes elements from both Mike Taylor's writing style and Harry Dry's writing style from the previous example. This is another example of meme unbundling, as discussed in "Meme Unbundling" on page 310:

```
Rewrite the article in the following style:

- Concise and to the point
- Professional and knowledgeable tone
- Relatable and accessible language
- Uses storytelling to convey ideas
- Relies on examples and case studies
- Mixes personal anecdotes with industry insights
- Provides actionable advice and tips
- Uses subheadings and bullet points for easy readability
```

In practice this part of the AI writing process is the most difficult to get right, and it's the only one that requires the larger and more expensive GPT-4 model to get passable results. If this part of the process isn't right, the user can be left doing a lot of manual editing to get the writing in the house style. Given the strategic importance of this prompt, it makes sense to do a round of prompt optimization (*https://oreil.ly/H3VtJ*), trying multiple approaches.

When optimizing prompts you can run the same prompt multiple times and check the average performance against an evaluation metric. As an example, here are the results of testing five different prompt approaches against an evaluation metric of embedding distance. The lower the score, the closer the embeddings of the response were to a reference answer (the text as rewritten manually is in the correct style). The prompts tested were as follows:

A

Control—the standard prompt as detailed in the preceding example.

B

One-shot writing sample—we provided one sample of text, and asked GPT-4 to describe the writing style.

C

Three-shot rewriting example—we gave three samples of the input text to GPT-4 and the rewritten version and asked it to describe the writing style.

D

Three-shot writing sample—same as previous, except without the input text, only the final samples of Mike's writing.

These prompts were tested in an experiment we ran (*https://oreil.ly/vRRYO*) against three test cases—memetics, skyscraper technique, and value-based pricing—which were snippets of text that were first generated by ChatGPT on a topic, for example: *explain value-based pricing*. We then manually rewrote the text in the style we desired to make reference texts for comparison. The embedding distance was calculated by getting the embeddings for the reference text (from OpenAI's `text-embedding-ada-002`) and comparing them to the embeddings for the output from the prompt, using *cosine similarity* (a method for calculating the distance between two sets of numbers), as detailed in LangChain's embedding evaluator (*https://oreil.ly/400gJ*) (Figure 10-1).

AVERAGE of embedding_distanc case variation	Memetics	SkyScraper Technique	Value-Based Pricing	Grand Total	+/-
A: Control	0.053	0.042	0.061	0.052	0.00%
B: 1-Shot Writing Sample	0.045	0.034	0.048	0.043	-17.75%
C: 3-Shot Rewriting Example	0.049	0.046	0.058	0.051	-1.71%
D: 3-Shot Writing Sample	0.044	0.037	0.052	0.045	-14.03%
Grand Total	**0.048**	0.040	**0.055**	**0.047**	

Figure 10-1. Test results from prompt optimization

As you can see from the results in Figure 10-1, some prompts work better than others, and some cases are easier for the AI to deliver on. It's important to test across multiple cases, with 10 or more runs per case, to get a realistic result for each prompt. Otherwise, the nondeterministic nature of the responses might mean you'll think the performance was better or worse than you can actually expect when scaling up usage of a prompt. Here was the final resulting prompt that performed best:

```
You will be provided with the sample text.
Your task is to rewrite the text into a different writing style.
The writing style can be described as follows:
1. Informative and Analytical: The writer presents detailed information
about different strategies, especially the main theme of the text, and breaks
down its benefits, challenges, and implementation steps. This depth of
information shows that the writer has a solid grasp of the topic.
2. Structured and Organized: The writing follows a logical flow, starting
with a brief overview of different approaches, delving into a deep dive on
the topic, and concluding with potential challenges and contexts where it
might be best applied.
3. Conversational Tone with Professionalism: While the information is
presented in a professional manner, the writer uses a conversational tone
("Here's how to implement..."), which makes it more relatable and easier for
readers to understand.
4. Practical and Actionable: The writer not only explains the concept but
also offers actionable advice ("Here's how to implement X") with step-by-step
guidance based on real world-experience.
5. Balanced Perspective: The writer doesn't just present the benefits of the
topic but also discusses its challenges, which gives a well-rounded
perspective to readers.
6. Examples and Analogies: To make concepts clearer, the writer uses
concrete examples (e.g., how much a company might save per month) and
analogies (e.g., making comparisons to popular frames of reference). This
helps readers relate to the concepts and understand them better.
7. Direct and Clear: The writer uses straightforward language without
excessive jargon. Concepts are broken down into digestible bits, making it
accessible for a broad audience, even if they're not well-versed in business
strategies. In essence, this writing style is a blend of professional
```

analysis with practical, actionable advice, written in a clear and conversational tone.

Evaluate Quality

Without testing the writing style, it would be hard to guess which prompting strategy would win. With a small amount of testing, you can be more confident this is the correct approach. Testing doesn't have to be highly organized or systematized, and the builders of many successful AI products like GitHub Copilot (*https://oreil.ly/vu0IU*) admit their eval process was haphazard and messy (but it got the job done!).

In this project we'll use this well-tested example, but you may take this opportunity to try to beat this score. The repository with the reference texts and code is publicly available on GitHub (*https://oreil.ly/O6RdB*), and please feel free to contribute to the repository if you find a better approach. One potential path to try is fine-tuning, which may get you better results in matching the writing style if you have enough samples (OpenAI recommends at least 50 (*https://oreil.ly/OMMKi*)). Even if you don't perform an A/B test (comparing two versions of a prompt to see which one performs better) on this prompt, these results should convince you of the value of testing your prompts in general.

Title Optimization

You can optimize the content's title by generating various options, testing them through A/B prompts, and gauging their effectiveness with a thumbs-up/thumbs-down rating system, as shown in Figure 10-2.

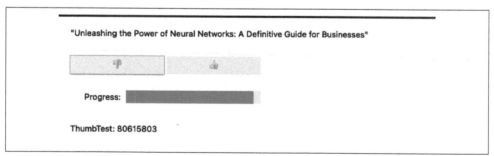

Figure 10-2. A simple thumbs-up and thumbs-down rating system

After evaluating all the prompts, you'll be able to see which prompt had the highest average score and the token usage (Figure 10-3).

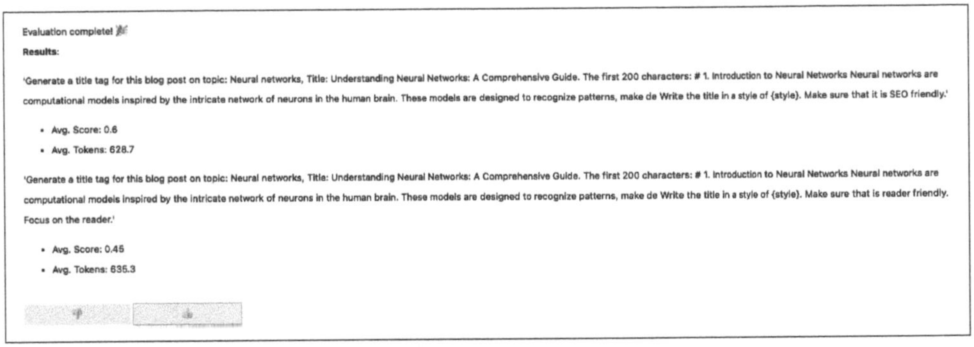

Figure 10-3. Example A/B test results after manually evaluating a prompt

If you still aren't getting the level of quality you need from this prompt, or the rest of the chain, this is a good time to experiment with a prompt optimization framework like DSPy (*https://oreil.ly/dspy*). Upon defining an evaluation metric, DSPy tests different combinations of instructions and few-shot examples in your prompts, selecting the best-performing combination automatically. See their documentation for examples (*https://oreil.ly/vercel*).

AI Blog Images

One thing you can do to make your blog look more professional is to add custom illustrations to your blog posts, with a consistent style. At its maximum this may mean training a Dreambooth model, as covered in Chapter 9, on your brand style guide or a mood board of images with a certain visual consistency or aesthetic quality you value. In many cases, however, training a custom model is not necessary, because a style can be replicated well using simple prompting.

One popular visual style among business-to-business (B2B) companies, Corporate Memphis (*https://oreil.ly/3UHQs*), is characterized by its vibrant color palettes, bold and asymmetric shapes, and a mix of both organic and geometric forms. This style arose as a costly signaling technique (*https://oreil.ly/haoTZ*), showing that the company could afford to commission custom illustrations from a designer and therefore was serious enough to be trusted. You can replicate this style with AI, saving yourself the cost of custom illustrations, while benefiting from the prior associations formed in consumers' minds. Figure 10-4 shows an example of Corporate Memphis style generated by Stable Diffusion, via the Stability AI API.

Input:

```
illustration of websites being linked together.
in the style of Corporate Memphis,
white background, professional, clean lines, warm pastel colors
```

Figure 10-4 shows the output.

Figure 10-4. Corporate Memphis: "websites being linked together"

Give Direction

Stable Diffusion is trained on many different styles, including obscure or niche styles like Corporate Memphis. If you know the name of a style, often that's all that's needed to guide the model toward the desired image. You can find a variety of art styles within this visual prompt builder (*https://oreil.ly/nxEzu*).

In our blog writing project we could ask the user for an idea of what image they want to accompany the blog post, but let's make it easier for them and automate this step. You can make an API call to ChatGPT and get back an idea for what could go in the image. When you get that response, it can form the basis of your prompt to Stability AI, a technique called *meta-prompting*, where one AI model writes the prompt for another AI model.

Input:

```
Describe an image that would go well at the top of this article:

{text}
```

Output:

```
A seamless collage or mosaic of diverse cultural elements from around the world,
including traditional dances, art pieces, landmarks, and people in various
traditional attires, symbolizing the interconnectedness of human cultures.
```

Stability AI hosts Stable Diffusion, including the latest models like Stable Diffusion XL, in their DreamStudio platform. You can also call them via API (*https://oreil.ly/ XD_jQ*) or via the Stability AI SDK (a library that simplifies the process of making the API call). In the following example, we'll create a function for calling Stability AI with our prompt.

Input:

```python
import base64
import os
import requests
import uuid

engine_id = "stable-diffusion-xl-1024-v1-0"
api_host = os.getenv('API_HOST', 'https://api.stability.ai')
api_key = os.getenv("STABILITY_API_KEY")

def generate_image(prompt):
    response = requests.post(
        f"{api_host}/v1/generation/{engine_id}/text-to-image",
        headers={
            "Content-Type": "application/json",
            "Accept": "application/json",
            "Authorization": f"Bearer {api_key}"
        },
        json={
            "text_prompts": [
                {
                    "text":'''an illustration of "+prompt+". in the style of
                    Corporate Memphis,
                    white background, professional, clean lines, warm pastel
                    colors'''
                }
            ],
            "cfg_scale": 7,
            "height": 1024,
            "width": 1024,
            "samples": 1,
            "steps": 30,
        },
    )
```

```
if response.status_code != 200:
    raise Exception("Non-200 response: " + str(response.text))

data = response.json()

image_paths = []

for i, image in enumerate(data["artifacts"]):
    filename = f"{uuid.uuid4().hex[:7]}.png"
    with open(filename, "wb") as f:
        f.write(base64.b64decode(image["base64"]))

    image_paths.append(filename)

return image_paths
```

```
prompt = """A seamless collage or mosaic of diverse cultural elements from
around the world, including traditional dances, art pieces, landmarks, and
people in various traditional attires, symbolizing the interconnectedness of
human cultures."""

generate_image(prompt)
```

Figure 10-5 shows the output.

Figure 10-5. A seamless collage or mosaic of diverse cultural elements from around the world

To encapsulate the whole system for image generation, you can bring the call to ChatGPT and the resulting call to Stability AI together in one function that uses the `outline_result.title`:

```
from image_generation_chain import create_image
image = create_image(outline_result.title)
```

The `create_image` function in *image_generation_chain.py* *(https://oreil.ly/cWpXH)* utilizes Stable Diffusion to create an image based on a generated title from GPT-4:

```python
import base64
from langchain_openai.chat_models import ChatOpenAI
from langchain_core.messages import SystemMessage
import os
import requests
import uuid

engine_id = "stable-diffusion-xl-1024-v1-0"
api_host = os.getenv("API_HOST", "https://api.stability.ai")
api_key = os.getenv("STABILITY_API_KEY", "INSERT_YOUR_IMAGE_API_KEY_HERE")

if api_key == "INSERT_YOUR_IMAGE_API_KEY_HERE":
    raise Exception(
        '''You need to insert your API key in the
        image_generation_chain.py file.'''
        "You can get your API key from https://platform.openai.com/"
    )


def create_image(title) -> str:
    chat = ChatOpenAI()
    # 1. Generate the image prompt:
    image_prompt = chat.invoke(
        [
            SystemMessage(content=f"""Create an image prompt
            that will be used for Midjourney for {title}."""
            )
        ]
    ).content


    # 2. Generate the image::
    response = requests.post(
        f"{api_host}/v1/generation/{engine_id}/text-to-image",
        headers={
            "Content-Type": "application/json",
            "Accept": "application/json",
            "Authorization": f"Bearer {api_key}",
        },
        json={
            "text_prompts": [
                {
```

```
            "text": f'''an illustration of {image_prompt} in the
            style of Corporate Memphis, white background,
            professional, clean lines, warm pastel colors'''
        }
    ],
    "cfg_scale": 7,
    "height": 1024,
    "width": 1024,
    "samples": 1,
    "steps": 30,
    },
)

if response.status_code != 200:
    raise Exception("Non-200 response: " + str(response.text))

data = response.json()
image_paths = []

for i, image in enumerate(data["artifacts"]):
    filename = f"{uuid.uuid4().hex[:7]}.png"
    with open(filename, "wb") as f:
        f.write(base64.b64decode(image["base64"]))
    image_paths.append(filename)
return image_paths
```

Here's the high-level process:

1. With the ChatOpenAI model, you'll craft an image prompt for your given title.

2. Using the Stability AI API, you'll send this prompt to generate an image with precise styling instructions.

3. Then you'll decode and save this image locally using a unique filename and return its path.

With these steps, you're not just prompting the AI to create textual content, but you're directing it to bring your prompts to life visually.

This system is flexible based on whatever style you decide to use for blog images. Parameters can be adjusted as needed, and perhaps this API call can be replaced in future with a call to a custom fine-tuned Dreambooth model of your own. In the meantime, however, you have a quick and easy way to generate a custom image for each blog post, without requiring any further input from the user, in a consistent visual style.

User Interface

Now that you have your script working end to end, you probably want to make it a little easier to work with, and maybe even get it into the hands of people who can give you feedback. The frontend of many AI tools in production is typically built using JavaScript, specifically the NextJS (*https://nextjs.org*) framework based on React. This is usually paired with a CSS library such as Tailwind CSS (*https://tailwindcss.com*), which makes rapid prototyping of design elements easier.

However, most of your AI code is likely in Python at this stage, and switching programming languages and development environments can be a daunting challenge. As well as learning JavaScript, NextJS, and Tailwind, you may also run into a series of issues getting a server running for your Python code, and a database live for your application and user data, and then integrating all of that with a frontend web design.

Instead of spending a lot of time spinning up servers, building databases, and adjusting button colors, it might make sense to create a simple prototype frontend to get early feedback, before investing too much at this stage in an unproven idea. Once you have built and tested a simple interface, you'll have a better understanding of what to build when you do need to get your app production-ready.

For launching simple user interfaces for AI-based prototypes, there are several popular open source interfaces, including gradio (*https://www.gradio.app*) and Streamlit (*https://streamlit.io*). Gradio was acquired by HuggingFace and powers the web user interface for many interactive demos of open source AI models, famously including the AUTOMATIC1111 (*https://oreil.ly/GlwJT*) Stable Diffusion Web UI. You can quickly build a Gradio interface to make it easier to run your code locally, as well as sharing the prototype to get feedback.

We've created an interface that allows you to automate the entire process within two steps. You can get access to the gradio source code here (*https://oreil.ly/HNqVX*).

Then run the gradio application by going into the chapter_10 folder (*https://oreil.ly/chapter10*) within your terminal and running python3 gradio_code_example.py. The script will ask you to enter a SERPAPI_API_KEY and a STABILITY_API_KEY in your terminal.

Then you can access the gradio interface as shown in Figure 10-6.

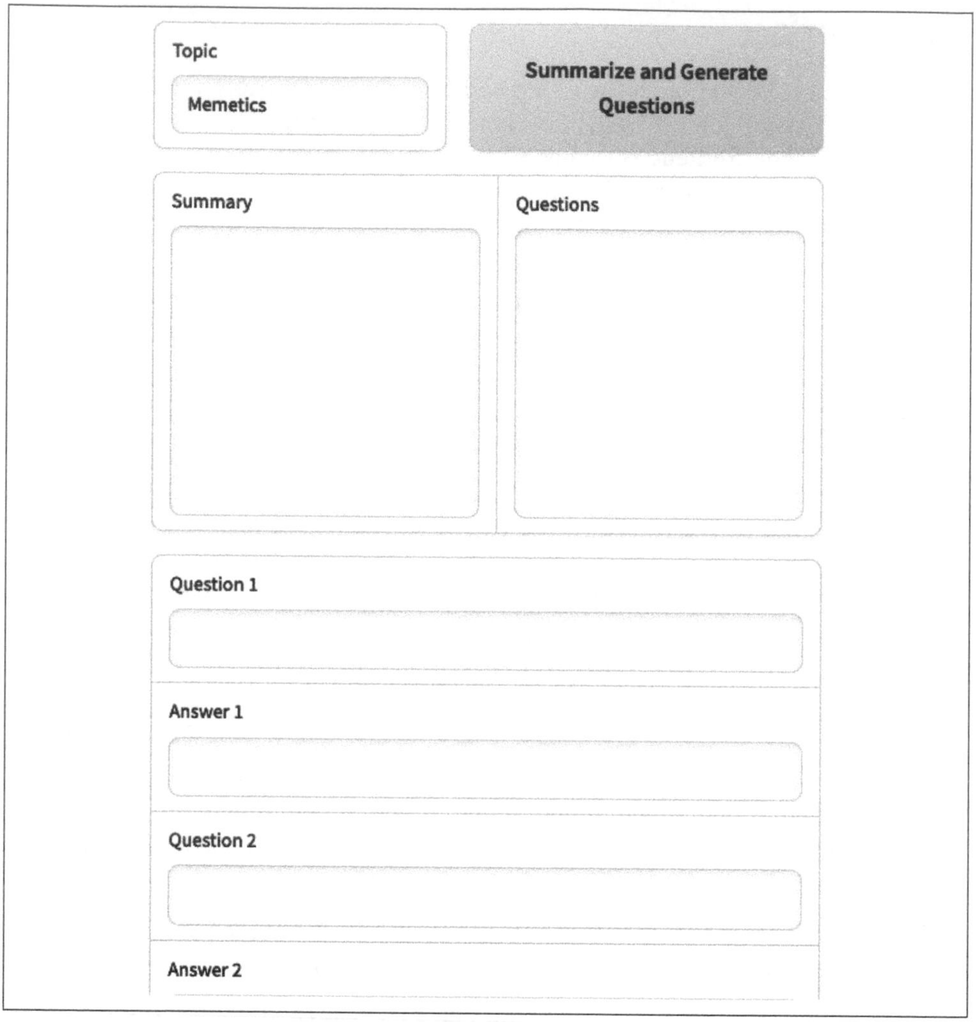

Figure 10-6. Gradio user interface

When you run gradio, you get an inline interface you can use directly or a URL that you can click to open the web interface in your browser. If you run gradio with the parameter `share=True`, for example `demo.launch(share=True)`, you get a publicly accessible link to share with friends, coworkers, or early users to get feedback on your prototype.

After initializing the interface, input a topic by clicking the Summarize and Generate Questions button. This will then collect and summarize the Google results as well as generate interview questions.

You'll then need to fill in the answers for each question. Finally, click the Generate Blog Post & Image button, which will take all the questions, answers, and summaries and will create an entire blog post and image using GPT-4!

Evaluate Quality

The most valuable evaluation data in AI is human feedback, as it has been the key to many AI alignment breakthroughs, including those that power ChatGPT. Asking for feedback from users via a user interface, or even building feedback mechanisms into your product, helps you identify and fix edge cases.

If you are building for research purposes or want to contribute to the open source community, consider sharing your gradio demo on Hugging Face Spaces. Hugging Face Spaces allows anyone to host their gradio demos freely, and uploading your project only takes a few minutes. New spaces can be created via the Hugging Face website (*https://oreil.ly/pSrP3*), or done programmatically using the Hugging Face API.

Summary

Congratulations! You've journeyed through the comprehensive world of prompt engineering for generative AI. You started with learning the prompt engineering principles and explored the historical context of LLMs, gaining awareness of their capabilities and the privacy concerns they pose.

You learned how to extract structured data, apply best practices of prompt engineering, and familiarize yourself with an LLM package called LangChain. Then you discovered vector databases for storing and querying text based on similarity and ventured into the world of autonomous agents.

Also, you immersed yourself in image generation techniques using diffusion models, learning how to navigate through this latent space. Your journey covered everything from format modifiers and art-style replication to inpainting and outpainting techniques. Moreover, you explored more advanced usage cases such as prompt expansion, meme mapping, and CLIP Interrogator, alongside many others.

Finally, you transitioned toward utilizing prompt engineering for content writing. You learned about creating a blog writing service that generates posts based on user responses, mimicking their writing styles, along with topic research strategies.

Overall, this journey not only enriched your knowledge but also equipped you with practical skills, setting you up to work professionally in the field of prompt engineering.

It's been our pleasure to guide you through the wide domain of prompt engineering for generative AI. Thank you for staying with us to the end of this book. We trust it will become a useful tool in all your future work with AI.

We would also greatly appreciate hearing your thoughts about the book, as well as any remarkable projects you create using the techniques we've discussed.

Please feel free to share your feedback or showcase your work by emailing us at *hi@brightpool.dev*. Once again, thank you! Your curiosity and perseverance are what shapes the future of this exciting field, and we can't wait to see what you contribute.

Happy prompting!

Index

About the Authors

Mike Taylor (*https://www.linkedin.com/in/mjt145*) cofounded a 50-person growth marketing agency called Ladder (*https://ladder.io*) with offices in the USA, UK, and EU. More than 400,000 people have taken his marketing and AI courses on LinkedIn Learning (*https://oreil.ly/mtaylor*), Udemy (*https://oreil.ly/QDWh0*), and Vexpower (*https://vexpower.com*).

James Phoenix (*https://www.linkedin.com/in/jamesphoenix*) builds reliable data pipelines for marketing teams, automating thousands of recurring tasks. He has taught 60+ Data Science bootcamps for General Assembly and partnered with Mike on the Udemy course (*https://oreil.ly/Nvkdm*), and Vexpower (*https://vexpower.com*).

Both authors been experimenting with prompt engineering since the GPT-3 beta in 2020. They slowly automated every part of their jobs with AI and now work as prompt engineers on various projects (*https://www.brightpool.dev*).

Colophon

The animal on the cover of *Prompt Engineering for Generative AI* is a screaming hairy armadillo (*Chaetophractus vellerosus*). This species of armadillo gets it name due to its habit of squealing, or screaming, when it is handled or threatened.

The screaming hairy armadillo resides in arid areas, specifically in regions in Argentina, Bolivia, and Paraguay. This animal prefers subtropical or tropical regions such as dry forests, scrubland, grassland, and deserts. White and light brown hair cover the animal's limbs and belly. A caparace, a thick armor made of keratin, covers the animal's body, a shield covers its head, and a small band exists between its ears. The animal typically reaches 12 to 22 inches in length, including its tail, and weighs less than 2 pounds, with male armadillos generally being larger than females.

The screaming hairy armadillo is an omnivore, eating small vertebrates such as frogs, toads, lizards, birds, and rodents, as well as fruits and vegetation. It can go long periods of time without drinking water.

Although the IUCN Red List designates the screaming hairy armadillo as Least Concern, it is heavily hunted in parts of Bolivia for its meat and carapace. Many of the animals on O'Reilly covers are endangered; all of them are important to the world.

The cover illustration is by Karen Montgomery, based on an antique line engraving from *Beeton's Dictionary*. The series design is by Edie Freedman, Ellie Volckhausen, and Karen Montgomery. The cover fonts are Gilroy Semibold and Guardian Sans. The text font is Adobe Minion Pro; the heading font is Adobe Myriad Condensed; and the code font is Dalton Maag's Ubuntu Mono.

Milton Keynes UK
Ingram Content Group UK Ltd.
UKHW051808200924
448583UK00001B/2